Praise for The Run of His Life

"Toobin deftly recounts the alternative realities of the Simpson case, explaining the personalities and strategies behind them. . . . [He] combines a talent for storytelling with an understanding of the trial process. . . . *The Run of His Life* offers a comprehensive, professional account, unburdened by the self-justifications of parties to the case or the banalities of ghostwriters."
—Wendy Kaminer, *The New York Times Book Review*

"[A] comprehensive summary of events. . . . Mr. Toobin is a scrupulous reporter, exercising sensible judgment."
—Philip Terzian, *The Wall Street Journal*

"Toobin's insight into the motives and mind-set of key players sets this Simpson book apart from the pack." —*People*

"Impressively informed . . . a book that delivers both the big picture and the telling details in fluid prose." —Sherryl Connelly, *Daily News*

"A well-written, profoundly rational analysis of the trial and, more specifically, the lawyers who conducted it . . . possesses fresh insights. . . . What sets Toobin's book apart from the growing pack of post-trial books from Christopher Darden, Robert Shapiro, Vincent Bugliosi, et al., is its calm, measured tone." —Deirdre Donahue, *USA Today*

"Toobin compiles the most compelling account to date. . . . What distinguishes Toobin's work is . . . its remarkable—and assiduously even-handed—reporting. . . . Toobin's book promises to be the one by which all O.J. chronicles are measured."
—Joseph P. Kahn, *The Boston Globe*

"For those wanting to read one—just one—good book on the case, *The Run of His Life* probably is it."
—Bruce Hight, *Austin American-Statesman*

"Toobin covers the case in exhausting detail, but what makes the book both important and entertaining is the way he fills in the gaps left by more partisan authors (Alan Dershowitz, Shapiro, Fay Resnick, Darden and others)."
—Patricia Holt, *San Francisco Chronicle Book Review*

THE RUN OF HIS LIFE

BY JEFFREY TOOBIN

JEFFREY TOOBIN

THE RUN OF HIS LIFE

The People v. O. J. Simpson

Random House
New York

2015 Random House Trade Paperback Edition

Copyright © 1996, 1997 by Jeffrey Toobin

Published in the United States by Random House, an imprint and division
of Penguin Random House LLC, New York.

RANDOM HOUSE and the HOUSE colophon are registered trademarks
of Penguin Random House LLC.

Originally published in hardcover in the United States by Random House,
an imprint and division of Penguin Random House LLC, in 1996,
and in different form in trade paperback by Touchstone Books,
an imprint of Simon & Schuster, Inc., in 1997.

ISBN 978-0-8129-8854-3
eBook ISBN 978-0-307-82916-0

Printed in the United States of America on acid-free paper

randomhousebooks.com

9   8   7   6   5   4

Book design by J. K. Lambert

To my favorite journalist,

MARLENE SANDERS,

my mother

Nicole:

Well, it seems that the worst part iş behind us.
I want you to know that whatever you might think
to the contrary I'v taken full responcibility for this.
It happen and I'm doing everything possible to assure
it doe'nt happen agan. But sooner or later we must
starte with our future. I love our time last weekend.
I know to you it may not have been much but it
showed we can get along.

I love you and losing you is the only thing that
madder to me. So lets not forget the past. Let's work
together (for the first time) to improve the futurr
live together. Know manner what I love you.

O.J.

Letter from O. J. Simpson to Nicole Brown Simpson,
following his plea of no contest to domestic violence
charges in 1989

CONTENTS

THE RUN OF HIS LIFE

One after another, the Jaguars, the BMWs, and the odd Porsche pulled off the Avenue of the Stars and slipped into the nearly deserted underground parking garage. The owners of these cars, about two dozen of the top lawyers in West Los Angeles, greeted each other with slightly embarrassed smiles. All white, virtually all men, and mostly in their early fifties, they reflected the culture in which they had thrived, one where workaholism was no virtue and a weekend in the office anathema. Yet here they were, on a glorious summer Saturday afternoon, June 25, 1994, forsaking golf and family for a meeting in a Century City tower. They came because everyone wanted a piece of this case—the defense of Orenthal James Simpson against charges that he had murdered his ex-wife Nicole and her friend Ronald Goldman.

Besides, they came because Robert Shapiro, Simpson's lead lawyer, had asked them. Many of these lawyers, who were among those closest to Shapiro, never knew precisely what to make of their friend. They could quickly catalogue his faults: his outsize ego; his self-obsession; his excessive comfort with the moral ambiguities of his profession. "Bob would have cocktails with Hitler," the wife of one of the lawyers at the meeting used to say. They chuckled at his endless socializing; Shapiro owned three tuxedos. He had once declined a lunch date with one of the lawyers, Alvin Michaelson, by explaining, without a touch of humor, "I only have lunch with people who can help me. It's part of my workday. I eat with clients, judges, and prosecutors." But so, too, these lawyers knew another side of Shapiro, that of the generous friend. When the wife of Roger Cossack, another lawyer at the meeting, had died a few years earlier after a terrible bout with cancer, Bob Shapiro had been the first person to arrive at Cossack's house to offer comfort after the funeral. When the Internal Revenue Service had begun investigating scores of professional athletes for evading taxes on the income they made from appearing at autograph shows, many had come running to Shapiro for assistance. He in turn had referred much of that business to his friends and, consequently, had paid for the additions to more than a few lawyers' houses. They remembered that. So they answered his call.

Shapiro greeted his colleagues on this Saturday with his trademark bear hugs and ushered them into a conference room. If you looked carefully out the window, you could make out Bundy Drive, in Brentwood, just three miles west. Thirteen days before this meeting, Nicole Brown Simpson and Ronald Goldman had been murdered near the front steps of her home on Bundy. A pair of late-night dog walkers had discovered the grisly scene: Nicole, at the foot of the front steps, her throat slashed down to the vertebrae; Ron, in a heap nearby, his torso and neck both savaged by fatal wounds. The following week, Shapiro had been retained to represent the prime suspect in the case, O. J. Simpson, who was Nicole's ex-husband as well as a very famous man. On June 17, the day Shapiro had agreed that Simpson would surrender to police, the former football star vanished. With virtually the entire nation watching on television, Simpson's friend Robert Kardashian read what sounded like a suicide note that Simpson had left behind. In the end, Simpson did not take his own life. He eventually turned himself in later that day, following a surreal, televised chase on the freeways of Southern California.

Technically, the space where the attorneys gathered was not really Shapiro's at all. Because he didn't have a conference room of his own, Shapiro had borrowed one from the large law firm where he rented space. Under the pressures of the Simpson case, Shapiro would come to use it so often that he eventually broke down and added the conference room to his sublet arrangement. Like most criminal defense attorneys, even the best known, Shapiro ran a lean business operation. He had a secretary and two young lawyers as associates. Every month, Shapiro wrote out by hand all the checks to cover his office expenses, including payroll. In recent years, he had had no trouble meeting that payroll—business was good—but Shapiro was ever mindful of the criminal defense attorney's dilemma: Successful though one may be, one can never count on repeat business. An unending supply of new clients must always be found. The quest for clients—his own and his friends'—was an important subtext for the gathering he had assembled this summer afternoon.

Summoning the participants by telephone earlier in the week, Shapiro had said he wanted to discuss the Simpson case. The preliminary hearing would begin the following Thursday, June 30. Shapiro said he wanted to pick the brains of the best in the business beforehand. Please help me, he said. I need your advice.

The lawyers came running, as Shapiro knew they would, for he understood that the invitation itself was a gift. The Simpson case was already a national sensation. In the gossipy, competitive Los Angeles legal world, Shapiro discerned that his conclave would be (in fact, already was) the talk of the city. Any lawyer would treasure the opportunity to mention the fact that Bob Shapiro had called to talk about the O.J. case. Friends, fellow lawyers, and, especially, clients (and even more especially *prospective* clients) would be impressed. The high end of criminal defense law operates almost entirely on a referral basis—that is, lawyers are hired because other lawyers recommend them—and Shapiro knew that his guests on this Saturday would not soon forget he had included them in this extraordinary session. A profitable referral to Shapiro would be the appropriate gesture of gratitude.

After the lawyers had settled in around the large oval table, Shapiro began the proceedings with a question.

"So," he said. "How many of you think O.J. did it?"

Everyone froze. After a moment, a few lawyers chuckled nervously and others rolled their eyes. In a flash, Shapiro had brought home just how strange this meeting was. Defense lawyers talk to each other about their cases all the time, often with brutal candor. Does my guy take a plea or not? Is my case triable? Winnable? In these discussions, guilt is a given; experienced criminal lawyers—the successful ones—harbor few illusions. These chats are private;

the cases are usually unknown to the public. But Shapiro was talking about what was well on its way to becoming the most sensational legal proceeding in American history. This was not the kind of question—or so it seemed—that an experienced criminal defense attorney would want answered in a quasi-public setting.

But Shapiro's question made a point. Though he was now, as Simpson's attorney, more famous than any of his friends around the conference table, he was still one of the boys. He still knew the score. He had no more illusions about this client than any other. The spotlight would never blind him to reality.

After his initial query brought only awkward silence, Shapiro moved quickly to introduce two of the guests—Skip Taft and Robert Kardashian, who were, for Shapiro's purposes, the most important audience for the meeting. Taft and Kardashian were lawyers, too, but that wasn't the point. Taft was O. J. Simpson's business manager, the man who would decide, among other things, how much Shapiro would be paid. Kardashian had known Simpson for thirty years, and in the days since the murders he had emerged as the defendant's closest friend and adviser. The gossip had already made the rounds that these two men had been instrumental in replacing Simpson's original lawyer, Howard Weitzman, with Shapiro. Attention had to be paid. It was for them that Shapiro had assembled this show of legal strength.

Almost everyone else knew one another. This was, as they sometimes joked, the West L.A. Jewish mafia. (Taft and Kardashian were among the very few non-Jews in the room.) In fact, as the group settled in, Alvin Michaelson whispered to his neighbor, "This is what it must have been like at Apalachin"—the infamous gathering of mob chieftains in upstate New York in 1957. It was a famously inbred group, and their connections to one another often stretched back decades. Among Shapiro's oldest friends in the room was Roger Cossack, who had pledged with Shapiro to the Zeta Beta Tau fraternity at UCLA in the early 1960s. (The Simpson case would transform Cossack's life as much as it did Shapiro's; Cossack became CNN's local expert on the trial, and when it was over, he quit the law altogether and moved to Washington to begin his own daily legal-affairs broadcast on the cable network.) When prosecutors began examining Kardashian's behavior in the aftermath of the murders, he hired Michaelson as his attorney. When Shapiro was later sued for libel in connection with the Simpson case, he asked another attendee, Larry Feldman, to represent him. (Feldman was ribbed mercilessly that Saturday because, due to go to a wedding, he came to Shapiro's office in black tie; for his part, Shapiro presided in an all-white designer sweat suit.) One of the few civil litigation specialists at the meeting was Patricia Glaser, a partner at the large law firm then known as Christensen White Miller Fink and Jacobs. A year and a half later, when the Simpson trial was over, her name would be added to the firm's name along with that of the newest partner—Robert Shapiro. Another of Shapiro's ZBT brothers, Mike Nasatir, was there, too, along with his longtime partner, Richard Hirsch. About fifteen years earlier, they had employed a Southwestern law student by the name of Marcia Kleks as an intern. (She later married Gordon Clark and took his name.) Johnnie Cochran, who was not part of Shapiro's social set, was not invited.

"I've asked you all here today because you all know how to try a case," Shapiro said, "and I'm not afraid to ask for your help."

But Shapiro actually asked few questions, and though he was pleased to have collected all these fine lawyers together, he didn't listen much to what they had to say. Shapiro's confidence was astonishing: He had the answer for O. J. Simpson. His client, he vowed, would go to trial and be acquitted. The strategy was set. Shapiro was caught up short only once. Michael Baden, the eminent medical examiner whom Shapiro had retained as an expert in the case, mentioned at the meeting that the autopsy results on the victims showed the possibility that more than one person had killed Nicole and Ron. Robert Shapiro paused to consider the implications. "So," he asked the group, "that means O.J. and who else did it?"

This remark, too, drew stunned silence, and the meeting soon broke up. Shapiro took several of the participants out to dinner at Nicky Blair's, a venerable (and now defunct) Hollywood hangout. A few hardy souls concluded the evening with drinks at the Beverly Hills estate of Shapiro's friend and former client Robert Evans, the movie producer whom Shapiro had steered clear of formal charges in the infamous Cotton Club murders of 1983.

Among the guests at Shapiro's meeting most pleased to have been invited was Marshall Grossman. Though he had enjoyed considerable success in the world of civil litigation, Grossman had never tried a criminal case, and the glamour and excitement of the Simpson case appealed to him. However, as Grossman later pondered what he had heard at the meeting, he hesitated. Grossman had tried cases for high stakes before, but he realized that this case, as Shapiro planned to defend it, would become something much bigger than the trial of a single defendant. If Shapiro had his way, it would come to involve (and possibly consume) the whole city of Los Angeles. Ultimately, Grossman decided this kind of public spectacle would not be for him.

The notion that Grossman might play a part in the Simpson case had generated excitement at his law firm, and he felt he owed his colleagues an explanation for his decision. At 11:12 A.M. on July 6, 1994, he sent an E-mail message around his firm that said, "I am sending a letter to the lead trial lawyer in the case this morning informing him of my decision" not to join the defense effort. The Simpson case, Grossman went on, "carries with it a high risk of racial divisiveness for our community, a situation which I don't wish to contribute to and would rather reserve the opportunity for a healing role if need be."

|||||

Johnnie L. (just "L") Cochran, Jr., loved appearing on *Nightline*— as well as the *Today* show, the *CBS Evening News,* and the *NBC Nightly News.* In the days immediately after the murders in Brentwood, he did them all, and the programs' producers were happy to have him, too. Cochran was a poised, accomplished, telegenic African-American lawyer, the answer to a network booker's dreams. Within a week of the murders, the *Today* show even made him a paid consultant.

As it happened, on the evening of June 17, 1994—the day Al Cowlings led the nation on the low-speed chase down the Los Angeles freeways—Cochran was booked to analyze the events of the day on *Nightline.* Though television viewers never knew it, Cochran's position in the case was considerably more complicated than that of the other legal experts who were surfacing in the media to analyze the case. Cochran had personal knowledge of what was going on behind the scenes. He was a friend of O. J. Simpson's—not, in normal circumstances, an intimate confidant, but certainly a long-term acquaintance. Since the day of the murders, Simpson had been on the phone with Cochran talking about his plight and asking the attorney to join in his defense efforts. On the air, Cochran was cautious and only mildly pro-defense. His comment that evening on *Nightline* was typical of what he was saying on all the programs: 'I think that the important thing for all Americans to understand is that this is a tragic, tragic case, but at this point he's still presumed to be innocent."

Off camera, though, Cochran, like Shapiro, could afford to be more blunt. For example, during a break in the broadcast of *Nightline* on June 17 in ABC's studios in Los Angeles, Cochran sized up the situation very differently from the way he did for the program's viewers. "O.J. is in massive denial," Cochran told a friend. "He obviously did it. He should do a diminished-capacity plea and he might have a chance to get out in a reasonable amount of time." When, the following week, Cochran traveled to Burbank for his early-morning duty to the *Today* show, he expressed the same sentiments—likewise to friends, off camera.

But in the days to come, as Cochran continued to listen to Simpson's entreaties, the lawyer learned that the defendant had no interest in pleading guilty. He wanted to go to trial and win—and he wanted Cochran to represent him. Cochran was torn. He enjoyed the broadcasting work; it was easy, flattering, low-stress, and, at several hundred dollars per appearance on *Today*, the money wasn't bad, either. But how could he turn down what was shaping up to be the trial of the century? Unlike Shapiro, Cochran's métier was trying cases, working before juries in a courtroom. Questioning Cochran on the June 20 edition of the *Today* show, Bryant Gumbel made note of the differences in the two men's reputations. "Mr. Shapiro has a great reputation as a plea bargainer," Gumbel said. "Do you think him the best man to represent O.J. in a criminal trial?" Cochran's response was a study in condescension toward Shapiro—and nothing less than an advertisement for himself.

"Well, again," Cochran told Gumbel, "I think there are lawyers and there are lawyers. He is a fine lawyer, but if the matter is to be tried, I think one needs one who is very well experienced and skilled in trying cases—a litigator, if you will. And I would not be surprised if you didn't see a lawyer—another lawyer, trial lawyer—come in and do that." Cochran, of course, did not let on that he was in fact at that very moment weighing whether to step in and take that trial lawyer role.

After the preliminary hearing ended on July 8 and Simpson was ordered to stand trial in sixty days, Cochran knew he had to make up his mind. He had a large circle of friends, and often liked to talk himself into (or out of) ideas by bouncing them off others. Cochran worked the phones.

One afternoon in mid-July, the phone rang in the office of a lawyer who also knew the stresses of high-profile cases. "You should do it," Cochran teased the lawyer, but he was really turning his own possible role over in his mind. The upside wasn't difficult to recognize. Any trial lawyer would relish the chance to perform in front of the biggest audience in American legal history. The downside, as Cochran explained it, was more complex. Simpson was a peer. "He's a friend," Cochran said, "and that's a mess when you start trying to represent a friend." Cochran wondered whether their relationship might hinder his ability to conduct the case the way he wanted. The last problem was in many ways the simplest, but also the most profound. Cochran's relationship with this friend was such that he could speak in a shorthand they would both understand. He hesitated for a while before he came out and said what was on his mind. If Johnnie Cochran's career had established anything at that point, it was that he liked to win. But he had talked to his prospective client and sized up the evidence against him. Ultimately, Cochran's problem with the Simpson case was a simple one.

"The case," said Cochran, "is a loser."

||||||

Of course they knew.

Of course Robert Shapiro and Johnnie Cochran knew from the start what any reasonably attentive student of the murders of Nicole Brown Simpson and Ronald Lyle Goldman could see: that O. J. Simpson was guilty of killing them. Their dilemma, then, was the oldest, as well as the most common, quandary of the criminal defense attorney: what to do about a guilty client.

The answer, they decided, was race. Because of the overwhelming evidence of Simpson's guilt, his lawyers could not undertake a defense aimed at proving his innocence—one that sought to establish, say, that some other person had committed the murders. Instead, in an astonishing act of legal bravado, they sought to create for the client—a man they believed to be a killer—the mantle of victimhood. Almost from the day of Simpson's arrest, his lawyers sought to invent a separate narrative, an alternative reality, for the events of June 12, 1994. This fictional version was both elegant and dramatic. It posited that Simpson was the victim of a wide-ranging conspiracy of racist law enforcement officials who had fabricated and planted evidence in order to frame him for a crime he did not commit. It was also, of course, an obscene parody of an authentic civil rights struggle, for this one pitted a guilty "victim" against innocent "perpetrators."

These conclusions are the result of more than two years of reporting on the Simpson case. The week after the murders, I was assigned to cover the story for *The New Yorker* magazine. In addition to attending Simpson's trial in Los Angeles Superior Court, I interviewed more than two hundred people, many of them repeatedly. I have had access to the full documentary record of the case—including internal memoranda of both the prosecution and the defense teams; advice provided by jury consultants to both the prosecution and the defense; the police "murder book," with its summaries of all LAPD interviews with witnesses; the written summaries of all witness interviews by members of the defense team; heretofore secret grand-jury testimony; and depositions from the pending civil case against Simpson. I have also reviewed the enormous coverage of the case in the news media, an especially important task in the context of this case. The participants in the Simpson case worked obsessively to influence press coverage. These efforts to shape the news—some successful, some not—had important and lasting consequences from the night of the murders to the morning of the verdict.

Indeed, the heart of the defense strategy featured an effort at public storytelling, the creation of a counternarrative based on the idea of a police conspiracy to frame Simpson. For this effort, the defense needed a receptive audience, which it most definitely had in the

African-Americans who dominated the jury pool in downtown Los Angeles. The defense strategy played to experiences that were anything but fictional—above all, the decades of racism in and by the Los Angeles Police Department. The defense sought to identify the Simpson case as the latest in a series of racial abuses by the LAPD, which featured such celebrated outrages as the Rodney King case and thousands of other insults and affronts great and small. This legacy of black distrust of the LAPD was the fertile soil in which the Simpson defense strategy grew. As the events of the case unfolded, the LAPD more than lived up to its reputation as one of the worst big-city police departments in the United States, one that tolerated sloth, incompetence, and racism. As it happened, though, bad as the LAPD was, it did not frame O. J. Simpson; no one planted or fabricated any evidence. In fact, the defense cleverly obscured the one actual police conspiracy that was revealed over the course of the case—that of the starstruck cops who in 1989 tried to minimize and excuse O. J. Simpson's history of domestic violence.

It is ultimately unknowable whether a brilliant effort by prosecutors in the Simpson case could have produced a conviction in spite of the defense effort to make the case a racial referendum. There was, alas, no such splendid performance. Indeed, despite the best intentions, the case was largely botched by the Los Angeles District Attorney's Office. The prosecutors were undone by the twin afflictions most common among government lawyers: arrogance (mostly Marcia Clark's) and ineptitude (largely Christopher Darden's). Drunk on virtue, the prosecutors squandered what little chance they had for victory.

At its core, the Simpson case was a horrific yet routine domestic-violence homicide. It metastasized into a national drama, one that exposed deep fissures in American society, for one reason: because the defendant's lawyers thought that using race would help their client win an acquittal. It did. That was all that mattered to them. More than a decade ago, Alan Dershowitz, one of Simpson's lawyers, gave a candid précis of the approach that would characterize the defense team's efforts. In his book *The Best Defense*, Dershowitz wrote, "Once I decide to take a case, I have only one agenda: I want to win. I will try, by every fair and legal means, to get my client off—without regard to the consequences."

1. DROP DEAD GORGEOUS

The geographic spine of Brentwood—indeed, the spine of wealthy West Los Angeles—is Sunset Boulevard. The legendary thoroughfare begins modestly, just a few blocks from the Los Angeles Criminal Courts Building, in the city's forlorn downtown, where it begins its twenty-mile trek west to the Pacific Ocean. From downtown, it passes through the honky-tonk precincts of Hollywood and then moves ever upscale, through Beverly Hills and then to Bel-Air. When Sunset then crosses the San Diego Freeway, the air clears—literally. The next community is Brentwood, where ocean breezes scrub the pervasive smog from the sky. Here, in its last stop before the ocean, Sunset Boulevard shimmies along the base of the foothills that lead up to the Santa Monica Mountains. When planners first laid out Brentwood in the 1920s, their model was Golden Gate Park in San Francisco. The little roads that sprout from Sunset still follow the curves of the hills. Big houses have always been the rule in Brentwood, in the usual stylistic mix for wealthy Los Angeles: Normandy farmhouse; English Tudor; English Cotswold cottage; Spanish Colonial Revival. In one respect, the houses in Brentwood differ from their wealthy cousins in the Hollywood Hills or Beverly Hills. It is a less showy neighborhood, with fewer modernist architectural gestures and rococo European follies—a conservative place.

The iron law of real estate in Brentwood is simple and unchanging: North of Sunset, sometimes called Brentwood Park, is better than south. On February 23, 1977, O. J. Simpson bought a house on a prime corner lot at 360 North Rockingham for $650,000. (Real estate agents say the house is probably worth about $4 million in 1996.) The home reflects the stolid grandeur of the hilly neighborhood north of Sunset Boulevard: 6,000 square feet in a timber-and-stone frame, with an adjoining pool and tennis court. A six-foot-tall brick wall protects the house's privacy. Some of Simpson's monthly expenses, as revealed in legal papers from his 1992 divorce from Nicole, give a sense of the scale of the place: $13,488 annually for utilities; $10,129 for gardening; and $4,371 for "Pool—Tennis Court Services."

Shortly after O.J. bought the house, he began seeing eighteen-year-old Nicole Brown, and then he separated from his wife, Marguerite. (At the time, O.J. was thirty and near the end of his professional football career.) O.J. and Marguerite divorced in 1979, the same year that their two-year-old daughter, Aaren, accidentally drowned in the pool at Rockingham. Nicole lived with O.J. in the Rockingham house for more than a decade, through their marriage in 1985, the birth of their daughter, Sydney, eight months later, and the birth of their son, Justin, in 1988. However, when they separated in February 1992, there was never any doubt that the house was his. As Simpson stated in a declaration filed as part of the divorce proceeding with Nicole, "Because of the nature of my estate and my existing obligations, I requested that [Nicole] sign a Prenuptial Agreement. There were substantial negotiations over a period of 7 to 9 months which resulted in a signed agreement essentially providing that all property rights would remain separate."

So Nicole and the two children moved to nearby 325 Gretna Green Way, in a quiet and pleasant part of Brentwood without gated estates on the southern side of Sunset. Her new house reflected one of the most common styles for modern California homes—what might be called Discount Mission. Spray-on stucco lined the exterior walls, a few wooden beams spruced up the sides, and clay tiles covered the roof. A two-car garage dominated the front.

As their divorce litigation went forward in 1992, it became clear that Nicole had many years earlier made herself a hostage to O.J.'s fortunes. In the divorce proceeding, Nicole pressed O.J. for both child and spousal support, stressing her complete financial dependence on him. "I am not currently employed and spend my time caring for my two young children," she declared in an affidavit. Her attorneys wrote in a brief that as a teenager, around the time she met Simpson, Nicole "worked as a waitress for two months. Prior to that, she worked as a sales clerk in a boutique. She worked there for a total of two weeks and did not make a single sale. These two jobs are the sum total of her employment experience." In a court-ordered meeting with a "vocational counselor," Nicole described herself as a "party animal" and said her personal goals were "to raise my kids as best I can; beyond that I haven't thought about me." She added, "I'm sure I will get a goal someday." It wasn't until Nicole was in her mid-thirties and divorced that she began to consider entering the business world. Her friend and fellow party animal Faye Resnick later reported in a book about Nicole that at the time of her death, the two women were hoping to open a coffeehouse in Brentwood called "Java Café or something like that," with "poetry readings and fabulous teas and coffees."

O.J. and Nicole's divorce was settled without a trial. On October 15, 1992, the parties agreed that O.J., whose after-tax income amounted to $55,000 monthly (that is, $660,000 a year), would pay Nicole $10,000 a month in child support. Nicole kept title to a rent-producing condominium in San Francisco, and O.J. agreed to make a one-time payment to her of $433,750. "It is the intent of the parties," the settlement stated, "that a substantial portion of this sum shall be used by [Nicole] for the acquisition of a residence."

||||||

Real estate agents in Brentwood speak about the extraordinary intimacy of their relationships with their clients. The brokers are often women who have entered the business as a new career in midlife. According to an experienced agent, "People are so wrapped up in their houses here that you become their confessors. It's amazing what I hear. People think nothing of telling their brokers that they were raped by their fathers." Nicole Simpson quickly developed a close friendship with Jeane McKenna, who had been a broker in Brentwood since 1978. They had much in common:

Both had been married to prominent athletes in Los Angeles. McKenna's ex-husband is Jim Lefebvre, the former Dodger infielder, whom she had met when she was a flight attendant. When the two women met in October 1993, McKenna learned that Nicole had been divorced for about a year. After a period of on-and-off reconciliations with O.J., she was finally ready to buy her own place.

Nicole needed to move quickly on a purchase. She had sold the rental property in San Francisco, and to avoid taxes on the sale, she was required to invest the proceeds promptly in another rent-producing property. According to Jeane McKenna, "She was paying five thousand a month at Gretna Green, which had a pool and a guest house, so when she bought a new place, she wasn't going to get everything she had before, but this would be her own." As it turned out, McKenna had just what Nicole wanted.

In exasperation, Jeane McKenna used to refer to 875 South Bundy Drive as her "career listing"—the house she couldn't sell. Bundy Drive is the main north-south artery of Brentwood, a noisy, busy, traffic-filled thoroughfare. McKenna's property was the north side of a two-family condominium building in an area real estate agents refer to as the Brentwood flats or, sometimes, the poor man's Brentwood. McKenna had had her name on a FOR SALE sign in front of that property for more than six months when she received a call from Nicole in October 1993. According to McKenna, "It's not exactly an ace area of Brentwood, south of Sunset. The windows were double-paned so you couldn't hear the noise on the street, and when I marketed the property, I told potential buyers, including Nicole, 'You're not going to be doing any outdoor entertaining, with all the buses and sirens screaming by.' " But the three-story condominium did have its advantages. It was modern, built in 1991, and it had a two-story living room, several skylights, and an assortment of high-end accoutrements, including a Jacuzzi, a Sub-Zero refrigerator, and a kitchen full of marble countertops. But McKenna couldn't sell it until Nicole came along.

Nicole liked the Bundy condo, in part because of its location near a school. Nicole wanted to be close to a playground because her children would no longer have a yard. McKenna negotiated a deal for Nicole to buy the house for $625,000, but she wound up paying an additional $30,000. "The seller was this television producer who was in financial trouble, so Nicole had to pay all the seller's closing costs, too," McKenna explained. "She just really wanted that place."

In January 1994, when Nicole moved into the Bundy condominium, her relationship with O.J. oscillated between reconciliation and a final breach, and the financial tensions between them escalated. The first point of conflict revolved around a man named Kato Kaelin. Although the Simpson affair made the name Kato synonymous with houseguest, his original relationship to Nicole was the more familiar one of tenant to landlord. Kaelin had rented her guest house at Gretna Green for five hundred dollars a month, a figure he could reduce somewhat by baby-sitting for her children. (During this period Sydney and Justin grew so fond of Kato that they named their pet Akita after him.) When Nicole moved to Bundy, she and Kaelin planned to continue the deal, with Kato paying to stay in a small guest suite wedged between the garage and kitchen. Shortly before the move, however, O.J. told Kaelin that although he had had no objections to his living in a separate guest house at Gretna Green, he didn't want him living under the same roof as his ex-wife. Simpson's solution was to give Kaelin a rent-free guest house at his home on Rockingham. O.J.'s offer thus simultaneously removed a potential rival for Nicole's affections and took money out of his ex-wife's pocket. It also led ultimately to Kaelin's prominent place in the history of freeloading.

In May 1994, O.J. and Nicole's final attempt at a reconciliation ended, leading to a financial controversy that dwarfed the dispute over Kato Kaelin. Around Memorial Day, less than six months after she and her children had settled into the Bundy condominium, Nicole called Jeane McKenna and said they would have to move out because O.J. was threatening to report her to the Internal Revenue Service.

When Nicole had sold her rental property in San Francisco she had invested the proceeds in the home on Bundy, but she apparently told the IRS that the new place was also a rental property. As a result, she had avoided tax on the initial sale. For tax purposes, she kept Rockingham as her official residence. Around Memorial

Day, O.J. told her that he would no longer permit her to use his address. "He's threatening to tell the IRS that I'm living in Bundy," Nicole told McKenna. As a legal matter, O.J. seems to have had a point, but McKenna scoffed at the idea that Simpson would force his children to move for the second time in a year. "Oh yes he is," Nicole told her broker. "Of course he is—the asshole." In the entry in her diary for June 3, Nicole quoted the exact words of O.J.'s threat: "You hang up on me last nite, you're gonna pay for this bitch, you're holding money from the IRS, you're going to jail you fucking cunt. You think you can do any fucking thing you want, you've got it comming—I've already talked to my lawyers about this bitch—they'll get you for tax evasion, bitch, I'll see to it. You're not going to have a dime left bitch etc."

On Monday, June 6, O.J. delivered on his threat. He put his warning in icily official terms, in a typed, formal letter to his ex-wife, which began: "Dear Nicole, On advice of legal counsel, and because of the change in our circumstances, I am compelled to put you on written notice that you do not have my permission or authority to use my permanent home address at 360 North Rockingham . . . as your residence or mailing address for any purpose. . . . I cannot take part in any action by you that might intentionally or unintentionally be misleading to the Internal Revenue Service . . ." Nicole showed the letter to her friend Cynthia Shahian on June 7. Not surprisingly, Nicole was horrified by it—especially by the prospect of being forced to move out of Bundy so soon after she and her children had moved in. The same day Shahian saw the letter, June 7, Nicole also telephoned the Sojourn shelter for battered women in Santa Monica to report that she was being stalked by O.J.

On Thursday, June 9, on Nicole's instructions, McKenna officially put 875 South Bundy up for lease, asking $4,800 a month. "Drop dead gorgeous 1991 townhome in the heart of Brentwood" was how McKenna described the property in the listing. Nicole told Jeane McKenna that if she stayed at Bundy, it would cost her $90,000 in taxes, which was just about all the money she had in the world. She didn't want to sacrifice that stake, so she decided to look for a new place to live with her kids.

The following morning, Friday, June 10, Nicole spoke with her friend Ron Hardy, a bartender and host at several Los Angeles nightspots. Nicole explained that she was just about to leave to go look at houses with McKenna. "She was happy," Hardy later recalled. "She said everything's great, she hadn't felt this good in a while. She felt that she had finally put O.J. behind her." Nicole made dinner plans with Hardy for Monday night, then spent the rest of the day with McKenna seeking a place to lease. "We were together all day, looking at houses," McKenna later recalled. "She knew the kids really liked Bundy and wouldn't want to move, so she wanted to do something special for them, to give them something they would want—especially a pool. And by the end of the day, we found a place for her in Malibu, a one-story contemporary with a pool and a view of the ocean, for five thousand a month. I remember walking up the hill there with her. We were smoking. Nobody smokes in Brentwood, so we used to sneak it together, and she was saying, like she couldn't really believe it, 'I can really do this. I can lease the house and move. I can really do this.' "

Nicole called McKenna on Saturday night to ask when the FOR LEASE sign would go up in front of her condo. "She was anxious to have it up," McKenna said, "because she wanted to get on with her life, but also because she wanted O.J. to see it, to say 'Screw you' to him." As it turned out, McKenna was then in the process of switching real estate agencies, so she couldn't locate an appropriate sign until the following day, Sunday, June 12. At about seven that evening, a colleague from McKenna's new office dropped off a sign with her just as she was leaving for a dinner party. McKenna figured she would put it up at Nicole's afterward. She put her hammer in the car.

McKenna's dinner party was in Beverly Hills, so as she was driving home she had to decide which way she was going to turn on Bundy. "At the time," McKenna remembered later, "I lived north on Bundy and she lived south. I remember looking at the clock in my car when I hit the intersection of Bundy and San Vicente. It was 10:15. It would have taken me five minutes to get to her house. I said, 'Screw it, I'll do it tomorrow.' "

||||||

On the night of June 12, 1994, Pablo Fenjves watched the top of the ten o'clock news with his wife, Jai, a costume designer, in their third-floor master bedroom. They lived about sixty yards north of

Nicole Simpson's condominium. Both Nicole's and Fenjves's back-doors opened onto the same alley, though they had never met. Nicole had moved into the neighborhood shortly after Fenjves. In fact, 875 South Bundy was on the market when Fenjves was look-ing at houses, and he had walked through it during his search. He had found it too narrow, too expensive, and too noisy, which were common opinions about the property.

Pablo Fenjves was forty-one years old in 1994 and starting to reap the benefits of many years' toil in Hollywood. His parents, Holocaust survivors from Hungary, emigrated to Venezuela, and young Pablo went to Illinois for college and to Canada for a brief apprenticeship in journalism. From Montreal, he ventured to Florida in the late 1970s, where he went to work writing "human interest stories" for the *National Enquirer*. Even though the job brought him the opportunity to interview such notables as the world's oldest Siamese twins (they were in their twenties and em-ployed in a traveling freak show), Fenjves quickly soured on the *Enquirer* and left after about a year. He has since made his living writing screenplays.

Fenjves's progress in the business was slow but steady. In 1986, he moved from the East Coast to an apartment in Santa Monica. There he began a long and fairly prosperous interlude in a sort of shadow Hollywood; he sold script after script, and they all lan-guished unproduced, yet still he sold more scripts. Finally, as the 1990s began, his luck changed. The turning point came, at least in part, courtesy of the surefire topic of interracial romance. HBO Showcase bought (and made) *The Affair*, the story of a black sol-dier who falls in love with a white woman during World War II. Fenjves bought a BMW and a Mercedes and decided to move to Brentwood. Since Pablo Fenjves would spend "only" about half a million dollars on a home, he was pretty much limited to south of Sunset.

Sometime after 10:00 on the night of June 12, Pablo and Jai began to hear the sound of a dog barking. The actual time, Pablo later testified, was right around 10:15. A few moments later, Pablo walked downstairs to his study to fiddle with a script called *The Last Bachelor*, a romantic comedy about an amorous baseball player. Shortly before 11:00, he walked back up to the bedroom, where his wife had been watching *Dynasty: The Reunion*. The credits on the show were rolling, and the barking had still not stopped. Fenjves remembered the sound because it was not the ordinary chatter of a neighborhood dog.

The sound of the dog, Fenjves later testified, was like "a plaintive wail—sounded like a, you know, very unhappy animal." Seven months before the murders, Fenjves had written a script called *Frame-Up*, a police drama that became a television movie on the USA Network. In the first scene of the screenplay, Fenjves wrote, "We hear the plaintive wail of a police siren." In the best Hollywood tradition, Fenjves plagiarized, if only from himself, a line that had brought him a brief moment of renown.

||||||

Pablo Fenjves was not Nicole's only neighbor who heard her grief-stricken Akita in the moments after 10:15. The "dog witnesses," as they came to be known, reflected the peculiar nature of the neighborhood. Almost none of the residents, for example, had what most Americans would describe as a job—that is, a place of employment where one had to appear five days a week, eight hours a day. Rather, Nicole's neighbors made their living as freelancers, mostly in the entertainment business—screenwriters, designers, and the like—and all were prowling for the big score that would catapult them north of Sunset. Many owned dogs, and in the atomized, car-oriented culture of Los Angeles, they tended to know only those neighbors who likewise walked their dogs. Finally, virtually every person in and around 875 South Bundy on the night of June 12 answered one question the same way: What were they doing at shortly after 10:00 P.M.? Watching television.

Steven Schwab watched reruns of *The Dick Van Dyke Show* seven nights a week. Like Fenjves, Schwab was a screenwriter. He had enjoyed less success in the business than Fenjves, however, and so lived more modestly, in an apartment on Montana Avenue, about three blocks from Nicole. The burly and bearded Schwab spoke in an almost eerie monotone, which seemed to match the extreme regularity of his habits. As he later testified, "During the week I would walk my dog between 11:00 and 11:30 so that when I got home I was able to watch *The Dick Van Dyke Show* on TV. On

the weekends I walked the dog between 10:30 and 11:00 because
The Dick Van Dyke Show ends at 10:30 on the weekend." As June
12, 1994, was a Sunday, he set out with his dog, Sherry, shortly
after his favorite program ended, at 10:30 P.M.

Schwab walked his regular route around the neighborhood, a
circuit he followed as religiously as he did his television schedule.
The route, he said, "is one that I designed to take about a half hour
to get me home so I can watch whatever shows I want." At about
10:55 P.M., when he passed the alley behind Nicole's home,
Schwab saw something unusual: a beautiful white Akita that was
barking at a house. It paused to look at Schwab and then barked at
the house again. Curious about the behavior and a little worried
about this seemingly abandoned animal, Schwab approached the
dog, let it sniff him, and examined its collar. He noticed that the
collar was expensive—"It wasn't something that I could afford to
get for my own dog"—but it did not give a name or address. As he
studied the dog more carefully, Schwab noticed something else.
There was blood on all four of the animal's paws.

Schwab couldn't figure out where the dog belonged, so he just
headed home. The Akita followed him. (In August 1994, the Akita
would be "interviewed" by Sergeant Donn Yarnall, the chief trainer
of the Los Angeles Police Department's "K-9 Patrol." Yarnall's report described the dog as having a "very nice disposition" but "inadequate instincts or courage to protect his territory, owner or
himself.") With the dog right behind him, Schwab made it home
shortly after 11:00, just after *The Mary Tyler Moore Show* had
begun. Eight months later, Schwab remembered that "it was an
episode that I had seen previously, involving Mary dating someone
from a rival station." Schwab told his wife, Linda, that a large dog
had followed him home. "You're kidding," she said, but then he
pointed to the Akita, which was waiting patiently on the landing
outside their second-floor apartment. While Steven and Linda
pondered what to do, they gave the dog some water. As they were
talking, at about 11:40 P.M. the Schwabs' neighbor Sukru Boztepe
walked into the apartment complex. A freelance laser printer re-
pairman who still speaks with the accent of his native Turkey,
Boztepe and his Danish-born wife, Bettina Rasmussen, had hosted
a garage sale with the Schwabs earlier that day.

After the two couples chatted for a few minutes, Boztepe agreed that he and his wife would keep the dog for the night. But when they took it inside, Boztepe later testified, the "dog was acting so nervous running around, scratching the door, and we didn't feel comfortable sleeping with such a big dog in the apartment, and we decide to take the dog for a walk. So we took it." They let the Akita lead them, and the dog pulled them back toward Bundy Drive—"It was getting more nervous and it was pulling me harder." Just after midnight, the dog stopped in front of a gate on Bundy that was labeled 875. Boztepe remembered that the area was so dark that he never would have looked down the pathway behind the gate if the dog had not called his attention to it.

What did he see there?

"I saw a lady laying down full of blood."

Officer Robert Riske of the Los Angeles Police Department was patrolling West Los Angeles in a black-and-white squad car when his radio summoned him at 12:09 A.M. on June 13. There had been a report of a crime from 874 South Bundy, in Brentwood. Four minutes later, Riske and his partner arrived at the address, which was the home of an elderly woman, Elsie Tistaert. She had called the police because a few moments earlier, a man and a woman—Sukru Boztepe and Bettina Rasmussen, it would turn out—had banged on her door. It wasn't the kind of thing that usually went on in the neighborhood, and Tistaert was scared. She called 911 and reported a possible attempted burglary of her home.

When Riske rolled up to the scene, he found Boztepe and Rasmussen, who were still tending to Kato-the-Akita, and the officer quickly straightened out the confusion about why the police were needed. Boztepe took Riske across the street and showed him the pathway to number 875. The officer shined his flashlight on the corpse of Nicole Brown Simpson.

Nicole was lying at the base of four stairs that led up to a landing and the front door. The pool of blood around her was bigger than she was. Blood covered much of the imitation-tile walkway leading to the stairs, a path that was bordered on both sides by shrubbery. When Riske pointed his flashlight to the right, he saw another body. It was a muscular young man with his shirt pulled up over his head. The man, later identified as Ronald Goldman, was slumped against the metal fence that separated 875 from the property next door. Near Goldman's feet, Riske identified three items: a black hat, a white envelope stained with blood, and a single leather glove. Turning back to Nicole, Riske made out a single fresh heel print in the blood next to her body. Perhaps the most important thing to Riske was what he didn't find: Despite all the blood, there were no bloody shoe prints coming out the front gate onto the sidewalk by Bundy Drive.

Careful not to make tracks in the blood, Riske tiptoed through the bushes to the left of the pathway, past Nicole's body, and up to the landing. From the landing, he shined his flashlight on a walkway that stretched the entire northern length of the property. Along this 120-foot-long corridor, Riske saw a single set of bloody shoe prints. It appeared that the killer had gone out the back way, to the alley that Nicole shared with Pablo Fenjves and other neighbors. On closer inspection, Riske noticed something else: fresh drops of blood to the left of those shoe prints. While leaving the scene, the killer might well have been bleeding from the left hand.

The front door to 875 South Bundy was open. Riske walked in to a scene of domestic calm. Nothing was out of place: no signs of ransacking or theft. Candles flickered in the living room. The officer walked up the stairs. There were lighted candles in the master bedroom and master bath, too, and the tub there was full of water. There were two other bedrooms, with a young girl asleep in one and a younger boy in the other.

Robert Riske knew his place in the chain of command. Once he had identified the dead and closed off access to the scene, his only responsibility was to summon the investigators, who would begin looking for clues. This was a major crime in an unlikely locale. (Eventually, there would be 1,811 murder victims in Los Angeles County in 1994, but these two were only the ninth and tenth of the year in the West Los Angeles division of the LAPD and the first two of the year in Brentwood.) As Riske prepared to summon assistance on his "rover," a portable walkie-talkie, he noticed a letter on the front hall table. The return address indicated that it was from O. J. Simpson. The former football star was also depicted in a poster on the north wall of the home. On closer inspection, Riske found photographs of Simpson among the family pictures scattered on tables.

These discoveries prompted a change in Riske's plans. He decided to call for help on the telephone because, as he testified later, "I didn't want to broadcast over my rover that there was a possible double homicide involving a celebrity." Reporters monitored the police bands, and if he had used his rover, he said, "the media would beat my backup there."

Robert Riske was only a four-year veteran of the LAPD when he made his grisly discoveries. His name had never even appeared in the *Los Angeles Times,* but as his actions demonstrated, he had already developed an interest in, and some sophistication about, the ways of the press. In this he was typical. More than any other police force in the nation, the LAPD was locked in a strange and complex symbiosis, of several decades' duration, with the media.

||||||

The modern Los Angeles Police Department was largely the creation of one man, William H. Parker. Born in 1902 and raised in the hard fields of South Dakota, Parker came to resemble in character the austere setting of his youth. He moved west to Los Angeles in 1923 and drove a cab to support himself while he studied at one of the many fledgling law schools that were springing up around the city. He joined the LAPD in 1927, worked a night shift on patrol, and became a member of the bar in 1930. Some years later, he made the acquaintance of another young LAPD officer, Gene Roddenberry, who eventually turned to writing science fiction and created *Star Trek.* The character of Spock is said to be based on Bill Parker.

Parker joined the force at a propitious time for an ambitious and incorruptible young officer. For years the LAPD, along with the rest of Los Angeles city government, had floated on a sea of graft and payoffs. The situation became so intolerable in the 1930s that the city's business leaders decided changes had to be made. They hired from out of town a series of reform-minded police chiefs, who brought with them the gospel of "professionalization" of the force. The new leadership improved training, cracked down on corruption, and worked to insulate the police from what was then seen as the sinister influence of elected officials. This last goal became the special mission of Bill Parker. Working in tandem with the police union, Parker drafted changes in Section 202 of the city charter, which put a cast-iron shield of civil-service law around all police officers. After voters approved these measures in 1937, it became virtually impossible to fire cops; they could only be dismissed by a panel of their invariably sympathetic brethren. The law even decreed that the police chief would be selected according to civil-service guidelines, which meant that the LAPD would determine for itself who would serve as its leader. Once selected, the chief would also enjoy the protection of the civil-service law, which amounted to lifetime tenure in the top spot of the LAPD. As Joe Domanick, a historian of the LAPD, has written of the changes in Section 202, "A quasi-military organization had declared itself independent of the rest of city government and placed itself outside the control of the police commission, City Hall, or any other elected public officials, outside the democratic system of checks and balances."

Parker became chief in 1950, when Los Angeles was in the midst of a period of spectacular postwar growth. At that point the city was no longer, in H. L. Mencken's phrase, "a double Dubuque"— an insular, nearly all-white outpost of the Midwest on the Pacific Ocean. But if Los Angeles was changing, the LAPD was not. Parker's model for his force was the Marine Corps, and so the police became tantamount to an army of occupation for those in the city who did not share Parker's ethnic heritage. As far as the rest of the world was concerned, though, the LAPD under Bill Parker became known as a model of efficiency and skill. This did not happen by accident. Shortly after Parker took charge, he became acquainted with a young radio producer named Jack Webb. In 1949, Webb had started a radio series, *Dragnet,* based on the exploits of the LAPD. At first Parker was suspicious of the show, worried that it might place his beloved department in an unflattering light. Aware of his discomfort, Webb proposed a deal: In return for the LAPD's cooperation, he would give the department the right to approve every script. Parker's suspicions eased. When *Dragnet* moved to television, Parker understood just how advantageous an arrangement he had struck. Sergeant Joe Friday became the paradigm of what Parker wanted in an LAPD officer: an incorruptible white man who, with scientific detachment, descended on neighborhoods where he had no personal or emotional ties to clean up the messes made by the vaguely distasteful residents of the city. Soon Parker was only too happy to have *Dragnet* conclude each week with the announcement "You have just seen *Dragnet,* a series of authentic cases from official files. . . . Technical advice for *Dragnet* comes from the offices of Chief of Police W. H. Parker, Los Angeles Police Department." Jack Webb, who later wrote an admiring biography of Parker, had created one of the longest-lived genres in television programming, the L.A. police drama, which has included, at various times, *The Mod Squad, Adam 12, Felony Squad, Blue Thunder, S.W.A.T., Strike Force, Chopper One, The Rookies, Hunter,* and *T. J. Hooker.* As Joe Domanick wrote, "For twenty-five consecutive seasons at least one LAPD police show was being aired on network television." They portrayed the LAPD in a manner that made Bill Parker proud.

Parker and his wife never had children, and the chief remained aloof from most of his colleagues on the force. He did, however, take a special shine to the young officer who was assigned to be his personal chauffeur—Daryl Gates. Together the two men refined a theory of "proactive policing," which featured relentless confrontations between heavily armed officers and the hostile populations they patrolled. Parker and Gates came of age in an era when white cops didn't have to rein in their feelings about African-Americans. When Watts exploded in 1965—a rebellion set off by a confrontation between a black motorist and a uniformed officer of the California Highway Patrol—Parker compared the black rioters to "monkeys in a zoo." A year later, a black man named Leonard Deadwyler was rushing his pregnant wife to the hospital when he was stopped by police for speeding. In the ensuing confrontation, the unarmed Deadwyler was shot dead. "Police are not supposed to stand by and watch a car speeding down the street at eighty miles per hour," Parker explained. "[The officer] did something he thought would successfully conclude a police action. All he is guilty of is trying to do his job."

True to the intent of the civil-service law, Parker served until he died, and Gates took over as chief in 1978. The selection process that led to Gates's appointment seemed designed as a direct affront to the city's black community: To head the internal review of candidates for the job, the LAPD brought in Curtis LeMay, the far-right-wing former air force general who had served as George Wallace's running mate in 1968 and earlier had promised to bomb North Vietnam "back to the Stone Age."

After Gates took over, the list of black victims of the LAPD grew ever longer. In 1979 Eulia Love, a thirty-nine-year-old black widow who was late in paying her gas bill, hit a meter reader on the arm with a garden shovel. The utility man summoned police officers, who, rather than defuse the situation, shot Love dead at point-blank range. In 1982, after a number of African-American men died from police choke holds, Gates observed that the deaths might have been caused by the distinctive physiology of the black victims: "We may be finding that in some blacks when [the choke hold] is applied, the veins or arteries do not open up as fast as they do on normal people." It mattered little that Los Angeles had had a black mayor, Tom Bradley, since 1973. The LAPD answered to no one.

A raid on a suspected narcotics operation in August 1988 may have been the paradigmatic LAPD operation. About eighty police officers (and one helicopter) swooped in on four apartments in two small buildings at Thirty-ninth Street and Dalton Avenue, on the periphery of the South Central district. The officers, armed with shotguns and sledgehammers, barreled through the rooms. They tore plumbing out of the walls, ripped a stairway from its moorings, pulled carpet from the floor, destroyed furniture and appliances, and kicked and punched the stunned residents. For all the terror it unleashed, the raid netted only two minor drug arrests. Nevertheless, the officers on the scene did find reasons to take thirty-two residents of the complex back to the local precinct, where the captives were forced to whistle the theme song from the 1960s situation comedy *The Andy Griffith Show*. Before they left the Dalton homes, some officers had spray-painted the words LAPD RULES on the walls.

Less than three years later, a passerby videotaped LAPD officers beating unarmed motorist Rodney King. On April 30, 1992, the four officers who administered the beating were acquitted in a trial that had been moved from downtown Los Angeles to the rustic (and largely white) Simi Valley. As it had in 1965, the city once again erupted in a riot of protest, rage, and frustration. A blue-ribbon commission, headed by future secretary of state Warren Christopher, after studying the King beating and its aftermath, delivered a deadpan verdict that was many years in coming. "The problem of excessive force is aggravated by racism and bias within the LAPD," the Christopher commission concluded. "These attitudes of prejudice and intolerance are translated into unacceptable behavior in the field."

At 12:30 A.M. on June 13, Officer Robert Riske telephoned news of the two homicides to his supervisor, David Rossi, the sergeant in charge of the West Los Angeles station at the time. Rossi promptly made a half dozen phone calls around the LAPD chain of command, setting in motion the police response to the crimes. In an ordinary case, even a homicide, Rossi would probably have made only two calls—to the detective on duty, who would investigate the scene, and to his own commander. But Rossi's supervisor immediately told him to reach higher in the command structure because of, as Rossi later put it, "the possible notoriety of this particular incident."

A steady stream of officers began converging on the murder scene at 875 South Bundy. Sergeant Marty Coon was the first supervisor to arrive. Riske and his partner put up yellow crime-scene tape to block access to this block on Bundy and to the back alley. Additional officers came to make sure no one passed through the tape. A squad car arrived to take the two children to the West L.A. station, and two more officers began walking through the alley, searching garbage pails for possible evidence and knocking on doors in an effort to find witnesses. By the time David Rossi arrived at the scene at 1:30 A.M., the tape was up and the scene quiet. Moments later, Rossi's boss, Captain Constance Dial, arrived as well. Riske took Coon and Rossi for a quick tour. Standing on the landing by the front door, Rossi saw what Riske had seen: the two bodies, the trail of blood heading toward the alley, the envelope, the knit hat, and the single leather glove.

Before leaving the station for the crime scene, Rossi had reached the chief of the West L.A. detective-homicide unit that would be in charge of the investigation, Ron Phillips, at home. A twenty-eight-year veteran of the LAPD, Phillips no longer investigated crimes himself; rather, it was his responsibility to visit the crime scene, talk with the uniformed officers who had discovered the bodies, and assign the case to one of the four homicide detectives who worked under him.

In the early morning hours of June 13, Phillips's on-call detective for the next case was Mark Fuhrman, who would be assisted by his more junior partner, Brad Roberts. Phillips called Fuhrman and Roberts at their respective homes and told them to meet him at the West L.A. station. Roberts couldn't get to the station as quickly as the other two, so when Phillips and Fuhrman met there at shortly before 2:00, they took an unmarked police car and proceeded together to the murder scene. They arrived at about 2:10 A.M. As Fuhrman approached the scene, he wore a shirt and tie but no jacket. According to the crime-scene log, Detective Mark Fuhrman was the seventeenth police officer to arrive at 875 South Bundy Drive.

Riske met Phillips and Fuhrman at the front of the house on Bundy and took them on a tour of the scene. They walked together toward the front door and hunched together in the shrubbery to the left of the pathway while Riske shined his high-powered flashlight on the female victim's body. But because the front pathway was so covered with blood, the three men decided not to try to tiptoe around it and up the stairs, as Riske had done when he first discovered the scene, but instead walked around the block, via Dorothy Street, to the back alley. Rossi was waiting for them in the alley, and he pointed out some blood on the rear gate to Phillips. Riske, Phillips, and Fuhrman then entered the house through the garage, passing a black Jeep Cherokee and a white Ferrari, and then walked up a short flight of stairs. On the bannister next to the stairs there was a partially eaten cup of Ben & Jerry's ice cream— Chocolate Chip Cookie Dough in flavor.

Riske led the two detectives through the house, including the second floor, and then back to the landing. There Phillips and Fuhrman could see the two bodies in front and the bloody shoe prints on the walkway leading to the back alley. Riske shined his flashlight around the scene once more, pointing out for the detec-

tives the envelope as well as the hat and the glove, which were partially obscured by the foliage. They went back into the house and
left through a door that opened onto the walkway that ran along
the northern edge of the property. Riske showed them at close
range the bloody shoe prints with the blood drops to the left. The
three men then went out the back gate, which was, Riske pointed
out, also stained with blood, especially on the handle.

After they completed their tour, Phillips and Fuhrman split up.
Phillips stayed outside to use his cellular phone. Fuhrman wanted
to make some notes of what he had seen. He wasn't writing a formal report at this stage, just his preliminary observations to refer
to as his investigation proceeded. Fuhrman reentered the house
through the garage and sat down on a couch in the living room to
scribble down some of what he had seen and been told. Number-
ing his entries, Fuhrman noted that Riske had discovered the bodies and made the initial report. The causes of death were still
unknown, and Fuhrman hadn't gotten close enough to the bodies
to make any definitive finding. The third item in his notes said the
victims had "Possible GSW"—gunshot wounds. Fuhrman made
reference to the two children who had been taken to the police station, the lit candles, the melting ice cream. Fuhrman noted the
blood drops to the left of the shoe prints on the walkway. "Suspect
ran through this area," he wrote. "Suspect possibly bitten by dog."
He made several mentions of blood on the rear gate, including a
note that said, referring to the handle that opened the gate from
inside the property, "Possible blood smudge and visible fingerprint." In all, Fuhrman listed seventeen items for follow-up. He
was writing his last entry—"Ski mask, one glove by feet of male victim"—when he was interrupted.

Brad Roberts had arrived and was asking for an update.
Fuhrman quickly walked his partner to the landing and showed
him the bodies, the hat, and the glove, and then they went back
along the walkway that was marked with the bloody shoe prints.
Afterward, Roberts headed around the block toward the Bundy entrance, and Fuhrman returned to the couch to work on his notes.
He was interrupted again. This time it was his boss, Ron Phillips.
Phillips told Fuhrman that the West L.A. team was off the case. It
was being turned over to Robbery-Homicide Division, the head-

quarters unit that handles especially complex or high-profile cases. Moments later, Fuhrman followed Phillips out of the house through the garage. It was about 2:40 A.M., and Mark Fuhrman's tenure as lead detective on this double homicide was over. It had lasted about thirty minutes.

||||||

Shortly after arriving at Bundy, Phillips had received a cellular phone call from one of the highest-ranking officers in the entire LAPD. Keith Bushey was the commander of operations for the western quarter of Los Angeles, a region that included not only West L.A. but the Hollywood, Pacific, and Wilshire divisions as well. Bushey had an order for Phillips. Since one of the victims was the ex-wife of O. J. Simpson—and because children presumed to be his had been removed from the house—he wanted Simpson personally informed of the murder. Bushey said he wanted to avoid a "Belushi situation." (When the actor and comedian John Belushi had died at the Chateau Marmont Hotel in 1982, the news media had learned of it almost instantaneously and broadcast the information before the LAPD had the chance to notify any family members in person. It had been painful for Belushi's family and embarrassing for the LAPD.)

Phillips hadn't had a chance to act on this order in his first half hour on the scene because he had, for the most part, been inspecting the evidence with Fuhrman. Then, at about 2:30 A.M., Lieutenant Frank Spangler, in charge of all detectives in West Los Angeles and thus Phillips's boss, arrived bearing the news that Phillips and his team were to withdraw from the case in deference to the Robbery-Homicide Division. In light of this change, Phillips decided that he would hold off on notifying Simpson as well.

Fuhrman pointed out some of the evidence, including the single glove and the envelope, for a police photographer who had arrived on the scene, but for the most part Fuhrman and Phillips stood around and waited for the detectives who were going to replace them. They stood together on Bundy chatting for almost an hour and a half, although at one point Fuhrman and Spangler did approach the male victim from the adjacent property to the north and together stared at the body through a fence.

At 4:05 A.M., Philip Vannatter, a Robbery-Homicide detective, arrived. Phillips mentioned to Vannatter that Bushey had ordered him to tell O. J. Simpson in person about the deaths. What should he do? Vannatter brushed off the issue, saying he would worry about it after he had seen the crime scene. At that point, Phillips walked Vannatter through the crime scene as he had been introduced to it by Officer Riske. At 4:30, Vannatter's partner, Tom Lange, arrived, and Phillips gave him the tour, too. The LAPD had about fourteen hundred detectives, and neither Phillips nor Fuhrman had ever previously met Vannatter or Lange.

When the two senior detectives had completed their walk-throughs, Phillips again raised the issue of Bushey's order for an in-person notification of Simpson. He was concerned about not having followed a very specific order from a high-ranking official. When was O.J. going to be notified? Vannatter said that since it was Simpson's ex-wife who had been murdered, he and Lange would need to interview him anyway. As Lange testified later, "I think it is very important to establish a rapport, especially with persons who are close to the victim, to get information." And besides, Simpson might be able to help them identify the male victim, whose name the police did not yet know. There was also the matter of the children. Simpson, who was bound to be upset at the news of the murder, might well need some assistance in collecting the boy and girl from the police station. So Vannatter decided that all four detectives would make the trip to Simpson's home. Vannatter and Lange would introduce themselves to Simpson, assist in the notification, and then return promptly to begin their investigation of the crime scene, while the two junior detectives would help Simpson retrieve his children. Before they left, they had to settle one obvious question: Where did Simpson live?

Fuhrman said he knew. He told Phillips that when he was a uniformed patrol officer in West L.A., he had gone on a radio call to the Simpson home. "I went up there a long time ago on a family dispute," Fuhrman said. "I think I can find it." He didn't remember the exact address, but Riske, who had run the plates on the Jeep parked in Nicole's garage, told Fuhrman that the plates had come back to 360 North Rockingham. In his report of the evening's activities, Lange summarized Fuhrman's information this way: "Mr. Simpson and victim had been embroiled in previous domestic-violence situations, one of these resulting in the arrest of Mr. Simpson." (Phillips later testified he did not remember any such discussion that evening, although it is possible he simply did not hear what Fuhrman said to Lange.) So, at just about 5:00 A.M., Phillips and Fuhrman led Vannatter and Lange in a two-car caravan from Bundy to Rockingham. The two-mile trip took about five minutes.

As the two cars made a right turn off Sunset Boulevard onto Rockingham Avenue, the terrain changed and the houses grew larger, grander. Traveling uphill along the silent street, the detectives strained to see the house numbers painted on the curbs. Earlier in his career, Vannatter had spent four years as a detective in West L.A., yet he had never driven on or even heard of Rockingham. It was not the kind of street that generated much police activity. Still, on that night he noticed one of the customs of the neighborhood. Rockingham was not a major artery, but it did serve as the conduit to Sunset for many smaller streets, and residents tended to avoid parking on it so that traffic could move freely. On this night, Rockingham was empty—except for a single vehicle. Just before the detectives reached the intersection of Rockingham Avenue and Ashford Street, Vannatter noticed a white Ford Bronco by the curb. On closer inspection, it appeared that the vehicle was slightly askew, as if it had been hurriedly parked. As it turned out, this car was stopped directly in front of number 360, which occupied the corner lot. The detectives turned right onto Ashford and parked their two cars near an iron gate set in the brick wall that surrounded O. J. Simpson's property.

A couple of lights were on in the house, and there were two cars in the driveway. Vannatter rang the buzzer by the gate. No answer. He rang some more, and then Phillips and Lange rang for a while. Still no response. A medallion posted near the house announced that it was protected by Westec, a prominent security firm in Los Angeles. By coincidence, a marked Westec car happened to drive by, and the detectives flagged it down. They persuaded the security guard to give them Simpson's home telephone number. (The guard also said that according to Westec records, a full-time housekeeper was usually on the premises.) At 5:36 A.M., Phillips began calling Simpson's number on his cellular phone, but Simpson's answering machine—"This is O.J.," the message began—took the call each time.

Fuhrman hung back while the other three detectives tried to raise someone in the house. Though he had been a police officer for nineteen years, he was a level-two detective while the others were at level three; in the hierarchical world of the LAPD, it was therefore his place to defer. So, with nothing to do, Fuhrman wandered around the corner, back to Rockingham, and over to the Bronco. He shined his small pocket flashlight into the back and saw papers addressed to O. J. Simpson. Fuhrman then studied the driver's door and noticed a small red stain just above the handle. Near the bottom of the door, on the exposed portion of the door-sill, he saw several more thin red stripes.

"I think I saw something on the Bronco," Fuhrman called to Vannatter.

The senior detective came by to study the vehicle more closely, and the two men agreed that the stains looked like blood. Vannatter directed Fuhrman to run the license plates and see who owned the car. The plates came back to the Hertz Corporation, whose products Simpson had long endorsed.

Vannatter and Lange conferred. They decided that Vannatter would radio a request for a police criminalist to come and test the stain and see if it really was blood on the Bronco door. More generally, as they testified later, Vannatter and Lange were growing concerned about what might have happened inside Simpson's property. They had just come from the scene of a brutal murder. Someone was supposed to be living at the Simpson home—at least a housekeeper—and there was no answer, even though lights were on. There appeared to be blood on the car outside. As Lange said later in court, "I felt that someone inside that house may be the victim of a crime, maybe bleeding or worse." Vannatter testified, "After leaving a very violent bloody murder scene, I believed something was wrong there. I made a determination that we needed to go over—to go into the property." Fuhrman—by far the youngest and fittest of the four detectives on the scene—volunteered. "I can go over the wall," he said. "Okay, go," said Lange. Fuhrman hoisted himself over the six-foot-high brick wall, then stepped to his right and manually opened the hydraulic gate. The four detectives entered O. J. Simpson's property.

|||||

Simpson's dog—a black chow—did not stir as the detectives passed it on their way to the front door. Vannatter knocked. No answer. They waited two or three minutes, knocked again, and still heard no stirring inside. The four detectives decided to take a look around, and so, still using flashlights in the moments before dawn, they walked together toward the rear of the house. There they saw a row of three guest houses, though they were really more like connected rooms, each with its own entrance. Phillips peered into one.

"There's—I see someone inside," he said.

Phillips knocked, and almost immediately a disheveled man who obviously had just awoken answered the door. Shaking his mane of blond hair out of his eyes, Kato Kaelin stared at Phillips, who identified himself and asked, "Is O. J. Simpson home?"

The groggy Kaelin said he didn't know, but suggested the officers knock at the adjacent guest house, where Simpson's daughter Arnelle lived. Phillips, accompanied by Vannatter and Lange, then knocked on Arnelle's door. Fuhrman stayed behind and asked Kaelin if he could come in. Fuhrman noticed that Kaelin seemed disoriented, even for someone who had just awakened. Fuhrman gave Kaelin a standard police test for intoxication: Holding a pen about fifteen inches in front of Kaelin's face, he watched to see if Kaelin could follow it with his eyes. Kaelin passed—he just *looked* zonked. Fuhrman asked to look around the small suite. As Fuhrman poked around—among other things, checking the shoes in the closet for blood—the detective asked if anything unusual had happened the previous night.

As a matter of fact, something unusual *had* happened. At about 10:45 P.M., while he was talking on the telephone, Kaelin said, there were some loud thumps on his bedroom wall, near the air conditioner. The jolts were so dramatic that a picture on the wall was jostled. He had thought there was going to be an earthquake.

The two men chatted a while longer, then Fuhrman walked with Kaelin into the main house, where the other three detectives were speaking with Arnelle Simpson. Fuhrman then decided to follow up on what Kaelin had told him. He left Kaelin in the house with the other detectives, walked back outside, and tried to orient himself to see what faced the south wall of Kaelin's bedroom—the wall where Kaelin had heard the loud noises. Fuhrman saw that the south wall faced the edge of Simpson's property, which was marked by a Cyclone fence, and that there was a narrow passageway between the back of the guest houses and the fence.

"I took out my flashlight and I started walking down the path trying to figure out the residence architecture to figure out where Kaelin's wall might have been," Fuhrman testified later. "I saw a long, dark path covered with leaves." When Fuhrman had walked about twenty feet along the path, he saw a dark object on the ground, but it wasn't until he was practically upon it that he realized what it was. "At some point," Fuhrman remembered, "I could tell that it was a glove."

It looked out of place. There were no leaves or twigs on it, and the glove looked moist or sticky, with some parts adhering to one another. Fuhrman stepped around the glove and kept walking along the path, but he started hitting cobwebs, which he had not previously encountered. He followed the path all the way to the end, which was an untended patch of dirt, then headed back out, passing the glove once more. He didn't touch it, but he noticed something about it: "It looked similar to the glove on the Bundy scene."

|||||

While Fuhrman had stopped in Kaelin's room to talk to him, the other three detectives had knocked on Arnelle Simpson's door, which she promptly answered. Phillips told her there was an emergency, and he needed to speak to her father—did she know how to reach him? Arnelle gestured to the main house and asked, "Isn't he there?" The officers told Arnelle that her father was apparently not there. Leaving her guest house, Arnelle began walking toward the Ashford gate to see if her father's car was there—that was where he usually parked it. The detective informed her that the Bronco was in fact parked on Rockingham. Using her key, Arnelle let them into the main house.

On the way they passed the third guest house—it belonged to the housekeeper, Gigi Guarin—and noticed that it was empty, the bed still made. Once they were inside the main house, Arnelle called Cathy Randa, her father's longtime secretary, who always knew O.J.'s whereabouts. Arnelle handed the phone to Phillips, who told Randa there was an emergency that required their speaking with Simpson. Randa said he had taken the red-eye flight to Chicago the previous night and was staying at an airport hotel, the Chicago O'Hare Plaza.

Phillips called the hotel at 6:05 A.M. and asked to be put through to O. J. Simpson's room. Though he recognized the voice, the detective still asked, "Is this O. J. Simpson?"

"Yes, who is this?"

Phillips chose his words carefully when he delivered news of Nicole's death to O.J. "This is Detective Phillips from the Los Angeles Police Department. I have some bad news for you. Your ex-wife, Nicole Simpson, has been killed."

Simpson was distraught. "Oh my God, Nicole is killed? Oh my God, she is dead?"

Phillips tried to calm him. "Mr. Simpson, please try to get ahold of yourself. I have your children at the West Los Angeles police station. I need to talk to you about that."

"What do you mean you have my children at the police station? Why are my kids at the police station?"

"Because we had no place else to take them," Phillips answered. "They are there for safekeeping. I need to know what to do with your children."

"Well, I'm going to be leaving out of Chicago on the first available flight," Simpson said. "I will come back to Los Angeles." Phillips then handed the phone to Arnelle, who agreed with her father that she would ask his friend Al Cowlings to pick up the children.

Phillips never spoke to Simpson again. Later, the detective found it worth noting what Simpson did *not* say in their brief conversation. Simpson never asked how or when Nicole had been "killed." Phillips had not said (and Simpson did not ask) whether she had been killed in an accident or a murder.

|||||

The drowsy children waited at the police station for someone to explain what had happened to them. At one point, eight-year-old

Sydney Simpson asked to make a phone call, and she dialed her home number. The answering machine picked up, and Sydney left a message: "Mommy, please call me back. I want to know what happened last night. Why did we have to go to the police station? Please answer, Mommy. Please answer, Mommy. Please answer, Mommy. Please answer. 'Bye."

The pace of events picked up quickly after Mark Fuhrman discovered the glove on the path behind Kato Kaelin's room. After Phillips spoke to Simpson in Chicago, Tom Lange had the melancholy duty of notifying Nicole Brown Simpson's parents of her death. LAPD policy called for detectives to notify a homicide victim's next of kin in person if possible, but Lange learned from Arnelle that Lou and Juditha Brown lived in Orange County, about seventy-five miles away. Lange knew the media would soon learn about the murders and suspected that if he didn't speak to Nicole's parents immediately, they would learn of their daughter's death from television news reports.

Lou Brown answered the telephone at 6:21 A.M. He took the news quietly. Lange did not know that Nicole's sister Denise, the oldest of the four Brown daughters, lived at the family home and that she had picked up the phone on another extension.

Denise began screaming, "He killed her! He finally killed her!"

"Who?" asked Lange.

"O.J.!" said Denise.

Meanwhile, behind the house, Fuhrman quickly appreciated the significance of what he had found. The detective later recalled in testimony that "when I found the glove back here on this pathway, I will have to—I have to admit to you that the adrenaline started pumping because I didn't really know what was going on. . . . When I found the glove and actually realized this glove was very close in description and color to the glove at the crime scene, my heart started pounding and I realized what I had probably found." One by one, Fuhrman took each of the other three detectives down the narrow pathway to study the glove without touching it. They all agreed that based on what they remembered, this right-hand glove looked like a match for the one at Bundy, but Vannatter sent Phillips and Fuhrman back to the murder scene to make a closer comparison. Lange would go back, too, to begin examining the evidence there, while Vannatter would await the criminalist at Rockingham.

The evidence stacked up quickly and led to a plausible theory of events: It appeared that the killer had dropped a left glove in a struggle at the murder scene and then suffered a cut on his exposed left hand. Bleeding, the killer then walked to a car in the back alley—very possibly Simpson's Bronco. He then traveled to Rockingham where, perhaps in an effort to hide his clothes on the narrow path behind Kato's room, he had dropped the other glove. "This is a crime scene," Vannatter declared at Rockingham.

After the other three detectives left for Bundy, Vannatter decided to take a look around O. J. Simpson's property. He stepped out the front door and onto the driveway, near the two parked cars. The sun was coming up at this point, and in the spreading daylight, Vannatter noticed what appeared to be a drop of blood on the ground. Then he found another . . . and another. The drops were all more or less in a row heading from the Rockingham gate to the front door. Vannatter opened that gate and took another look at the Bronco parked nearby. He stared in from the passenger side and noticed blood on the console between the two seats—and more blood on the inside of the driver's door. Vannatter thought back to what he had seen at Bundy. The individual drops to the left of the bloody shoe prints leaving the two bodies resembled in size, shape, and color the drops here at Rockingham. Vannatter went back into O. J. Simpson's home and found more blood drops in the foyer, just beyond the front door. The trail of blood now led right into Simpson's home.

The criminalist, Dennis Fung, arrived at Rockingham at 7:10 A.M. and did a quick test of the red stain on the exterior of the Bronco. It was only a presumptive test, and so not 100 percent definitive, but it suggested the presence of human blood. Fuhrman returned from Nicole's condominium a few moments later. He said the glove at Bundy was for a left hand, and told Vannatter that it did indeed look like a match for the right glove found behind Kaelin's room.

That's it, said Vannatter. We need to get a search warrant for this place. Vannatter left for the West Los Angeles station to write one up. Once there, he decided to touch base with deputy district attorney Marcia Clark. Vannatter and Clark had recently completed work together on a murder case that focused on blood and other trace evidence, and the detective wanted a second opinion on the facts he had gathered so far in this case. Checking with a prosecutor made sense for a detective; lawyers usually had better antennae than cops for determining whether a judge would grant a search warrant. For her part, Clark was only too pleased to receive Vannatter's call at home shortly after eight on that Monday morning. A workaholic, and something of a crime junkie, she relished the details of criminal investigations as much as courtroom prosecutions.

Vannatter told Clark about the apparently matching gloves and then summarized the trail of blood—which wound from the left side of the shoe prints at Bundy, to the Bronco on Rockingham, to the driveway, and then to the foyer of Simpson's home. Clark listened to Vannatter dispassionately and was struck only by one thing: the fancy neighborhood where the murders had taken place.

"Marcia," Vannatter said. "It's O. J. Simpson."

"Who's that?" Clark replied.

"You know, the football player, actor, *Naked Gun*."

Marcia Clark had never followed sports. She went to the movies only once in a while. Just about her only connection to mass culture was when she listened to her Doors albums. For relaxation, she read novels about serial murderers.

"Sorry," Clark said. "Never heard of him."

On hearing the facts of the case, Clark thought there was more than enough evidence to get a search warrant—probably enough to arrest Simpson himself. But Vannatter said they should take it one step at a time, and he hung up. Then he began drafting the affidavit he would be required to submit in order to get a search warrant.

In his affidavit, Vannatter said he had been a police officer for over twenty-five years and a detective for fifteen. He wrote that after examining the crime scene, he and his partner had traveled to 360 North Rockingham to notify O. J. Simpson of the murder of his ex-wife. When they examined the Ford Bronco, Vannatter went on, they "noticed what appeared to be human blood, later confirmed by Scientific Investigation personnel to be human blood on the driver's door handle of the vehicle." Vannatter continued, "It was determined by interviews of Simpson's daughter and a friend Brian Kaelin [that Simpson] had left on an unexpected flight to Chicago during the early morning hours of June 13, 1994, and was last seen at the residence at approximately 2300 hours, June 12, 1994."

A magistrate signed the warrant in the late morning, and Vannatter returned to the Rockingham estate at just about noon on Monday, June 13, which was, as it happened, almost the same time O. J. Simpson arrived home from his abbreviated trip to Chicago.

|||||

Simpson's friends often used the same expression to describe him: "He loved being O.J." That was, in many respects, his occupation—being O.J. By 1994, he was long retired from his days of football glory. He had modest visibility as a sports broadcaster and some minor success as an actor in occasional self-mocking roles in the *Naked Gun* movies. He judged beauty contests. He shilled for Hertz. He pitched in an infomercial for an arthritis cure. At the time of his arrest for murder, Simpson had only a vaporous, peculiarly American kind of renown: He was famous for being O.J. (When Nicole Brown Simpson called 911 on October 25, 1993, and complained that her ex-husband was "going nuts" outside her home, she assumed that his name would be immediately recognizable; but having heard it, the dispatcher asked, "Is he the sportscaster or whatever?")

The event Simpson planned to attend in Chicago on Monday, June 13, demonstrated how he made his living as a "sportscaster or whatever." He was due that day at the Mission Hills Country Club, in suburban Northbrook, to play in the Hertz Invitational, the rental car company's annual tournament for its top corporate customers in the neighboring thirteen-state area. In 1994, playing golf was pretty much all O. J. Simpson did for Hertz, though he did a lot of it. (The previous week, he had played for Hertz in Virginia.)

It had been a different story when he first signed with Hertz in the 1970s, when he was still playing football. At that time Simpson starred in some of the best-known television advertisements of the era, which featured the handsome athlete leaping over furniture in airports to make a swift connection to his rental car. "Go, O.J., go!," a grandmotherly matron shouted after him. At the time Hertz even tied its corporate slogan to its celebrity spokesman, touting itself as "the superstar in rent-a-car." But a decade and a half later, the company paid him about half a million dollars a year to be, as his friends put it, "the house golfer for Hertz."

The creation of a public image—that is, defining what "being O.J." meant—had been Simpson's life work. In the years before he was arrested for murder, O. J. Simpson was interviewed countless times about his life story, and he would invariably invoke the same themes, even the same anecdotes. Though it is now difficult to remember in light of the notoriety of the murder case, Simpson for many years enjoyed a clean-cut and lovable image. This was a man who, after all, had been sanctified with a nationally televised "roast" by Bob Hope before he was twenty-five years old. So Simpson often went out of his way to boast in interviews about his hardscrabble origins and rascally past—a history that would take on a more sinister cast after his arrest.

Orenthal James Simpson was born on July 7, 1947, the third of four children of James and Eunice Simpson, in San Francisco. (His unusual first name, which O.J. loathed, was an aunt's suggestion of obscure origin.) His father was an intermittent presence in his life; in later life, he came out as a homosexual, and he died of AIDS in 1985. His mother, who worked nights as an orderly and then a technician in the psychiatric ward of San Francisco General Hospital, supported the family as best she could.

In an authorized, highly laudatory biography published in 1974, when O.J. was twenty-seven, Larry Fox wrote of Simpson's childhood: "There was the throwing rocks at buses, the shoplifting (after all, they were too young to *buy* beer and wine), the breaking up of parties, and, above all, the fights, the constant fights." And Simpson himself admitted in an extensive *Playboy* interview in 1976, "If there wasn't no fight, there wasn't no weekend. . . . Sports was lucky for me. If I hadn't been on the high school football team, there's no question but that I would've been sent to jail for three years."

When asked about his formative influences, Simpson repeated one story from his adolescence over and over again. The year was 1962, and Simpson, a sophomore in high school, was in trouble. In some versions of the story, he had been caught stealing from a liquor store; in others, he had been arrested for a fight involving his gang, the Persian Warriors, in his Potrero Hill neighborhood. Simpson was asleep in his apartment when there was a knock at the door. Knowing of O.J.'s troubles, as well as of his athletic promise, a concerned adult had arranged for Willie Mays, the legendary center fielder for the San Francisco Giants, to pay a call.

"Willie didn't give me no discipline rap; we drove over to his place and spent the afternoon talking sports," Simpson told *Playboy*. "He lived in a great big house over in Forest Hill and he was exactly the easygoing friendly guy I'd always pictured him to be." (In a revealing segue in the interview, Simpson went on to defend Mays because "a short time after that, Jackie Robinson took a shot at Mays by saying he didn't do enough for his people." But, Simpson protested, "Mays always put out good vibes.") Of the Mays visit Larry Fox wrote, "Willie's message was not so much in his words. It was in his achievements and what these achievements had brought him in the way of material goods." Telling the Mays story in the book *I Want to Tell You*, which he nominally wrote later from his prison cell, Simpson said, "It was the first time I saw the pot of gold at the end of the rainbow."

Getting a big house and putting out good vibes became the leitmotif of Simpson's professional life. After high school, he spent two years playing football and running track at the City College of San Francisco, a local junior college. He averaged more than ten yards per carry at CCSF, so the recruiters from the big four-year schools came calling in droves. But Simpson only had eyes for the University of Southern California. As a boy, O.J. had admired the pageantry of USC football—the Trojan wearing a suit of armor seated atop a great white stallion. But as a prospective Trojan himself, Simpson saw that USC delivered media exposure—and thus potentially lucrative contacts—beyond that of any other college football program in the land.

Almost half a century earlier, the USC football machine had been willed into existence by one man, an obscure, Illinois-born academic named Rufus Bernhard von KleinSmid. After bouncing around several different universities after the turn of the century, Dr. K, as he was known, became president of USC in 1921. There he faced a dilemma familiar to college presidents. "Supported by tuition, possessed of virtually no endowment (hardly more than $1 million by 1926) with which to finance its expansion, U.S.C. needed money," the historian Kevin Starr has observed. "Football offered a solution." Dr. K invested in recruiting, bands, and a magnificent new stadium, the Coliseum, which would serve as the centerpiece of the 1932 Olympic games in Los Angeles. Von KleinSmid's gamble paid off beyond even his own imaginings. Trojan football became one of the few activities to unite the fractured metropolis of Los Angeles. When USC defeated Notre Dame on a last-second field goal in 1931, a crowd of 300,000, one third the population of the city, greeted the returning team at the train station. The passage of time did not dim the school's (or the city's) enthusiasm for the sport. By the 1950s, the Trojans' greatest star was Frank Gifford, about whom a fellow student, the novelist Frederick Exley, would observe, "Frank Gifford was an All-America at USC, and I know of no way of describing this phenomenon short of equating it with being the Pope in the Vatican."

In 1967, at the University of Southern California, O. J. Simpson became pope—and then some. He quickly established himself as the best running back in the school's history on what was perhaps the best team in USC history. He gained 158 yards rushing in his third game and 190 in his fourth. Southern Cal had not beaten Notre Dame in South Bend since 1939, but in 1967 Simpson and his teammates routed the Irish there, 24–7. In the final week of O.J.'s first season, USC played crosstown rival UCLA in a game freighted with even more significance than usual. Both schools, with just one loss each, remained in the hunt for a national championship, and likewise both teams needed only to beat the other to win a bid to go to the Rose Bowl. Finally, the game matched the leading contenders for the Heisman trophy, awarded annually to the best player in the nation—Gary Beban, the senior UCLA quarterback, and O. J. Simpson, the USC junior. Late in the fourth quarter, the game came down to a single play. UCLA led 20–14, and the Trojans had the ball on their own thirty-six-yard line. The drive looked like it would be Southern Cal's last chance to score. It was third down and eight yards to go.

In the huddle, Toby Page, the USC quarterback, called a play that did not involve Simpson, but he changed his mind at the line of scrimmage and called out, "Twenty-three blast!"—signaling to his teammates that he was calling an audible. In the reconfigured play, Page handed the ball to Simpson, who took off—first right and then back against the grain to the left, all the while trailing UCLA defenders. Simpson outran his own blockers as well as the defense, and his touchdown gave the Trojans the game. Decades later the play remains known to USC faithful as, simply, "the run." USC went on to beat Indiana in the Rose Bowl, where Simpson was named player of the game, and to win the national championship. (Beban, however, still won the Heisman in a close vote.)

As a senior, Simpson picked up where he had left off. He gained 236 yards in the season opener against Minnesota, 220 against Stanford, and a career high of 238 yards against Oregon State. Southern Cal was tied by Notre Dame in its last regular season game and lost the Rose Bowl to Ohio State, but as a senior Simpson won the Heisman in a landslide. The number of O.J.'s jersey—32—was retired at the end of his career. To be sure, his success at USC was limited to the athletic arena. In those days, before the NCAA began to regulate seriously the recruiting and schooling of college athletes, Simpson received virtually no education at USC. Even today, he can barely write a grammatical sentence. As he confided to *Playboy*, "My only interest in school was in gettin' out, so I took courses like home economics, and didn't exactly kill myself."

Simpson was the first player selected in the 1969 professional draft and, in a characteristic gesture, parlayed that first year into a book deal as well as a lucrative contract with the Buffalo Bills. *OJ: The Education of a Rich Rookie*, which was cowritten by Pete Axthelm, is for the most part a stupefyingly dull game-by-game account of the season ("We spent the week working on the I-formation . . ."), but there are casually revealing moments as well. On the very first page, Simpson wrote, "I have been praised, kidded, and criticized about being image-conscious. And I plead guilty to the charge. I have always wanted to be liked and respected." In fact, his good looks and cheerful demeanor with reporters and fans paid dividends as soon as he left college.

Before he had played a single professional game, Simpson won endorsement contracts with Chevrolet and Royal Crown Cola, and a broadcasting deal with ABC. "I'm enjoying the money, the big house, the cars; what ghetto kid wouldn't?" Simpson went on in that first book. "But I don't feel that I'm being selfish about it. In the long run, I feel that my advances in the business world will shatter a lot of white myths about black athletes—and give some pride and hope to a lot of young blacks. And when I'm finished with the challenges of football, I'm going to take on the challenge of helping black kids in every way I can. I believe I can do as much for my people in my own way as a Tommie Smith, a Jim Brown, or a Jackie Robinson may choose to do in another way. That's part of the image I want, too." Simpson had put his views on race more starkly in a 1968 interview with Robert Lipsyte of *The New York Times*. As the country smoldered with racial tensions—and some black athletes, like Robinson and Muhammad Ali, jeopardized their careers to participate in the civil rights movement—Simpson told Lipsyte, "I'm not black, I'm O.J."

Simpson's professional football career started slowly. His first Bills coach, John Rauch, favored a pass-oriented attack, and O.J. did not come close to winning the Rookie of the Year award. He missed most of his second year with an injury. In his third year, the Bills won only one game. But after that season, the owner of the team, Ralph Wilson, made a decision to reorient the entire Bills operation around O. J. Simpson. He fired Rauch and brought in Lou Saban, who favored a running attack. The team began using its draft choices on blockers, building the group that would become famous as the Electric Company—because they "turn on the Juice." In 1972, the first season under Saban, Simpson ran for 1,251 yards, the best in the league, and his professional career was launched.

Shortly before the next season, Simpson spoke on the phone with Reggie McKenzie, his lead blocker on the Bills. As O.J. recalled it for Larry Fox, he said, "You know, with the guys we've got to block, I think I should gain 1,700 yards this year. Maybe I'll even have a shot at Jim Brown's [single-season] record."

McKenzie disagreed. "Why don't we go for the two grand?"

A 2,000-yard season—something never before done in professional football—became Simpson's obsession. O.J. gained 250 yards in the Bills' season opener against the New England Patriots, a new single-game record for the league. As he built his totals with similar performances throughout the 1973 season, football fans followed his race against Brown's record 1,863 yards and beyond. The hoped-for number had a magical quality. It was one of those round figures that have defined many of sports history's greatest dramas: the 4-minute mile; the .400 batting average; the 2,000-yard season.

As the year wore on, nearly every story about Simpson noted the contrast between him and Jim Brown. The great Cleveland player, who had been a dour, brooding presence in the game, had churned out his record by crushing everyone in his way, and he was something of a black activist to boot. Simpson relied on speed and agility more than on brute strength. These differences in style, it was said, were reflected in the two men's temperaments—the militant Brown versus the cheerful Simpson. To the public, Simpson was the anti-Brown, the smiling celebrity, the chipper pitchman, the one who ran around, rather than over, defenders and who never said a discouraging word before the cameras. In fact, these portraits amounted to little more than sportswriters' tinny conceits, but they affixed Simpson with a glowing image that would last through his arrest for murder in 1994. Simpson did, of course, break the magical barrier in 1973, finishing with 2,003 yards as the nation's sports fans cheered.

In Simpson's years as a professional athlete and then afterward, his life amounted to a lesson on the manufacture and maintenance of an image—albeit one that bore little resemblance to the realities of his life. He gave the black community little more than his own example; his charitable activities were minimal. In the seventies, he did a memorable television commercial for sunglasses that ended in a cuddly embrace among Simpson, his wife, Marguerite, and their two little children, Arnelle and Jason. But the marriage—which took place shortly before Arnelle's birth, in 1968—was a sham. Simpson philandered compulsively, both before and after he met Nicole Brown in 1977, when she was eighteen years old. Nicole had already moved into the Rockingham house when the divorce from Marguerite became final two years later, the year that also marked the end of his football career. O.J. didn't marry Nicole until she was pregnant with Sydney, in 1985. When he was inducted into the football Hall of Fame that same year, he said Nicole "came into my life at what is probably the most difficult time for an athlete, at the end of my career, and she turned those years into some of the best years of my life."

After his football career, Simpson enjoyed a perpetual boyhood, and he drifted between golf games and long lunches, always surrounded by the sycophants who cluster around star athletes. From broadcasting, acting roles, and business investments, he could count on about a million dollars a year in income in the late 1980s. He was charming and courteous to strangers, and would sign autographs interminably without complaint. He was no prima donna. Several production workers at NBC Sports, which he joined in 1989 after several unsuccessful years at ABC, recalled that Simpson was the only on-air talent who gave them Christmas presents. Ironically, in light of how his trial would unfold, Simpson always had a special fondness for police officers, and over the years many of them came by the house on Rockingham to use the pool or shoot the breeze. The cops turned out to be valuable friends, especially when it came to the events of January 1, 1989.

At 3:58 A.M. on that New Year's Day in Los Angeles, the phone rang in front of 911 operator Sharyn Gilbert. At first she heard no one at the other end, but her console indicated that the call was coming from 360 North Rockingham, in Brentwood. Then there were sounds—a woman screaming, then slaps. "I heard someone being hit," Gilbert later recalled. There was more screaming, and then the call was cut off. Though no one ever said any words to her, Gilbert rated the call a "code-two high," which meant that it required immediate police response.

Officer John Edwards and his partner, a trainee named Patricia Milewski, went to the scene. Edwards pressed the buzzer at the Ashford gate to the property, and a woman who identified herself as the housekeeper came out. She said, "There's no problem here," and told the officers to leave. Edwards said they couldn't go anywhere until they spoke with the woman who had called

911. After a few minutes of this back-and-forth, a blond woman—
Nicole Brown Simpson—staggered out from the heavy bushes
behind the gate. She was wearing just a bra and a pair of dirty
sweatpants.

Nicole collapsed against the inside of the gate and started
yelling to the officers, "He's going to kill me! He's going to kill me!"
She pounded on the button that opened the gate and then flung
herself into Edwards's arms.

"Who's going to kill you?" Edwards asked.

"O.J."

"O.J. who?" Edwards asked. "Do you mean O.J. the football
player?"

"Yes," Nicole said. "O. J. Simpson the football player."

"Does he have any weapons?"

"Yeah," she replied, still breathless. "Lots of guns. He has lots
of guns."

Edwards shined his flashlight on Nicole's face. Her lip was cut
and bleeding. Her left eye was black-and-blue. Her forehead was
bruised, and on her neck—unmistakably—was the imprint of a
human hand. As Nicole calmed down, Edwards learned that O. J.
Simpson had slapped her, hit her with his fist, and pulled her by
the hair. Just before Edwards placed her in the squad car to warm
up, Nicole turned to him and said with disgust, "You guys never do
anything. You never do anything. You come out. You've been here
eight times. And you never do anything about him." She then
agreed to sign a crime report against her husband.

As Edwards turned to the house, he noticed O. J. Simpson,
wearing a bathrobe, walking toward him. Simpson was screaming,
"I don't want that woman in my bed anymore! I got two other
women. I don't want that woman in my bed!"

Edwards explained that he was going to place Simpson under arrest for beating his wife.

"I didn't beat her," Simpson said, still furious. "I just pushed her
out of bed." Edwards repeated that he was going to have to take
him in.

Simpson was incredulous. "You've been out here eight times before and now you're going to arrest me for this? This is a family
matter. This is a family matter."

Edwards requested that Simpson go back into to his house, get dressed, and return to be taken in to the station. As Simpson walked off, the housekeeper, Michelle Abudrahm, went over to Nicole, who was in the squad car, and implored, "Don't do this, Nicole. Come inside." The housekeeper was actually tugging on Nicole from outside the car, and Edwards came over and shooed her away. Moments later Simpson, now dressed, returned to the gate and began lecturing Edwards. "What makes you so special? Why are you doing this? You guys have been out here eight times before, and no one has ever done anything like this before."

Edwards explained that the law required him to take Simpson in to the station. When Edwards turned to brief a second set of officers who had arrived on the scene, the officers saw a blue Bentley roar out of another gate at the property, this one on Rockingham.

Edwards got into his car and took off after Simpson—and four other police cars soon joined in the chase—but they couldn't catch up with him. Returning to Nicole, Edwards asked what had prompted her husband's attack. She said she had complained because there were two other women staying in their home, and O.J. had had sex with one of them earlier in the day. Edwards never saw Simpson again.

With Nicole having signed a police report, the police were obliged to bring the case against O.J. at least to the next step. The case was assigned to Officer Mike Farrell, who reached O.J. by telephone on January 3. Simpson explained that after he and Nicole had returned home from a New Year's Eve party, where they had been drinking, they had had a verbal dispute "that got out of hand." O.J. said it then turned into "a mutual-type wrestling match. That was basically it. Nothing more than that." Accompanied by her two children, Nicole came into the West Los Angeles police station the next day, and she, too, minimized the dispute. She said she didn't really want to go through with a full-fledged prosecution. Farrell mentioned the possibility of resolving the case through an informal mediation with the city attorney's office. "I would like to have that," the twenty-nine-year-old Nicole said. "I think that would be neat."

Still, under the law, Farrell had to present the case to the city attorney's office, which would have the final say over whether Simpson would be prosecuted for misdemeanor spousal abuse. The prosecutors were torn, as they so often are in domestic-violence cases. If this really was just a single drunken brawl after a New Year's Eve party, a prosecutor told Farrell, then maybe they should just let it drop. After all, they had a reluctant victim as their only witness. Farrell was told to ask around the West L.A. station and determine whether there had been other incidents at the Simpson home. If there was a pattern, they would prosecute.

So Farrell asked around—and heard nothing. Both O.J. and Nicole had acknowledged that the police had come to the house eight times to stop O.J. from hurting Nicole, but at first Farrell couldn't find a single cop who admitted to going to Rockingham. (O.J. had entertained about forty officers at his home at various times, and with their silence, the officers may have been repaying his hospitality.) Eventually, out of all the cops who had handled calls at the Simpson home, one spoke up. Yes, this officer said, he had been out to the house on a domestic-violence incident. Farrell asked him to write up the incident in a memo, and the officer wrote on January 18, 1989, "To whom it may concern":

During the fall or winter of 1985 I responded to a 415 family dispute at 360 North Rockingham. Upon arrival I observed two persons in front of the estate, a black male pacing on the driveway and a female wht sitting on a veh crying. I inquired if the persons I observed were the residents, at which time the male black stated, "Yeah, I own this, I'm O. J. Simpson!" My attention turned to the female who was sobbing and asked her if she was alright but before she could speak the male black (Simpson) interrupted saying, "she's my wife, she's okay!" During my conversation with the female I noted that she was sitting in front of a shattered windshield (Mercedes-Benz I believe) and I asked, "who broke the windshield?" with the female responding, "he did (pointing to Simpson) . . . He hit the windshield with a baseball bat!" Upon hearing the female's statement, Simpson exclaimed, "I broke the windshield . . . it's mine . . . there's no trouble here." I turned to the female and asked if she would like to make a report and she stated, "no."

It seems odd to remember such an event but it is not everyday that you respond to a celebrity's home for a family dispute. For this reason this incident was indelibly pressed in my memory.

The author of the letter was Mark Fuhrman. Farrell passed it to the prosecutors, and on January 30 they decided to bring a case against O. J. Simpson.

As his lawyer, Simpson hired Howard Weitzman, a predictable choice given the latter's reputation. Since winning an acquittal for John Z. DeLorean in a drug-possession case, Weitzman had run a well-publicized criminal and civil practice in Century City. Weitzman was also an active USC alumnus and big sports fan. In Simpson's case, the lawyer quietly worked out a deal. First there would be several adjournments, which would diminish the already minimal media attention the incident had received. (The *Los Angeles Times* covered Simpson's arrest with a 142-word story on page four of the sports section.) Weitzman arranged for Simpson to plead "no contest" to the charge—which is legally identical to "guilty" but sounds better in the press—in return for a sentence of probation and community service.

Weitzman pushed hard for Simpson. The day after Simpson made his plea, Weitzman filed a brief asking that Simpson's case be "diverted." Diversion is a legal process that allows a defendant, if he is not subsequently arrested, to lose the stigma of a criminal record. In his brief Weitzman observed, "Mrs. Simpson has indicated she did not want criminal charges filed against her husband nor will she voluntarily appear as a witness against her husband on behalf of the State." This case, Weitzman wrote, involved a "minor physical injury (nonetheless significant to Mrs. Simpson) inflicted by a first-time offender who could be helped to refrain from repeating the offense with the proper counseling." The city attorney objected to a diversion, however, and Simpson did in fact have to plea to the misdemeanor. On May 24, 1989, he received a suspended sentence, twenty-four months of probation, and fines totaling $470. He was ordered to "perform 120 hours of community service through the Voluntary Action Bureau" and to receive counseling twice a week. (Weitzman persuaded the prosecutor, Rob Pingel, to excuse Simpson from the customary group counseling sessions for batterers and instead allow him to receive his counseling from a private psychologist, Burton Kittay.) Finally, Simpson was directed to pay $500 as "restitution," to the Sojourn Counseling Center, a battered women's shelter in Santa Monica. (This was the same center that Nicole would call on June 7, 1994, five days before her death, to complain that O.J. was stalking her.)

Weitzman—and Simpson— did not cease playing the angles after the imposition of sentence. Simpson never reported to the Voluntary Action Bureau, which can assign convicts to such tasks as picking up trash by the highway or cleaning bedpans at hospitals. Instead, Simpson took it upon himself to select his own form of community service: organizing a fund-raiser for Camp Ronald McDonald, a children's cancer charity, at the Ritz-Carlton Hotel in Laguna Beach, where O.J. and Nicole had a vacation home.

When Simpson went back to court on September 1, 1989, to report on the progress of his probation, his form of community service was questioned by the judge. Simpson's response—indeed, his behavior at the hearing, where no journalists were present—was a mixture of indignation and self-pity.

"I want to know specifically what you did," the judge, Ronald Schoenberg, asked the defendant.

"Everything," said Simpson. "I closed up my office at the beginning of June and moved my office to Laguna. I created this affair. I didn't just work for them. I created this affair. When my lawyer informed me before the sentence that I would have to do community service . . . in the spirit of all of this, I went out on my own and created this event. I talked everyone into it from Coca-Cola to—I flew to Atlanta. I flew to New York and met with Hertz. I flew to Boston to meet with sponsors like Reebok. I went to Ritz-Carlton, spent time with them to get them to pick up some of the cost of the event. . . . I wrote personal letters and contacted corporate America to see if they would participate in this event. . . . We put on what I felt was the finest event they ever had in that area. At least that's what the press said."

Judge Schoenberg finally cut off the monologue. "When you're talking to other people, they're interested in the results and what you did for them," he began deferentially. "I'm not interested in that. I'm interested in the work that you did, the hours that you put in, and what you were doing. I know you're used to talking to people that are interested in what results you achieved, and I'm not."

Simpson replied, "Well, I was told, Your Honor, that I had to put in time. I think I put in not only the time that was required of me but far beyond those hours. . . . I guess what I'm trying to say is I wasn't trying to get a hundred hours into community service. I tried to do a good job, and it just so happened that I put in more than the hundred hours that I was sentenced to by the court."

The prosecutor, Rob Pingel, was frustrated—and obviously feeling snookered by how Simpson's entire case had unfolded. He complained that by organizing the fund-raiser, Simpson had merely engaged in business as usual, rather than submitting to the customary kind of community service.

After Weitzman stepped in to defend the worthiness of Simpson's work, Judge Schoenberg asked a clever question, albeit with considerable solicitude. "There's a question I'm afraid to ask, and that is this: If this whole case hadn't come about, would Mr. Simpson have done the same thing for the charity?" Simpson replied, "Certainly not the hours that I put in. . . . I went into this full-time . . . hoping to influence the court." Simpson added sarcastically, "I know that's not a worthy charity, it seems, in this room."

The judge raised the prospect of Simpson doing a more conventional form of community service before being formally released from supervision. Weitzman informed the judge that this would not be possible: Simpson was moving to New York. "He's moving Sunday," Weitzman said. "Football season starts." (Simpson was moving to NBC to cohost its pregame shows on Sundays.)

Remembering that Simpson had also agreed to undergo counseling as part of his sentence, the judge asked, "What's going to happen with the other condition about counseling?"

"I mean, I'm sure there are counselors in New York," Simpson answered. "I've gone to that religiously. I don't know how often I can discuss one incident in my entire life, but I'll continue to do that."

"For whatever it's worth, Your Honor," Weitzman then said, "I think the counselor did indicate that he believes whatever problem existed doesn't exist any longer. The counselor said, if necessary, he'd be willing to do it via telephone. . . ."

Simpson apparently couldn't help himself from adding, "Maybe I'm wrong in saying this, but I just don't understand. At that point when we're talking about counseling, I'm more than willing to do it, and I've been doing it religiously. It's just, how long can I—I mean, I really have reached a point where I can write a book about all of this. I don't even know what else to talk about. I come in. I sit down with him. We start talking about other things that are happening in my life at this point. I can't talk about one incident. I mean, I just don't know how long, sir, I can talk about one incident in my entire life.

"I think I've been a great citizen. My wife has indicated we have a great marriage. We had one bad night in our life."

The judge allowed Simpson to be counseled by telephone. He never had to appear in court again. He wrote Nicole a series of apologetic letters reflecting his hope that they could continue their marriage. In an interview, later in 1989, with Roy Firestone on *Up Close,* a sports talk show on ESPN, Simpson described the incident by saying, "We had a fight. We were both guilty. No one was hurt. It was no big deal and we got on with our lives. It wasn't that big of a deal."

Simpson's probation expired uneventfully, and he had no more formal contact with the criminal justice system for almost five years—until, that is, June 13, 1994, the day after his ex-wife's death, when he returned to his home in Brentwood and found that the police urgently wanted to speak with him.

||||||

After the judge granted the search warrant, Vannatter returned to the Rockingham house shortly before noon on June 13. At that point, the detective gave an order to Donald Thompson, one of the uniformed patrol officers guarding the perimeter of Simpson's property. Since the entire area was now considered a crime scene— and since Vannatter now had a warrant to search the house and the Bronco—he did not want Simpson or anyone else allowed inside. If Simpson arrives, Vannatter instructed Thompson, detain him and let me know he's here. The precise words Vannatter used with regard to Simpson later became a point of some controversy. Thompson remembered that Vannatter said, "Hook him up"—that is, handcuff him. Vannatter recalled that he simply said Simpson should be detained until detectives could speak with him.

Simpson had indeed caught the first available flight from Chicago to Los Angeles, and he made his way home at about 12:10 P.M. Curiously for a man who had been told only that his ex-wife had been killed, not necessarily murdered, Simpson had telephoned from his hotel room in Chicago to arrange for a criminal defense attorney to meet him upon his return home. That was Howard Weitzman, who had represented him so successfully in his abuse case. So Weitzman—as well as Simpson's longtime secretary, Cathy Randa; his business lawyer, Skip Taft; and an old friend, Robert Kardashian—were waiting for Simpson on the sidewalk when he arrived at his house. Under the watchful eye of several news cameras, Simpson left his bags with Kardashian and hurried up to the front door. At that point, Weitzman, Randa, and Kardashian were not allowed on the property. Simpson was escorted to the front door by Detective Brad Roberts, Mark Fuhrman's partner, who was assisting in the search of the house.

According to Roberts's written report, Simpson pointed to the cops milling around his property and asked him, "What's all this?"

"It relates to the phone call you got earlier about the death of your ex-wife."

"Yeah, so?" Simpson replied.

"Well, I'm not the detective on the case," Roberts explained, "but we came here because a blood trail led us here from the scene."

Simpson started hyperventilating. "Oh, man. Oh, man. Oh, man," he muttered to himself.

Acting according to his understanding of Vannatter's instructions, Officer Thompson placed a hand on Simpson to slow him down as he approached the front door. He could have handcuffed him right there. But like Robert Riske, the first officer to see the bodies on Bundy, Donald Thompson was a media-savvy cop. (Of the dozens of Los Angeles law enforcement officials with roles in this case, Thompson was also the only African-American.) As a nine-year veteran, Thompson knew that informal LAPD protocol for dealing with celebrities dictated that he refrain from making a show for the cameras. Instead, he guided Simpson over to another part of the yard, where there was an elaborate play set that had been set up for Nicole and O.J.'s two children. There, in an area he thought was out of the cameras' range, Thompson shackled Simpson's hands behind his back. The officer later recalled that he applied the cuffs in this sheltered location "for the dignity of the defendant."

It almost worked. The swarm of photographers and camera operators who had shot Simpson as he walked up the driveway strained against the iron gate on Rockingham to get a better view. Ron Edwards's sixth sense, honed over twenty-five years as a local news cameraman, told him to break away from the pack. By himself, Edwards quietly walked around the corner toward Ashford. There, the six-foot-four-inch Edwards stood on tiptoes so that he could point his KCOP camera over the six-foot-high brick wall surrounding the property. Thus, Edwards alone got a shot of Thompson handcuffing Simpson. After a moment, O.J. noticed the lone camera, and he sought to hide his manacled hands in the doorway of his children's plastic playhouse.

Vannatter—a beefy, slow-moving cop with a helmet of caramel-colored hair—ambled over to Simpson and Thompson. He allowed Weitzman to join them, and the lawyer immediately asked that the cuffs be removed. Vannatter agreed, and unlocked them himself. As he was working the key, the detective noticed something: a bandage on the middle finger of Simpson's left hand. Vannatter thought this was important, because he knew there were drops of blood to the left side of the shoe prints leaving the murder scene.

Vannatter told Simpson that they had some questions for him about the death of his ex-wife. Would he come down to police headquarters and talk?

O.J. agreed without hesitation.

Simpson got in the backseat of Vannatter and Lange's car, and they made their way to Parker Center in downtown Los Angeles, about twenty miles from Brentwood. (The LAPD command center is named for former chief Bill Parker.) Weitzman and Taft followed in another car.

Once everyone was reunited in the Robbery-Homicide Division reception area, Weitzman had a request. Could he speak to his client alone for a moment? The detectives gave Weitzman a conference room and told him to take as long as he wanted. Weitzman, Taft, and Simpson then conferred for about half an hour. When they emerged, Weitzman said that Simpson still wanted to talk to the officers but that he and Skip Taft did not want to be present. Weitzman's only request was that the detectives tape-record whatever went on among them. So Vannatter and Lange and their tape recorder replaced Weitzman and Taft in the small room with Simpson.

"We're in an interview room in Parker Center," Vannatter began. "The date is June 13th, 1994, and the time is 13:35 hours. And we're here with O. J. Simpson. Is that Orenthal James Simpson?"

"Orenthal James Simpson," O.J. confirmed.

Vannatter began by reading Simpson his constitutional rights, in the form of a Miranda warning. "Okay, do you wish to give up your right to remain silent and talk to us?" Vannatter then asked.

"Ah, yes."

"Okay," Vannatter continued. "And you give up your right to have an attorney present while you talk?"

"Mmm-hmmm, yes," Simpson replied.

Vannatter began, "We're investigating, obviously, the death of your ex-wife and another man . . . and we're going to need to talk to you about that. Are you divorced from her now?"

Simpson said they had been divorced for about two years.

"What was your relationship with her?" Vannatter asked.

"Well, we tried to get back together, and it just didn't work. It wasn't working, and so we were going our separate ways."

Vannatter quickly changed the subject. "I understand that she made a couple of crime . . . crime reports or something?"

"Ah, we have a big fight about six years ago on New Year's, you know, she made a report. I didn't make a report. And then we had an altercation about a year ago maybe. It wasn't a physical argument. I kicked her door or something."

"Were you arrested at one time for something?" Lange asked.

"No, I mean, five years ago we had a big fight, six years ago, I don't know. I know I ended up doing community service." (Later in the interview, Simpson explained the 1989 incident this way: "We had a fight, and she hit me. And they never took my statement, they never wanted to hear my side, and they never wanted to hear the housekeeper's side. Nicole was drunk. She did her thing, she started tearing up my house, you know? And I didn't punch her or anything, but I . . . wrestled her, is what I did. I didn't slap her at all. I mean, Nicole's a strong girl, one of the most conditioned women. Since that period of time, she's hit me a few times, but I've never touched her after that. . . .")

"So you weren't arrested?" Vannatter asked.

"No, I was never really arrested."

After Vannatter asked how much sleep Simpson had had the previous night—the answer was very little—Lange said to his partner, "Phil, what do you think? We can maybe just recount last night." Vannatter agreed. "Yeah, when was the last time you saw Nicole?"

"We were leaving a dance recital. She took off and I was talking to her parents." O.J. and Nicole's daughter, Sydney, had performed on Sunday night at Paul Revere Middle School in Brentwood. "It ended at about six-thirty, quarter to seven, something like that, you know, in the ballpark, right in that area. . . . Her mother said something about me joining them for dinner, and I said no thanks." Simpson added that he left the scene in his Bentley, and Vannatter asked him where he went from there.

"Ah, home, home for a while, got my car for a while, tried to find my girlfriend for a while, came back to the house."

"So what time do you think you got back home, actually physically got home?" Vannatter asked.

"Seven-something. . . . Yeah, I'm trying to think, did I leave. You know, I always . . . I had to run and get my daughter some flowers. I was actually doing the recital, so I rushed and got her some flowers, and I came home, and then I called Paula [Barbieri, his girlfriend] as I was going to her house, and Paula wasn't home. . . . I mean, any time I was . . . whatever time it took me to get to the recital and back, to get to the flower shop and back, I mean, that's the time I was out of the house."

This was an incomprehensible answer. Did Simpson buy flowers for Sydney before or after the recital? (She was holding flowers in a photograph taken at the recital.) Or were the flowers for his other daughter, Arnelle? Did he actually go to Paula's house? If not, where did he go? Intentionally or not, Simpson gave the officers absolutely no way to check his story and determine if he was telling the truth. The officers could, of course, have pursued the issue and tried to pin Simpson down, yet Vannatter's follow-up question was "Were you scheduled to play golf this morning someplace?" Yes, Simpson said, in Chicago, with Hertz clients.

Vannatter then established that Simpson had taken the 11:45 P.M. flight to Chicago the previous night. He followed that with a question about Simpson's Bronco. When did Simpson park it on Rockingham?

"Eight-something, seven . . . eight, nine-o'clock, I don't know, right in that area." This was another meaningless answer, yet the detectives did not ask Simpson to estimate his arrival any more specifically than this two- or three-hour window. Rather, they established that Simpson had come home from the recital in his Bentley and then got into the Bronco.

"In the Bronco," Simpson explained, " 'cause my phone was in the Bronco. And because it's a Bronco. It's a Bronco. It's what I drive, you know. I'd rather drive it than any other car. And, you know, as I was going over there, I called [Paula] a couple of times, and she wasn't there, and I left a message, and then I checked my messages, and there were no messages. She wasn't there, and she may have to leave town. Then I came back and ended up sitting with Kato."

"Okay," Lange now said. "What time was this again that you parked the Bronco?"

"Eight-something, maybe. He hadn't done a Jacuzzi, we had . . . went and got a burger, and I'd come home and kind of leisurely got ready to go. I mean, we'd done a few things."

Neither detective asked anything about this trip for a burger. Where exactly did they go? What time did they go? Who saw them? Did he use the cellular phone again that night?

Instead the detectives pursued a new subject: "How did you get the injury on your hand?"

"I don't know," Simpson replied. "The first time, when I was in Chicago and all, but at the house I was just running around."

"How did you do it in Chicago?" Vannatter asked.

"I broke a glass. One of you guys had just called me, and I was in the bathroom, and I just kind of went bonkers for a little bit."

"Is that how you cut it?"

"Mmm, it was cut before, but I think I just opened it again. I'm not sure."

Lange asked, "Do you recall bleeding at all in your truck, in the Bronco?"

"I recall bleeding at my house, and then I went to the Bronco. The last thing I did before I left, when I was rushing, was went and got my phone out of the Bronco." Lange asked where the phone was now. Simpson told him, but there is no evidence that the detectives ever examined it.

"So do you recall bleeding at all?"

"Yeah, I mean, I knew I was bleeding, but it was no big deal. I bleed all the time. I play golf and stuff, so there's always something, nicks and stuff here and there." Lange asked where Simpson had gotten the Band-Aid he was wearing on his left middle finger. "Actually, I asked the girl this morning for it."

"And she got it?"

"Yeah," Simpson continued. " 'Cause last night with Kato, when I was leaving, he was saying something to me, and I was rushing to get my phone, and I put a little thing on it, and it stopped."

The detectives never returned to the subject of the cut on his left hand, even though Simpson had not answered the most basic question about it: How had he first injured his hand? Again, the detectives changed the topic. They established that O.J.'s maid, Gigi, had access to the Bronco; that he had not argued with Nicole at the recital; and that he had worn black pants and Reebok tennis shoes the previous night. (Simpson said he left these clothes back at the house; the detectives did not even ask where, precisely—in the laundry? on a coat hanger?—Simpson had put them. They were never found, and Simpson's lawyers never produced them, either.)

Finally, Vannatter said, "O.J., we've got sort of a problem."

"Mmm-hmm."

"We've got some blood on and in your car, we've got some blood at your house, and sort of a problem."

"Well, take my blood test," Simpson volunteered.

"Well, we'd like to do that," Lange responded. "We've got, of course, the cut on your finger that you aren't real clear on. Do you recall having that cut on your finger the last time you were at Nicole's house?"

No, Simpson said. "It was last night. . . . Somewhere when I was rushing to get out of my house."

Vannatter, in effect, just threw up his hands and asked, "What do you think happened? Do you have any idea?"

"I have no idea, man. You guys haven't told me anything. I have no idea. When you said to my daughter, who said something to me today, that somebody else might have been involved, I have absolutely no idea what happened. I don't know how, why, or what. But you guys haven't told me anything. Every time I ask you guys, you say you're going to tell me in a bit."

"Understand," Lange said a few moments later, "the reason we're talking to you is because you're the ex-husband. . . ."

"I know I'm the number one target, and now you tell me I've got blood all over the place."

"Well," Lange said, "there's blood at your house in the driveway, and we've got a search warrant, and we're going to go get your blood. We found some in your house. Is that your blood that's there?"

"If it's dripped, it's what I dripped running around trying to leave. . . . You know, I was trying to get out of the house, I didn't even pay attention to it. I saw it when I grabbed a napkin or something, and that was it. I didn't think about it after that. . . . That was last night when I was . . . I don't know what I was . . . I was getting my junk out of the car. I was in the house throwing hangers and stuff in my suitcase. I was doing my little crazy what I do. . . . I mean, I do it everywhere. Anybody who has ever picked me up say that O.J.'s a whirlwind, he's running, he's grabbing things, and that's what I'm doing."

And after a few more desultory exchanges, the interview drew to a close. At 2:07 P.M., Lange said, "We're ready to terminate this." LAPD investigators never had the opportunity to speak with O. J. Simpson again. The interview on June 13 had lasted thirty-two minutes.

|||||

It became known almost immediately that Simpson had given a statement to the detectives, and the news media's legal "experts"— a group that became a ubiquitous presence in the case (and that often included me)—promptly excoriated Howard Weitzman for allowing his client to answer questions. This was understandable, for it rarely works to a prospective defendant's advantage to commit himself to a single version of the facts at an early stage of the investigation. In the months afterward, Weitzman often said in his own defense that he had tried and failed to stop Simpson from talking. It is true that such a decision is always the client's to make. And given Simpson's vast ego, he undoubtedly thought he could talk his way out of trouble—and similarly, he probably dreaded the humiliating prospect of the police leaking word to the public that O.J. had been afraid to talk.

But the debate over Weitzman's role missed the larger significance of the detectives' interview of Simpson. The real lesson there concerned Vannatter and Lange—and the LAPD as a whole. In both the 1989 abuse incident and the murder case five years later, the police behavior suggested a fear of offending a celebrity. In the domestic-violence case on New Year's Day, the officers could have—and probably should have—put handcuffs on O.J. as soon as they arrived on his doorstep. But they let him go upstairs to change out of his bathrobe—and then, inexplicably, allowed him to get into his car and drive off. (And Simpson, of course, was never punished for what might be seen as a rehearsal for his more celebrated flight from arrest in 1994.) Simpson was then prosecuted only because a single police officer out of the many who had seen the results of his past mistreatment of Nicole had the integrity to step forward. This crime then earned Simpson an almost comically inadequate punishment—an opportunity to network with the advertisers he longed to cultivate.

Then, on the afternoon of June 13, 1994, though Vannatter and Lange already had considerable evidence that O. J. Simpson was likely a murderer, they too treated him with astonishing deference. Time after time, as Simpson gave vague and even nonsensical answers, the detectives failed to follow up. The entire purpose of a police interrogation is to pin a suspect down, so that the prosecution can, if necessary later on, demonstrate in minute particulars that his story is false. An effective interrogation forces a suspect to repeat, in ever greater detail, his version of the facts. Incredibly, Vannatter and Lange never forced Simpson to account specifically for his whereabouts between the end of Sydney's dance recital and his departure for the airport. (This failure allowed Simpson's attorneys to claim later, as they did at various times, that their client spent this period sleeping, showering, and chipping golf balls in the dark.) The detectives never pressed him to describe completely what clothes he was wearing and what had happened to them.

Even if Simpson had said he could not remember these basic facts, such a failure of recollection might have been highly incriminating. In a murder case, it is common for the police to question a suspect for many hours, but Vannatter and Lange surrendered after barely half an hour—even before Simpson himself could ask for a break.

When the prosecutors heard the tape, they knew immediately how dreadfully the detectives had botched this opportunity. They seethed with frustration—in private. To berate Vannatter and Lange would have been futile, and might also have damaged a partnership that faced a long and difficult investigation. But among themselves the prosecutors had a nickname for the police interview of the defendant on June 13: "the fiasco."

4. "I CANNOT PROMISE JUSTICE"

By noon on Monday, June 13, the media frenzy surrounding the case had begun in earnest. At about 10:00 A.M., just ten hours after the bodies were discovered—and before the coroner had removed them—the first local news satellite trucks showed up at the Bundy crime scene. By noon, several stations were transmitting live pictures of Nicole Brown Simpson's bloodstained walkway. Shortly after the cameras appeared at Bundy, several more were set up outside O.J.'s home. Even though nothing conspicuous was going on there, the growing corps of police officers at the Simpson house suggested that something was up, and soon there were twice as many cameras at Rockingham as at Bundy. Media people and cops gathered, watching each other. The two journalists whose actions that week would have the longest-term implications for the case never came to either scene, but Dennis Schatzman and James Gaines nevertheless studied with care the events unfolding in Brentwood.

A forty-five-year-old black man with a salt-and-pepper beard, oversize tortoiseshell glasses, and a predilection for brightly colored African robes, Dennis Schatzman covered the Simpson case for the Los Angeles *Sentinel*, a paid-circulation weekly devoted to the city's African-American community. His reports were syndicated to many other black papers around the country, and Schatzman was interviewed frequently on black-owned radio stations. More than anyone else, he set the black conversational agenda on the Simpson case.

The *Sentinel*, which was founded in 1934, is a broadsheet, with a red, white, and blue logo framed by the slogans "The Largest Black-Owned Newspaper in the West" and "Education Will Lead to the Truth." In 1994, its circulation was just short of twenty thousand, and falling; it lost many readers when, in the post–Rodney King riots of 1992, many of the small stores that sold the paper were looted and closed. The *Sentinel* is fairly typical of the bigger black papers around the country. Generally, the political views reflected in its pages are conventionally liberal; the paper's dominant theme, not surprisingly, is pride in African-American accomplishments, but it is expressed without the ideological excesses of, say, Louis Farrakhan. In many respects, the *Sentinel* is old-fashioned, with extensive reporting about the cotillions and awards banquets of black society; the paper aims its coverage at a settled and reasonably prosperous middle-class audience—the kind of people who, among other things, tend to answer a summons for jury duty.

A single moment from the events of June 13 stood out for Schatzman: the televised image of Simpson being handcuffed, then released. After first broadcasting Ron Edwards's scoop exclusively, KCOP, an independent local station, later allowed its competitors to use it, and the scene was rebroadcast frequently. The handcuffing was probably not the most famous videotaped moment to come out of the case, but for one audience in particular, African-Americans in Los Angeles, it immediately linked the Simpson case to their long and tortured relationship with the LAPD. From the beginning, while the mainstream press was using the Simpson case mainly to focus on the issue of domestic violence, the *Sentinel* was presenting the story of a black man searching for justice in a white system.

Schatzman's first article on the case, in the issue dated June 16, 1994, set the tone. It began: "Los Angeles police officers first handcuffed, then unhandcuffed, football Hall of Famer O. J. Simpson before whisking him from his Brentwood mansion to police headquarters for questioning." On June 13, of course, Simpson was never actually arrested. Of all the issues raised by the murders on Bundy Drive, the *Sentinel*'s coverage focused on how and why Simpson had been handcuffed. The headline on a front-page sidebar, also by Schatzman, asked, WERE THE HANDCUFFS

REALLY NECESSARY? In the breezy style that characterized many of Schatzman's stories, the sidebar started thus: "Think hard. How many times did you see convicted cannibal Jeffrey Dahmer hand-cuffed during his well-publicized arrest and subsequent trial? If you say 'none' then you get the prize." Schatzman went on to note that a police spokesman never directly answered his questions about why Simpson was cuffed. "So why was he handcuffed?" Schatzman wrote. "Still no satisfactory answer. The black/white double standard just won't go away."

From the outset, Schatzman viewed the case not as an anomaly but rather as an especially important moment in Los Angeles black history. To him, it never mattered that Simpson had previously made a conscious choice to play a negligible role in that history. Schatzman wrote in his initial story, about the handcuffing, "And, it just didn't happen to O.J.; this is not an isolated incident with prominent black men and local law enforcement." It was true that in the years leading up to the Simpson case, taxpayers in Los Angeles had had to pay substantial amounts to settle lawsuits alleging that the LAPD had illegally detained, in separate incidents, the former baseball star Joe Morgan and the track-and-field Olympian Al Joyner. "When O.J. got handcuffed without being charged, that was the thing," Schatzman explained later. "With the brothers on the corner, the attitude was 'There they go again.' You see, these things happen to us every day."

At just about the same time Schatzman was deciding to lead the *Sentinel* with the handcuffing angle to the Simpson story, Jim Gaines also had a choice to make. At the end of the first week after the murder, the managing editor of *Time* magazine contemplated what he later would call the "decision that is in a way the culmination of every week: the choice of a cover." From the moment the bodies were discovered in the early morning of Monday, June 13, there was never any doubt that the Simpson story would lead the magazine, which sells about 4 million copies of each issue. Early that week, *Time* had commissioned a painting of Simpson, and as the days passed, the magazine's New York headquarters was inundated with a multitude of photographs as well. Then, at 2:00 A.M. on Saturday—just hours before *Time*'s deadline—the LAPD released Simpson's mug shot. As a final option, Gaines later wrote in the magazine, "we decided to commission another artist's portrait, using the mug shot as a starting point. For this assignment we turned to Matt Mahurin, a master of photo-illustration (using photography as the basis for work in another medium, in this case a computerized image). Mahurin had done numerous other *Time* cover portraits in the same genre, including the one of Kim Il Sung two weeks earlier. He had only a few hours, but I found what he did in that time quite impressive.

"The harshness of the mug shot—the merciless bright light, the stubble on Simpson's face, the cold specificity of the picture—had been subtly smoothed and shaped into an icon of tragedy," Gaines elaborated in the self-dramatizing idiom of *Time*. "The expression on his face was not merely blank now; it was bottomless. This cover, with the simple, non-judgmental headline, 'An American Tragedy,' seemed the obvious, right choice." A simpler way of describing the cover is this: *Time* darkened the mug shot.

And the roof fell in. As *USA Today* put it in a prominently played story just a day after *Time* hit the newsstands, "If a picture is worth a thousand words, then Time's 'photo-illustration' cover this week of a darker O. J. Simpson is speaking volumes—and raising charges of racism. 'The way he's pictured, it's like he's some kind of animal,' says NAACP Director Benjamin Chavis Jr. . . . 'The photo plays into the stereotype of the African-American male as dangerous and violence prone,' Chavis said." The civil rights community rose up as one in outrage. "The cover appeared to be a conscious effort to make Simpson look evil and macabre, to sway the opinion of the reader to becoming fixated on his guilt," said Dorothy Butler Gilliam, president of the National Association of Black Journalists. And on CNN, Jesse Jackson ascribed the *Time* cover to "the devastating dimension of something called institutional racism."

Today, at some remove from the controversy, it is not clear that *Time* should have been judged so harshly. (It is also interesting to ponder whether anyone would even have commented on *Time*'s cover had *Newsweek* not used an unaltered version of the same mug shot on its cover that week.) Magazines have used doctored photographs for years; as long as they are properly labeled (as *Time*'s was) they have prompted little, if any, debate. Journalists make implicitly political choices every time they run a photograph—should President Clinton be smiling or frowning this week?—and these decisions generally pass unnoticed. The cry of racism about the *Time* cover is especially perplexing. Were Chavis et al. suggesting that darker-skinned blacks are more threatening, more evil, than their lighter-skinned brethren? If so, that seems far more racist than anything conveyed by the editors at *Time*. In any event, *Time*'s transgression does seem to have prompted a disproportionate response. Still, the magazine did what the mainstream press always does when faced with the charge of racism: It denied any malign intent, offered a tepid justification for its actions, and then fell on its sword. "It should be said (I wish it went without saying) that no racial implication was intended by *Time* or by the artist," Gaines wrote in a full-page apologia the following week.

The fallout from both the *Time* cover and the *Sentinel*'s coverage lasted the entire duration of the case. Regardless of Simpson's feelings for the black community—on CNN, Jesse Jackson had referred to him as "a kind of de-ethnicized Negro"—the first week saw his case immediately move to the top of the civil rights movement's agenda. For Dennis Schatzman and the black press generally, Simpson's cause became their own. For the mainstream press, fearful of enduring a *Time*-like ordeal, the priority became how to avoid giving offense to that black leadership. No one recognized these developments faster, or exploited them more, than O. J. Simpson's lawyers.

|||||

Marcia Clark received Vannatter's call on the morning of June 13, and she learned a great deal about O. J. Simpson over the course of that day. Vannatter asked her to come out to the Rockingham house and monitor the situation while detectives executed the search warrant. The magnitude of the case dawned on Clark gradually. She had helped plan a bridal shower in honor of her closest friend, fellow deputy district attorney Lynn Reed Baragona, for lunch on that Monday. Clark called at the last moment to say she couldn't make it.

"How can you cancel?" Baragona asked. "You're throwing this thing."

"I have to do this search warrant," Clark answered. "It could end up being kind of big. I'll tell you about it later."

It didn't take long for Clark to size up the situation to her satisfaction. The following morning, back in her office downtown, a friend stopped Clark and asked whether she thought O.J. had committed the murders.

Of course, Clark snapped. She was confident the tests on the blood at Bundy and at his home would come back to implicate Simpson. "He's evil," Clark said. "He beat his wife. He's evil."

It was a characteristic reaction—atypical only in that Clark did not describe Simpson as "fuckin' evil." Quick-witted and quick to judge, cheerfully and relentlessly profane, Clark was the paradigmatic "lifer"—the term prosecutors use to describe those among them who cannot conceive of switching sides to criminal defense work. She saw her cases—and the Simpson case in particular—as struggles between good and evil, Us versus Them. O.J. had killed Ron and Nicole; that was all that mattered to her. But for better or worse, trials, especially this trial, are about something more than whodunnit. The Simpson case blurred the lines between the good guys and the bad in a way that Clark had never before encountered.

||||||

Marcia Clark belonged to the smallest, and most intense, subspecies of lifers, the trial addicts. She learned this about herself the hard way. By the spring of 1993, when she was almost forty, Clark had been trying cases in the D.A.'s office for twelve years, the last four of them in the special-trials unit, which handled the county's most complex and sensitive investigations. Around the time she was prosecuting two men charged with murdering two parishioners during a church service in South Central Los Angeles, Gil Garcetti, the district attorney, felt that Clark had earned a promotion. She became a supervisor, overseeing the bulk of the office's career-criminal cases and advising the deputy district attorneys who would actually be appearing in court. Her salary, which had been around ninety thousand dollars a year, broke into the six-figure bracket, with the prospect of more increases to come. Relieved of the pressure and stress of trying cases, Clark moved into management.

The change was a disaster. This is not altogether uncommon, since many good trial lawyers make weak administrators. But most prosecutors are so eager to escape trial work (and to get a raise) that they hang on to their new jobs and, thanks to the civil-service system, take root in them. Trials wear lawyers out—especially prosecutors, who must orchestrate what happens in a trial—everything from making sure the witnesses show up in the correct order to putting the exhibit stickers on the evidence. The logistical burdens are enormous. The hours are long. Witnesses are usually uncooperative or, almost as often, criminals themselves. The police, ostensibly prosecutors' allies, may be lazy or incompetent or both—or worse. And prosecutors bear the burden of knowing that it is essentially up to them whether a murderer (or other criminal) walks out the door when it's all over. Small wonder, then, that many supervisors content themselves with war stories, second guesses, and long lunches.

What happened to Marcia Clark's career as an administrator was unusual. "I hated it," Clark said not long after she took on the Simpson case. "I begged them to let me back in the courtroom. I learned that all I wanted to do was try cases." As it happened, she had returned to the special-trials unit just a few weeks before the murders on Bundy Drive. So when Vannatter called, Marcia Clark had some time on her hands.

|||||

Marcia Clark graduated from Southwestern University School of Law in Los Angeles in 1979, then worked briefly as an apprentice criminal defense attorney in a top-flight firm. At first her cases involved mostly drugs—sale and possession—and as a child of her era, she had few qualms about defending participants in these "victimless," if illegal, transactions. But early in her tenure, she also drew the assignment of helping to defend James "Doc" Holiday, a leader of the notorious Black Guerrilla Family. The case against Holiday included a charge of attempted murder. According to Clark, "Doc had lured this woman called Vicki D into a car, and then stabbed her about a million times and left her for dead—just a horrible, vicious crime. That's what happened, but the fact was that the government's proof was very thin, and I was assigned to draft the brief asking the judge to dismiss the case. I knew that it was a winner of a motion, and one night I was working on it and I just choked. I said to my husband, 'I can't do this kind of work.' My husband said, 'Pick up your pen. We have to pay the rent,' and, of course, I did. But when I heard that we really did win the motion, I just said, 'Oh my God!' My boss at the firm said I should probably join the D.A.'s office. When I went for my interview with John Van de Kamp, who was the D.A. at the time, I basically threw myself at his feet. I said to him, 'You're going to decide whether I practice law. I can't do criminal defense, won't do civil. This is the only job I want.' "

Clark joined the Los Angeles District Attorney's Office in 1981, and she took to the work immediately. "Marcia and I were hired around the same time, and we were the only two deputy district attorneys in the Culver City courthouse for a year," said her friend Diane Vezzani. "From the start, she just loved trying cases. I never saw anyone with more energy. And it wasn't just in court. She'd read the advance sheets"—reports of appellate-court decisions—"and boil them down to an index-card file. She must have twenty-five boxes of cards now. I used to tease her that she'd have a nervous breakdown if she didn't get a chance to read the advance sheets." Clark's dedication quickly won the attention of her superiors. The turning point in her career came when she found herself under the wing of one of the office's legendary prosecutors.

By the time of the Simpson trial, Harvey Giss, who has the angular face of a film-noir detective, spoke with a valedictory air about his years as a top homicide prosecutor in Los Angeles. Like many lawyers who try murder cases, he tired of the strain and shifted to a lower-stress existence, in his case fighting auto insurance fraud. Clark was assigned to work with Giss in 1985, just four years after she joined the D.A.'s office. The defendant in the case that brought them together was, like O. J. Simpson, a widely admired figure in Los Angeles. According to Giss, "James Hawkins was a big local hero here for a while. He worked at his father's grocery store, in Watts, and one day in 1983 he shot a gang member who was accosting passersby. After the shooting, the gang firebombed the store, and everyone, including the mayor, praised Hawkins for standing up to the gangs." But Giss subsequently obtained evidence that Hawkins had actually killed the gang member not by accident, as Hawkins claimed, but intentionally, about half an hour after the attack on the passersby. What was more, Giss charged Hawkins in an unrelated double murder. "I knew I needed some help in the double murder," Giss said. He got Marcia Clark. "We were like two peas in a pod," he went on. "As I got to know her, I could see she was the real deal. I told her I didn't believe in working with anyone who wasn't my equal, so I told her we were going to try it halfsie-halfsie."

Giss assigned Clark the toughest part of the case—the ballistics evidence. Ironically, the prosecution's biggest break came after Hawkins escaped from jail just before jury selection. The police tracked him down and then engaged him in a huge shoot-out, where 180 rounds of ammunition were fired. Police thought one of the guns seized from Hawkins after the shoot-out was the same one he had used in the double murder. As ballistics experts examined the gun, however, they discovered that its barrel had been scraped with an instrument, perhaps a file. Knowing that the grooves on gun barrels are unique, like fingerprints, Hawkins had evidently tried to alter them before he used the gun again. But Clark, by presenting meticulously prepared expert testimony to the jury, was able to make a strong case that the murder weapon in the double homicide and the altered gun seized from Hawkins after the shoot-out were one and the same.

According to Barry Levin, who represented Hawkins, "The trial was like a war. There were six months of jury selection, and the actual trial in front of the jury lasted thirteen months. Marcia was very junior at the time, so what's unusual about her is that she cut her teeth on murder cases. Harvey was the most tenacious prosecutor in the L.A. D.A.'s office. You could just see Marcia grow in the course of the case. Not only was she competent, but she was unflappable. It was a death-penalty case, and after my client was convicted, Harvey had Marcia get up and do one of the summations in the penalty phase. In truth, I wasn't too worried, because she had been so low-key up to that point, but then she made the most impassioned plea about why my client should die. As it turned out, the jury gave him life instead. But you could see Harvey's influence on Marcia. She was a tiger."

Giss's influence was great, and traces of it linger in Clark's style. The thorough preparation of both testimony and scientific evidence; the aggressive response to defense attacks; the passion and the fire for the jury—all became Clark's hallmarks, as they were Giss's. But differences between the two also stand out. For Giss, trials were basically about defendants; for Clark, they were, for the most part, about victims. This was apparent in Clark's most celebrated trial before the Simpson case.

In 1989, Rebecca Schaeffer was an up-and-coming twenty-one-year-old actress who had starred in the television comedy *My Sister Sam*. On July 18 of that year, Robert John Bardo, an obsessive fan of Schaeffer's who, unbeknownst to her, had been stalking her for two years, rang the doorbell of her home. When Schaeffer opened the door, Bardo shot her dead with a .357 magnum.

"Rebecca was killed Tuesday morning, July 18, 1989, and my husband and I flew down that afternoon," Danna Schaeffer, Rebecca's mother, said later. "The next morning, we went into Wilshire Homicide, and she was sitting there in a pink suit looking very beautiful and serious, and she said, 'My name is Marcia Clark and I'm going to be your prosecutor.' " Bardo was caught within a day of the murder, and he immediately confessed to the shooting. The major issue in the case—a nonjury trial before Judge Dino Fulgoni—was whether Bardo was mentally fit to commit the crime of first-degree murder. According to Danna Schaeffer, "There were a million hearings and continuances, and many times afterward Marcia called us and reported to us what was going on." Finally, as the trial was set to begin, in September 1991, the victim's mother received a letter from Marcia Clark.

It was three pages long, handwritten on a yellow pad—and a very unusual thing for a prosecutor to do. "Even as I'm writing this I'm crying again—as I feared, once you start letting yourself feel, it's an endless thing," Clark wrote. "If all goes well the miserable, slimy piece of cow dung will be convicted of everything. . . . I will do everything in my power to see that her loss is avenged—I cannot promise justice because to me justice would mean Rebecca is alive and her murderer is dead." Clark concluded, "The one thing I can promise you is that when this is all over I will honestly be able to tell you that I gave it my all, my very best, without reservation. Beyond that you have my love and empathy forever."

The trial, one of the first to be covered by Court TV, featured extensive psychiatric testimony from experts on both sides. Judge Fulgoni convicted Bardo of first-degree murder and sentenced him to life in prison without the possibility of parole. Clark's trademark became her facility with complex scientific evidence, whether psychiatric or, later, DNA. In 1992, for example, she won the conviction of a man named Christopher Johnson in a "missing body" murder case (the one on which she had worked with Detective Vannatter). Johnson had been arrested driving a car in which investigators found a single drop of blood under the rear passenger seat. In a more ambitious use of DNA technology than the prosecution would ever attempt in the Simpson case, Clark used evidence from members of the family of the man presumed to be Johnson's victim to establish that the blood in the car belonged to the missing man.

The case that best summed up Clark's career before Simpson was the double homicide at the Mount Olive Church of God in Christ. Even in a city that had grown increasingly inured to violence, the facts of that case stood out as particularly appalling. On the evening of Friday, July 21, 1989, a man wearing a mask and carrying a twelve-gauge shotgun walked into the Mount Olive Church. In the chaos set off by his arrival, a seventy-six-year-old woman named Eddie Mae Lee panicked and tried to run to the ladies' room to hide. The man pumped the shotgun and fired, killing her. Then, as he appeared to be searching the pews for someone, he stopped when he saw a man named Peter Luke, and shot him, too. (Luke survived.) Before the gunman left the church, he noticed Patronella Luke, Peter's wife, who was sitting toward the back of the church, and he shot her dead.

Though none of the eyewitnesses could identify the masked gunman, police quickly fixed on a pair of suspects. One was Albert Lewis. After his wife, Cynthia, left him, he began stalking her, sometimes in the company of his half-brother, Anthony Oliver, the other suspect. On July 21, Cynthia was supposed to be playing the organ at Mount Olive, but—unbeknownst to Lewis and Oliver— she had taken the night off. Peter and Patronella Luke were Cynthia Lewis's cousins. "We set up a surveillance on Lewis's house, and we saw Lewis and Oliver taking a barrel of a shotgun out,"

Richard Aldahl, the detective in charge of the case, said later. "After that, we got a search warrant and found the rest of the gun and shotgun shells that matched those at the crime scene. At that point, we were certain we had our guys." One problem remained, however. "Albert Lewis had an alibi," said Aldahl. "He said he was with his girlfriend, Jeanette Hudson, and she stuck with him on this. We had a real issue in dealing with the alibi."

Clark assigned herself the task of refuting the alibi. According to Aldahl, "It turns out Jeanette had been living in fear of Albert for ten or fifteen years. She was really a battered woman. Marcia started spending a lot of time with Jeanette, talking with her, learning about her situation. Some prosecutors want you to interview the witnesses yourself and then just ignore them until they're brought in for testimony at the trial. Marcia was different. She wants to meet everyone in person, get to know everyone. When she puts a witness on the stand, she wants to know there will be no surprises." The work with Jeanette Hudson paid off, and in more ways than one. "After Marcia started talking to her, she came around and admitted not only that the alibi was a lie but also that she had seen the two guys with the guns right after the murders," Aldahl said. "It broke the case open." But Clark's efforts did not stop with recruiting a witness. "Marcia got Jeanette into a program for battered women, and Jeanette got her life back together as a result."

The trial, which took place in 1993 in the courtroom next door to the one where O. J. Simpson would be tried, was a tour de force for Clark. "These criminals violated the one safe haven we have in this troubled world, the place where we go to enrich and glorify what is best in us, where we reaffirm our faith in all that is good and righteous, where we renew our souls and seek solace in the spiritual from a troubled world, a house of God," Clark told the jury in her summation in the penalty phase of the trial, on March 15, 1993. "This was no liquor-store robbery. This was no bank-robbery murder. This was murder in a church. . . .

"We speak of justice for a defendant, but what about the victim? If the tragic deaths of Eddie Mae Lee and Patronella Luke mean anything, the punishment must be fitting. The death penalty may be the most you can do, but, ladies and gentlemen, in this case it is the least that you can do. . . .

"Their voices are forever silenced and the love they gave so freely and to so many is now cut off, and now mine is the only voice that is left to speak for them, to cry out for justice on their behalf, and on their behalf and in the name of justice I ask you to impose the only punishment that can possibly fit this crime. I ask you, ladies and gentlemen, for both of these defendants, Anthony Oliver and Albert Lewis, to impose the punishment of death." The jurors did.

For many prosecutors, the Mount Olive case would have marked the culmination of a career. For Clark, however, it simply comprised many of the elements that had run through her cases. Like the Hawkins and Johnson cases, it featured a mountain of scientific evidence that the defense lacked the expertise or wherewithal to challenge; like the Bardo case, it featured victims whom a jury would understand and admire. And like virtually all her cases—indeed, like most murder cases prosecuted in a big-city D.A.'s office—it involved utterly unsympathetic defendants. In all these respects, however, these cases could not have differed more from the one against O. J. Simpson.

|||||

Marcia Clark couldn't wait to charge O. J. Simpson with murder. From the moment Vannatter called her on that Monday morning, she had thought there was enough evidence to arrest Simpson for the murders. Nevertheless, in what she regarded as an abundance of caution, Clark agreed to put off filing the case against Simpson until the initial blood tests were reviewed. But she didn't want to waste any time.

No one did. Shortly after seven the following morning, June 14, Dennis Fung was hunched over a lab bench in the serology unit of the Scientific Investigation Division of the LAPD. Fung had gathered before him what he regarded as some of the best evidence he had collected the previous day—the gloves and various samples from the trail of blood that appeared to go from Bundy to Rockingham. He also had a blood sample from O. J. Simpson. After the detectives interviewed Simpson the previous afternoon at Parker Center, they had taken him to police nurse Thano Peratis, who had drawn a blood sample from him. Peratis had given the sample to

Vannatter, who had then traveled the twenty miles back to Rockingham in the late afternoon and given the test tube to Fung.

At the lab bench, Fung handed Simpson's blood and the rest of his samples to Collin Yamauchi, the LAPD criminalist who would perform the initial testing. Yamauchi had been tipped off the previous day that he might be involved in the Simpson case, so he had watched the television news that evening with considerable interest. As far as he could tell from initial news reports, Simpson was in Chicago at the time of the murders—he had an "airtight alibi." So Yamauchi expected his tests would exclude Simpson as a possible source of the blood from the crime scenes.

Yamauchi spent two days, June 14 and 15, testing the samples. (During that time, he also was given reference blood samples from Nicole Brown Simpson and Ronald Goldman, obtained during their autopsies.) Ordinarily, in an initial test like this, Yamauchi might have used conventional ABO typing to categorize the blood samples; these experiments, which have existed for decades, separate blood types into six basic categories. But because of the high stakes involved in the Simpson case—particularly the risk of making a very public mistake—Yamauchi's boss had asked him to use DNA typing on the blood samples. Yamauchi conducted one of the simplest kind of DNA tests, one known as DQ-alpha. Instead of merely dividing blood types into six categories, DQ-alpha uses finer discrimination, placing individuals into one of twenty-one categories.

The results surprised Yamauchi. The blood drops on the pathway at Bundy matched Simpson's type—a characteristic shared by only about 7 percent of population. And the blood on the glove found behind Kato's room at Rockingham was consistent with a mixture of Simpson's and the two victims'. The prosecutors learned of the results late on Wednesday, June 15.

Thursday was decision day on the eighteenth floor of the Criminal Courts Building in Los Angeles, where the top county prosecutors have their offices. The corridors on the floor are decorated with completed jigsaw puzzles, and Marcia Clark felt that by the morning of June 16 they had enough pieces of the Simpson puzzle to arrest him. The bloody trail led from the murder scene to his house; the blood on that trail was consistent with Simpson's; and the glove found behind his house appeared to have the blood of the victims as well as his own blood on it. Further, more refined DNA tests would surely tie the noose tighter around Simpson's neck. All that—plus O.J.'s history of abusing Nicole—meant that he should be brought in immediately. Clark's supervisor, David Conn, agreed.

Bill Hodgman thought it over. From his corner office, Hodgman, the director of central operations, supervised most of the prosecutors in the Criminal Courts Building. Cautious, sober, methodical to the point of occasional dullness, Hodgman didn't want to rush into anything. Yet there was substantial evidence that Simpson was a murderer, and prosecutors arrest murderers—period. Clark and Conn were right. It was time to bring Simpson in.

Late Thursday, Hodgman planned logistics for the next day with Clark and Conn. Vannatter and Lange had already spoken briefly with Simpson's new lawyer, Robert Shapiro, who had replaced Howard Weitzman. Shapiro had secured the detectives' promise that they would not arrest Simpson in the event they decided to file murder charges against him. In return, Shapiro had vowed that he would arrange for Simpson to surrender at any time the detectives chose. This was a fairly standard arrangement between prosecutors and defense lawyers in cases where both sides agreed that the defendant posed no risk of flight. While these agreements are routine in white-collar crime cases, they are rarer when violent crimes are involved.

At 8:30 A.M. on Friday, June 17, the prosecutors agreed, Lange would telephone Shapiro at home, inform him of the charges, and demand that Simpson surrender at 11:00 A.M., at Parker Center. At 11:30 A.M. Simpson would be transported the two blocks to the Criminal Courts Building for his arraignment—a legal proceeding that usually takes less than five minutes. At 11:45 A.M. the prosecutors would hold a news conference in their eighteenth-floor conference room. Fifteen minutes later, the police spokesman would answer questions at Parker Center.

Hodgman felt matters were well in hand when he left for home on Thursday night, so he decided to take the next day off to go to a Father's Day celebration at his children's preschool. Hodgman thought the events of Friday, June 17, 1994, would be rather routine.

At 8:30 A.M. on Friday, as planned, Lange reached Shapiro at home. He and Vannatter had worked nearly all night to prepare the paperwork for the arrest, and Lange was tired and in no mood for a long conversation. He told Shapiro that the police had an arrest warrant charging O. J. Simpson with the double homicide, with "special circumstances," of Nicole Brown Simpson and Ronald Goldman. Under California law, "special circumstances" refers to a list of designated aggravating factors that change the legal landscape of a murder case. The special circumstance charged against Simpson was a double homicide. Two implications jumped out immediately at Shapiro. First, the charge made Simpson eligible for the death penalty. (The final decision on whether the prosecution would seek execution would come later.) Second, California law does not allow for bail in special-circumstances cases. So Shapiro knew immediately that O. J. Simpson was going to jail on June 17 and that he would remain there for the duration of his trial—many months at the least.

The conversation between the two men was polite, and each heard what he wanted to hear. Lange did not view the call as an invitation to negotiate. He knew that it should take less than an hour for Simpson to travel from his home in Brentwood to Parker Center. He told Shapiro that Simpson had two and a half hours to surrender—that is, until 11:00 A.M. Shapiro saw Lange's comments as more of a request than a command. The lawyer mentioned some concerns about his client's mental state—he might be suicidal—

but said that he would do his best to bring Simpson in on time. The two men agreed to stay in touch as the day progressed.

When he received the call from Lange, Robert Shapiro had been O. J. Simpson's lawyer for less than seventy-two hours. He had been hired in a way that revealed much about his client, himself, and the case as a whole. It was Howard Weitzman, of course, who had represented Simpson when he returned from Chicago and went on to be interviewed by the police on Monday, June 13. Word that Simpson had given a statement to the police leaked out that evening, and the news prompted a strong reaction in wealthy television executive Roger King, who was monitoring events from New Jersey. King, the chairman of King World, which syndicates *Oprah* and *Wheel of Fortune,* among other television shows, was a sometime resident of Los Angeles and knew Simpson from playing the occasional round of golf with him. Appalled that Weitzman had allowed Simpson to be questioned by the police, King called O.J. and told him so—and recommended that Simpson find a new lawyer. "I'll get you Bob Shapiro," King promised. He then tracked Shapiro down to where he was having dinner, at the House of Blues, a popular Hollywood nightspot, and asked him to take the case. Shapiro agreed. He was hired by Simpson on Tuesday and entered the case officially on Wednesday.

What makes this transaction curious is that none of the participants really knew one another. O.J. and Roger King saw each other rarely, but King was the kind of man Simpson admired. O.J. believed King when he said that Weitzman had let him down. (This also allowed Simpson to blame someone else for his own decision to speak to the police.) More remarkably, King had never even spoken to Shapiro before he reached him at the House of Blues. The entrepreneur couldn't name a single client the lawyer had represented, but he had some general sense of Shapiro as a skilled defender of celebrities. For his part, Shapiro did not hesitate before saying he wanted the case. And to Simpson, as always, image was everything: Robert Shapiro became his lawyer because he fit the image of a smart lawyer in the eyes of a fellow who fit O.J.'s image of a smart guy. (The Shapiro-for-Weitzman exchange also provided grist for these two lawyers' longstanding feud, one that was based largely, it seems, on their similarity to one another.) Shapiro took over the case on Tuesday, June 14, and the following morning Weitzman issued a public statement saying that he had resigned from the case because of his friendship with O.J. and his obligations to other clients. Shapiro delighted in telling friends that Weitzman's statement was a lie and that he had in fact been fired. The truth probably lies somewhere between the two versions— along the lines of a job departure once described by Casey Stengel: "We call it discharged because there is no question I had to leave."

Shapiro had a very busy first week, organizing his initial efforts with Simpson's medical and legal well-being in mind. Simpson told Shapiro that he was innocent, but lawyers are used to hearing this sort of thing from clients, especially at the beginning of a case. The first thing Shapiro did was arrange for Simpson to take a polygraph examination, which is something many criminal defense lawyers do. These tests are generally inadmissible in court, but lawyers often use them to force their clients to come clean, face reality, and make the best deal they can. Shapiro called his friend F. Lee Bailey, who is a national authority on polygraphs, for a recommendation on which expert to use. Bailey suggested Edward Gelb, who ran a firm called Intercept out of a set of nondescript offices on Wilshire Boulevard. (Bailey knew Gelb because they had hosted a short-lived television series together in 1983. Called *Lie Detector,* the program showcased Gelb and Bailey examining UFO sighters and other fringe figures to determine whether they were telling the truth.)

Gelb was out of town, so the test was administered by his top deputy, Dennis Nellany. Simpson took what is known as a "zone of comparison" polygraph examination, which measured three of his physiological responses to questions—heart rate, breathing, and the electrical sensitivity of his skin. Lie detectors do not, strictly speaking, detect lies. Rather, the examiner interprets the subject's responses on a sliding scale in which negative numbers indicated deception and positive numbers, truthfulness. According to the test Nellany administered, any score higher than plus-6 meant that Simpson was telling the truth; any number lower than minus-6 meant he was lying. A score between plus-6 and minus-6 would be ambiguous.

Simpson scored a minus-24—total failure. The score was so catastrophic that some people around Simpson tried to attribute it to his distressed emotional state at the time of the examination. Bailey in particular tried to say that Simpson was so upset that the result should not be seen as dispositive. Nellany, however, regarded the polygraph as conclusive evidence of Simpson's guilt in the murders, and he reported that view to Shapiro.

Shapiro weighed his options—which included an insanity defense. To that end, he called in another expert on Wednesday, June 15, one who could serve two purposes. As a respected psychiatrist with a private practice in Beverly Hills, Saul Faerstein could examine O.J. and prescribe medication. But Faerstein also had a national reputation as an expert witness in the field of forensic psychiatry. Shapiro thus viewed him as a hedge in case Simpson wanted to raise a diminished-capacity defense to the murders.

Faerstein went to the house on Rockingham and joined Simpson on the couch in the living room. Simpson talked and talked—about himself. The press was out to get him now; his image would never recover; it was all so unfair. What struck Faerstein most were the gaps in Simpson's narrative—there was no sadness for the loss of the mother of his children, no concern for his children's future, no empathy for Nicole. Simpson worried only about himself. His reactions were inconsistent with what Faerstein would expect from an unjustly accused man, yet Simpson was obviously not insane in any legal sense. So, as with Nellany's examination, Faerstein's report offered Shapiro no help in constructing a defense. Faerstein returned to see Simpson many times over the next two months to continue his course of psychiatric treatment. Like Shapiro, Faerstein was convinced early on of Simpson's guilt in the murders.

On that same Wednesday, June 15, which was also the day of the viewing of Nicole's body at a funeral home, Shapiro asked an internist, Robert Huizenga, to give O.J. a detailed physical examination. Shapiro wanted Huizenga to check on Simpson's medical condition, but he also asked the doctor to document with photographs any bruises or abrasions on Simpson's body at that point, which was less than three days after the killings; his lack of any major injuries would become a central part of his defense at trial. Also in those first two days on the job, Shapiro had recruited two of the nation's leading forensic experts to Simpson's team—Henry Lee, the chief police scientist for the state of Connecticut, and

Michael Baden, the former chief medical examiner of New York City. By Thursday, June 16, both Lee and Baden had arrived in Los Angeles. In spite of all the activity, Shapiro found the time to make a characteristic gesture. On the night of June 16, he took Baden to a glamorous Hollywood screening of the Jack Nicholson movie *Wolf,* which was opening the next day.

Detective Lange's call on Friday morning, June 17, presented Shapiro with a dilemma. What he could have done—indeed, should have done—was simple: make a direct effort to locate Simpson and then take him in to Parker Center, and thereby make the 11:00 A.M. deadline with ease. But the situation was more complicated than Lange knew when he made the call, for Simpson was not at home at Brentwood, as the police investigating his case had assumed. On Thursday, June 16, following Nicole's funeral earlier in the day, Simpson had participated in an elaborate ruse to convince the vast media encampment outside his home that he had in fact returned to Rockingham. The person who was actually hustled into the property with a jacket over his head was his old friend Al "A.C." Cowlings. Simpson had been taken to his friend Robert Kardashian's home in Encino, in the San Fernando Valley. Remarkably, this operation was engineered by an off-duty LAPD sergeant, Dennis Sebenick, who was moonlighting as a security guard for the murder suspect. Sebenick did not, of course, apprise his colleagues on the force of the whereabouts of their prey. This kind of solicitude typified Simpson's relationship with the LAPD.

Shapiro, therefore, had to retrieve Simpson from Encino, which was slightly farther from downtown than Brentwood. In his years of dealing with celebrity clients, Shapiro had learned the value of deference. He did not, for example, telephone ahead to Kardashian's place and tell O.J. to get ready to leave. Defending his actions later, Shapiro said that he had acted this gingerly because he feared Simpson might harm himself if he were dealt with more harshly. Shapiro also knew that Simpson's friends had just orchestrated Howard Weitzman's departure in part because they thought he had been insufficiently zealous in protecting Simpson's interests. Shapiro did not want to meet the same fate. If the choice was between offending the LAPD or his client, Shapiro would take his chances with the cops. While still at home, Shapiro called Faerstein, the psychiatrist, and asked him to meet him at Kardashian's house; together they would break the news to O.J.

At 9:30 A.M., Shapiro arrived at Kardashian's vast white villa, a garish affair resembling a Teheran bordello, all marble and mirrors. Simpson, who had been sedated, was still in the first-floor bedroom he was using during his stay. His girlfriend Paula Barbieri was with him; she had been at his side for much of the week. (After Simpson's criminal trial, in a deposition in the victims' civil case against O.J., Barbieri testified that she had left a telephone message breaking off her relationship with Simpson on the morning of the murders, June 12. But her actions the following week seem inconsistent with the notion that she was trying to end their affair.)

Shapiro and Kardashian woke O.J. and told him that they would be taking him to Parker Center to surrender. Again, they did not force him to leave. Instead, they explained that Doctors Huizenga and Faerstein were on their way to examine him before they had to leave for jail. Within moments, the house was buzzing with people. First Faerstein arrived, followed by Huizenga, who was accompanied by an entourage of assistants. Then came Henry Lee and Michael Baden. Kardashian's girlfriend, Denice Shakarian Halicki, who also lived at the house, suggested that Al Cowlings be called, and he was summoned to join the group as well. Huizenga wanted to evaluate some swollen lymph nodes he had noticed in his initial examination of Simpson, particularly because O.J. had a family history of cancer. (Later tests showed no malignancy.) In addition—incredibly—Huizenga took the time to do some additional examinations to bolster Simpson's defense, taking more photographs to demonstrate that Simpson had no significant wounds. Granted the privilege of being allowed to surrender, Simpson was missing his deadline so that he could, in effect, conduct his defense.

Shapiro was on the phone every fifteen minutes to the LAPD—stroking, consoling, explaining that these things take time and that Simpson would be on his way shortly. Patiently, but with some indignation, Shapiro gave a series of increasingly high-level officers the same message: "I have always had a good relationship with the police department. I've always kept my word. You have to trust me here. I will be there when I say I can be there." After all, Shapiro told the cops, what difference did it make if Simpson surrendered at 11:00 A.M. or 1:00 P.M.?

Simpson, too, had his demands. In the hour or so after Shapiro's arrival, the entire group gathered in a large second-floor study just off the master bedroom. When Huizenga finished taking blood and hair samples there, O.J. said he wanted to take a shower, then talk to his mother and his children. Simpson, Barbieri, and Cowlings went back down to O.J.'s bedroom on the first floor. When he arrived, Faerstein had wanted to keep a close eye on Simpson to make sure he wouldn't harm himself. But he had no qualms about Cowlings monitoring O.J.; the psychiatrist assumed that Cowlings, too, would make sure Simpson remained safe.

Finally, Vannatter and Lange grew fed up waiting for the lawyer to drive the defendant to Parker Center. They had been reaching Shapiro on his cellular phone, so they did not even know where he and Simpson were. (Marcia Clark, who was beginning the grand-jury proceedings against Simpson that day, took a break from those labors to have her own indignant conversation with Shapiro.) At around noon, the detectives said they would wait no longer for Simpson to surrender. They wanted to send a squad car to pick him up. As always, the LAPD was concerned about the media. A news conference had been scheduled for noon, and now that had to be put off. It was just after noon when Shapiro put Faerstein on the phone with an LAPD commander, in an effort to explain the reasons for the delay.

"There is a warrant for this man's arrest," the commander said, "and we have to come get him. Now, where are you?"

Faerstein stalled. "I don't think I'm at liberty to tell you where we are."

"I don't think you understand, Doctor. There are laws relating to aiding and abetting fugitives. Now, you tell me where you are—"

"Just a minute," Faerstein said, and then handed the phone to Shapiro, who finally agreed to provide Kardashian's address. Ever the negotiator, Shapiro secured the commander's promise that Shapiro and Faerstein could accompany Simpson on his trip downtown.

Moments later, at about 12:10 P.M., a squad car arrived at Kardashian's, and a police helicopter began circling overhead. Shapiro and Faerstein answered the door. Even then, after all the delays, the lawyer had another request. Shapiro and his professional colleagues—Faerstein, Huizenga, Lee, Baden, and Kardashian—had been gathered upstairs. O.J. was in a back bedroom talking with Barbieri and Cowlings. Shapiro asked the officers if Faerstein, the psychiatrist, could break the news to O.J. that the police had arrived. (Simpson had not even been told that the police were coming to get him.) The officers, who at that point had every right to barge in and take Simpson away, agreed. Faerstein walked back to the bedroom where O.J. and A.C. were talking. A moment later Faerstein returned, alone. "He must be somewhere else," Faerstein told the officers.

One at a time, the people in the house fanned out. A few walked upstairs. With each passing second, the pace of everyone's steps increased. O.J. wasn't upstairs. Chests constricted. There was a brief ray of hope when they realized they had not checked the garage. Maybe O.J. went to get something out of the trunk of his car. But there was no one in the garage. Panic. They talked to Otto "Keno" Jenkins, Bob Shapiro's chauffeur. He hadn't seen O.J. And then the realization dawned on them that no one had seen Barbieri or Cowlings, either.

"No one leaves," one officer said when he realized what had happened. "This is a crime scene."

As he had done when the officers came for him in 1989 for beating Nicole, so he did when they came for him in 1994 for killing her: O. J. Simpson disappeared.

|||||

The LAPD's considerable press apparatus had put out the word early in the morning: There would be an announcement regarding the Simpson case at noon. Reporters drifted in to Parker Center over the course of the morning and then learned that the briefing had been delayed. This was no great surprise, because most such events start late. Then there was a bomb scare at police headquarters, and the media people were told they could vacate the building if they wanted. No one left—media machismo. At 1:53 P.M., the reporters got the two-minute warning: The briefing was about to begin.

Commander David Gascon was the chief spokesman for the LAPD. With his neat black hair, obligatory mustache, and tight-fitting uniform, Gascon cut a typical figure for the department he represented. He was also fairly relaxed and approachable, and he had a good rapport with most of the reporters who covered the LAPD. They noticed, when he stepped to the podium, that he looked . . . different. He seemed shaken, and his voice quavered slightly.

"Okay, I have an official announcement from the Los Angeles Police Department," Gascon said.

"This morning," Gascon said, his voice unsteady, "detectives from the Los Angeles Police Department, after an exhaustive investigation which included interviews with dozens of witnesses, a thorough examination and analysis of the physical evidence both here and in Chicago, sought and obtained a warrant for the arrest of O. J. Simpson, charging him with the murders of Nicole Brown Simpson and Ronald Lyle Goldman.

"Mr. Simpson, in agreement with his attorney, was scheduled to surrender this morning to the Los Angeles Police Department. Initially, that was 11:00. It then became 11:45. Mr. Simpson has not appeared."

The room stirred.

"The Los Angeles Police Department right now is actively searching for Mr. Simpson."

An experienced group of reporters were gathered in that room, and yet none of them could ever recall having heard the sound they issued at that moment: a sort of collective gasp. And then one journalist, name lost to history, let out a long and very astonished whistle.

"Mr. Simpson is out there somewhere," Gascon said, "and we will find him."

Shortly after it became clear that Simpson and Cowlings were really gone, Kardashian materialized in the foyer of his house with an envelope that contained a letter. Shapiro and Faerstein sat on the bottom step of the winding marble staircase and read it. They agreed that it seemed like a suicide note written by O.J. Meanwhile, the cops asked the assembled group where they thought Simpson had gone.

Someone suggested Nicole's grave, near her parents' home in Orange County. Someone else said the Los Angeles Coliseum, site of O.J.'s greatest moments of football glory at USC. "He might kill himself in the end zone," Faerstein said.

In fact, no one had any idea where he was.

After Shapiro and Kardashian spoke to the officers on the scene and recounted the events of the morning to their satisfaction, the two men left for Shapiro's office in Century City. (They also determined that Paula Barbieri had left the house shortly before O.J. and A.C., but not with them.) "The two Bobs," as they were sometimes known, asked the officers if Faerstein could leave with them, but the police weren't yet finished talking to the psychiatrist. Though the letter was clearly important evidence of Simpson's state of mind and his possible plans, Kardashian took it with him rather than mentioning it, much less giving it to the police, who were looking for O.J.

From the moment Simpson vanished, Robert Shapiro focused on his top priority: Robert Shapiro. He knew immediately how furious the police and prosecutors were about Simpson's disappearance, and he knew they would hold him responsible. Shapiro had embarrassed them in front of the entire country. Worse, Shapiro didn't like what the cops were insinuating about his role in Simpson's flight. Even though Shapiro had committed no crime in harboring Simpson for the morning, the mere fact that he might be investigated worried him. Shapiro decided he was finished dealing with underlings—Lange, Clark, and the like. Shapiro decided to call the district attorney himself, Gil Garcetti.

Everything had been shaping up so well for Gil Garcetti. Elected overwhelmingly in 1992, he had an ideal ethnic and political résumé. The son of Mexican immigrants and the grandson of an Italian, the fifty-three-year-old politician had spent his entire professional career in the D.A.'s office. (He was, in fact, a neighbor of O.J.'s in Brentwood, thanks not to his civil-service earnings but rather to the wherewithal of his wealthy wife.) Even his steely-gray hair came with an uplifting tale: It had changed color after Garcetti underwent chemotherapy in a successful battle with lymphoma in 1980. As a tough-on-crime prosecutor and yet a Democrat, he had a promising political future. One problem hovered—

his office's remarkable record of futility in high-profile cases. The D.A. had failed to obtain convictions against the proprietors of the McMartin Preschool in a lengthy child abuse case; against several motion picture industry figures in connection with the deaths of two people on the set of *Twilight Zone—The Movie;* against the Menendez brothers for killing their parents; and, most notoriously, against the police officers who beat Rodney King—acquittals that set off the riots of 1992. As Garcetti would frequently (and correctly) point out over the course of the Simpson case, evaluating an office of nearly a thousand prosecutors on the basis of how they did in a few "big ones" was pretty unfair. (Still, in his campaign against his predecessor, Ira Reiner, Garcetti himself hadn't hesitated to play the can't-win-the-big-one card.) These murders presented Garcetti with a case that was likely to dwarf the other "big ones" in media attention. Suddenly, though, he had a bigger problem than trying to *convict* O. J. Simpson—he couldn't even *find* the guy.

So Garcetti focused on *his* top priority: Gil Garcetti. When Shapiro got on the phone with the D.A., the defense attorney began reciting a version of the same speech he had been giving the cops all day: You know me, Gil, I don't pull this kind of stuff. I arranged Erik Menendez's surrender from Israel. Name-dropping even at a time like this, Shapiro then became nearly unhinged, practically weeping over the phone: "I didn't know he would run, Gil. You have to believe me." The two men were old acquaintances; Shapiro had even contributed $5,000 to Garcetti's campaign. But at this moment Garcetti addressed Shapiro with barely controlled rage: "Just get him in here, Bob. That's all we're thinking about now."

At 3:00 P.M., just after he got off the phone with Shapiro, Garcetti went to give his own press conference, on the eighteenth floor of the Criminal Courts Building. Flanked by Marcia Clark and David Conn, Garcetti looked even more distraught than Gascon had in his briefing an hour earlier. He looked right at the cameras, which were broadcasting his words live.

"I want to say something to the entire community," Garcetti said. "If you in any way are assisting Mr. Simpson in avoiding justice, Mr. Simpson is a fugitive of justice right now. [His feelings were garbling his usually adequate syntax.] And if you assist him in any way, you are committing a felony. Think about it. And I'll guarantee you that if there is evidence establishing that you've assisted Mr. Simpson in any way to avoid his arrest, you will be prosecuted as a felon.

"Now," Garcetti added, stumbling again a bit, "you can tell that I am a little upset, and I am upset. This is a very serious case. Many of us, perhaps, had empathy to some extent. We saw, perhaps, the falling of an American hero. To some extent, I viewed Mr. Simpson in the same way. But let's remember that we have two innocent people who have been brutally killed. . . . It's a serious case. We will continue to treat it seriously."

Through more than a half hour of hostile questions, Garcetti had nothing but polite things to say about the LAPD, but his frustration did surface toward the end.

Rewording a question that had already been asked approximately twenty times at the press conference, one reporter ventured, "The question so many people are asking—and perhaps this needs to be addressed to the LAPD, and it already has—is how can this possibly happen? The entire world is focused on this man. Is there any way to answer that?"

"I can't," Garcetti said simply.

"Surely you're wondering that yourself."

"Aren't we all?" said the district attorney.

|||||

Garcetti's press conference did nothing to ease Shapiro's anxiety. He knew he remained the villain in the minds of the Los Angeles law enforcement establishment. So Simpson's lawyer decided, in effect, to take his case to the public. He told reporters that he would be making a statement about the day's events at 5:00 P.M., which was barely an hour after Garcetti's briefing ended. Unlike every other event that had been planned for June 17, this press conference started right on time. Robert Shapiro was anxious to go. He stepped to a podium in a makeshift briefing room on the ground floor of his Century City office building and spoke calmly and methodically, with no notes.

Shapiro, too, started with a plea to the camera. But he was aiming for an audience of one. "For the sake of your children," he told O.J., "please surrender immediately. Surrender to any law enforce-

ment official at any police station, but please do it immediately."
There was an odd calm about Shapiro, a lack of affect to his presentation. For all the turmoil of the day—and the sheer strange-
ness of all the occurrences—he spoke without passion or even
inflection. In retrospect, his agenda at the press conference appears utterly transparent: Whatever else had happened today, this
mess was not going to drag him down with it.

Shapiro began by summarizing the day's events: the early morning call from the detectives, his journey to Kardashian's home, his
passing the news of the arrest warrant to Simpson, and the defendant's sudden disappearance. "I have on numerous occasions in
the past twenty-five years made similar arrangements with the Los
Angeles Police Department and the district attorney's office and
Mr. Garcetti. All of them have always kept their word to me, and I
have always kept my word to them. In fact, I arranged the surrender of Erik Menendez from Israel on a similar basis. We are all
shocked by this sudden turn of events."

It was an extraordinary tale, and the reporters, along with the
national television audience, listened with rapt attention.
Shapiro's account was also highly incriminating of his client.
Simpson's actions, as described by Shapiro, did not seem to be
those of an innocent man. In light of Simpson's escape, Shapiro
might have had an obligation to recount this story to the police,
but the lawyer was certainly under no obligation to share it with
the public at large. Indeed, by some reckonings, much of what had
gone on that morning at Kardashian's house may have been protected by the attorney-client privilege—a privilege that only Simpson had the right to waive. Yet Shapiro told all. He had hung his
client out to dry in order to save himself.

Yet Shapiro's statement was only the beginning of the proceedings at this press conference. "Now," Shapiro continued, "I would
like to introduce to you Mr. Robert Kardashian, who is one of Mr.
Simpson's closest and dearest friends, who will read a letter that
O. J. Simpson wrote in his handwriting today. Thank you."

|||||

He became one of the most familiar, if least known, figures in the
Simpson saga: loyal friend Robert Kardashian, the one with the

white stripe in his hair. Heir to a meat-packing fortune in Los Angeles, Kardashian attended USC a couple of years before Simpson and served there as the student manager of the football team, the prototypical hanger-on position. He graduated from law school but quickly dropped practice for the business world. He started a music magazine and sold his share for $3 million in 1979. At the time of the murders he was running Movie Tunes, a company that played music in movie theaters between shows.

For many years Simpson and Kardashian shared lively and similar social lives. In 1978, Kardashian met his future wife, Kristen, when she was seventeen and he thirty-four; Kardashian had been there the previous year when O.J., then thirty, met Nicole Brown, then eighteen. Bob and Kristen Kardashian would ultimately have four children (Kourtney, Kimberly, Khole, and Robert, Jr.), and they often joined O.J. and Nicole for vacations. The two couples separated around the same time, too, and Kardashian's divorce papers suggest that his marriage was beset by some of the same troubles as O.J. and Nicole's. During the divorce, Kristen Kardashian obtained a restraining order that barred either party from "molesting, attacking, striking, threatening, sexually assaulting, battering, or otherwise disturbing the peace of the other party."

Strangely, Kardashian seemed to have an attack of poverty during his divorce. In an affidavit filed on January 11, 1991, he wrote that he had been terminated from his job the previous December. "I AM NOW UNEMPLOYED AND HAVE NO INCOME," the document stated. Yet at the time of the murders, Kardashian was living in the vast house in Encino, and from the moment Simpson was arrested, Kardashian suspended all other work, reactivated his law license, and toiled full-time on O.J.'s defense for more than a year. His Rolls-Royce became a fixture at the county jail. His devotion to Simpson had a desperate, frantic quality. In September 1994, he placed a full-page advertisement in *Hits* magazine, a trade publication, bearing the words JUSTICE FOR THE JUICE. In the ad Kardashian used the name of Movie Tunes' executive vice-president, Michael Ameen, without Ameen's permission. Ameen promptly quit, telling *The Hollywood Reporter,* "Robert's commitment to this case has overwhelmed every other corner of his life."

Kardashian's divorce from Kristen pained him, especially because she left him for Bruce Jenner, the former Olympic decathlon champion. Jenner and Kristen later married, and at the time of the murders they were starring in a frequently played infomercial for a thigh-exercising device. According to a close associate of Kardashian's, "It bothered him that she was on TV all the time with the Thighmaster. This case was his way to step over them. This was better than infomercials."

Head bowed, with no words of introduction or explanation, Kardashian followed Shapiro to the podium at the June 17 press conference and began speaking into the nest of microphones. His audience surely dwarfed that of any infomercial. "This letter was written by O.J. today," Kardashian said. Actually, it was not. The letter was headed "6/15/94," two days earlier. Then Kardashian began reading: *"To whom it may concern . . ."*

||||||

Suicide notes vary. Some tell the truth; some don't. Some reflect a genuine intention to commit the deed; some merely display a taste for melodrama. There is, of course, no way to tell for sure what O. J. Simpson truly intended to do when he composed the letter that Robert Kardashian read to the world on the afternoon of June 17, 1994. It is safe to say, however, that Simpson intended his letter to be understood as a suicide note—and as a public last will and testament. As such, it provides both intentional and unintentional clues to the nature of its author—and in particular to the banality, self-pity, and narcissism that are the touchstones of his character.

First everyone understand nothing to do with Nicole's murder. I loved her, allways have and always will. If we had a promblem it's because I loved her so much. Recitly we came to the understanding that for now we were'nt right for each other at least for now. Dispite our love we were different and thats why we murtually agreed to go our spaerate ways.

Kardashian edited as he went along, first by omitting the date at the top of the letter. Shapiro had suggested that Simpson had given this and two other letters to Kardashian right after he wrote them. But if O.J. had actually written them two days earlier, Kardashian might have had a clue that Simpson was contemplating not surrendering. By leaving out the date, Kardashian avoided uncomfortable questions about his own role in O.J.'s disappearance.

Kardashian also began his recitation by quoting the letter as saying "First, everyone understand *I had* nothing to do with Nicole's murder." The text illustrates that Simpson in fact omitted these two important words. The "suicide note" showed that Simpson was a terrible writer and speller, so it is difficult to draw any conclusions from his errors except about his near-illiteracy. However, it is tempting to infer some psychological significance from Simpson's failure to render correctly this most important sentence of his letter. (Most newspapers that printed excerpts of the letter cleaned up the grammar and spelling, thereby leaving the impression that Simpson was more literate than he was.)

Two days earlier, standing before Nicole's body at the O'Connor Mortuary in Laguna Beach, her mother, Juditha, had asked O.J. whether he had anything to do with Nicole's death. Staring at Nicole's corpse as he answered, Simpson used words similar to those in this note: "I loved her," O.J. told Nicole's mother. "I loved her too much." From both the letter and the remark, it seems that O.J. believed his love for Nicole was in some way excessive.

It was tough spitting for a second time but we both knew it was for the best. Inside I had no doubt that in the future we would be close as friend or more. Unlike whats been in the press, Nicole + I had a great relationship for most of our lives together. Like all long term relationships, we had a few downs + ups. I took the heat New Years 1989 because that what I was suppose to do I did not plea no contest for any other reason but to protect our privicy and was advise it would end the press hype.

Kardashian rendered that last sentence in a considerably more grammatical way than Simpson wrote it.

I don't want to belabor knocking the press but I cant beleive what's being said. Most of it tottally made up. I know you have a job to do but as a last wish, please, please, please leave my <u>children</u> in <u>peace.</u> Their lives will be tough enough.

Leaving aside the question of whether a criminal conviction for spousal abuse and Nicole's repeated pleas to 911 qualified as something more than "a few downs + ups," it is Simpson's self-obsession that is so striking here. He not only denies responsibility for beating Nicole but congratulates himself for accepting the blame for it. Ironically, there was in fact very little "press hype" about the 1989 beating incident. Notwithstanding his criminal conviction, Simpson received generally glowing press coverage from 1989 until even the week after the murders. That O.J. should have been so wounded by what little criticism there was again demonstrates his vast self-regard.

I want to send my love and thanks to all my friend. I'm sorry I can't name every one of you. Especially A.C., Man, thanks for being in my life. The support and friendship I receive from so many, Wayne Hughes, Louis Marx, Frank Olson, Marc Packer, Bender, Bobby Kardashian I wish we had spend more time together in recite years.

Hughes is a USC benefactor and the owner of a chain of private warehouse facilities; Marx is a private investor who sold off his father's toy company at great profit; Olson is the longtime chief executive officer of Hertz; Packer is a New York–based restaurateur; Bobby Bender is a garment-industry executive in New York. As for Kardashian, the letter suggests that even Simpson was astonished by the extent and intensity of his friend's sycophancy.

My golfing buddie, Hoss, Alan Austin, Mike, Craig, Bender, Wyler, Sandy, Jay, Donnie Sofer, thank for the fun.

The first four mentioned were all playing partners of O.J.'s at the Riviera Country Club, near Simpson's home in Brentwood. "Hoss" is Bob Hoskins, a Los Angeles–based businessman; Alan Austin ran a women's wear boutique in Beverly Hills for many years; Mike Melchiori was a semiretired printing executive (he died of a heart attack in April 1996); and Craig Baumgarten, a former senior executive at Columbia Pictures, is now an independent movie producer. Wyler is Bender's partner in the garment business. Sandy, Jay, and Don Soffer (correct spelling) were Simpson's East Coast golfing companions. It is worth noting, given the way his case unfolded, that in this list of O.J.'s fifteen best friends, all of them except Cowlings are wealthy, middle-aged white men.

All my teammatte over the years. Reggie, you were the soul of my pro career. Ahmad I never stop being proud of you. Marcus you got a great lady in Katherine Don't mess it up. Bobby Chandler thanks for always being there.

When he turned to his fellow athletes, the style of the letter shifted to that of a high school yearbook. Reggie McKenzie was Simpson's top blocker on the Buffalo Bills; Ahmad Rashad played

wide receiver for the Bills and later the Minnesota Vikings and was
O.J.'s colleague and sometime rival at NBC Sports; Marcus Allen,
who won the Heisman as a running back thirteen years after Simpson at USC, had a magnificent professional career with the
Raiders and Kansas City Chiefs; Chandler, a teammate of O.J.'s at
USC, played for the Raiders in the NFL. (He would die of cancer
while O.J. was in jail during his trial.)

The reference to Allen was especially intriguing. Marcus Allen
was in some ways O.J.'s protégé, the man who came closest to
equaling his feats at USC and in the professional ranks. Not surprisingly, their relationship generated tensions, which were exacerbated by Allen's on-and-off affair with Nicole. Some of O.J. and
Nicole's friends believe that it was jealousy about Allen in particular that ultimately drove Simpson to murder her. O.J. apparently
knew about this affair and at least forgave Allen for it, allowing
Marcus and Kathryn (the correct spelling) to marry in his home on
Rockingham in 1993. But the instruction to Allen about his marriage—"Don't mess it up"—may be a subtle reminder that O.J.'s re-
sentments against him lingered.

*Skip + Cathy I love you guys without you I never would have made
it this far. Marguerite thanks for those early years. We had some fun.
Paula, what can I say, You are special I'm sorry we're not going to
have our chanc. God brought you to me. I now see, as I leave, you'll
be in my thoughs.*

Skip Taft was O.J.'s business manager; Cathy Randa, his secretary; Marguerite, his first wife and the mother of Jason, Arnelle,
and Aaren, the child who drowned in the pool at Rockingham. Barbieri was, of course, his principal—but far from exclusive—girlfriend during the period after his separation from Nicole. The only
women mentioned in the suicide note are secretaries, wives, and
girlfriends—an apt summary of O.J.'s view of the place of women
in the world.

By the end, the letter came to resemble the speech Simpson
gave on August 3, 1985, upon his induction to the professional
football Hall of Fame in Canton, Ohio. O.J. thanked many of the
same people, in much the same style. (". . . I wouldn't be here if it
wasn't for Skip Taft and Cathy Randa . . .") Notwithstanding the
macabre circumstances, Simpson seems to have composed his sui-

cide note in the manner of the celebrity intent upon allowing a few friends to share in his reflected glory.

I think of my life and feel I'v done most of the right things. so why do I end up like this. I can't go on, no matter what the outcome people will look and point. I can't take that. I can't subject my children to that. This way they can move on and go on with thair lives. Please, if I'v done anything worthwhile in my life, let my kids live in peace from you (press).

Simpson demonstrated a certain prescience here. Even though he was ultimately acquitted, he did become a pariah; people do look and point. But what is peculiar is how he converted his own inability to cope with unpopularity into a problem for his children: "I can't subject my children to that." Sydney and Justin had lost their mother. A more rational and generous reaction might have been to hold them close and assure them that they were not going to lose their father, too. Simpson's ego compelled him to imagine that his own problems with the public would torture his children—when of course it was he, not they, who could not abide the humiliation.

I'v had a good life I'm proud of how I lived, my momma tought me to do un to other. I treated people the way I wanted to be treated I'v always tryed to be up + helpful so why is this happening? I'm sorry for the Goldman family. I kwow how much it hurts. Nicole and I had a good life together, all this press talk about a rocky relationship was no morr than what ever long term relationship expriences. All her friends will confrim that I'v been tottally loving and understanding of what she's been going through. At times I'v felt like a battered husband or boyfriend but I loved her, made that clear to everyone and would take whatever to make us work.

Though it is theoretically possible that the 5-foot-5-inch, 129-pound Nicole battered her husband, a 6-foot-2-inch, 210-pound football player, there is apparently no record of O.J.'s seeking medical assistance because of her physical abuse.

Don't feel sorry for me. I'v had a great life made great friends. Please think of the real O.J. and not this lost person. Thank for making my life special I hope I help yours. Peace + Love O.J.

Inside the O in his name, Simpson scrawled a happy face—a flourish that is almost too perverse to contemplate.

For all that the content of the letter reveals of its author, what is perhaps most striking is something that is absent from it. Simpson portrays himself as an unjustly accused murderer, but his letter does not even request the police to locate the "real" killer of his ex-wife and her friend.

|||||

Shapiro handled the questions from the reporters at the press conference. One asked why Kardashian had read the letter. After all the letter, on the whole, was highly incriminating of Shapiro's client. "We read it because it is the only words that we have from O.J.," Shapiro replied. This answer says much about the care and feeding of celebrity clients. O.J. wanted it done, so it was done. It is possible that Simpson wanted the letter read only in the event that he committed suicide. (Others who attended the meeting at Kardashian's house were appalled that the letter was read to the public.) There would have been no harm in Shapiro's waiting a while and then deciding whether to read the letter. But reading the letter simultaneously granted O.J.'s last wish and served Shapiro's own interests, by demonstrating that the lawyer had been duped by a despondent and possibly deranged man. Elaborating on the question of why he had the letter read, Shapiro went on, "I have never felt worse in my professional career as a result of what has happened today." In other words, Shapiro had it read, in part, because it made him feel better.

Another question again illustrated the way Simpson's status as a celebrity affected the way his case was conducted. Shapiro mentioned that three letters had been found at Kardashian's house—one to the public (which Kardashian had read out loud), one to his children, and one to his mother. A reporter asked if Shapiro had read all three. No, the lawyer said. "They are under seal and will be turned over to the persons to whom they are addressed." All three letters constituted crucial evidence in locating a fugitive accused of murder. First and foremost, it was the police who were entitled to seize and read those letters. Yet Shapiro and Kardashian blithely walked out of the house with them and then announced that the fugitive, not the police, would determine who read them. This was so much the natural order of things in Los Angeles that the removal of the letters from the house scarcely drew a word of comment in the local media.

Nor was that Shapiro's most remarkable answer at the press conference. "What were the last words you heard from O. J. Simpson?" a reporter asked.

This question called for him to reveal a communication that may have been subject to Simpson's attorney-client privilege, yet Shapiro did not hesitate to answer. "My personal words with him were of a complimentary nature to the way I had been with him and for him to thank me for everything I had done up-to-date," he replied. The response raised another question (which went unasked): If Simpson was offering you valedictory thanks about your efforts on the case, why didn't you think he was about to flee?

Many lawyers with a client on the run would have gone straight to their desks and worked the phones to sniff out any clue of the missing man's whereabouts. But Shapiro had never liked to spend any more time than necessary at the office. After the press conference, he simply went home. His wife, Linell, greeted him at the door.

"Where have you been?" she asked. "He's on television, Bob."

|||||

The LAPD had put out an all-points bulletin for Al Cowlings right around the time of Gascon's press conference, at 2:00 P.M. Around that time, Vannatter, Lange, and their colleagues put in their first calls to the many police departments whose jurisdictions abut that of the LAPD. But because the police had never seized Simpson's passport, the cops had to cast an even wider net. They alerted the U.S. Border Patrol, as well as the airlines, the U.S. Customs Service, and the Mexican Judicial Police.

It wasn't until just after Shapiro's press conference ended, however, at around 6:00 P.M., that the Los Angeles media confirmed the description of the car the police were seeking: a 1993 white Ford Bronco with California license plate 3DHY503. Not surprisingly, perhaps, given the vast public interest in the case, it was the broadcast announcement, not the law enforcement effort, that produced almost immediate results.

Chris Thomas had been watching television at home in Mission Viejo when he learned Simpson was on the run. At 6:25 P.M., he and his girlfriend, Kathy Ferrigno, were heading north on Interstate 5, the Santa Ana Freeway, on their way to a weekend of camping. They had been joking about O.J.'s disappearance, studying in a halfhearted way the cars coming toward them, seeing if Simpson might be among them, on his way to Mexico. After a few minutes of this, Ferrigno looked into the passenger-side rearview mirror and started saying, "Oh my God!—Chris, Chris, Chris!" Thomas slowed down and in a moment Ferrigno was face-to-face with Al Cowlings. When he noticed that she was staring at him, Cowlings glowered at her. Their location at that moment was about eighty miles south of Kardashian's house in Encino, near the El Toro interchange on Interstate 5. They were about a five-minute drive from the gravesite of Nicole Brown Simpson. The Bronco—and this later proved important—was heading north, that is, back toward Los Angeles and away from the Mexican border.

Ferrigno jotted down the Bronco's license plate, and Thomas pulled to the side of the freeway by a call box. Thomas called the California Highway Patrol and gave the dispatcher his impression of Cowlings's demeanor: "We looked at him, you know, and he like stared us down, like he was death."

As Simpson described it in his deposition in the civil case, he and Cowlings left Interstate 5 intending to go to Nicole's grave, but they retreated when they saw that the cemetery was staked out by police. Just a few minutes after Thomas's telephone call, Orange County sheriff's deputy Larry Pool saw the Bronco heading on an on-ramp returning to the northbound Santa Ana. Pool sped alongside the Bronco and looked inside. Cowlings smiled nervously at him. The officer then radioed in to check the plate on the Bronco and learned that it was a match for Cowlings's.

"Ten-four, I'm behind it," Pool said into his radio, and with that, all air traffic on the police radio band receded into a stunned silence.

As the Bronco began to move on the freeway through the city of Santa Ana, the traffic grew heavier and then came to a complete standstill. Pool and a colleague in another car, Jim Sewell, used the opportunity to leave their cars and, with guns drawn, advance by foot on the Bronco.

"Turn off your engine," the officers shouted to Cowlings.

Cowlings started screaming and pounding his left hand on the side of the door. "Fuck, no!" he said. He was banging the car so hard that it was rocking in place. "Put away your guns! He's in the backseat and he's got a gun to his head."

Fearing bloodshed, the officers held their ground and watched Cowlings drive off as the traffic ahead of him cleared. The Bronco began moving again at moderate speed, still heading north. Returning to their black-and-white squad cars, the Orange County officials simply began following the Bronco, and radioed for backup assistance. The chase was on.

Cowlings turned on his car's four-way flashers and called 911 from his car phone shortly after the confrontation. "This is A.C.," he told the dispatcher at 6:46 P.M. "I have O.J. in the car."

"Okay, where are you?" the dispatcher asked.

"Please," Cowlings said. "I'm coming up the Five freeway . . . Right now, we all, we're okay, but you got to tell the police to just back off. He's still alive. He's got a gun to his head."

"Hold on a moment. Okay, where are you?" the dispatcher responded. "Is everything else okay?"

"Everything right now is okay, Officer. Everything is okay. He wants me to get him to his mom. He wants me to get him to his house."

The dispatcher patched through another voice, who asked Cowlings his name.

"My name is A.C.," he bellowed. "You know who I am, goddammit!" Cowlings hung up and continued driving north, in the general direction of Brentwood.

The police, of course, were not the only people looking for Cowlings that afternoon. As soon as the LAPD announced that O.J. was missing, Bob Tur, the dean of the L.A. media's helicopter journalists, also began scheming to find O.J. and A.C. Mulling over Simpson's predicament with his wife, copilot, and video cameraperson, Marika, Bob Tur reached the same conclusion as the doctors who were treating Simpson. Tur guessed that he would try to visit his ex-wife's grave in Orange County. So he and Marika steered their KCBS chopper to Ascension Cemetery in Lake Forest. Tur noticed that the cops had staked the place out, likewise waiting for Simpson. Then Tur drifted over to the Santa Ana Freeway and caught sight of the Bronco, apparently just after Cowlings's confrontation with Pool and Sewell. The backup units—there would be a dozen in all—were falling in at a safe distance behind Cowlings and Simpson as they headed north. KCBS began broadcasting live, and the other stations, with their own helicopters, picked up the chase a few moments later.

It was, to be sure, an unusual moment in journalism, but not quite as rare as many people thought. The freeway chase, broadcast live by cameras mounted in helicopters, is a staple of television news in Los Angeles. Local stations break into programming on a regular basis to follow the most routine chases, even some that emerge out of traffic infractions. Bob Tur had had 128 previous journeys like this one, and local pilots all know the drill; they follow police transmissions on their scramblers. Even though the Bronco was picked up on camera about seventy miles from the house on Rockingham, the helicopter pilots' intimate knowledge of the local terrain meant that they could, and did, project exactly where the Bronco was going. As a result, for those watching in the Los Angeles area, there was no mystery about Simpson's plans or his route.

For the national audience, however, it was another story. One after another, the networks broke into their regular programming to pick up the chase live. (NBC skittered back and forth from the Bronco to the fifth game of the National Basketball Association championship series, between the New York Knicks and Houston Rockets.) The network anchors were far less familiar with the customs of these helicopter chases and completely ignorant of Los Angeles freeway topography. Their narratives, accordingly, reflected only bewilderment at the scene unfolding before them. On ABC, for example, Peter Jennings repeatedly confessed that he did not know where the Bronco was or where it was going. These uninformative nondescriptions somehow made the chase even more hypnotizing for the rest of the nation.

Simpson's televised journey into the unknown transformed a tabloid murder into an international phenomenon. Approximately 95 million Americans watched some portion of the chase on television, which exceeded that year's Super Bowl audience by about 5 million.

With the helicopters gathering above, the Bronco continued north on the Santa Ana, passing Disneyland in Anaheim, and then headed west on the Artesia Freeway. It was here, in the period just after 7:00 P.M. Pacific Time, that word of the chase spread and television coverage became ubiquitous. Seven news helicopters followed the Bronco's trail.

Crowds began forming in Compton, a small, heavily black city just south of Los Angeles. The numbers were small at first, just a few dozen people drawn to the spectacle by what they had seen on television. Cowlings turned off the Artesia, traveling less than a mile south on the Harbor Freeway, and then west on I-405, the San Diego Freeway. These moves confirmed what Cowlings had told the police; though he still had a good thirty miles to go, he was en route to Simpson's house in Brentwood. The San Diego Freeway took Simpson through Torrance, a community not at all like nearby Compton. Mark Fuhrman, in his distinctive style, once explained the difference. His taped interviews with aspiring screenwriter Laura Hart McKinny contained the following description: "Westwood is gone, the niggers have discovered it. . . . Torrance is considered the last white middle-class society." The reaction to the Bronco was different in "the last white middle-class society." No supporters lined the highway, and O.J. and his helicopter entourage passed through without fanfare. In Inglewood and at the edge of Watts, the largely African-American communities to the north, the spectators returned. They were shouting encouragement at this point. "Go, O.J.!" many screamed. "Save the Juice!"

The helicopters had to pull back briefly when the Bronco, curving gently north along the contour of the Pacific Ocean, passed by Los Angeles International Airport. The scene on television became even stranger for a moment when the cameras from the choppers showed several jetliners landing beneath them. Their airspace clear, the helicopters then resumed the chase as the Bronco moved into the densely populated West Side. Hundreds of people lined the overpass at Venice Boulevard, another area with a heavy minority population. Several people held up encouraging signs, and many were yelling in support of O.J.

Knowledgeable television broadcasters had been speculating for some time that Cowlings would leave the San Diego Freeway at the Sunset Boulevard exit, since it was the most direct route to Simpson's home in Brentwood. Yet notwithstanding the advance notice, the crowd of people at the Sunset exit was modest, perhaps a couple of dozen. That area, of course, is the edge of Bel-Air, perhaps the wealthiest and whitest community in all of Los Angeles. Only a handful of the people there turned out to cheer for O.J.

Cowlings indeed left I-405 at Sunset, then he dodged traffic for about a mile until he could make a right turn into the privileged, hilly precincts of Brentwood. He knew a shortcut. Instead of making a right onto Rockingham, he turned north off Sunset one street earlier, onto Bristol Avenue. With the helicopters still tracking him among the gated homes, Cowlings then made a left onto Ashford, from which he could turn into O.J.'s driveway. Cowlings, however, almost didn't make it. There were so many television satellite trucks parked on tiny Ashford that Cowlings had to slow to nearly a full stop to inch his way past them. With dusk fast approaching, Cowlings finally managed to pull into the driveway at 360 North Rockingham. The Bronco's flashers illuminated the cobblestones in the driveway from which, earlier that week, police had scraped blood samples. It was shortly before 8:00 P.M.

||||

At about 7:15 P.M., when A.C. and O.J. were still wending their way to Brentwood, Detective Tom Lange had reached Cowlings on the cellular phone in the Bronco. In their conversation, Cowlings confirmed that he was heading to O.J.'s home and that Simpson remained suicidal. Lange did his best to calm the situation. Without telling Cowlings, Lange also arranged for the LAPD's SWAT team to go to the Rockingham house and prepare to arrest Simpson there. A team of about twenty-five SWAT specialists, with their arsenal of stun grenades and night-sighted weaponry, arrived at Rockingham about fifteen minutes before Cowlings did. Several of Simpson's friends had set up a vigil there, but the officers evicted everyone except Kardashian and O.J.'s twenty-four-year-old son, Jason. True to form, though, the LAPD did invite one outsider to tag along: Roger Sandler, a photographer for *Time* and *Life* magazines.

The SWAT team's plans nearly went awry immediately. As soon as the Bronco stopped in the driveway, Jason sprang from the front door and began yelling at Cowlings, who seemed to be equally hyped up. The 6-foot-5-inch Cowlings, a defensive lineman taken out of USC by the Buffalo Bills the year after they selected Simpson, stuck his long arm out the driver's window and pushed Jason away. There was a considerable poignancy to the scene. Jason's relationship with his father had long vacillated between poor and nonexistent. Cowlings's pokes made clear the status of the pudgy and unathletic son: He was not wanted in his father's moment of crisis. A pair of officers gingerly approached Jason and all but dragged him back into the house.

Jason's approach unnerved Cowlings. He started screaming that the police had to get back, get away. He even stepped out of the car and caught sight of one of the officers posted on the wall along Ashford. "He's got a gun!" Cowlings screamed before he reentered the car. "Don't do anything stupid! Get the police away!"

The police, of course, were not going to go away. Lange had handed over negotiating duties to the SWAT team's Pete Weireter, who was posted inside O.J.'s house. Weireter reached O.J. on the cellular phone and attempted to talk him into surrendering.

Minutes passed, and the world waited to see if O. J. Simpson would blow his brains out on live national TV. Unaccustomed to chases of this duration, the local television stations agreed that they could share one another's pictures of the scene so each helicopter would have a chance to refuel. Suddenly, there was very little to see: just the Bronco parked in the driveway. Close observers noticed one spectator with the best view of all. Jason had brought Kato, the white Akita that had apparently witnessed the murders, to live at Rockingham. The dog, which Jason would later rename Satchmo, wandered around the Bronco as O.J. and A.C. lingered inside it.

The silence at the driveway standoff contrasted dramatically with the scene unfolding at the foot of Rockingham, on Sunset Boulevard. A raucous crowd several hundred strong had gathered there, drawn to the drama. Sunset was impassable; even residents of the area couldn't get home. (Shapiro had asked Michael Baden and Saul Faerstein to meet him at O.J.'s home, but the wall of people prevented either doctor from reaching Rockingham.) Local reporters broadcasting live from Sunset found a stark racial division at the scene. The whites, a minority of the revelers, were curiosity seekers—"looky loos" in the LAPD phrase—who had come simply to experience the bizarre scene. The African-Americans, on the other hand, had mostly come to show solidarity, and their chants and shouts made their feelings clear. "Free O.J.!" they repeated again and again. Interviewed on KCBS, one of them said, "I feel that the black people ought to come together. They're trying to make us extinct." A woman then added, "First it was Michael [Jackson] and Mike Tyson and Rodney King. I'm calling for the unification of the black race!"

Up at the Rockingham house, Weireter eventually obtained Simpson's promise that he did not intend to hurt anyone except himself. The negotiator told O.J. that his children needed him. Simpson asked to speak with his mother, who had checked into a San Francisco hospital for stress-related symptoms. No problem, said Weireter, just come inside. He seemed to be making progress when the battery in O.J.'s phone went dead. Cowlings went into the house to fetch a replacement. Finally, Simpson agreed to give up.

"You'll have to come to us," said Mike Albanese, chief of the SWAT unit. After a pause, Simpson hesitantly put a foot out the door of the Bronco. It was 8:53 P.M., nearly an hour after Cowlings had arrived at Simpson's home. In his hands, O.J. held a couple of family pictures, which he had been clutching in the car. He staggered into the foyer and collapsed into the officers' arms. "I'm sorry, guys," Simpson kept repeating. "I'm sorry I put you through this." Albanese allowed Simpson to use the bathroom and gave him a glass of orange juice to drink while he called his mother on the telephone. Deferential even then, the officers finally asked whether Simpson was ready to go. He nodded. The officers put handcuffs on him and led him out the front door—with Roger Sandler behind them, recording the moment for posterity and *Time*. The police had forbidden the news helicopters from shining their powerful lights down on the scene, so the public never saw Simpson being placed in an unmarked cruiser for the trip downtown.

With Simpson gone, other members of the SWAT team examined Cowlings's Bronco. (When he was booked at the police station, Cowlings had $8,750 in cash in his pockets.) In what appeared to be Simpson's travel bag, they found O.J.'s passport and a plastic bag that contained a fake goatee, a fake mustache, a bottle of makeup adhesive remover, and three receipts from Cinema Secrets Beauty Supply, dated May 27, 1994. The officers also found a fully loaded Smith & Wesson .357 magnum blue steel handgun. It was registered to Lieutenant Earl Paysinger, yet another of Simpson's friends on the LAPD. About five years earlier, at a time when Paysinger was providing security for O.J., the lieutenant had bought his client the gun.

An eighteen-car caravan escorted Simpson to his booking at Parker Center. He was then transported to the L.A. county jail for his first night in custody, which he spent on suicide watch. In his book *I Want to Tell You,* Simpson wrote, "The first week I was in jail I thought about Jesus being crucified."

Simpson was arraigned in municipal court on the following Monday, June 20. He was physically transformed from any O. J. Simpson the public had seen before. Looking dazed and bewildered, he staggered from the holding pen to the defendant's table before Judge Patti Jo McKay. He wore a black suit and white shirt, but he was denied a tie, belt, and shoelaces—even, apparently, collar stays—for fear that he might turn them into instruments of suicide. Head cocked to one side, Simpson stared vacantly around the courtroom. Asked his name, he appeared confused, and Shapiro had to prompt his answer. Asked his plea, Simpson muttered quietly, "Not guilty." The proceeding was over in moments, and in the only real business transacted, Judge McKay scheduled the preliminary hearing for ten days hence, June 30.

Both sides held press conferences the same day. There was, of course, nothing that required the lawyers on either side to answer reporters' questions at that time, and much to recommend silence. Shapiro had a client who had acted like a very guilty man the previous Friday. The circumstances seemed to call for a discreet weighing of options. Garcetti's prosecutors, on the other hand, faced the prospect of convicting a popular celebrity. Their task seemed to call for a serious, untheatrical getting down to business. The worst thing they could do was appear unduly zealous. Yet the adversaries could not resist an attempt to posture and spin. Shapiro fancied himself a master at manipulating the press. Likewise, Garcetti—under the tutelage of his ever-present director of communications, ex-prosecutor and ex–local news anchorwoman Suzanne Childs—had similarly high regard for his own talents in this realm. In fact, throughout the case, many efforts at press management by both sides failed, and that was never more true than after the parties' first day in court.

Shapiro faced a bank of television cameras at his Century City office shortly after the arraignment. Looking almost as sorrowful as his client had in court, Shapiro offered Simpson only lukewarm support. Shapiro portrayed himself less as an advocate than as someone who was looking for answers just like everyone else. "At the present time," he said, "I have not discussed at any great length the facts of the case with [Simpson]." The lawyer was asked about the possibility of raising an insanity defense—that is, one based on the premise that Simpson had committed the murders. "Every possible defense has to be considered by any trial lawyer," Shapiro responded, "and I certainly would reserve all possibilities." His lawyerly words made Simpson look even more guilty.

Yet the prosecutors made even more trouble for themselves. Since the murders, Garcetti had turned himself into a virtual interview machine. In addition to his press conferences, he appeared on ABC's *Nightline, CBS Evening News, NBC Nightly News, Today,* and a special nighttime edition of *Good Morning America.* Garcetti did use these appearances to focus, in part, on his longstanding and heartfelt devotion to the issue of domestic violence, but the promiscuity of his efforts suggested he was seeking attention for himself as much as for any issue. In an especially surreal touch, Garcetti appeared live on ABC to describe the freeway chase as it was happening. "We're all hurting right now," Garcetti told Peter Jennings as the Bronco sped on. "We're all sharing a very painful experience." But in truth, over these first fevered days, Garcetti didn't looked pained at all; rather, he looked like he was exploiting the moment for all it was worth. He even strayed into some dubious ethical territory, predicting that Simpson would ultimately admit to committing the murders. Appearing on yet another national program, *This Week with David Brinkley,* on Sunday, June 19, Garcetti said, "Well, it's not going to shock me if we see an O. J. Simpson, sometime down the road—and it could happen very soon, it could happen months from now—say, 'Okay, I did do it, but I'm not responsible.' We've seen it in Menendez. It's going to be a likely defense here, I believe, once the evidence is reviewed by the lawyers."

Marcia Clark's June 20 press conference only contributed to a perception that the prosecution camp was celebrating. It was the public's first real view of Clark, and a revealing one at that. She was a formidable extemporaneous speaker. There was also no mistaking the sincerity of her passions—or the fixity of her beliefs. Like her boss, Clark did not even pay lip service to such legal niceties as the presumption of innocence. She was, if anything, more categorical than Garcetti in her judgments of the accused. Although it had been just two days since the arrest—and only eight days since the murders—Clark announced, "It was premeditated murder. It was done with deliberation and premeditation. That is precisely what he was charged with because that is what we will prove." Thus, in a single breath, Clark wrote off the possibility of arguing that Simpson had murdered his ex-wife in a fit of jealous passion—a perfectly reasonable theory of the case. Asked about the possibility of accomplices, Clark again spoke with total confidence, even arrogance: "Mr. Simpson is charged alone because he is the sole murderer." Of course, no responsible prosecutors would have filed charges against Simpson unless they felt he was guilty. But Clark and Garcetti put their case at risk when they let themselves, rather than the evidence, do the talking—and they heedlessly limited their options at trial by rushing into a single theory about how the crime had occurred.

Clark was an accomplished lawyer but a far from obvious choice to prosecute such an important case. In fact, Garcetti never really assigned Clark to the Simpson case at all; she had simply taken Vannatter's call on Monday, June 13, and stayed with the case through the tumultuous first week. It is difficult to say whether Garcetti, given a real choice, would have picked Clark. She had prosecuted several murders, but other senior deputies had tried more, and more difficult, cases. Moreover, Clark's June 20 performance suggested that for all her competence, there may have been good reason not to choose her. Among those with long memories of the Los Angeles District Attorney's Office, Clark's behavior at the press conference raised disquieting echoes. The office's losing streak in big cases was well known. What was less known—or at least less commented upon in the media—was that most of those cases had been lost by women prosecutors with pugnacious demeanors, among them Lael Rubin in McMartin Preschool; Lea D'Agostino in *Twilight Zone;* and Pamela Bozanich in Menendez. All of these prosecutors came across as aggressive and outspoken, just as Marcia Clark did at her postarraignment press conference. Of course, it might have been just a coincidence that it was female prosecutors in Los Angeles who had failed in the high-profile cases—just as the harsh judgments of them might have been the result of sexism—but Shapiro and his colleagues on the defense team regarded these perceptions as important. From the beginning, they thought that, like the other prominent and unsuccessful prosecutors, Clark would come across as unduly harsh; consequently, they were delighted she had the case.

Ironically, the public relations concerns that guided the district attorney's office made Clark's position on the case unassailable. Because the events of the first week had been so public—and Clark such a visible part of them—removing her would have caused a considerable stir. During that week, Clark herself had clearly committed no gaffe that would have justified her being pulled from the case. Whether or not Garcetti admitted it, a decision to remove her would have been seen as at least partially driven by her gender, as well as the office's history of failure by female prosecutors. Garcetti's base of liberal Democratic supporters would have rebelled, and the media would have rushed to the story.

And there was another, less public, reason Garcetti was bound to stay with Clark, this one rooted in the arcane internal politics of the district attorney's office. Clark's best friend in the office was prosecutor Lynn Reed Baragona. Several years earlier, Lynn Reed, as she was then known, had sued Gil Garcetti, then just a supervisor in the D.A.'s office, alleging sexual discrimination in promotions. The case was settled to Reed's satisfaction before it was adjudicated, but the rancor between Reed and Garcetti was long established and well known. (The D.A.'s office abounds in these sorts of interwoven connections. Though the office has nearly a thousand prosecutors, the same set of senior people has run the office for decades, and the personal, social, and professional relationships among them yield a byzantine web of rivalry, grudge, and affection. For example, Lynn Reed had once dated prosecutor Peter Bozanich, who later married the prosecutor who would go on to lead the first Menendez brothers trial. At the time, Peter Bozanich was sharing an office with fellow prosecutor Lance Ito, who in turn was dating prosecutor Jackie Connor. Connor went on to marry yet another prosecutor, James Bascue, who would become a superior court judge and Ito's mentor in the district attorney's office and, later, on the bench. Connor later became a superior court judge as well, and she presided over Marcia Clark's biggest case prior to Simpson—the Mount Olive Church murders.) If Garcetti had taken Clark off the case, Clark's supporters might have suggested that he was retaliating against her for her friendship with Lynn Reed Baragona, and thus raised the issue of the sexual discrimination claim. The district attorney had no interest in stirring up that old controversy.

Besides, Garcetti gave little thought to replacing Clark that first week because everything seemed to be going so well. With Simpson reeling, Garcetti and Clark's instincts told them to keep the pressure on. The hiring of Shapiro had also buoyed the prosecutors. No one could remember the last time Shapiro had taken a murder case to trial in superior court. (In fact, he never had.) Shapiro had the reputation for trying to delay cases into oblivion and then, when the heat died down, striking a plea bargain. That, after all, was what happened in most cases: Defense lawyers stalled; prosecutors pushed. True to their customary role, the prosecutors tried to skip the June 30 preliminary hearing altogether.

|||||

The California tradition of holding preliminary hearings is a relative anomaly in American criminal law. "Prelims," as they are known, are essentially miniature trials held in front of a judge rather than a jury. For many years, California law required prelims—a municipal judge would determine, in a felony case, if there was "probable cause" that the defendant had committed the crime. In fact, prosecutors almost never lost preliminary hearings—that is, judges rarely tossed out cases on the grounds that the government had failed to meet its burden. Still, prosecutors loathed prelims, which forced them to offer up their witnesses for cross-examination by defense lawyers at a very early stage in the game. An effective cross-examination of a government witness at a prelim sometimes rendered that person virtually useless at trial or, at the very least, gave the defense a road map to weaknesses in the prosecution's case. (Not surprisingly, defense lawyers loved prelims.) So, as part of the law-and-order movement that swept California in the 1980s and 1990s, prosecutors fought to cut back on prelims. Specifically, in a referendum proposed by the law enforcement community and passed by state voters in 1990, the government won the right to present most cases, including murder cases, to grand juries rather than at preliminary hearings.

By contrast, prosecutors love grand juries, whose deliberations are secret. Most important, defense lawyers are not allowed to cross-examine witnesses, or even to attend the proceedings. Asked by a prosecutor to indict someone, grand juries invariably do. Grand juries allow prosecutors to move cases to trial without exposing more than a small fraction of their evidence—and they obviate the need for preliminary hearings. So in the Simpson case, the prosecutors set out to have the grand jury issue an indictment before the preliminary hearing was to begin on June 30. That meant Clark had to move quickly. In fact, she had begun her presentation to the grand jury on Friday, June 17, even before Simpson was tracked down and arrested.

The grand jury met in the downtown Criminal Courts Building—a fact of considerable significance in one of the biggest controversies of the case. Since the murders had occurred in Brentwood, prosecutors theoretically had the right to try the case in the Santa Monica branch of superior court—and thus to have access to that court's substantially white jury pool. The differences in the jury pool between Santa Monica and downtown were dramatic: in Santa Monica, 80 percent white and 7 percent black; downtown, 30 percent white and 31 percent black. (Latinos and Asians accounted for most of the remainder in both areas.) Why, it has long been asked, did prosecutors choose to try a popular black celebrity in front of a heavily black jury pool?

In fact, the prosecutors made no such choice. A variety of factors made a trial in Santa Monica impossible from the outset.

First, the courthouse there had sustained considerable damage in the Northridge earthquake, which took place just six months before the murders. It was in no shape to receive the onslaught of media and public demands that would accompany the Simpson trial, and damage to the district attorney's offices there had left them all but uninhabitable. Second, the county had set up metal detectors and other logistical accoutrements to lengthy, high-publicity cases on the ninth floor of the downtown courthouse; the judges insisted that all such cases be tried there. Third, the D.A.'s office had placed the special-trials division—Marcia Clark's unit—in the Criminal Courts Building just so that it would be near those ninth-floor courtrooms. And finally, there was a grand-jury room in the Criminal Courts Building, but not in Santa Monica; cases indicted by the downtown grand jury usually stayed there for trial. In light of all this, trying the Simpson case downtown was such an obvious decision that the prosecutors never even discussed any alternative possibilities that first week.

It was Gil Garcetti who muddied the waters on the downtown versus Santa Monica issue. Shortly after Simpson's arrest, Garcetti told several reporters that he wanted the Simpson trial held downtown because a verdict rendered there would have more "credibility" than one in Santa Monica. He said a downtown jury would contribute to the "perception of justice" surrounding the case. These remarks were typical of the elliptical way the participants in the case discussed race in its early stages, but Garcetti's message was clear: A downtown jury would have substantial African-American representation, and its judgment on a black American hero would be respected. In addition, as a Democrat elected with substantial African-American support, Garcetti had to pay homage to his base, and trying the case downtown was one way to do it. Even more important, Garcetti lacked the stomach for the kind of fight an effort to conduct the trial in Santa Monica would have provoked. He would have had to argue that he wanted to be in Santa Monica because he wanted white jurors—a politically unpalatable prospect, especially on a issue where he was probably doomed to lose anyway. Garcetti's coded remarks about "credibility" and the "perception of justice" came at a time of, and as a result of, the prosecution's first blush of confidence after the Bronco chase. At that point the D.A. and the prosecutors on the case had no doubt about their ability to win the case, wherever it was tried. There seemed little harm in the district attorney's boasting about his concern for the sensitivities of a crucial constituency.

In fact, Garcetti's remarks would backfire dramatically. Once the case began to turn against the prosecution and racial issues emerged at the center of the trial, reporters began pestering Garcetti with questions about why he had decided to have the case tried downtown—i.e., why he had given up the opportunity for a much "whiter" jury. (Of course, if he had tried to keep the trial in Santa Monica, these same reporters would have demanded to know whether his attempt to keep the case away from downtown was "racist.") In answering these questions long after the original decision to go downtown, Garcetti fell back on the truth: that the earthquake damage to the Santa Monica courthouse and other factors had tied his hands. But because Garcetti's past remarks suggested that he had made a *choice* to go downtown, the issue dogged him. It was a classic example of the phenomenon of a lawyer's "spin" returning to haunt him. But Garcetti's answer—his last answer, anyway—was the truth: The Simpson case could never have been tried anywhere except the dreary and decaying Criminal Courts Building in the civic heart of downtown Los Angeles.

||||||

On Friday, June 17, the grand-jury investigation of O. J. Simpson began with the sound of a telephone jarring Kato Kaelin awake at 6:00 A.M. Seeking relief from the chaotic scene at Rockingham after the murders, Kaelin had moved in temporarily with a friend, Grant Cramer. In the early morning call, an LAPD detective informed Kaelin that he would be coming to Cramer's home at 8:00 and escorting Kaelin downtown for more interviews with the police. At the appointed hour, a pair of detectives arrived with a grand-jury subpoena demanding that Kaelin provide testimony that very afternoon.

Marcia Clark had not yet met Kato Kaelin, but the detectives had warned her about this skittish and eccentric witness. Clark and David Conn worried that he might be manipulated by Simpson's lawyers if they had a chance to get to him first. (In fact, though the prosecutors didn't know it at the time, Kaelin had already spoken to Shapiro.) The prosecutors felt that they needed to lock in Kaelin's story under oath or it might change to help the defendant. This was a highly unusual, and confrontational, way to proceed. Grand-jury witnesses invariably receive more than a few hours' notice.

Through friends, Kaelin had managed to arrange for a criminal defense lawyer to meet him at the district attorney's office. Escorted into Marcia Clark's office on the eighteenth floor late Friday morning, Kaelin tried to stall until his lawyer, Bill Genego, arrived. Kaelin made small talk with Clark about the poster of Jim Morrison that adorned her office, but he fended her off when she tried to discuss the murders. Not for the last time, he left Clark a thoroughly frustrated woman.

Finally, Genego arrived to intervene.

"It's five to one," Clark said. "You can have three minutes with your client before we take him down to the grand jury. He's going on at one o'clock."

"That's insane," Genego replied. "You don't subpoena someone for the same day he's going to testify."

"He's going in," Clark said. "That's that."

After Genego and Kaelin conferred briefly in Conn's office, the defense lawyer renewed his plea for a little time to talk the situation over. No deal, said Clark. Get in the elevator.

Downstairs, in a small anteroom, Genego made a final plea to Clark just before she was to take Kaelin inside the grand-jury room to testify. "Look," said Genego, "let's just put this off until Monday."

"No way," said Clark.

"If you force him to go in there, I'll just tell him to take the Fifth and you won't get anything from him."

"He's already spoken to the cops on Monday," Clark said, then handed Genego a copy of the police report of Kaelin's statement. She asked Kaelin, "Aren't you going to say the same thing you said before?"

Genego put up his hand. "I told you I don't want you asking him any questions."

Clark was incensed. "I'll ask him questions if I want, and if you try to interfere I'll have you arrested for obstruction of justice."

An experienced criminal lawyer, Genego had never before been threatened this way by a prosecutor. Left no alternative, Genego scribbled out a page of instructions and handed them to Kaelin before Clark escorted him into the grand-jury room. Clinging to his lawyer's script, Kaelin picked his way through the jurors, who were seated classroom-style in front of the witness stand, and flopped into the chair.

After he gave his name and took the oath, Clark asked him, "Mr. Kaelin, were you acquainted with a woman by the name of Nicole Simpson?"

"On the advice of my attorney," Kaelin stated, "I must respectfully decline to answer and assert my constitutional right to remain silent."

"You seem to be reading from a piece of yellow paper, and there is some writing on that paper," the prosecutor said. As Clark would soon know only too well, Kaelin could never have uttered such a cogent sentence if left to his own devices. Kaelin admitted that he had been reading his answer.

Clark tried again, asking, "On the night of June 12, 1994, were you in the company of Mr. Orenthal James Simpson?" (Among prosecutors, it would become sort of a trope, even a badge of honor, to use Simpson's ungainly full name, no matter how stilted it made them sound.)

Kaelin kept reading the same response to her questions, and Clark soon excused him to speak with Genego, who was waiting outside. After a moment, Kaelin returned to the grand-jury room and repeated his refusal to answer questions.

Then, at Clark's direction, the foreperson of the grand jury read a stern message to Kaelin: "Mr. Kaelin, I advise you that this grand jury is a lawfully constituted legal body and that your refusal, without legal cause, to answer questions before this grand jury does constitute contempt and will subject you to imprisonment pursuant to the laws of this state." (Recalling the scene for the man who later wrote his "instant" biography, Kaelin described his reaction in his own terms: "It sounded like something out of an old *Dragnet* rerun on Nickelodeon.") When Kaelin still wouldn't answer, the foreperson officially found him in contempt of the grand jury and ordered the bewildered houseguest to the courtroom of Judge Stephen Czuleger.

Before Judge Czuleger, the prosecutors erupted in fury and indignation. Kaelin, they said, was not a suspect in the case but only a witness; therefore, he had no right to invoke the Fifth Amendment privilege against self-incrimination. Genego replied that Kaelin certainly had been treated like a suspect that morning, and it was undeniable that Kaelin had received unusually rough treatment for a mere grand-jury witness. Under those circumstances, Genego argued, Kaelin had every right to refuse to answer. A thoughtful judge, Czuleger seemed put off by the prosecutors' strong-arm tactics. What was more, even though Czuleger (like the rest of the world) had never heard of Kato Kaelin at that point, his reaction to Kaelin's puppy-dog persona offered a preview of the response of the public at large. What was the harm, Czuleger asked Conn, in giving Kaelin a weekend to talk to his lawyer, "putting aside he may flee the country and be in Brazil by morning." Everyone in the courtroom laughed at the ridiculous prospect of Kato Kaelin on the run.

Conn had to admit that the weekend probably wouldn't make much difference, and Czuleger put off the confrontation until Monday, June 20. "Trust me," the judge, momentarily stern, told Kaelin. "Don't go anywhere. You wouldn't like the alternative. Be here Monday at 8:30 in the morning." Czuleger then moved to recess the hearing—but not before he learned from his bailiff, and told the astonished audience, that O. J. Simpson had been located and was at that moment part of a televised car chase across the Los Angeles freeways.

The wisdom of Judge Czuleger's decision was proven on Monday morning, when Kaelin agreed to testify without invoking his Fifth Amendment right. The weekend-long delay had defused the legal confrontation, but the rocky introduction set the tone for Kaelin's relationship with the district attorney's office. When he took the oath and answered Clark's questions, she found that the core of his story remained largely unchanged from the moment he had first told it to the detectives at Rockingham just hours after the murders. Kaelin told the grand jury, as he had told the detectives, that on the night of the murders he and O.J. had gone to McDonald's for hamburgers shortly after 9:00 and returned at about 9:40 P.M. (The grand jury also marked the on-the-record debut of

Kaelin's singular diction. He said, for example, that at McDonald's he had ordered a "McGrilled chicken sandwich deal.") At about 10:45 P.M., while he was talking on the telephone in his room, Kaelin said, he heard the three loud thumps on his wall. Shortly before 11:00, Kaelin said, he had helped Simpson put his bags in the limousine for the trip to the airport.

It was, for the most part, an incriminating story. Most important, it established that Simpson's whereabouts were unaccounted for at the time the murders took place. Kaelin gave O.J. no alibi. His testimony also established that someone, possibly Simpson, had been rummaging around in the precise location where the bloody glove was found just a few hours later. Some details in Kaelin's recounting did favor Simpson. For one thing, as Kato described it, Simpson's demeanor during their trip to McDonald's hardly seemed that of a man who was moments away from slaughtering his ex-wife. Still, that kind of nuance might have evolved in the prosecution's favor if Kaelin had come to trust the prosecutors and confront the truth about his benefactor.

One way of drawing a fuller story out of Kaelin might have been to stroke him, accommodate him, and try to persuade him that the prosecutors would stand by him and, just as important, that he had nothing to fear from O.J. and his friends. But that kind of approach wasn't Clark's style; she relied far more on the stick than the carrot. Clark and Conn had decided to put the fear of God into Kaelin by rushing him before the grand jury. They succeeded only in alienating him.

|||||

Another grand-jury witness was Jill Shively. If the glamour of O.J. and Nicole's lives represented one archetype of Los Angeles culture, the reality of Shively's represented another—a more common, if less celebrated, saga of the city.

Though the great migration of white midwesterners that created modern Los Angeles had slowed by the 1970s, it never entirely stopped. Jill Shively's newly divorced mother, Nancy, arrived from Indiana in 1979 and settled in Santa Monica. Nancy Shively worked as a medical transcriber, and the family struggled to maintain a middle-class existence. At the age of thirty-two, in 1994, Jill found herself working intermittent hours in a film-supply business and living in a tiny one-bedroom apartment. On most nights, Jill cared for a young niece, the daughter of Jill's sister, whose personal problems left her unable to act as a parent. Diminutive, athletic, long on schemes for success but short on good luck and results, Shively lived one mile and a world away from Nicole Brown Simpson's condominium on Bundy Drive.

On June 12, Shively had been battling the flu all day and had eaten nothing. At around 10:45 that night, she decided to drive to San Vicente Boulevard to a favorite salad bar. Gunning her Volkswagen to beat the store's 11:00 closing time, she raced along San Vicente, going east. As she approached the intersection where Bundy crosses San Vicente, Shively accelerated to make the light. A large white vehicle heading north on Bundy raced in front of her against the light. Shively slammed on her brakes, as did the white car, which then ran up partially on San Vicente's raised center median. A third car, a gray Nissan heading west on San Vicente, also stopped suddenly, trying like Shively to avoid the white car that had raced in front of them.

Briefly, the three cars were frozen next to one another. Then Shively noticed that the driver of the white car began honking his horn and screaming—"Move your damn car! Move it! Move it!"—for the driver heading west on San Vicente to let him pass. Shively noticed that the driver of the white car was black, and on second glance, she thought she recognized him. Her mind raced.

That's . . . that's . . . Marcus Allen!

Then she heard him scream again, and she realized that she recognized the voice. It's wasn't Marcus Allen; it was O. J. Simpson. The stunned driver of the gray Nissan was finally gathering his wits to move on. At last he did, and Simpson peeled off on Bundy, but not before Shively had a chance to look at and remember the license plate of the white car: 3CZW788.

Shively wrote off the incident and continued her search for salad. Her car lacked a radio, so when she went to work the next morning, she had no idea about the murders until her mother called her at her job. "Did you hear that Nicole Simpson was murdered last night?" Nancy Shively asked.

Jill said she hadn't. "That's weird," she went on. "O.J. nearly ran me down last night."

Later that day Shively called the police, and a pair of detectives came to interview her the following day. On Saturday, June 18, a detective came to her home with a grand-jury subpoena ordering her to testify on Tuesday, June 21. By Sunday, June 19, her name had leaked out as a witness and reporters were banging on her apartment door. The next morning, she called Patty Jo Fairbanks, whose name she had been given as a witness coordinator for the district attorney's office. Shively later recalled Fairbanks saying that she could give no interviews until after she had testified in front of the grand jury; Fairbanks remembered telling her to speak to no one at all. In any event, on Monday, June 20, Shively decided to give an interview. She went to the Paramount lot in Hollywood, found her way to the set of *Hard Copy,* and sat down to make a little money.

|||||

Long-established policies at virtually all outlets of the mainstream press, from newspapers to television networks, categorically prohibit journalists from paying interview subjects. For many years, only the operators on the disreputable fringe of the print world, the supermarket tabloids, paid for news. But thanks to two seemingly unrelated phenomena, the "cash-for-trash" business exploded in the early 1990s.

The first was the birth of a new and successful genre of television program, the tabloid, or infotainment, program, which parlayed celebrity news and scandal into tremendous ratings. *A Current Affair* (Fox), *Inside Edition* (King World), and *Hard Copy* (Paramount) boomed in popularity. Produced by entertainment companies with no history of journalistic enterprise or ethics, the television tabloids had the money to buy stories and did so with abandon. The supermarket tabloids, led by the *National Enquirer,* which has a weekly readership of nearly 20 million, had no trouble keeping pace.

The second factor was a decision of the United States Supreme Court. The so-called Son of Sam law was passed by the New York state legislature in 1977 to prevent David Berkowitz (who sent notes to the police signed "Son of Sam") from capitalizing on his notoriety as a serial killer. The measure made it illegal for criminals to earn income from selling stories about their misdeeds. In 1991, however, the Supreme Court ruled that the law violated the First Amendment. The tabloid industry saw the Supreme Court's decision as a vindication of its ways.

Because witnesses who take money from tabloids automatically raise questions about their credibility—and because defense attorneys can successfully vilify those witnesses on cross-examination—the practice of buying and selling interviews seriously threatens prosecutors' abilities to win high-profile cases. In the William Kennedy Smith rape trial, for example, defense attorney Roy Black skewered a critical government witness who had sold an interview to *A Current Affair*. Ironically, the print and television tabloids that fuel this industry have been widely denounced for their supposed rush to convict celebrity defendants before their trials; in his early press conferences, Robert Shapiro often complained about their unfairness to O. J. Simpson. As it happens, though, the tabloids can so taint government witnesses that tabloid infotainment may actually be the greatest friend a famous defendant can have.

In the Simpson case, the LAPD addressed its cash-for-trash problem in a little-noticed coda to the first public announcement of the murders. After giving the basic facts about the case, such as the names of the victims and the place where the bodies were found, Commander Gascon, the police spokesman, issued a plea to the news media. "Over the next few days, detectives will continue to interview possible witnesses and gather and analyze evidence," Gascon said on June 13. "Detectives are requesting that the media not attempt to contact potential witnesses in this case, as those contacts may delay and negatively impact the course of this investigation. I need to stress that. It's critically important."

If the tabloids heard Gascon's plea, it didn't change their behavior. They offered cash to virtually every major participant (and many fringe figures) in the Simpson case. One night shortly after the murders, Mike Walker, the gossip columnist for the *National Enquirer*, announced on *Larry King Live* that his paper was offering Al Cowlings $1 million for an interview—and Walker held up a cardboard check in that amount to clarify his point. For the interview that she gave *Hard Copy* on June 20, Shively got a relatively small amount—$5,000. Displaying her subpoena for the cameras at Paramount, Shively adapted nicely to the tabloid idiom in her interview, declaring that Simpson looked "like a madman gone mad, insane." The producers at *Hard Copy* even gave her a little extra present. They said a friend of theirs at the supermarket tabloid *Star* would give her another $2,600 if she would allow him to use the text of the *Hard Copy* interview and pretend that it had actually been with him. Shively said sure. Then the following morning, June 21, Shively presented herself downtown, and Marcia Clark walked her through her story for the grand jury.

That night, *Hard Copy* ran the interview with Shively. Clark was apoplectic when she learned of it. In a brief conversation with Shively just before she had testified in the grand jury, Clark and Conn had asked her if she had spoken to anyone about the subject matter of her testimony. Just her mother, Shively had replied. Now it was clear that she had spoken to *Hard Copy* as well. Clark demanded that Shively return to the courthouse to explain herself.

Shively was terrified, and she brought her mother with her to the Criminal Courts Building on June 22. They waited nearly all day for an audience with Clark. When it came, Clark lashed out at her: "You lied to us! How could you?"

Shively tried to explain that she thought Clark and Conn had asked her who was the *first* person she told about the incident. That had been her mother. Shively said she didn't realize they wanted to know all of the people she had told.

Clark scoffed. "We've got plenty of circumstantial evidence," she said. "We don't need you. We're going to make an example out of you."

Clark ordered her to return the next day, June 23, to explain herself before the grand jury. That night, Shively looked in the Yellow Pages for a lawyer on call twenty-four hours a day so that she would have someone to protect her from Clark's wrath in the morning.

Accompanied by her lawyer, Shively returned to Clark's office for another tongue-lashing. They then trooped in silence to the grand-jury room. There, Clark asked Shively why she had misled the prosecutors in the interview before her grand-jury appearance.

Shively explained again that she thought they had only wanted to know the first person she had told. "I was nervous and hadn't slept all week, and wasn't really thinking," Shively said. "I wasn't trying to hide anything, because I knew it was being aired the next day."

Shively was ushered out after only a few minutes, and then Marcia Clark asked for a moment to address the grand jury. "Ladies and gentlemen of this jury," she said. "Because it is our duty as prosecutors to present only that evidence in which we are 110 percent confident as to its truthfulness and reliability, I must now ask you to completely disregard the statements given and the testimony given by Jill Shively in this case."

Jill Shively presented a kind of problem that a midlevel prosecutor like Clark would never have encountered before. (To be sure, *Hard Copy* had never come calling on the witnesses in any of Clark's earlier cases.) In part, Clark's denunciation of Shively to the grand jury reflected a high degree of prosecutorial ethics, because prosecutors should never present evidence they find less than fully believable. But there was a kind of self-defeating sanctimony in Clark's posture as well. Prosecutors deal all the time with witnesses who take a while to tell the full truth. Some lie far more extensively than Shively did before they get around to a credible story. And Shively's "lie" seems more pathetic than evil; as Shively herself pointed out, she could not have expected that the prosecutors were going to miss the fact that she had spoken to a national television program. But Clark thought she could summarily dispose of Shively. A simple and unadorned request to the grand jury to disregard Shively's testimony would have more than satisfied Clark's ethical obligations. Instead, in a fit of pique, Clark denounced Shively in terms that made her permanently useless to the government.

But Marcia Clark felt she could afford it. After all, the prosecution had plenty of witnesses.

|||||

If Robert Shapiro had one great strength as a lawyer, it was that he usually knew what he didn't know. In the first few days after the murders, Shapiro bought himself an enormous amount of help—high-priced experts in their respective fields. He didn't know much about autopsies and crime scenes, so he called Michael Baden and Henry Lee. He knew nothing about DNA, so he recruited two lawyers from New York, Barry Scheck and Peter Neufeld. Shapiro had not gone to trial on many complex crimes—and he had never tried a murder—so he summoned his old friend F. Lee Bailey. On the day Shapiro was hired, he called Bailey and said, "I need you to help me hold on to this case." Shapiro knew that he needed Alan Dershowitz as well.

Of course, Shapiro didn't get to Dershowitz first. Whenever any legal or criminal proceeding makes news, talk-show bookers instantly summon the Harvard Law School professor for analysis, and Dershowitz gladly delivers the goods in well-rounded sound bites. Alan Dershowitz has an enviable life—a prestigious professorship, lucrative deals for books and speeches, a full plate of wealthy clients eager to pay him for legal work—and yet he seemingly will appear on any program and talk about anything. His lust for publicity has a manic quality, as if the bookish yeshiva boy from Brooklyn still cannot believe that others care what he thinks. So when the calls came from the media in the immediate aftermath of the murders in Brentwood, Dershowitz was, as usual, available.

Besides, the timing was propitious. Dershowitz was just completing a book called *The Abuse Excuse—and Other Cop-Outs, Sob Stories, and Evasions of Responsibility*. In it, he wrote that a whole series of excuses—such as the "battered-woman syndrome," the "abused-child syndrome," and the like—were "quickly becoming a license to kill." Some of these excuses, Dershowitz wrote with disdain, reflected "politically correct" sentiments that sought to apply different criteria of culpability to people from disadvantaged groups. "In effect," he wrote, "these abuse excuse defenses, by emphasizing historical discrimination suffered by particular groups, seek to introduce some degree of affirmative action into our criminal-justice system." The Simpson case seemed to fit right in. On Monday, June 20, 1994—the day the haggard Simpson mumbled his not-guilty plea in court—Dershowitz expounded on this thesis when he appeared in his legal-expert persona on public television's *Charlie Rose*. On the broadcast, Dershowitz speculated that the Simpson case "may end up not with a bang but a whimper. I mean, this may end up in something like a hung jury. It may end up in a plea bargain." Indeed, Dershowitz went on, the Simpson case might wind up having sinister implications. "It may end up with a terrible message. It may end up with a Menendez- or Bobbitt-type verdict, which will send a message out, 'Gee, you can get away with this kind of stuff.' "

Dershowitz's comments irritated Shapiro when they got back to him. He told a friend, "How can we shut that guy up?" After a pause, he said, half jokingly, "I guess we'll have to hire him." And the day after Dershowitz appeared on *Charlie Rose*, Robert Shapiro called Alan Dershowitz and invited him to join the defense team. Dershowitz dutifully informed Shapiro that he had made some less than supportive comments in the media. Shapiro didn't care. Alan, he said, we need you.

No law, or even any ethical rule, prevented Dershowitz from accepting the assignment. (Shamelessness is a moral, rather than a legal, concept.) As Dershowitz himself cheerfully noted in his memoir *The Best Defense*, "Almost all of my own clients have been guilty." In the Simpson case, Dershowitz was an observer one day, an advocate the next—a shift that reflected, as Anthony Kronman, the dean of Yale Law School, once aptly put it, "the indifference to truth that all advocacy entails." Lawyers live by such distinctions, even as they fuel public cynicism about their profession. (Kronman himself later changed his mind about his own mordant observation.)

For Dershowitz, though, the call from Shapiro did not come completely out of the blue. The two lawyers had worked together before. And although Dershowitz sometimes comes across as a preening clown on television, he is in fact a superb defense attorney, who specializes in identifying and exploiting the weaknesses in the government's case. Dershowitz had played a behind-the-scenes role in the defense of Shapiro client Christian Brando, who eventually pleaded guilty to killing his sister's boyfriend. Shapiro now told Dershowitz that he had also hired a lawyer who had worked with them on the Brando case: Gerald Uelman, who was, like Dershowitz, a law school professor but was in many ways his opposite. Soft-spoken, with pale skin and white hair that seemed at times to render him nearly invisible, Uelman served as dean of Santa Clara University law school, in San Jose. Although the two professors differed in style and temperament, they shared an aggressive philosophy about how to defend a criminal case. Above all, they believed that the defense had to stay on the offensive—challenging, protesting, complaining, and endeavoring in every respect to create chaos in the prosecution camp.

Dershowitz and Uelman discovered their first opportunity to do this in the extraordinary onslaught of publicity the Simpson case was receiving. It is a truism among judges in criminal cases that pretrial publicity hurts the defendant, and much incriminating information about Simpson did come out immediately after the murders. However, as the Simpson case illustrated so dramatically, pretrial publicity can hurt the government's case as well. Simpson's lawyers knew they could portray their client as the helpless victim of a publicity-seeking prosecutor and an irresponsible news media. The question was how to turn that sympathetic picture of the client to their legal advantage.

Simpson's lawyers hit on the idea of challenging the grand jury. They would allege that the pretrial publicity had so poisoned the minds of the grand jurors that they would have to be recused en masse and the case would have to be sent to the June 30 preliminary hearing after all. There was only one problem with this theory: Apparently, no grand jury in history had ever been disbanded for this reason. Still, Dershowitz and Uelman figured, it didn't hurt to take a shot. Besides, on Wednesday, June 22, the government presented the defense with another unintentional gift. On that day, the Los Angeles City Attorney's Office, acting on media requests, released the audiotape of Nicole Brown Simpson's heartrending telephone call to 911 on October 25, 1993. "Can you get someone over here now? He's back. Please," the trembling voice of Nicole said on a tape that was played repeatedly on television and radio. "He's O. J. Simpson. I think you know his record. . . . He's going to beat the shit out of me." While the tape did contribute to a poisoning of attitudes against Simpson, its release also added to the defense's claim of excessive pretrial publicity.

So, with Uelman working out of San Jose and Dershowitz in Jerusalem on unrelated business, the lawyers put together the first of the 393 legal motions that would be filed in the Simpson case. They called it an "Emergency Motion for Voir Dire of Grand Jurors and Determination of Prejudice from Improper Pretrial Publicity." The most the defense lawyers really hoped for was that a judge would agree to voir dire—that is, question—each of the jurors and then determine the impact of the publicity on them. Almost as an afterthought, they threw in the completely unprecedented request that the grand jury be disbanded. Though it meant that Dershowitz had to run up a telephone bill of $800 at the King David Hotel, the defense was able to file its indignant brief on the morning of Friday, June 24. In it, the defense urged the court to take "certain essential steps to alleviate the prejudicial impact of the improper release and massive publicity given to inadmissible evidence in this case [and] prejudicial and improper expressions of personal opinions by prosecutors." Listing the calumnies that had been heaped on their client by Garcetti and Clark, the defense lawyers wrote, "The District Attorney speculated that the ex–football star eventually might admit killing his ex-wife and her friend but would claim a defense similar to that of the Menendez brothers." In another example, the defense noted with dismay a statement from Garcetti quoted in the *Los Angeles Times* of June 19: "It wouldn't surprise me if at some point we go from, 'I didn't do it,' to 'I did it, but I'm not responsible.'" (Meanwhile, of course, Dershowitz had said practically word for word the same thing on national television on June 20!)

The defense motion had the intended effect of throwing the prosecutors off their stride. The release of the tapes had already complicated their task. Concerned about his base in the black community, Garcetti didn't want it to look like he was treating Simpson unfairly, so the district attorney publicly criticized the city attorney's office for releasing the 911 tapes in the middle of his office's investigation. (The district attorney, who prosecutes felonies, and city attorney, who handles misdemeanors and civil matters, are elected separately and have separate staffs.) The airing of the tapes also created legal problems for the prosecutors. After the 911 tapes had been released on June 22, several people around the courthouse overheard some grand jurors talking about them, although the tapes had not been presented as evidence to the grand jury. Broadcasts of the tapes were so widespread that they were, of course, nearly impossible to avoid. The prosecutors realized they might have an ethical obligation to tell a judge about what the jurors had said. The judge, in turn, might want to question the jurors individually or let defense lawyers interrogate them. That might take days—and reveal new complications that the defense could exploit. In addition, going forward with a tainted grand jury might infect the case with a legal error that could jeopardize a conviction on appeal. Seeing the defense motion on the morning of June 24, the prosecutors thought it might make more sense simply to give up on the grand jury and go forward with the preliminary hearing after all. Garcetti was still weighing his options when, in a brief court hearing that Friday morning, June 24, Marcia Clark denied that prosecutors had exploited the publicity in the case and instead accused Shapiro of doing just that.

In reaction to the defense motion and the prosecutors' concerns, Cecil Mills, the supervising judge of the Los Angeles Superior Court, conducted his own brief investigation and learned that several jurors had indeed heard the 911 tapes. The district attorney's office decided to join in the motion to disband the grand jury. In a terse ruling from the bench, Judge Mills said, "Given the request of both Counsel for Mr. Simpson and the Los Angeles County District Attorney . . . this Court recuses the 1993–94 Grand Jury from further consideration of this matter."

In a news conference after Mills's ruling, Shapiro did not try to restrain his glee. "We are very pleased the judge agreed with our position," he said in a packed hallway of the Criminal Courts Building. "We look forward to finally presenting this evidence in a public courtroom . . . to hearing live testimony under oath from the witnesses." There would be a preliminary hearing after all.

|||||

Marcia Clark had only four days to put it together. During the truncated grand-jury proceedings, the prosecutors had learned that Simpson had recently bought a large knife at Ross Cutlery, a store in downtown Los Angeles. A preliminary comparison with the autopsy findings suggested that Simpson's recent purchase might be the murder weapon. So on Tuesday, June 28, Clark obtained a warrant to allow the police to search Simpson's home again, this time for the knife. Cops turned the place upside down but came up empty-handed.

The next day, in the L.A. county jail, Gerald Uelman showed O. J. Simpson the police affidavit underlying the June 28 search. "Where's the knife?" lawyer asked client.

After receiving instructions from Simpson, Uelman returned to Rockingham and went upstairs to the master bedroom, where a set of shelves was set behind mirrored doors. Uelman opened the doors and found, in a box, the knife that O. J. Simpson had purchased just a few weeks earlier. It appeared pristine—as Simpson had promised Uelman it would be. Apparently, the police had never looked behind the mirrored doors.

The discovery called to the law professor's mind an old story in legal circles. As the tale goes, a lawyer named Harry Levine is sitting in his office when the phone rings. A voice on the phone says, "Mr. Levine, I just shot my wife. I've got the gun in my hands. What should I do?"

Levine weighs his options. At last he replies, "Oh! You must be looking for Harry Levine the lawyer!"—and hangs up.

Much as the option of throwing up his hands looked appealing at that moment, Gerald Uelman had to decide what to do. It was a profound ethical dilemma. Here was a piece of evidence the prosecution clearly regarded as important. If Uelman were to touch the knife, he would immediately become a witness in the case; and in light of the cops' embarrassing failure to find the knife, they might accuse Uelman of planting or hiding it. But doing nothing—the "Levine option," as it were—didn't seem like the right thing, either. The knife's pristine appearance seemed to reflect favorably on Simpson, so the defense would want some way to safeguard its condition. How was Uelman supposed to preserve the knife as evidence without touching it himself? And how could he avoid tipping the defense's hand on this subject to the prosecution?

Uelman kept his options open by simply closing the mirrored door. A night of feverish consultations among the defense lawyers yielded a plan.

The first thing the following morning, Thursday, June 30— which also happened to be the first day of the preliminary hearing—Uelman and Shapiro went in secret to the chambers of Judge Lance Ito of the superior court. (They chose Ito because he was, at that time, the judge who handled all miscellaneous criminal matters.) The lawyers asked Ito to appoint a "special master"—that is, a neutral arbitrator—to go to O. J. Simpson's house, note the knife's condition, and remove it to the custody of the court. Ito agreed, and that very morning asked retired superior court judge Delbert Wong to go to Rockingham and pick up the knife. Wong did as asked and brought to Ito a heavily taped envelope with the knife in it. No one—not the public and not the prosecutors—was any the wiser.

Uelman and Shapiro were delighted. From Ito's chambers, they raced to the courtroom of Judge Kathleen Kennedy-Powell for the opening moments of the preliminary hearing. The atmosphere there did not match Shapiro's cheery mood, so he made a wan effort to break the ice as soon as the judge appeared on the bench.

"This is the quietest courtroom I've ever been in, Your Honor," Shapiro said.

The silence, of course, came from the tension. It had been just eighteen days since the murders, but already the case had generated extraordinary media attention. Now, for the first time, all the principals in the case, including the families of the victims, were arrayed in one place under the scrutiny of a live national television audience: All three networks, as well as CNN and Court TV, had preempted regular programming to broadcast Simpson's preliminary hearing live.

"Good morning," said Judge Kennedy-Powell, attempting to conduct business as usual. "Now, there are a number of matters on calendar today. I think there is one matter that can be resolved in fairly short order, and that relates to . . . an order for a hair sample."

Police had discovered hairs, apparently of African-American origin, inside the knit cap found at the murder scene. Prosecutors wanted to obtain hair samples from Simpson so they could be compared with the hairs in the cap. It was, as the judge suggested, a routine matter. The courts have held for many years that a defendant does not have a Fifth Amendment right to withhold a hair sample.

But, as would become the pattern in the case, this was not treated as routine. The first issue in court would give the prosecution a flavor of the defense it would be facing in this trial.

Kennedy-Powell said that the defense was not objecting to providing a hair sample as long as it was just that—a single hair. Prosecutors objected.

"Ms. Clark, how much hair do the People need?" the judge asked.

Clark was indignant. "Well, Your Honor, hair samples—as I'm sure the defense must be aware—in order to be effectively compared with an evidence sample recovered from a crime scene, have to be taken from each area of the suspect's head, and that means that a minimum of 5 to 10 hairs from each area, which usually amounts to about 100 hairs.

"Any scientist, no matter how inexperienced, is aware of that fact," Clark declared. "You cannot do an effective comparison between a known standard and an evidence standard without that size of sample."

"So you're asking for 100 hairs?"

Clark exhaled. "We're asking for as many hairs as the criminalist or expert determines is necessary to effectively compare the standard hairs. . . . And I've never seen a court attempt to restrict that."

Kennedy-Powell asked Shapiro for his view.

"Your Honor," Shapiro said, "according to Dr. Henry Lee, our chief criminalist, who is the head of the department of criminology in Connecticut, he tells us one to three hairs are sufficient." Shapiro—and Lee—were being cute. Only a few hairs are necessary for DNA testing. But many more hairs are needed for conventional microscopic analysis, which the prosecution also wanted to do.

Characteristically, Shapiro was more muted than Clark, but he did not skimp on indignation, either. "I think 100 hairs is unduly invasive, makes the inventorying of the hairs a very, very difficult task, and certainly allows for the possibility of commingling of samples, which could contaminate any test. So we would ask for a hearing on this."

"This is what I'm prepared to do at this point in time," the judge said, "that is, to order no more than ten hairs at this point."

Clark couldn't believe it. The collection of hair samples was a standard, invariably uncontested matter of criminal procedure. Kennedy-Powell had reacted to the issue with great caution, to avoid making a very public mistake. In the extremely unlikely event that a defendant even contested the hair issue in a run-of-the-mill case, most judges would have ordered the hair samples without a second thought. Clark thought ten hairs would probably be sufficient, but the ever-aggressive prosecutor wanted to put the defense—and the judge—in their place. Rather than leave the issue alone, she fought back: If they want a hearing, we'll give them a hearing. Michele Kestler, the assistant director of the LAPD crime lab, happened to be in court to offer testimony on another matter. Clark figured Kestler could handle the hair issue as well, and so she called Kestler to the stand that very first morning.

On the stand, Kestler dutifully said that when she heard the defense wanted to limit the sample to one hair, "I was shocked at best. . . . I said, 'You've got to be kidding.' " But Shapiro knew what to do with her on cross-examination. He established that Kestler had worked most recently as a bureaucrat rather than as a scientist and that her academic qualifications were rather meager—along the lines of taking in-house LAPD training courses like "How to Turn Your Work Group into a Winning Team."

"Are you familiar with a gentleman by the name of Dr. Henry Lee?" Shapiro asked.

Kestler was.

"Have you seen his fifty-page curriculum vitae recently?"

Kestler, it appeared, had no great expertise on hair samples. At the lunch break, Clark scrambled to find a certain criminalistics textbook written by Dr. Lee, that suggested that about 40 hairs were needed for proper microscopic testing. That proved enough for the judge, and after several hours of this literal and figurative exercise in hairsplitting, Kennedy-Powell said the prosecution could have "at least 40 but no more than 100 hairs." After making her ruling, Kennedy-Powell asked Clark to call her first witness.

In addition to the public attention, the Simpson preliminary hearing was atypical in another way. As a result of a California voter initiative in 1990, prosecutors now had to present considerably less evidence than they once had in preliminary hearings. Under Proposition 115, as the law was known, prosecutors could (and usually did) present their cases in prelims primarily by using hearsay evidence. Many prelims involved the testimony of only a single police officer, who would explain what evidence had been collected and what witnesses had said. This kind of presentation insulated most government witnesses from cross-examination. But the D.A.'s office in the Simpson case decided not to conduct a "Prop 115" prelim. Displaying their characteristic concern for public relations—in this respect at the expense of the long-term prospects for their case—the prosecutors decided to call many of the actual witnesses instead of merely relying on hearsay. They felt it was important to show prospective jurors (and Garcetti's constituency) just how much evidence they already had.

So the prosecution decided to start out with a bang. By this point, David Conn, Marcia Clark's direct superior, was off the case, having returned to his primary assignment of leading the retrial of the Menendez brothers. In his place as coprosecutor with Clark, Garcetti had named Bill Hodgman. As director of the Bureau of Central Operations, the forty-one-year-old Hodgman served as one of the highest-ranking prosecutors in the office. (During Clark's brief stint as an administrator, she had worked as Hodgman's special assistant.) Cool where Clark was hot, calm where she was excitable, Hodgman served as a good foil for Clark, in Garcetti's view. It was Hodgman who called the first witness to the stand in the prelim.

Allen Wattenberg and his brother operated one of the more unusual businesses in downtown Los Angeles. Ross Cutlery was nestled in a corner of the historic Bradbury Building, whose magnificent iron-and-glass interior courtyard has long served the city's moviemakers, most famously in Ridley Scott's dystopic meditation on the future of L.A., *Blade Runner*. A mere three blocks from the Criminal Courts Building, Ross Cutlery was surrounded mostly by Latino fast-food joints, evangelical churches, and discount clothing stores. On May 3, 1994, the sidewalk in front of Ross Cutlery served as the setting for a scene in a pilot for an NBC series, *Frogman*, starring O. J. Simpson. Allen Wattenberg testified that during a break in filming that day, Simpson had come into the store to browse among its hundreds of gleaming blades and scissors. Simpson chose a fifteen-inch folding lock-blade knife with a handle carved from deer antlers. A few days before the hearing, LAPD detectives had bought an identical model from Ross Cutlery, and Hodgman displayed the sinister-looking item on a board for the judge (and, of course, the television camera). Simpson had paid the $81.17 price with a $100 bill. And then, providing just the malevolent touch prosecutors love, Wattenberg added that even though the knife was brand-new, Simpson had asked for it to be sharpened before he took it home.

In private, Shapiro and Uelman laughed. The prosecutors were using the Ross Cutlery witness to insinuate that the knife Simpson purchased on May 3 was the murder weapon. But the defense lawyers had actually seen the knife—as the government had not—and they knew that it appeared to be in pristine condition. The prosecutors got what they wanted: large and sinister photographs of the knife in virtually every newspaper in America. But as would happen so often in the case, the quest for a public relations advantage led the seekers only to folly. Yes, the knife looked evil, but when its purchase led nowhere, it was the prosecutors who looked bad.

There was another reason, besides high drama, that Hodgman and Clark wanted Wattenberg on the stand first. His employee Jose Camacho had testified in front of the grand jury the previous week. After he testified, Camacho had been approached by representatives of the *National Enquirer* seeking an interview for pay. Camacho had agreed. In the prelim, Hodgman asked Wattenberg, "Do you expect to profit in some manner from your brother and your employee Mr. Camacho having signed such an agreement?"

"Yes, I do," Wattenberg replied.

"Would you explain to us, please, how you expect to profit?"

"My brother and I, being equal partners in the business, are going to divide this money up three ways. Mr. Camacho will receive one third, my brother one third, and myself one third."

"What sum of money are we talking about?"

"The figure, I believe, is $12,500."

The courtroom stirred. The prosecutors underwent a swift education. They discovered that their tabloid problem went beyond just Jill Shively. (And had they known at the outset that Shively was going to be only one of several witnesses paid by the tabloids, Clark might not have been so hasty to disown her in front of the grand jury.) With Wattenberg and Camacho, who followed his boss to the witness stand in the prelim, the prosecutors had figured that the mutually corroborating nature of their stories would trump the taint of tabloid money.

The saga of the Ross Cutlery knife had a bittersweet conclusion for the defense lawyers who had conjured the clever scheme to preserve it as evidence. After accepting the envelope containing the knife from neutral arbitrator Delbert Wong, Judge Lance Ito left on vacation and turned the package over to his boss, Cecil Mills, the chief superior court judge. Mills apparently failed to understand the secret nature of the defense lawyers' negotiations with Ito. Mills simply turned the envelope over to Judge Kennedy-Powell, since she was presiding over the preliminary hearing. She, too, had no idea of the story behind the envelope, and brought it out on the bench with her when she received it. The media promptly dubbed it the "mystery envelope," but given its size and the timing of the disclosure, Clark and Hodgman had no trouble figuring out what was inside. Shapiro and Uelman were disappointed that they could never spring the surprise of the envelope's existence, but they did succeed in spooking the prosecutors into not mentioning the Ross Cutlery knife again; indeed, they would never attempt to identify a specific knife as the murder weapon. Eventually, the defense obtained the court's permission to test the knife in the envelope. It was found to be in mint condition.

|||||

The publicity-infected grand jury . . . the tabloid-tainted "knife witnesses" . . . the hairsplitting saga of Michele Kestler . . . they all demonstrated that the defense was going to take the offensive at every opportunity. But they were merely a warm-up for the most important defense effort at the preliminary hearing. Shapiro and Uelman made their first attempt to have evidence in the case suppressed—an enterprise that reflected the defense's dual legal and public relations priorities. For the judge, Uelman wanted to establish that the detectives' first search of Simpson's home violated the law. For the television cameras, Shapiro wanted to establish that O. J. Simpson was yet another black victim of the LAPD.

Customarily, police officers must obtain a search warrant before entering a suspect's property. But under the expansive interpretations of government power that have been the rule in criminal law over the past two decades, courts have established several exceptions to the warrant requirement for searches. One of them holds that in an emergency—in "exigent circumstances"—the police can search without a warrant. The question for Judge Kennedy-Powell was whether there was any emergency that justified four detectives—Vannatter, Lange, Phillips, and Fuhrman—entering Simpson's property in the early morning hours of June 13.

Vannatter first offered his justification for the search of Simpson's property at the preliminary hearing, and it immediately drew a skeptical reaction. The detective insisted that Simpson was simply receiving the normal, courteous service the LAPD provides to any relative of a murder victim. Vannatter insisted that the detectives traveled from Bundy to Rockingham not because Simpson was a suspect in the murders but because they wanted to inform him of the murders and arrange for him to pick up his children. Once at O.J.'s home, Vannatter decided to have Fuhrman vault the wall because the blood they found near the handle of the Bronco made him think that Simpson might also be injured. As Vannatter testified at the preliminary hearing, "I was concerned that something had occurred there, whether I had a second murder scene, whether I had someone injured, whether I had someone that was stalking Mr. Simpson and his wife, whatever."

When it came time to argue the illegal-search motion before Judge Kennedy-Powell, Uelman made his point nicely: "We are told that four detectives . . . all converged on the residence of Mr. Simpson simply for the purpose of informing him of the tragedy that had taken place at the Bundy location, a purpose that could just as easily have been accomplished by the placing of a telephone call." Uelman pointed out that the drop of blood on the Bronco door "was just as consistent with a dripping taco or a driver with a hangnail." No, Uelman insisted, the detectives' purported concern for Simpson's welfare merely served as a pretext for their desire to tie him to the murder of his ex-wife. Another factor made the police behavior even more suspect: One of the four detectives, Mark Fuhrman, had been to the house before to investigate an altercation between husband and wife; that history might certainly have made the officers view Simpson as a suspect.

After arguments from both sides, Kennedy-Powell faced a stark choice. According to the prosecution, the detectives' behavior amounted to normal service to a bereaved citizen. According to the defense, the cops had acted like jackbooted thugs intent on violating a black man's rights. The truth may well have been reflected in a third view—one that neither side would have wanted the judge, or the public, to believe. From the moment the murders were reported, the LAPD investigated this case with one eye fixed on the news media. As soon as Detective Phillips arrived on the scene, Commander Bushey ordered him to get over to Simpson's home and make sure that O.J. didn't find out about the murders from media reports. In Bushey's view, that kind of insensitivity to a celebrity might have led to bad press for the LAPD. As Simpson's own previous experience with the LAPD demonstrates, the police wanted nothing more than to coddle and please celebrities. The four detectives may simply have been as starstruck as the West L.A. patrol cops who used to lounge in O.J.'s pool.

As the circumstances of this case evolved, neither side could put its actions in their true light. The defense never wanted to acknowledge that the police viewed O.J. with anything other than hostility and suspicion. The police, in contrast, could not admit that instead of investigating the crime scene, they preferred to hobnob with a celebrity. Once the detectives entered O.J.'s property and found evidence linking him to the murders, Vannatter had to construct a believable pretext for why they had gone there in the first place. It worked in the short term: Judge Kennedy-Powell decided not to suppress the evidence, although the defense had the right to renew the motion in superior court.

This prosecution victory came at a price. The suppression motion shifted the public debate on the case, at least in part, from whether O.J. was guilty to whether the police had acted appropriately. And on the latter question, Shapiro made considerable progress. He was able to portray Vannatter as incompetent at best, sinister at worst. He showed that Vannatter's search warrant affidavit contained significant errors: Simpson's trip to Chicago had not been "unexpected," and the substance on the Bronco door tested only presumptively, not positively, for the presence of blood. Although they failed to persuade the judge, the defense lawyers planted the idea with a pool of potential jurors that the police had a secret, nefarious agenda to get Simpson. That alone made the preliminary hearing worthwhile for the defense.

Simpson "lost" the prelim, of course. After five days of testimony spread on both sides of the July Fourth holiday weekend, Judge Kennedy-Powell ruled on July 8 that Simpson had to stand trial in superior court. But notwithstanding his reputation as a deal maker, Shapiro had shown the prosecutors that in this case he would be battling them every step of the way—for the audiences both inside and outside the courtroom. All the legal action, as well as an unending stream of well-wishers visiting him in jail, considerably buoyed the spirits of Shapiro's client. By the time O. J. Simpson was arraigned in superior court following the prelim, he looked like O. J. Simpson again. With his tie and belt returned to him, he cut a dapper figure once more, and he greeted his supporters in the gallery with a wink and a thumbs-up. And when the judge asked him to repeat his plea to the charges of double murder, this time Simpson needed no prompting.

"Absolutely, 100 percent not guilty," he said.

The month after Simpson's arrest went better than Shapiro had any reason to expect. The team of experts he had gathered was already beginning a meticulous examination of the prosecution's case. The defense had eliminated the grand jury, and in the prelim had forced many important government witnesses to commit themselves under oath to their version of events. The police detectives had been put on the defensive about their conduct on the night of the murders. Much public support for O.J. remained, although his poll numbers were dipping daily. So the news was, up to a point, good.

Successful criminal defense attorneys permit themselves no illusions, and for all the good that came out of the prelim, the hearing forced Shapiro to face reality as well. Clark had concluded her presentation of the evidence to Judge Kennedy-Powell with the first public airing of the government's blood evidence in the case. Since the first week, when Collin Yamauchi did the initial DNA tests, LAPD scientists had continued refining their results. For the purposes of the hearing, Clark thought it best to offer testimony only about conventional testing of the blood. Such testing offers somewhat less refined results than the best DNA tests, but Clark knew the judge would admit it into evidence without an evidentiary hearing. According to the tests disclosed at the preliminary hearing, the blood drops to the left of the shoe prints at Bundy matched Simpson's—and that of only .43 percent of the population. In other words, 99.57 percent of the population could be excluded as sources of that blood.

It was devastating evidence. DNA tests, which were pending, would surely further incriminate Simpson. Even with the clever half steps he had taken so far, Shapiro could not win a simple jury referendum on whether his client had killed those two human beings. He knew, however, that he might win a referendum on a different subject—say, the racism of the Los Angeles Police Department.

||||||

The revelation that tabloid outlets had paid several prosecution witnesses for interviews led, indirectly, to my own involvement in the Simpson case. Around the time of the murders, I was completing a story for *The New Yorker* about "cash for trash." My article focused almost entirely on how the investigation of Michael Jackson for sexual abuse of minors had been severely compromised because so many potential prosecution witnesses had been paid by the tabloids. I had a chance to add a few details about the tabloids' role in the early days of the Simpson case—specifically, with regard to Jill Shively and the Ross Cutlery witnesses—and my story appeared on newsstands on Tuesday, July 5, 1994.

Later that week, unbeknownst to me at the time, the editor of *The New Yorker,* Tina Brown, asked the photographer Richard Avedon to travel to Los Angeles to take pictures of the defense and prosecution teams in the Simpson case. He and Susan Mercandetti, an editor at *The New Yorker* who often works with Avedon, spent the bulk of that week negotiating with Shapiro and his colleagues about how and when the defense-team photographs would be taken. The photo shoot of the prosecutors went off fairly smoothly, but dealing with Shapiro turned out to be a tense and frustrating experience for my colleagues. First the session was on, then it was off. Some people were included in the picture, and then they were not. The problem, as Shapiro explained it to Susan, was that the makeup of the defense team was in flux. (Though he did not say so at the time, the key issue was whether Johnnie Cochran would be joining the team.)

In the end, Shapiro proposed a compromise to Avedon and Mercandetti. Shapiro could not produce the entire defense team for a photograph, but he could produce . . . Shapiro. He would agree to sit for a solo portrait. He proposed this solution as if it had not been his hope all along, and Avedon ultimately did take Shapiro's photograph. Shapiro knew that the process leading up to the portrait had been bumpy, to say the least, so he made a peace offering to the *New Yorker* team. He and his wife would take Avedon and Mercandetti to dinner at Eclipse, a trendy West Hollywood restaurant. Mercandetti, who had given birth to a daughter just a couple of months before, wanted nothing more than to go home to Washington, but she agreed to go to dinner.

At the restaurant Shapiro was in his glory. Producers and agents paid court at the banquette. Shapiro basked. Avedon, in an expansive mood, felt compelled to share with the table the fact that Susan was a nursing mother. On learning this news, Shapiro rose theatrically from his seat and spoke to Bernard Erpicum, the suave maître d' of Eclipse. Moments later, Bernard reappeared with a package for Susan: a breast pump. Needless to say, Susan had not requested this gift, but she managed to mumble a stunned thank-you. She spent the rest of the meal mortified by Shapiro's presumptuousness (however well intentioned), and contemplating a departure from the business altogether.

In any event, Tina Brown told me on Monday, July 11, that Shapiro had told Susan he might—*might*—agree to be interviewed by me about the case. Tina said I should make plans to go to Los Angeles the next morning. I made an airplane reservation, but I doubted anything would come of it. It didn't sound like Shapiro had made much of a commitment to Susan, and I worried that I would just be stuck out there with nothing to write.

Tina had no patience for my agonizing. "Look," she said. "There's no story in New York. Just go." I went.

|||||

I did have one possible lead. While I was still in New York, I had had a brief telephone conversation with Alan Dershowitz, who had by then joined Simpson's defense team. Ten years earlier, I had taken Dershowitz's first-year criminal law class at Harvard Law School, and we had spoken occasionally in subsequent years. In the course of a rambling and unfocused talk, Dershowitz went on a lengthy tirade about one of the detectives involved in the case. Knowing that in my previous career as a prosecutor I had been a junior

THE RACE CARD ||| 147

member of the Iran-contra Independent Counsel's staff, Dershowitz described the detective in question to me: "He sounds like Oliver North, looks like Oliver North, and lies like Oliver North." I had thought little of the comment at the time, but reviewing my notes on the flight to California, I thought it might be worth pursuing the subject.

When I arrived late Tuesday, I found out there had been no progress in my getting an audience with Shapiro. So, on the morning of Wednesday, July 13, I decided to follow up on what I had heard from Dershowitz. There was, I was sure, no news in the fact that Dershowitz thought ill of the detective. But if the detective really did have a bad record, there was bound to be an official file. I began by calling the LAPD and asking if I could see the detective's disciplinary record. I was not allowed to see anything in his file, but I was told there had been no formal adjudications against him. In short, no help. So I thought of another tack. From my days as a prosecutor, I knew that law enforcement officials were often sued for violating the civil rights of people they encountered. Perhaps there had been judgments against the detective. I decided I would go look.

But before I set out to find any records, I had to settle something. From my hotel room, I placed a call to David Kirkpatrick, a fact checker for *The New Yorker*. I asked him to check the spelling of the name Dershowitz mentioned.

"I have it in my notes as F-U-R-M-A-N, but that looks wrong to me," I said.

Kirkpatrick set me straight: F-U-*H*-R-M-A-N.

Shortly after ten, I parked near the long, low Los Angeles County Courthouse and made my way inside. About halfway down the corridor that runs the length of the main floor, I found the room where all cases are indexed on microform. I sat down to see if Mark Fuhrman had ever been sued.

No—not exactly. But the file did indicate that on August 24, 1983, Fuhrman himself had filed a lawsuit. And the defendant, curiously enough, was the City of Los Angeles Fire and Police Pension System. I showed the clerk the case number—C 465,544—and asked where I might find the paperwork. She told me that since it was so old, it would be in closed files in the archives, across

Hill Street. Following her directions, I found myself staring at an elevator door that seemed to have been planted by itself near the side of the street. I stepped aboard the elevator and saw that there was, of course, nowhere to go but down. I rode it to the bottom.

There I discovered a ghostly subterranean Los Angeles, a network of cool, deserted corridors connecting the buildings above to one another. I followed the signs to the archives, which turned out to be housed in a vast, hangarlike chamber where everything, especially the employees, seemed to exist in a fluorescent haze. I filled out a form and then watched the clerk disappear into the endless stacks of forgotten papers. After less than ten minutes, she called my number and handed me a file about two inches thick. I took it to a table and began to study the contents.

||||||

The case file amounted to a miniature autobiography of Mark Fuhrman: born February 5, 1952; grew up in Washington State; a brother died of leukemia before Mark was born; father a truck driver and carpenter; parents divorced when he was seven. In 1970, Fuhrman joined the marines, then served in Vietnam as a machine gunner. He thrived in the service until his last six months there. As Fuhrman later explained to Dr. Ronald R. Koegler, a psychiatrist, he stopped enjoying his military service because "there were these Mexicans and niggers, volunteers, and they would tell me they weren't going to do something." As a result of these problems, in 1975 Fuhrman left the marines and went almost directly to the Los Angeles Police Academy.

Fuhrman excelled at the academy, finishing second in his class, and his career at the LAPD had a promising start. His early personnel ratings were high. One superior wrote, "His progress is excellent and with continued field experience he would progress into an outstanding officer." But in 1977, Fuhrman's assignment was changed to East L.A., and his evaluators began to show some reservations. "He is enthusiastic and demonstrates a lot of initiative in making arrests," a superior wrote at the time. "However, his overall production is unbalanced at this point because of the greater proportion of time spent trying to make the 'big arrest.'" Dr. Koegler wrote, "After a while he began to dislike his work, especially the 'low-class' people he was dealing with. He bragged about violence he used in subduing suspects, including chokeholds, and said he would break their hands or face or arms or legs, if necessary."

Fuhrman was moved into the pursuit of street gangs in late 1977, and while his job ratings remained high, he reported that the strains of the job affected him. "Those people disgust me, and the public puts up with it," he told Dr. John Hochman, another psychiatrist, referring to his gang work. Fuhrman said that he was in a fight "at least every other day" and that he had to be "violent just to exist." In just one year, he said, he was involved in at least twenty-five altercations while on duty. "They shoot little kids and they shoot other people," he told Dr. Hochman. "We'd catch them and beat them, and we'd get sued or suspended. . . . This job has damaged me mentally. I can't even go anywhere without a gun." Fuhrman explained, "I have this urge to kill people that upset me."

The stress of police work took such a toll that in the early 1980s, Fuhrman sought to leave the force. His lawyers asserted that in the course of his work, Fuhrman "sustained seriously disabling psychiatric symptomatology" and as a result should receive a disability pension from the city. To get that pension, Fuhrman waged a protracted legal battle. The extensive case file documenting his efforts, replete with detailed psychiatric evaluations of the officer, was paradoxical. In all of Fuhrman's own briefs, he was portrayed as a dangerously unbalanced man; as one of them put it, Fuhrman was "substantially incapacitated for the performance of his regular and customary duties as a policeman." In the city's answers, however, he was called a competent officer, albeit one involved in an elaborate ruse to win a pension. Dr. Hochman observed, "There is some suggestion here that the patient was trying to feign the presence of severe psychopathology. This suggests a conscious attempt to look bad and an exaggeration of problems which could be a cry for help and/or overdramatization by a narcissistic, self-indulgent, emotionally unstable person who expects immediate attention and pity." In either case—whether Fuhrman was a psychotic or a malingerer—the picture of him was an unattractive one. Fuhrman lost his case and, as a result, remained on the force.

As I studied the file, its implications were obvious. The Fuhrman disability case had the potential to thrust the specter of Rodney King into the middle of the Simpson case. The officer depicted in this battle over a pension seemed the archetype of the bigoted, bullying L.A. cop. If Simpson's lawyers chose to use this file—and I wondered at the time whether they even knew about it—it could transform the case, which to that point had been regarded as largely apolitical. Would that change? Having seen Fuhrman's file, I decided it was now all the more important that I speak to Shapiro.

||||||

It turned out that Simpson's lawyers did know about Fuhrman's disability-case file. Several months after I located the documents, I learned how the defense had found out about them.

The name Mark Fuhrman rang a bell with Zvonko Pavelic, but he couldn't remember how. Bill Pavelic, as he is known, was born in Croatia in 1949, and after more than three decades in the United States, he still retained a slight residue of Central Europe in his speech. His family came to Cleveland in 1961 and to Los Angeles two years later, when Pavelic was fourteen. In 1974, when he was twenty-five, Pavelic became an officer with the LAPD. Looking back, he regarded it as important that he was a little older than many other cops were when they joined the force; he felt it made him more independent, more trusting of his own judgments. Pavelic worked South Central L.A. for almost his entire career. Early on, he prospered, moving quickly up the ranks to detective. But his career stalled when he began speaking out against what he saw as the pervasive racism in the department. He investigated other cops, including those involved in the infamous 1988 raid on the apartments at Thirty-ninth Street and Dalton Avenue, in which homes were trashed and residents terrorized. Eventually Pavelic made a name for himself as an in-house critic, which is a difficult role in any police department and was a nearly impossible one in the LAPD. His profile is a fairly common one for whistle-blowers: He is regarded as courageous and honorable by some, egocentric and bizarre by others.

After the Rodney King beating in 1991, Pavelic began speaking out in public against the LAPD, and it then became clear that his days on the force were numbered. He quit after eighteen years, in

1992, with a stress-and-asthma-disability pension, telling a doctor he would "rather go to the gulag" than return to work. According to a doctor Pavelic consulted for his disability application, he said he had "prior thoughts of homicide toward LAPD management." (Pavelic later denied making that statement.) In any case, after leaving the force Pavelic hired himself out as a "consultant" to those with grievances against the LAPD. His work resembled that of a private investigator, but Pavelic, ever prickly, did not want to register as a private eye and subject himself to any regulation by the state. So he did what he called "biopsies" of both criminal and civil cases, looking for lapses by the LAPD that his clients might exploit. Robert Shapiro had called Pavelic to do just that the day after he himself had been hired to work on the Simpson case. So Pavelic had watched the preliminary hearing with more than passing interest.

Mark Fuhrman piqued Pavelic's interest, but the ex-cop couldn't figure out why. Pavelic knew they had never been assigned together. They certainly weren't friends. But Fuhrman did look familiar. Pavelic was still puzzling about the detective after the prelim concluded: How did he know Mark Fuhrman? Then, suddenly, the name hit him.

Johnny Carson.

Shortly before he left the force, Pavelic, like many LAPD officers, had moonlighted as a security guard. He had done some work for the host of *The Tonight Show,* and so, Pavelic remembered, had Mark Fuhrman (as had Fuhrman's boss, Ron Phillips). The Carson memory triggered another one in Pavelic. In the spring of 1993, Pavelic had done a bit of work for a civil lawyer named Robert Deutsch in a case for a client, Joseph Britton. In 1988 Britton had robbed a man at an automatic teller machine where Fuhrman and his partner had set up a stakeout. In the chase after the robbery, Britton was shot. He ultimately pleaded guilty to the robbery, but he later filed a civil suit alleging that the police—Fuhrman and his partner—had used racial epithets in the course of the arrest and had placed a knife at Britton's feet to justify the shooting. In the course of pretrial discovery in Britton's civil case, Deutsch had uncovered the matter of *Fuhrman v. City of Los Angeles Fire and Police Pension System,* Number C 465,544—the same case I had found in the archived files. A few days after he was hired in the Simpson case, Pavelic, through Deutsch, rediscovered the case file and mentioned it to his new boss, Robert Shapiro.

‖‖‖

On the day I discovered the Fuhrman file, I had no appointment with Shapiro. I was not expected or, I imagine, much wanted. But I decided the best thing I could do at that moment was simply to arrive at Robert Shapiro's office. I drove from downtown L.A. to Century City.

The directory in the lobby of Shapiro's office tower indicated his office was on the nineteenth floor. I went to the elevator and pressed the button. No response. I tried another elevator. Same thing. The floor had obviously been blocked off. I assumed this must have been because of Shapiro. I had read about how inundated he was with callers; he must have decided that he would not admit anyone unless he first summoned them. I figured there was no way I could talk his secretary into letting me upstairs without an appointment, and I prepared to leave in disappointment. But since I was in the building anyway, I figured I would satisfy my curiosity about a rumor I had heard.

I wandered over to the security guard and asked, "Is it true that Ronald Reagan has his office here?" Yes, this friendly fellow responded immediately, and then he volunteered the floor number. I figured I might as well push my luck. So I asked, "The elevator seems to be giving me some trouble. How do you get up to nineteen?"

"Reception is on eighteen," he said. "Just go there, and they'll direct you."

I took the elevator to eighteen and looked around. There was a spiral staircase between floors. I put my head down and, trying to look like I belonged, hustled past the front desk and up the stairs one flight. It was a big building, but as it happened, Shapiro's office was right near the stairs. He was sitting at his desk. Susan Mercandetti had told me his secretary's name was Bonnie Barron.

"Hi, Bonnie!" I said, with perhaps excessive enthusiasm, to the middle-aged woman outside Shapiro's office. "I'm Jeff Toobin with *The New Yorker,* but I have to confess that I don't have a cake with me."

In the course of courting Shapiro for the photo, Susan had sent a cake to his office as a joke. Susan told me she had been surprised by how enthusiastically it was received. Barron smiled—my new best friend. In a rather pathetic effort to justify my unannounced arrival, I had put a copy of my cash-for-trash article in an envelope, on the theory that I could say I was merely "delivering" it to Shapiro. (Never mind that he hadn't asked for it, and probably didn't want it.) I told Barron, "I have something for Bob, and I thought I might drop it off for him."

Shapiro looked out to see who was talking to his secretary. I thought I had one chance.

Standing in the doorway, I introduced myself and said, "I had a very interesting morning looking at Mark Fuhrman's employment records."

"You saw those?" Shapiro asked.

"Yeah, about how he hates blacks and all that. It's pretty interesting."

"Jesus, you're the only guy who's found those. Come in here and sit down." I did. "Where did you say you were from?"

"*The New Yorker.*"

"*The New Yorker?*"

"Yes," I answered.

"That's different from *New York?*" he asked.

I nodded.

"Son of a bitch!" He pounded his fist into his palm. "That Susan Mercandetti is the nicest woman. I wanted to do her a favor, so I talked to this guy from *New York*. I got them mixed up." (I checked *New York* magazine for the next several weeks, but never found anything that looked like it could have come from Shapiro.)

"Well, anyway," I said, "here I am."

Shapiro was full of energy, excited. Unshaven, he was wearing a work shirt and blue jeans. His messy office was long and narrow, distinguished only by his stunning desk, which appeared to be a genuine Napoleonic antique, full of inlaid woods and brass ornamentation.

I asked him what he made of the Fuhrman records. "There's worse stuff, too," he told me. "This is a guy who used to wake up every day and say to his ex-wife, 'I'm going to kill some niggers this morning.' " He paused. "You understand this stuff. I want to work with you on this."

I asked what he thought Mark Fuhrman meant for the Simpson defense effort. "Just picture it," he said, growing more animated as he spoke. "Here's a guy who's one of the cops coming on the scene early in the morning. They have the biggest case of their lives. But an hour later you're told you're not in charge of the case. How's that going to make that guy feel? So now he's one of four detectives heading over to O.J.'s house. Suppose he's actually found two gloves at the murder scene. He transports one of them over to the house and then 'finds' it back in that little alleyway where no one can see him." Discovering the glove would turn Fuhrman into "the hero of the case."

"This is a bad cop," Shapiro said a few moments later. "This is a racist cop."

I was stunned. The thought that Fuhrman might have planted the glove at Rockingham had never occurred to me. But I immediately realized how clever the suggestion was as a defense tactic. It was what some lawyers call a "judo defense," in that it seeks to turn the strength of the prosecution's case against the prosecution. The idea was to transform the gloves from strong evidence of Simpson's guilt—who else but Simpson could have been at both Nicole's house and his own that night?—to evidence of a police conspiracy. If Fuhrman had transported the glove, then the bloody gloves became, for the defense, harmless at worse and exculpatory at best. I immediately realized that Shapiro's theory, while ingenious, was also monstrous. In a criminal trial, the defense has no burden of proof, so it looked like the defense would attempt to persuade a jury of Los Angeles citizens—largely through innuendo— that one of their own police officers, acting out of racial animus, had planted evidence to see an innocent man convicted of murder and, potentially, sent to the gas chamber.

Trying to process all those thoughts, I briefly found myself at a loss for words. Shapiro, too, suddenly seemed to withdraw from the conversation. He picked up a stack of mail he had been reading—mostly letters to Simpson in jail—and for a moment I watched him read. Shapiro then tossed me a handwritten note from Larry King requesting that Shapiro appear on his show. "He writes me every day," Shapiro said.

We had never discussed ground rules for our interview. Technically, since nothing had been said to the contrary, I could quote him directly. But I felt I owed him the right to clarify his understanding of the terms of our talk. I make it a point never to use the phrases *off the record* or *on background* with sources, because most people—including most journalists—don't really understand what those terms mean. So I asked, "Can I quote you by name?"

"No," he said. "That's too much like an interview."

"So it's okay if I say 'a member of the defense team,' " I said.

"Something like that."*

And then, simple as that, our conversation was over. It had lasted no more than fifteen minutes. Not only was I having trouble keeping up my end, but I realized I was, at that very moment, due in Culver City to conduct a radio debate about the propriety of tabloids' paying for interviews. (My adversary was the *National Enquirer*'s Mike Walker, who would go on to play his own curious role in the Simpson story.) We said our goodbyes, and Shapiro and I agreed to keep in touch.

After my belated appearance on the radio show, I drove to *The New Yorker*'s L.A. office to write up a draft of my article and fax it to the editors in New York. I spent the next day, Thursday, July 14, conferring with other members of the defense team, polishing the story and filling in holes. That night I took the TWA red-eye home to New York. (The in-flight movie was *Naked Gun 33 1/3*, starring, among others, O. J. Simpson.)

Friday morning, back in my office to close the piece, I realized that one issue still gnawed at me. This would be, I realized, a very damaging story to write about someone. I had called the public-affairs office of the LAPD and had been told that it would have no comment on any matter relating to the Simpson case. And no, I certainly could not interview Mark Fuhrman. That bothered me. I called around the LAPD to try to find a phone number for Fuhrman. It didn't take more than five minutes to locate it. I dialed.

"Fuhrman," a man answered.

---

* In a conversation many months later, Shapiro gave me permission to recount that conversation in this book. Also, in his own book, Shapiro disclosed that he was the source for my story.

"Is this Mark Fuhrman?" I asked.

"Yes," he said.

I figured this conversation would not last long, so I identified myself and got right to the point. I explained that I was working on a story that said the defense was planning to charge that Fuhrman had planted the glove on Simpson's property. I asked him if he had planted the glove.

Fuhrman paused, then said, "That's a ridiculous question."

I found that answer curious. Indulging, perhaps, in a taste for overdramatization, I thought of what Bob Woodward and Carl Bernstein used to call "nondenial denials." During Watergate, White House spokesmen like Ron Ziegler would answer reporters' questions by assailing the queries as "preposterous," "absurd," and "ridiculous"—but would not really address the underlying facts.

So, following up, I asked Fuhrman again straight out if he planted the glove.

"Of course it didn't happen."

So much for Ron Ziegler. Fuhrman said he couldn't talk any more and hung up.

|||||

My story appeared on Monday, July 18. All through the editing process, the title had been "Playing the Race Card." But at the last moment, someone at *The New Yorker* thought that was too similar to another headline in the issue, so mine was changed to "An Incendiary Defense." I wrote that in a series of conversations the previous week, "leading members of Simpson's defense team floated [a] new and provocative theory. Those conversations revealed that they plan to portray [Mark Fuhrman] as a rogue cop who, rather than solving the crime, framed an innocent man." Though I summarized the defense hypothesis and explained its basis in the court records from Fuhrman's pension case, I did not suggest that the theory was true—that is, that Fuhrman did indeed plant the glove. And, of course, I included Fuhrman's denial prominently.

It is important to remember just how early in the case this was: Nicole and Goldman had been dead for just about a month. Indeed, I noted that "for all its bravado last week, the defense has not foreclosed any option, including a claim that Simpson did kill his ex-wife and Goldman but was suffering from some sort of insanity. Even a plea bargain remains a possibility. . . . The new strategy may simply be a form of desperation; the race card may be the only one in Simpson's hand."

Was it plausible that Fuhrman had planted the glove? It was, at that point, impossible to say. No one—not the prosecutors, not the defense lawyers, and certainly not reporters like me—knew many details about the case. Few of the DNA tests had been completed. The gloves themselves had scarcely been examined; certainly at this time prosecutors did not know where or when this pair had been purchased or by whom. In testimony at the preliminary hearing, the movements of police investigators, including Fuhrman, in the early morning hours of June 13 had only been hastily sketched.

In retrospect, what mattered most about my story—as well as a similar item about Fuhrman by Mark Miller that appeared in *Newsweek* the same week—was what they promised about how the case would unfold. The issue of race had, to this point, hovered around the edges of the case, with the prosecutors, the press, and even the defense unwilling to acknowledge its explosive potential. Now it was out in the open. I wrote in my article, "If race does become a significant factor in this case—if the case becomes transformed from a mere soap opera to a civil rights melodrama; that is, from the Menendez brothers writ large to Rodney King redux—then the stakes will change dramatically." At the time, I thought I might be overstating the case when I added, "It appears that the case is about to enter a new phase—one with the potential to affect the city of Los Angeles as a whole, and not just one of its most famous residents."

Robert Shapiro had a parochial, if accurate, reaction after his Fuhrman-as-racist-villain theory appeared in my story. On the day that issue of *The New Yorker* appeared, Shapiro called F. Lee Bailey in London and said, "It's over. I won the case."

8. HORRIBLE HUMAN EVENT

I had an early taste of what the reaction might be to my story. *The New Yorker* sent out copies to the wire services on Sunday night, July 17, and it was the lead story on many newscasts around the nation. At 8:00 on Monday morning, Maurie Perl, *The New Yorker*'s chief of public relations, received an early morning call from public television's Charlie Rose, asking if I could be on his program that night. Similar requests came in all day. For me, the week passed in a haze of television talk shows and radio "phoners." Maurie's indefatigable staff computed that, based on Nielsen ratings, approximately 170 million people heard a reference to the "Incendiary Defense" story in *The New Yorker* in the first two days after it was published.

By far the most important experience for me came on Monday night, July 18, when I traveled to Washington to be the first guest on that night's *Larry King Live*. King would come to occupy an unusual niche in the Simpson case. By the time of the trial, King had decided to devote the bulk of his program to the case, and he even moved his base of operations to Los Angeles for long periods. I eventually made several dozen appearances on the show, and King's CNN studio on Sunset Boulevard came to resemble a sort of Hyde Park Corner for the Simpson case. On any given day that I appeared, I was likely to find a defense lawyer, an expert witness, or some other witness or peripheral figure lingering in the makeup room. For me, a reporter who was actually covering the case, the visits amounted to priceless opportunities to chat with these people in a quiet and intimate setting. So many people involved with the case developed relationships with King that he became a quasi-participant himself. Robert Shapiro, though he never appeared on the show until the trial was over, became a friend of King's; so did Skip Taft, Simpson's business manager, who never even agreed to appear on the show. On the air King always maintained a scrupulous nonpartisanship. His renowned even-handedness extended to his famously busy social life. During the trial King simultaneously dated Jo-Ellan Dimitrius, the defense team's jury consultant, and Suzanne Childs, Gil Garcetti's director of communications.

On July 18, 1994, King started his show this way: "The charge is simple and stunning, and it's already touched off a fresh round of fierce debate in the O. J. Simpson case. The claim from the defense, made public today through a pair of respected magazines, is this: O.J. was framed. Set up as a murderer by a racist cop, who planted one of the famous bloody gloves at the Simpson mansion . . ." After the introduction, King turned to me and asked, "How did you get the story?"

"I got the story by being tipped off by the defense to go look in the court records. And I burrowed down two stories in the archives of the L.A. Superior Court, and looked in an index under Mark Fuhrman's name and found a case called *Fuhrman v. The City of Los Angeles.*"

"You were in L.A.?" King asked.

"Yeah."

"The tip came from the defense?"

I answered, "Tip came from the defense."

The interview proceeded for the remainder of the hour, and I never gave a second thought to my answers until about a week later. At that point, I checked in with Dershowitz, whose vague tirade had led me to look at the court records in the first place. I had no special agenda with him, but rather called to ask what was up.

"Bob is very pissed at you," Dershowitz said.

"Why?"

"Because you said on *Larry King* that we had given you the records."

"I don't think I said anything like that. It's not true."

"No," Dershowitz continued confidently. "We've reviewed the transcript, and that's what you said. Bob is very pissed."

We've reviewed the transcript, I thought. They've got a client looking at the gas chamber, and they're reviewing transcripts of *Larry King Live?* I mumbled a vague dissent and steered the conversation in another direction. Much later, when I had a chance to look at the transcript, I came to believe that Shapiro did have a point, although not the one Dershowitz had raised. I never said on *Larry King* that the defense gave me the court records, but I did say that the defense tipped me off to their existence. That was a mistake. They had only spoken vaguely about Fuhrman; I had sought out the records on my own. Still, I wondered, why did Shapiro care? He had gotten his point across. Why was he upset?

|||||

Robert Shapiro always wanted to be liked. In the eighth grade of his public school in Los Angeles, he and his friend Joel Siegel— now the lavishly mustached and preternaturally cheerful entertainment reporter for ABC's *Good Morning America*—had an experience they still talked about forty years later. A clique that called itself the Idols was having a meeting one day, and neither Shapiro nor Siegel was invited. So they just hung around together and moped until the meeting ended. The slight festered. It was as if from that day forward Bob Shapiro, like an updated Scarlett O'Hara, made a vow: With God as his witness, he would never be unpopular again. And he never was.

He was born in Plainfield, New Jersey, in 1942 and the family moved to Los Angeles a year later—an advance guard in the great Jewish migration to West Los Angeles that followed World War II. His mother was a housewife, and his father did a lot of things— drove a lunch wagon, worked in a factory—but Marty Shapiro's real passion was playing the piano in a small band that did gigs at bar mitzvahs and weddings around the West Side. An only child much loved by his parents and his grandparents, who lived downstairs in their apartment building, Bob sought early on never to disappoint them, and he rarely has.

By the time he arrived at UCLA, at the dawn of the sixties, Shapiro had a showman's moxie and a taste for action. His taste for the high life earned him the nickname Trini, after the stylish singer Trini Lopez, and fellow students recall his big hair and powder-blue polyester suit with "zero lapels." He was always a joiner, first of Zeta Beta Tau, a Jewish fraternity (with a rowdier reputation than the stereotypes suggest), but also of a campus booster organization called the Kelps. Resplendent in their blue-and-yellow caps, the Kelps didn't do a lot more than cheer for the Bruins at football games, but they were distinctive at UCLA nonetheless. At a time when campus life was rigidly, if unofficially, segregated by race and religion, the Kelps were a diverse group. This appealed to Bob Shapiro, who collected friends promiscuously and who, decades later, would still attend Kelp reunions.

Shapiro went to law school because, well, the frat practically went en masse. Smart and a quick study, Shapiro thrived at Loyola Law School in Los Angeles, even though he went through a quick marriage and annulment while there. He was so nervous about California's notoriously difficult bar exam that he compulsively tore out his eyebrows, but he passed on his first try and began work as a deputy district attorney in the relative backwater of Torrance.

Shapiro spent three years as a prosecutor—a successful if unremarkable tenure—before he caught the eye of the man who would change his life. The way he found his ticket out of Torrance said a good deal about both Shapiro and where he was going. The criminal defense lawyer Harry Weiss, overwhelmed with work, had hired one junior associate, Peter Knecht, and he needed another one in 1972. (Around this time, Weiss asked a young lawyer named Johnnie Cochran to join him. Cochran demurred and gave Weiss a revealing explanation. "I don't want to work for Harry Weiss," Cochran said. "I want to *be* Harry Weiss.") Weiss had also seen Robert Shapiro in action, and found the young lawyer "presentable and charming," as he later recalled. But something Knecht told Weiss about Shapiro really stuck in his mind. "You know," Knecht told his boss, "Shapiro is the only deputy D.A. I know who drives a Bentley." It was, to be sure, only a used Bentley, and Shapiro had no great fortune in those days, but it was all Weiss needed to hear.

||||||

In his current entry in *Who's Who*, Robert Shapiro lists his occupation during the period of 1972 to 1987 this way: "sole practice L.A." In fact, during most of this period Shapiro was Harry Weiss's associate, and during all of it, in an informal sense, he was Weiss's partner. But after Shapiro became famous in the 1990s, he found it convenient to minimize, and then consign to oblivion, their relationship. The Weiss name—and the Weiss style—did not comport with Shapiro's later pretensions. Once, during a break in the Simpson trial, I made the mistake of mentioning to Shapiro that I had just met Harry Weiss. Shapiro looked at me as if he had never before heard the name. But for fifteen years, the formative period of his professional life, Bob Shapiro was Harry Weiss's protégé. And that fancy Napoleonic desk Shapiro sat behind in Century City? A gift from Harry.

At the age of eighty, Harry Weiss—bearing his trademark monocle and two-tone shoes—remains a familiar figure along the corridors of the Los Angeles Criminal Courts Building. He works every day, just as he has since he was four years old and a child star in vaudeville. He had six sisters, and they traveled as a family around the Midwest on the Orpheum circuit, the largest and most prestigious network of vaudeville theaters. As a four- and five-year-old, in the years around 1920, Harry would close the act by demonstrating the now lost art of "recitation." These were monologues—anything ranging from the Gettysburg Address to soliloquies from *Hamlet*—addressed directly to the audience. "I used to stop the show," Weiss boasted three quarters of a century later.

The Weiss act ended with the decline of vaudeville and the advent of child labor laws in the twenties, and the family moved to Los Angeles in 1929. Harry became a lawyer in 1940 and never let the skills honed onstage go to waste. From the beginning, long before the era of celebrity defense attorneys, there was something rakish and theatrical about Weiss's style of practice. In a way, Weiss's law business reflected his roots in vaudeville—more mass than class, just shy of total respectability. He had his share of famous clients—Peter Fonda, in a marijuana case, and John Lennon, in an immigration dispute—but mostly Weiss believed in volume. There was a saying: Every hooker in Hollywood has Harry's card.

The seventies, the heyday of Shapiro's association with Weiss, were boom years for their law practice. They shared a penthouse suite at 8600 Sunset Boulevard, which boasted a private swimming pool to go with the palatial offices for Weiss, Shapiro, and

Knecht. Harry always began his workday the same way, with a conference call at seven in the morning to go over the day's court appearances. This was no simple matter, because at the time Harry Weiss may have had the biggest criminal law practice in the United States. In an office that never had more than half a dozen lawyers who appeared in court, there might be a hundred appearances to be handled in courthouses that were sometimes twenty miles from one another. (Weiss provided chauffeurs for his top lawyers to help them make their rounds; Shapiro, for a time, hired his own father to drive for him.) The morning conference calls would feature a rotating cast of characters, but there were four regulars: Harry Weiss, Shapiro, Knecht, and Sammy Weiss, Harry's nephew. (Sammy's surname was originally Greene, but he changed it to Weiss to bathe in Harry's reflected glow.) Both Sammy Weiss and Peter Knecht, who drove a Ferrari and dated starlets, had active social lives that made the early morning phone calls an unwelcome chore.

"Are we all here?" Harry would begin.

Sammy Weiss at this point might reply with a slight groan.

"Sammy?" the senior Weiss would ask.

"Wha . . ."

"SAMMY!"

"What!?"

"You been out again, Sammy? Out dancing or whatever?" Harry would continue at deafening volume. "This is what you have to do. You go get an enema. You listening?"

"Leave me alone, Harry," Sammy would mumble.

"Listen to me, Sammy!" Harry would shoot back. "Mae West told me that's why she looks so good. She's seventy-six years old, she gets enemas. You should too!"

After a little more in this vein it was usually Shapiro, the most levelheaded member of the group, who would interrupt to suggest that Harry move on to the case assignments, and so another day on the circuit would begin. Mostly, Weiss and Shapiro cut deals for their clients. This was imperative, given the number of clients they had to service, but it also reflected the nature of their cases and the personalities of the lawyers. In the mid-1970s the police in Los Angeles still arrested large numbers of people for so-called victimless crimes—prostitution, drug usage, and some consensual-sex offenses. The firm specialized in the speedy and painless resolutions of these matters. Weiss, in particular, always had many clients in Los Angeles's gay community, and in the days when Shapiro worked with him, the police were still routinely arresting men for having sex with one another. According to Weiss, "Bob handled many of these cases—vag lewds, we called them. The cops always had these guys dead-bang, and no one ever wanted to go to trial. In those days, the men couldn't stand the embarrassment of fighting it in public, and anyway, judges never came down too hard on them. So you had to make deals, and Bob made deals. That's the way you've got to do it. He learned."

Deal making suited Shapiro's temperament. He has an unusual quality for a successful lawyer—a strong aversion to conflict. Plea bargains please him; both sides win. He is, to be sure, an effective trial attorney, but the area of the law where he truly excels is the cultivation of clients, a skill he honed from his earliest days with Weiss. Shapiro always had ambitions that went beyond the profitable, if low-prestige, Harry Weiss assembly line. He married a beautiful model, Linell Thomas, in 1970. They had no children for a decade, a period that Shapiro spent developing the social contacts that later blossomed into law clients. He and Linell had lunch almost every Sunday at the Beverly Hills Hotel with one high-powered friend or another. One of them was Dale Gribow, a personal-injury lawyer. Gribow introduced Shapiro to Dennis Gilbert, then a successful insurance salesman. In time, Gilbert became one of the biggest agents in professional baseball. When, as sometimes happened, Gilbert's clients were arrested, he referred them to Shapiro, who became something like house counsel to ballplayers in trouble, a group that came to include Jose Canseco (gun possession), Darryl Strawberry (tax evasion), and Vince Coleman (throwing a firecracker at a group of fans).

There was a pattern to many of Shapiro's big cases: The facts were usually undisputed; the only issue was punishment—that is, how a bargain could be structured with the prosecutor and judge. This was no secret. On the day he was retained to represent Christian Brando, Marlon's son, for murdering his half-sister's lover, Shapiro told the *Los Angeles Times* that he would meet with prosecutors and try to resolve the case without a trial. Many lawyers would view such a statement as a pointless surrender of bargaining power, but Shapiro had great confidence in his ability to cut a deal. There was another pattern, too, in the celebrity cases. Shapiro cleverly treated these clients as loss leaders, charging them little or nothing in fees, a practice that did not hurt in attracting even more celebrity clients—and, of course, in drawing the lesser-known souls whom Shapiro would make pay through the nose. (The quest for clients was never far from Shapiro's thoughts. When the Simpson defense team pulled the ludicrous stunt of establishing an 800 number for tips to help them identify the real killer, Shapiro, quite naturally, gave callers the option of pressing 4 if they wanted to retain his services. Embarrassed by the public attention to this feature, Shapiro quickly had it removed, and the number itself was shut down a little while later. Not surprisingly, the 800 number provided no useful information.)

Shapiro cut so many deals so successfully—the celebrities he represented almost never went to jail—that it contributed to an impression that he didn't know how to try a case. It was true that Shapiro did not relish that side of the job. For example, he hated having to visit his clients in jail. This became a problem in a difficult federal narcotics trial Shapiro conducted in 1989. His client, George Guzman, who had been stopped in a car that contained cocaine, complained bitterly that Shapiro never came to see him; Guzman was even more offended that Shapiro had instructed him not to speak to him in court. Yet when the time came for summations in the trial, Shapiro became so swept away by the emotion of the moment that he embraced his client in front of the jury and shouted, "This man is innocent!" The theatrics drew an astonished rebuke from the judge, but that was nothing compared to Guzman's surprise: The prisoner recoiled so quickly that he threw out a muscle in his back. But he never complained; the jury acquitted him.

Many of Shapiro's cases attracted intense media interest, and Shapiro came to fancy himself an expert on dealing with reporters. In January 1993, more than a year before the murders on Bundy Drive, Shapiro wrote a casually revealing article in *The Champion*, a trade publication for criminal defense lawyers. Entitled "Using the Media to Your Advantage," it offered a step-by-step guide for attorneys handling high-profile cases. The article was full of sensible advice—be truthful, be courteous, be prompt—and yet it was written with profound ignorance about the larger implications of what he had to say. In some respects, Shapiro figured out clever ways to deal with the frenzy generated by the media in big cases. His advice was cynical, but probably justified under the circumstances. For example: "I tell the reporters in advance that I will be making a statement at the end of the day, and I direct them to an area outside the courthouse. I prefer a lawn with trees or some other attractive background. . . . The most important lead story on an hour newscast allots only 15 or 20 seconds for a statement from an interview. These 'sound bytes' [sic] must be concise and easily understood. . . . Pick and choose the questions you want to answer. You do not have to be concerned with whether the answer precisely addresses the question, since only the answer will be aired. . . . In dealing with all members of the press, avoid clichés. Referring to a case as a tragedy or to a client as being framed does not convey a thoughtful message. To describe an unfortunate death situation, I use the term 'a horrible human event.' " (Shapiro practiced what he preached. On June 11, 1990, when he took over as counsel for Christian Brando, the third paragraph of the *Los Angeles Times* story read: " 'It's a horrible human event,' Shapiro said of the fatal shooting last month of Dag Drollet.")

On close inspection, the calculated sincerity of the Shapiro method certainly may look a little smarmy, but there was little harm in it for a case about a Hollywood peccadillo. Yet Shapiro learned at his peril that the Simpson case was different—because the subject of race is different. In his conversations with me and *Newsweek*'s Mark Miller, Shapiro had raised the subject in American life that is least amenable to compromise and deal making. No "lawn with trees or some other attractive background" could help him here. Shapiro was suddenly out of his league, and he knew it. That was why he was mad at me.

|||||

Still, Shapiro's irritation with me amounted to little more than a minor annoyance. Fundamentally, he was having the time of his life. He did not give interviews, but he was happy to be courted by the American media royalty. It wasn't just Larry King who wrote him every day. ABC's Barbara Walters appeared to pay homage, as did CBS's Connie Chung. For the moment, Shapiro played coy; there would be no interviews—not least because he didn't want to be asked on camera whether he thought Simpson was guilty. (He was, however, happy to pose for photographs—by Avedon for *The New Yorker*; by Annie Leibovitz for *Vanity Fair*; and in his boxing trunks for *People*.) So Shapiro took Walters and Chung to dinner, and they agreed to stay in touch.

It was a heady time, and Shapiro loved the action. One day shortly after he was hired, he was waxing nostalgic on the telephone with his old friend Joel Siegel. Siegel was urging Shaps—Bob's junior high school nickname—to keep a diary of his experiences in the Simpson case. "Just be purely subjective about your feelings about it, and at the end of the trial you'll have a book," Siegel said. "You know, we're not getting any younger, all of us, and this book will be around forever." Shapiro demurred for the moment, even if he enjoyed the attention. In the middle of the conversation, Shapiro asked Siegel if he could put him on hold. He had to take another call. In a moment, Shapiro was back.

"Joel," Shapiro said, "say hello to O. J. Simpson."

Siegel unexpectedly found himself on a conference call with America's most famous murder defendant and his lawyer. Simpson knew Siegel worked in the media, of course, and the defendant started venting his anger at what he regarded as the unfair treatment he had received in the press. "Why don't they talk to my friends?" Simpson said. "I'm not a wife beater."

Shapiro said he wanted to raise another subject. They had made great progress in hiring legal and scientific experts, but there was still the matter of a trial lawyer. Shapiro was looking at some people they might want to bring in to help at the trial. There were three main candidates. Astonished at what he was hearing, Siegel could not resist sharing his good fortune. Without telling Shapiro (or, needless to say, Simpson), Siegel patched in Roger Cossack, another old chum of his and Shapiro's from Los Angeles. In this bizarre four-way phone call, O. J. Simpson evaluated the lawyers who might defend him in court.

Simpson didn't like one of the candidates, which was actually a team, Leslie Abramson and Gerald Chaleff. Simpson didn't know Chaleff, a well-regarded Santa Monica–based defense attorney who had represented Angelo Buono in the "Hillside Stranger" case. It was Abramson who was the problem. Simpson just didn't cotton to the frizzy-haired counsel to Erik Menendez.

The second possibility was Johnnie Cochran. Simpson liked Cochran well enough, and he wasn't willing to dismiss him as a possibility.

But the third candidate had become Simpson's favorite. O.J. had seen Gerry Spence on television for years. Dressed in his trademark cowboy hats and fringed leather jackets, the sage of Jackson Hole, Wyoming, had deployed his cornpone charm for clients as diverse as Karen Silkwood and Imelda Marcos. O.J. thought he was great.

"Get me Gerry Spence," the defendant said.

One of the enduring fictions of the Simpson case was the notion of the defendant himself as "involved" in his defense. Press reports persistently portrayed Simpson as virtually a member of his own defense team. O.J., it was said, was "plotting strategy" and "planning his own defense." Simpson's attorneys manufactured this idea primarily as a gift to their client and as a way of remaining in his good graces. Moreover, the idea of Simpson as a formidable figure in his own right—an African-American of stature—helped rally black support to him. In addition, the lawyers knew that many journalists would take their line about Simpson's level of involvement at face value, even as it was transparently false. Treating Simpson as the equal of his lawyers fit nicely with the paternalistic approach many mainstream journalists take in writing about race. According to these informal standards, white reporters can write with candor about the intellectual limitations of their fellow whites, but not blacks. Absurdly, black sensibilities are thought to be too tender for the truth. Indeed, it is thought to be flirting with a charge of racism to draw attention to the intellectual limitations of any African-American, especially a prominent one like Simpson. So accepting the idea of Simpson as the peer of his attorneys relieved the mainstream press of confronting the obvious truth about him—that he was an uneducated, semiliterate ex-athlete who could barely understand much about the legal proceedings against him.

O.J. didn't even understand the nature of the defense strategy Shapiro had constructed. Shapiro was, for example, incredulous that Simpson wanted Gerry Spence as his lawyer. Shapiro had nothing against Spence, but he regarded the Wyoming attorney as self-evidently the wrong man for the job. The defense in this case would be race—Shapiro had decided that from the very beginning. What could Spence offer to, in Shapiro's preferred code words, "a downtown jury"?

In truth, Shapiro didn't really want any other lawyers added to the team. In the first week after the murders, he had assembled all the supporting players he wanted, and he regarded any more high-profile assistance as superfluous, not to mention a threat. But O.J.'s friends—much the same group that had lobbied Simpson to evict Weitzman from the case—felt otherwise. They worried about Shapiro's reputation as a plea bargainer. They fretted about his relative lack of trial experience. The informal leader of O.J.'s kitchen cabinet, Wayne Hughes, a private-warehouse mogul, made clear that he and his peers wanted another high-powered trial attorney on the team. Shapiro reluctantly agreed. But O.J. wanted Gerry Spence.

Out of a sense of obligation to his client, Shapiro went so far as to invite Spence to California for consultations about the case. On Friday, July 15, Spence came to Los Angeles for a secret meeting, held at the Beverly Hills home of Shapiro's friend Michael Klein. Shapiro presented the possibility of Spence joining the defense team in terms he knew the lawyer would reject. "I will be the lead counsel," Shapiro told the famously strong-willed Spence. Shapiro also told Spence of his plans to make race a key part of the defense, and in particular of his intention to use Mark Fuhrman as the focus of that strategy. (Though Shapiro had spoken to me about Fuhrman on Wednesday, July 13, my story would not hit the newsstands until the following Monday, after Spence's visit to Los Angeles.) As Shapiro could have surmised, Spence had neither the experience nor the inclination to defend this double-murder case based on a nonexistent conspiracy of racist police officers. And, again as Shapiro surely predicted, Spence had no desire to play second fiddle to anyone. "I have to be captain of the ship," he told Shapiro.

In the course of their meeting, Shapiro mentioned to Spence in passing that he was also talking to Johnnie Cochran about joining the team as a trial lawyer. Who else but the foremost black attorney in Los Angeles to conduct a defense based on race? Spence averred that Cochran sounded like a much better fit. Shapiro agreed. So did Wayne Hughes, and so, ultimately, did all of Simpson's friends who were consulted. For a time, only O.J. demurred. He liked Cochran, had even talked to him several times since the murders, but he wasn't sure if he wanted him as his lawyer. It is one of the richer and more revealing ironies of the case that only O. J. Simpson—"I'm not black. I'm O.J."—failed to understand the preeminent place of race in his own defense. Simpson was himself so alienated from the world of his fellow black Angelenos that he alone failed to recognize what was obvious to whites and blacks alike: that Johnnie L. Cochran, Jr., had been waiting his whole life for this case, and this case had been waiting for Johnnie Cochran as well.

|||||

Shapiro and the others prevailed upon Simpson to put aside his infatuation with Spence, and Cochran was hired officially on Monday, July 18. Since the day of the murders, Cochran had been commenting on the case almost daily for the *Today* show and other programs, presenting himself as a nominally independent outside analyst of the case. In fact, he had been laying the groundwork all along for the role that he saw would probably be coming his way. Shortly after the freeway chase, for example, Cochran told Bryant Gumbel on *Today*, "I think Mr. Cowlings is probably a hero and helped save O. J. Simpson's life. I would urge all your viewers to keep an open mind until you've heard all the evidence, and don't prejudge the case, so that hopefully we can get a fair trial." During the preliminary hearing, Katie Couric asked Cochran on *Today* if he thought the police had violated Simpson's rights in searching his house. "I think it's a little more in favor of the defense right now," Cochran said. "They were there, it seems to me, looking for suspects, and they created this fanciful justification for their having gone over the wall after the fact. These officers had the Fourth Amendment backward. Search first, then ask permission." All in all, as Cochran put it another time on *Today*, "I think the defense made a very strong showing. . . . I think this case is now clearly about the Fourth Amendment and whether or not it's alive and well in Los Angeles County."

Boundless confidence and infectious enthusiasm served as touchstones of Cochran's character, and Simpson quickly absorbed his new lawyer's good cheer. Cochran had a standard greeting for friends and colleagues. "Are you okay, my brother?" he would ask, and then continue, without pausing for an answer, "I'm okay. Are you okay? I'm okay." It was patter more than conversation, but it tended to work. On the first day Cochran appeared beside him as his lawyer, O.J. looked better than he had at any time since his arrest. That was at the arraignment on July 22, 1994, when Simpson boomed out his "Absolutely, 100 percent not guilty." Simpson's spirits reflected Cochran's attitude—upbeat, positive, even chipper. Once Cochran signed onto the case, the question of whether Simpson had in fact murdered his ex-wife and her friend became immaterial. Cochran had a gift, and he knew it. Preeminently in his generation of lawyers, Johnnie Cochran had perfected the art of winning jury trials in downtown Los Angeles. Now he was going to do it for O. J. Simpson.

|||||

As the strap on the burlap sack rubbed his shoulder raw and his young man's fingers turned cramped and gnarled under the Louisiana sun, Johnnie L. Cochran, Sr., had only one thought: This is not for me. He was working the fields in the tiny town of Caspiana, about twenty miles south of Shreveport, and for the first time in his life, harvest duties on the family's eight-acre patch of cotton had fallen to him.

It was June 1935, and Johnnie had just turned nineteen. Northern Louisiana was desperately poor country. But the Cochrans were ambitious, even in tiny Caspiana, which had only about thirty families. As an only child, Johnnie was blessed with as much good fortune as a sharecropper's son might reasonably allow himself to expect. His father valued education, and forgoing the young man's help in the fields, he sent young Johnnie to live with an aunt in Shreveport so that he could go to high school.

There Johnnie L. Cochran, Sr., would find his life's work: insurance sales. After graduating from high school, he plugged into one of the most important social and financial networks in early twentieth century African-American life, albeit one mostly invisible to the white world. Cochran went to work at Louisiana Life, which was one of several black-owned insurance businesses that had cropped up around the turn of the century. In an era when white-owned banks and insurance companies refused to do any business with black folks, these small and often struggling insurance companies represented practically the only way African-Americans could save for their future. Just as important, jobs at these companies represented nearly the only employment options, outside of the ministry, for white-collar work in the black community. The slogan of one of the best-known black insurance companies—"The Company with a Soul and a Service"—reveals that they saw their mission as something more than merely commercial. They were also cautious instruments of black empowerment. The tension between these motives—between God and mammon, the spiritual and the earthly—formed a central theme of the Cochran family story.

Every payday, the dapper young insurance agent would go door-to-door in Shreveport's black neighborhoods. He collected about a nickel a week for the policies, which paid death benefits of about $100. Polite yet dogged, Cochran built a business and a life in the late 1930s. He was promoted to manager and married a local girl. From 1937 to 1940, he and his wife, Hattie, had three children in rapid succession: Johnnie junior, Pearl, and Martha. As it did for so many other families, the specter of World War II threw their ordered lives into tumult.

Hattie was in frail health much of her life, and when the draft was reinstated, she feared having to care for her children alone. Johnnie Senior was rated 1-A by the draft board, which made him a prime candidate for service overseas. So the family realized that the only way to keep the patriarch out of harm's way was for him to find civilian war work, which was scarce in Louisiana. But Johnnie had an aunt who lived in San Francisco, and she said employers there needed an endless supply of able bodies to staff all the factories that were gearing up around the Bay Area. So Johnnie hopped the fabled Sunset Limited train and made for the coast.

It became a well-worn path. The Cochran family joined one of the greatest internal migrations any country has ever seen: the black flight from the South during and after the war. Kinship and custom dictated the destinations: Mississippians went to Chicago; North Carolinians headed to New York; and Texans and Louisianans, like the Cochrans, went to California. Johnnie quickly found work as a shipfitter for Bethlehem Steel, building vast troop ships in Alameda, next door to Oakland. He rented a three-bedroom apartment and sent word for Hattie and the kids to join him.

The war may have put welding tools in his hands, but Johnnie Cochran, Sr., was still determined to keep in touch with the white-collar world. After long days at the docks, he took correspondence courses to hone the sales techniques that would serve him in peacetime. Within weeks of V-J day, the Golden State Mutual Life Insurance Company, the biggest of the black-owned companies on the West Coast, tracked down Cochran in Alameda and offered him a job on the spot. Johnnie quit the shipyard that day. He thrived. Promoted to manager in 1947, he was appointed to open a San Diego office in 1948 and then went on to a bigger job in Los Angeles the following year.

Having lived in subsidized housing during the war, Johnnie senior had accumulated a considerable nest egg by this point, and he had a notion of buying an apartment building as an investment in the booming Los Angeles real estate market. He told Hattie the family could live in one of the flats. She wouldn't hear of it. She wanted a house for her family—a big one. And Johnnie, as was his custom, deferred to her wishes and bought her a house on a pleasant street in an integrated neighborhood called West Adams. Johnnie junior, his mother's favorite, was about to start high school, and Hattie Cochran was determined that he would have nothing but the best.

|||||

Easy Rawlins, the private eye in Walter Mosley's novels, once described the Los Angeles of the early fifties this way: "California was like heaven for the southern Negro. People told stories of how you could eat fruit right off the trees and get enough work to retire one day. The stories were true for the most part but the truth wasn't like the dream. Life was still hard in L.A. and if you worked every day you still found yourself on the bottom." Such was—and in many respects still is—the paradox of black life in the city. After World War II, thousands of African-Americans bought real estate in Southern California, worked in factories for good pay, and shared in the American dream to a degree that would be difficult to fathom in, say, Caspiana, Louisiana. But no one (and especially not black Angelenos) confused their hometown with paradise. The realities of racism, most visible in the blue uniforms of the Los Angeles Police Department, lingered like the smog.

Hattie Cochran was determined that no son of hers was going to wind up on the bottom. She and her husband had already escaped from the ghetto, so her hopes for Johnnie junior called for success on a wider stage, a life of accomplishment and prominence. For all the pluck it took to bring his family into the middle class, the elder Cochran had a diffidence about him, finding contentment in the small things, like family, home, and church. Hattie Cochran hungered for greater success, and she fastened those ambitions onto her firstborn son. The life of the lawyer Johnnie Cochran, Jr., stands as confirmation of a famous observation of Freud's: "If a man has been his mother's undisputed darling he retains throughout life the triumphant feeling, the confidence in success, which not seldom brings actual success with it." Johnnie's mother determined that education would be his route, and she had a simple formula for the kind of place that would push students in the right direction: a school with white children.

So Hattie pushed and pulled and made sure that young Johnnie came to be one of about thirty black students out of the two thousand or so at Los Angeles High School, even though he didn't live in the district. For Hattie's son, the experience among the children of doctors and lawyers would prove, as she had predicted, transforming. "If you were a person who integrated well, as I was, you got to go to people's houses and envision another life," Cochran has said of those years. "I knew kids who had things I could only *dream* of. I remember going to someone's house and seeing a swimming pool. I was like, 'That's great!' Another guy had an *archery range* in his loft. An archery range. I could not believe it. I had never thought about archery! But it made me get off my butt and say, 'Hey, I can do this!' " These slices of life among his largely Jewish peers were every bit as important to Cochran as an afternoon with Willie Mays had been to O. J. Simpson. For Simpson it meant that sports was the route out; for Cochran it meant that education was the way up.

Cochran went to the city's great public university, UCLA, which was then in the midst of its own postwar boom, admitting sons and daughters of the striving middle class and vaulting past its crosstown rival, the private USC. (Indeed, the Simpson case illustrated rather starkly the changing fortunes of the two schools. In earlier decades the private USC traditionally supplied Los Angeles with its leaders, but the public UCLA could count among its alumni not only Cochran but also Robert Shapiro, Marcia Clark, and Lance Ito—who were all smart kids of modest means when they arrived at the Westwood campus. Only one former USC student figured prominently in the Simpson trial: the defendant.) Cochran thrived at UCLA, where he joined the elite black fraternity Kappa Alpha Psi and made a lasting bond with an older Kappa by the name of Tom Bradley. While still in college, Cochran also polished his considerable verbal skills selling insurance for Golden State Mutual, but he recognized quickly that the most profitable outlet for his talents lay in the law.

Cochran graduated from Loyola Law School in 1962 (six years before Shapiro did) and faced the classic dilemma of the newly minted lawyer: to do good or to do well. He thought he could do both. The first stirrings of the civil rights movement were beginning in Los Angeles, and Cochran and his new wife, Barbara, a schoolteacher who had attended UCLA with him, had heard Dr. Martin Luther King, Jr., when he visited the pulpit of their Second Baptist Church. His message had moved them both. But so, too, did the lessons of his father's business. Serving the black community, he decided, could also serve Johnnie Cochran. He spent his first three years in practice as a prosecutor with the city attorney, trying misdemeanor cases and building a reputation as a trial lawyer. When he left the government, he set up shop as a defense lawyer, with one office near downtown and another in largely black Compton. When Watts exploded in the riots of 1965, Cochran basically sat out the controversy. And when the NAACP and other civil rights organizations launched efforts to integrate the fire department and local schools, Cochran left no mark on these struggles. Notwithstanding these absences, young Johnnie Cochran did find his way into the public eye in a case that reflected the city's painful racial dilemmas.

In May 1966, Leonard Deadwyler, who was stopped for speeding while rushing his pregnant wife to the hospital, was shot and killed by an LAPD officer. Self-defense, said the police. The Deadwyler family hired Cochran to represent them, and the resulting coroner's inquest was televised to a rapt citywide audience. According to the peculiar procedure of the inquest, Cochran had no right to address witnesses himself but instead had to ask the deputy district attorney on the case to pose questions for him. The twenty-nine-year-old lawyer scarcely said anything at the inquest, but the government lawyer's words as he relayed the questions—"Mr. Cochran wants to know"—became something of a mantra heard around the city. After the inquest, the district attorney brought no charges against the officer, and Cochran lost the family's civil suit against the city. But Cochran's career—and his issue—were launched. Many years later, shortly before the murders of Nicole Simpson and Ron Goldman, Cochran summed up the impact of the Deadwyler case in an interview with Gay Jervey of *American Lawyer*. "What *Deadwyler* confirmed for me was that the issue of police abuse really galvanized the minority community," Cochran said. "It taught me these cases could really get attention."

|||||

Cochran's public relations triumph in the Deadwyler case contributed to a feeling of invincibility on his part, and this attitude extended to his personal life. In 1967, Cochran began living an extraordinary double life—one that required, among other things, astonishing bravado.

Over the course of that year, Barbara Cochran began to suspect that her husband was having an affair. Night after night, he worked late, and he took what she regarded as suspicious trips on weekends. Barbara hired a private detective, who reported that Johnnie was in fact spending those evenings at the home of Patty Sikora, a blond legal secretary. When Barbara confronted Johnnie, she later wrote in a book, he turned violent, and he beat her on several occasions. Pounding his hands on her head above the hairline, Cochran yelled, "I'm going to hit you where there won't be any bruises!" (Cochran has denied hitting Barbara.) Not long after these incidents, Barbara threw him out of the house they shared with their young daughter. Cochran, however, vowed to mend his ways, and Barbara took him back after a brief separation.

The beatings stopped, but Cochran kept seeing Patty Sikora, telling her that he was in the midst of a drawn-out divorce battle with Barbara. Patty believed him, and their relationship continued. Awaiting the formal end of Johnnie's marriage to Barbara, Patty went so far as to change her legal name to Cochran. Indeed, while he was still living with Barbara, Cochran entered into a quasi-marriage with Patty; they traveled together, bought property together, and had their own group of friends. As Barbara pieced it together years later (with Patty's help), Johnnie would "stop over at Patty's after he left the office. He'd read, help April [Patty's daughter from a previous marriage] with her homework, or watch TV while Patty made dinner for the family. After April was in bed, they might have some intimate time together. Then John would leave and come home to our house." Barbara simply thought her husband still worked late.

Incredibly, Cochran managed to juggle these two lives for ten years. Over the course of this period, Patty had a son with Johnnie, and Barbara had another daughter with him. Both women had their suspicions—Patty, that no divorce would ever happen, and Barbara, that there was another woman—but neither made a final move to put Cochran out of her life. At last, in 1977, Barbara ceased playing the fool and moved out of the elegant home they had purchased five years earlier in the tony Los Feliz district of the city. The 1970s had been prosperous years for Cochran, and he had purchased what he later called "my first Rolls" to go with the fancy new house. Facing a potentially expensive divorce settlement, however, Johnnie Cochran decided to make a change. A crusading young liberal named John Van de Kamp had been elected the new district attorney that year, and Johnnie agreed to join him as the number three prosecutor in the office.

|||||

As always, Cochran's motives were mixed. Reducing his income at that moment allowed him to pare down his divorce settlement with

Barbara. Also, his having done a stint in a prominent public position would help his law practice when he returned to it. But Cochran brought unfeigned passion for racial justice to his job as a prosecutor, and he made a special effort to leave a legacy on the issue that mattered most to him.

Cochran had come to focus his practice on the racial abuses of the LAPD. He had no shortage of material. His most prominent case after Deadwyler involved the murder prosecution of former Black Panther Geronimo Pratt, who was convicted over Cochran's vehement insistence that he was framed. The case became, and remains, a cause célèbre in black Los Angeles. Later, Cochran joined the D.A.'s office in the middle of the investigation of the police shooting of Eulia Love, a woman whose chief crime seemed to have been the failure to pay her gas bill. As a top prosecutor, Cochran had finally arrived in a position where he could take on the LAPD on nearly equal terms. He and Van de Kamp organized what became known as the "rollout unit," a special cadre of deputy district attorneys who would independently investigate all police shootings in the city. The LAPD despised the rollout unit, and the powerful police union went so far as to picket a Van de Kamp fundraising event in protest, yet the unit still seems to have had an impact in reducing the unjustified use of force. The rollout unit also demonstrated the small-world nature of the Los Angeles legal world. Cochran's subordinate, who ran the unit on a day-to-day basis, was deputy district attorney Gil Garcetti. (Ironically, as district attorney in 1995, Garcetti reluctantly disbanded the unit because, among other reasons, the Simpson trial was draining so many of his office's resources.)

The three-year tour in the district attorney's office only added to Cochran's professional luster. By the 1980s, Cochran discovered that there was big business in the LAPD's misdeeds, and his office became a regular port of call for victims of excessive police force. In little more than a decade of filing civil suits based on these incidents, Cochran amassed more than $40 million in damages against the city—which meant that, according to legal-industry custom, Cochran netted about $15 million in fees from those cases alone. Thanks to his friendship with his fraternity brother (and, later, mayor of Los Angeles) Tom Bradley, Cochran took his place at the head of a growing black establishment in the city. Bradley named him to the Board of Airport Commissioners, which runs the Los Angeles International Airport, and that in turn fed a growing corporate law practice for the dozen or so lawyers in the firm known as the Law Offices of Johnnie L. Cochran, Jr. His personal life also settled down during this period. He separated from Patricia shortly after his divorce from Barbara, and entered into a happy marriage with his current wife, marketing consultant Dale Cochran, in 1985. All of Hattie's children thrived. Johnnie's sister Pearl became a high-ranking administrator in the L.A. school system, and her husband ultimately reached the post of the deputy chief of the L.A. Sheriff's Department. Martha became a real estate broker and married an accountant. A much younger brother, Rolonzo, born in 1955, has prospered somewhat less and works as a trainer for a long-distance telephone company.

Even though Cochran had official duties on behalf of Tom Bradley's government, that did not stop him from milking the city's coffers on behalf of his clients. The lawyers in his firm, all members of minority groups, worked with great zeal to exploit the city's racial climate for profit. In the aftermath of the 1992 riots in Los Angeles, for example, Cochran took on a civil case on behalf of Reginald Denny, a white truck driver who was removed from his vehicle in South Central Los Angeles and beaten by an African-American mob. Cochran's civil suit on behalf of Denny did not seek damages from the black men who had nearly beaten him to death (after all, the assailants were poor) but rather from the city of Los Angeles, whose police officers intervened and saved Denny's life. Cochran's audacious theory posited that the LAPD was engaged in racial discrimination by devoting insufficient forces to the black neighborhood where Denny was injured. (The case is still pending.) Whatever the case, civil or criminal, prosecution or defense, Cochran worked reliable magic with black jurors, at least in part because he could turn anything into a racial issue. Cochran knew that a black defendant could scarcely go wrong crying racism in the downtown Criminal Courts Building, and he exploited that phenomenon with singular determination and success.

It was, for example, a stretch to see the racial dimension in the trial of Todd Bridges, a black child actor who once starred in the situation comedy *Diff'rent Strokes*. The case generated a good deal of media attention in its day, and the district attorney's office brought in one of its rising stars to try it—small world again—Bill Hodgman. The facts of the case were not really in dispute. On February 2, 1988, convicted drug dealer Kenneth "Tex" Clay, also an African-American, was shot eight times in a South Central L.A. cocaine "rock house." At the trial Clay testified that Bridges, a frequent cocaine customer of the drug den, had come to the house with a friend and shot him while he shouted, "I told you, Tex! I told you!" Three other eyewitnesses corroborated the victim's version of events.

Cochran called the twenty-five-year-old Bridges in his own defense. He testified that at the time of the murder he had been in the midst of a "four-day cocaine binge. Round the clock. Twenty-four hours a day." He said that he remembered going to Clay's house at the time of the murders: "I decided to kick the door in to see if we could scare Tex into leaving." After that, though, Bridges said, he remembered nothing. Asked by Cochran if he recalled shooting Clay, Bridges replied, "I don't think I did. I didn't know who did. That's one of the side effects of the drugs."

In his summation, Cochran skirted the facts surrounding the murder and instead lashed out at what he called the Los Angeles entertainment establishment, which he said had driven Bridges into the grip of his cocaine addiction. Cochran said that Bridges, an actor since the age of six, had been exploited by the white establishment, which was, by implication, the same establishment that was then conspiring to convict him of this murder. Cochran asked the jury to stand up to these malign forces by acquitting the young man. There were two trials, both before predominantly black jury panels. The first ended in acquittals on the major charges and mistrials on the rest. The second ended in a complete acquittal.

Cochran's legend grew. Although he was little known in the broader white world, his reputation was matchless in black Los Angeles, especially among the *Sentinel*-reading, jury-serving middle class. He was, in fact, a longtime fixture in publications read by black Angelenos. On December 8, 1994, for example, a large front-page picture in the *Sentinel* showed Cochran receiving the annual award of the Brotherhood Crusade, a fraternal organization in Los Angeles. Three weeks later, the *Sentinel* devoted more than a full page, including fifteen photographs, to the ceremony at which Cochran was honored. The president of the Brotherhood Crusade, Danny J. Bakewell, Sr., was quoted as saying of Cochran, "He is, in a time when people reflect upon African-American males in a way that is often condescending and shallow, an individual who serves as a tireless warrior against those who would deny justice for all." In February 1995, the very week of his opening statement in the Simpson case, Cochran was honored with a plaque at a Watts park's "Promenade of Prominence Walk of Fame." Taking note of his role in the Simpson case, the article in the *L.A. Watts Times* said that Cochran was "a leader whose task has been likened to Moses demanding that Pharaoh let God's people go."

In the years leading up to the Simpson case, Cochran expanded his racial appeals on behalf of clients beyond the courtroom. He began using the press as well. When he represented singer Michael Jackson in the child-abuse investigation launched by the district attorney's office, Cochran orchestrated a press conference in support of Jackson by a dozen of the top black ministers in Los Angeles. The event was a peculiar one, to say the least. The ministers had never voiced support for Jackson in the past, and the singer, to be sure, had never before been a presence in their lives or churches. But at the widely covered news event, the ministers lashed out at the "prosecution frenzy" surrounding the case—even though Jackson had not been charged with anything and, in fact, never was. Cochran had requested that his own minister, William Epps of the Second Baptist Church, organize the press conference, and his words there could have been Cochran's own. "I would like to think that it's not racially motivated," Epps told the cameras of the investigation of Jackson. "It does seem strange, however."

So the Johnnie Cochran who came to the Simpson case represented a known quantity in Los Angeles legal circles. Hiring Cochran represented the logical next step in the theory of the defense Shapiro had outlined for his circle of lawyer friends the first week after the murders. Cochran had enjoyed a lifetime of success by using the same theme over and over again: that his clients (even a white man like Reginald Denny!) were the victims of official white conspiracies. So it would be with O. J. Simpson. But Cochran gave this theory immeasurably more force than Shapiro or any other white lawyer ever could. It apparently mattered little that Cochran would be investing his vast credibility and reputation in service of a lie. He took the case with the goal of conveying a simple syllogism: Cochran stands for the cause of all African-Americans, therefore Simpson does, too. To do this, Cochran started by casting aside his previous (if private) doubts about Simpson's innocence. As Cochran put it in an interview with Katie Couric on the *Today* show shortly after he was hired, "In the O. J. Simpson case, I think winning takes on the form of him being found not guilty and getting out, because this is one of those cases where, from the very beginning, he said, 'I'm innocent.' "

"And you believe him?" Couric asked.

"And I believe him," Cochran replied. "I believe him. Absolutely."

Couric pursued the issue, asking, "A hundred percent, in your heart, that he is not guilty?"

Cochran was adamant. "In my heart, I believe that, absolutely."

At first, Cochran made a seamless transition onto the defense team. At the arraignment on Friday, July 22—when Simpson said he was "absolutely, 100 percent not guilty"—Judge Cecil Mills announced that he had assigned the case for trial to Judge Lance A. Ito, of the superior court. Because Ito's wife, Margaret York, served as a captain in the LAPD, Mills gave the defense the opportunity to have Ito removed from the case with no questions asked. But Cochran and Shapiro agreed that Ito would suit them fine. Ito brought the parties together in his courtroom for the first time the next Monday.

The defense team regarded Ito as about as good a choice as they could expect. Since Jerry Brown had left the governorship of California in 1978, the Republicans who followed him had named a steady stream of conservative law-and-order ex-prosecutors to the state's trial and appellate courts. Ito seemed to reflect this trend. After spending virtually his entire professional career as a deputy district attorney in Los Angeles, he had been named to the municipal court bench in 1988 by Governor George Deukmejian and promoted to the superior court the following year. But unlike many of his colleagues, Ito had a reputation as a judge who could be reasoned with, one who would at least listen to the arguments of defense lawyers—especially these defense lawyers. Cochran and Shapiro knew him well. During his own stint in the D.A.'s office, Cochran had supervised Ito. Shapiro, ever the networker, had also crossed paths with the judge any number of times over the years.

When, shortly before the murders in Brentwood, the Century City Bar Association named Shapiro "Defense Counsel of the Year" for 1994, Ito sent him a note calling the award "well deserved and overdue." (Shapiro explained to F. Lee Bailey that he had approved the judge "because Lance Ito loves me.")

Ito was also known as an energetic judge, and this was important, because speed remained the defense's objective. Both Shapiro and Cochran saw Simpson's popularity as a dwindling asset, and they viewed an expeditious trial as imperative. The judge obliged by scheduling jury selection to begin sixty days hence, on September 20. By California standards, Ito's schedule amounted to warp speed; in ordinary circumstances it often took one or two *years* for a complex murder case to come to trial. But these delays invariably came at the request of defendants who hoped the cases against them would grow stale. In the Simpson trial, by contrast, the defense lawyers believed that additional time would only allow the prosecution to refine its scientific evidence against their increasingly unpopular client.

For their part, Clark and Hodgman's strategy never changed much after the preliminary hearing. Using Kato Kaelin and Allan Park, they would prove first that Simpson had had the time and the opportunity to commit the crimes—establishing, through Kaelin, that Simpson was alone after about 9:40 P.M. on June 12, and showing, through Park, that the house at Rockingham appeared empty between 10:35 and 10:55 P.M. Before the jury, the prosecutors would add the specter of domestic violence to establish Simpson's motive. The core of their case would always remain the physical evidence tying Simpson to the murder scene and the victims to him: hairs and fibers, shoe prints, and, above all, blood. The prosecutors regarded the defense's rush to trial as an inconvenience, but by both law and custom, government lawyers almost never seek delays. After charging someone with a serious crime, the theory goes, prosecutors are obligated to put up or shut up. Regardless of when Ito scheduled the trial, Clark and company vowed to be ready.

In the summer months before jury selection, the defense, too, did little more than elaborate on the themes it had struck at the preliminary hearing. Of course, the defense lawyers never had any evidence (or hope of finding evidence) that someone other than Simpson had committed the murders. That left them with one option: chipping away at the believability of the government's case. For this, they had several approaches. First, they would attack the government's chronology—its "time line"—in an attempt to show that Simpson did not have time to commit the murders. Then they would allege that the LAPD had collected the blood and other physical evidence in a shoddy manner, thus reducing the probative value of the tests on that evidence. And the defense team would allege, as Shapiro did in his interview with me, that at least one police officer had engaged in a conscious effort to frame Simpson for the crimes. These approaches all constituted variations on the principal theme of misfeasance, malfeasance, and nonfeasance by the LAPD, and the defense lawyers sought to elaborate on them in their initial appearances before Judge Ito.

As would so often be the case in this trial, each side had both legal and public relations agendas in the early weeks in superior court. Virtually all of the motions the defense filed over the summer asked Judge Ito to redress some perceived wrong that had been inflicted on its client by law enforcement. These ranged from renewing the claim that the LAPD had illegally searched Simpson's home shortly after the murders to asserting that the prosecution had improperly failed to share blood samples with defense-team scientists. As the defense well knew, most of these entreaties were doomed to failure. Republican-appointed judges in California, as well as on the United States Supreme Court, have greatly narrowed the rights of criminal defendants in recent years, and thus judges scarcely ever suppress evidence. But in the unique circumstances of the Simpson case, the defense could still "win" in losing these motions. The court hearings over the summer raised a continual drumbeat of accusations against the police—amplified by intense media coverage—for the benefit of prospective jurors in the case. The defense even made a little progress with Ito. Although the judge declined to suppress the fruits of the police search of Simpson's house on Rockingham, Ito excoriated Detective Vannatter in making his ruling. He said that Vannatter's error-filled affidavit (in which he wrote that the substance on Simpson's Bronco was confirmed to be blood and that O.J. had gone to Chicago unexpectedly) was "at least reckless"—words that the defense was only too pleased to see widely reported in the news media.

The defense lawyers also brought an ample load of cynicism to their early pleas before Judge Ito. Immediately after the arraignment, for example, they filed an "emergency" motion asking Ito to suspend all prosecution DNA tests on the blood in the case. They said they wanted a portion of all the samples so that defense DNA experts could conduct their own tests on the evidence. The issue raised difficult technical questions about how much blood the various laboratories needed to perform the different DNA tests, and Ito was plainly feeling his way as he went along, admitting at one point that he was "a political science major who never set foot on the south side of the campus [where the laboratories are] at UCLA." Still, after days of complex hearings over what became known as the "split" issue, Ito reached a reasonable accommodation for both sides. The prosecution could conduct its tests as scheduled, but to the extent it was possible, the judge ordered that the government reserve 10 percent of each sample for the defense to do its own DNA experiments.

Months later, however, it became clear that, for all its anguished demands for samples of the blood, the defense never did do any of its own refined DNA testing. Raising the "split" issue was simply another excuse to portray its client as a victim of official misconduct, a mistreated defendant denied access to the evidence in the case. Indeed, from this small episode, one can reasonably conclude that the defense lawyers did not want the blood at the crime scene tested because they knew what the results would be.

|||||

By summer both sides had largely set their basic trial strategies. Each side then turned, in its own way, to the next and most important challenge on the horizon: how to identify and select the jury that would be the most receptive to its case.

As ever, Shapiro went for the best person he could find. He hired Jo-Ellan Dimitrius, a jury consultant based near Los Angeles, whose previous clients included the defendants in the McMartin Preschool case and the police officers accused of beating Rodney King. (As for her work for King's assailants, Shapiro worried about results, not ideological purity.) Shapiro asked Dimitrius to conduct all the surveys and focus groups she needed to, and then promised to consult her closely when it came time to select the jurors for trial.

The prosecutors, in contrast, followed a more tortuous route to jury selection. Their efforts in this critical area reflected, in microcosm, the problems that beset them from the start—the consequences of their starchy insistence on high ethical standards; their arrogance; their recurring bad luck; and above all, their inability to surmount the ever-present problem of race. In particular, jury selection showcased Marcia Clark's peculiar mix of virtues and flaws, which in the end combined to render her and her colleagues spectators to the trial unfolding around them.

Shortly before jury selection began, the prosecution honorably forfeited one advantage it might have had as the case proceeded: Garcetti's office announced it would not seek the death penalty. "Death-qualified" jurors, as they are known—that is, jurors who have stated that they are willing at least to consider imposing the death penalty—are well known for being more likely to convict as well. As a defendant without an extensive criminal past, Simpson was an unlikely candidate for the death penalty, but the prosecution did yield an important strategic advantage when it excluded even the possibility.

In ordinary circumstances, government lawyers do little to prepare for jury selection in a criminal trial. Prosecutors' offices almost never have the funds to hire jury consultants, so the lawyers generally rely on their experience and gut feelings to do the best they can. All along, Marcia Clark thought a business-as-usual approach would best serve her team. One can see why. Prosecutors tread on dangerous ground when they make decisions about jurors based on generalizations about their ethnic backgrounds—which is, after all, the reason jury consultants conduct surveys and focus groups. In crude form, such actions by prosecutors are flatly unconstitutional. Since the *Batson v. Kentucky* case, in 1986, the Supreme Court has held that prosecutors may not systematically remove prospective jurors from a criminal case solely because of their race. *Batson* and some cases that have followed it leave prosecutors considerable leeway on what constitutes racial bias in jury selection, but the subject still gives honorable prosecutors pause. By the summer of 1994, public surveys had already shown profound racial differences in attitudes about the Simpson case. Why, Clark wondered, bring that sort of divisiveness right into the prosecution camp?

Besides, Clark had her own ideas about jury selection. While trying many cases in the Criminal Courts Building, she felt she had always developed a special rapport with one group in particular: black women. In case after case, she won their smiles, their nods, their sympathy. After trials, Clark would often speak to jurors, and the ones who always gave her the warmest greetings were the African-American women. She even had a fan club of sorts, a group of former jurors, all black women, who wrote her letters and kept in touch well after their trials had ended. Clark felt that these women—*her* women—would respond to the story she would tell of Nicole Brown Simpson's death. After all, African-American women were disproportionately the victims of domestic violence. They would understand how Simpson's violence had built inexorably to murder. Clark didn't need any outsider to tell her what she felt in her trial lawyer's bones.

Yet a consultant did appear—and not just any jury consultant. In 1976, Donald Vinson was a respected if obscure marketing professor at the University of Southern California when he received a surprise phone call from lawyers at Cravath, Swaine & Moore. The New York firm was representing IBM in a complex antitrust case, and they wondered if Vinson might apply some of his work in the social sciences to the art of jury selection. Spurred by Cravath, Vinson invented a new field. Using the most sophisticated research techniques—including focus groups, survey research, and even the hiring of "shadow jurors," who would sit in court and give lawyers day-by-day critiques of their efforts—Vinson transformed the way well-heeled trial lawyers prepare for court. He quit USC, founded a company called Litigation Sciences, developed it into the leader in the field, and sold out for many millions of dollars to the Saatchi and Saatchi advertising agency in 1987. When his non-compete agreement expired in 1989, Vinson started from scratch and created a new firm, DecisionQuest, which he promptly transformed into the new industry leader. By the time of the Simpson trial, Vinson employed two hundred people and had an itch for bigger challenges and a wider stage.

Actually, the hankering had started a little earlier. Vinson had been appalled in January 1994 when the first trial of Lyle and Erik Menendez had ended in hung juries. Immodestly perhaps, Vinson felt this failure of the district attorney's office reflected, at least in part, government prosecutors' lack of access to experts like himself. Vinson felt that even a temporary escape of such obviously guilty figures as the Menendez brothers brought the whole judicial system into disrepute. He and his friend John Martel, a prominent civil lawyer in San Francisco, discussed the situation and decided to volunteer their services for the next Menendez trial. In March 1994, the two men met with Gil Garcetti and David Conn, who would be leading the retrial, and the prosecutors accepted Vinson's offer. After an initial round of focus groups, both Garcetti and Conn immediately became boosters of Vinson's work, and they touted him to Clark. Vinson was game for another pro bono project, and Clark reluctantly agreed to see what he had to offer.

The first test came on July 23, 1994, when Vinson organized a focus group at the Plaza Research Center, an anonymous-looking office building near Los Angeles International Airport. Decision-Quest recruited ten "jurors" for what Vinson called a "mock trial." Clark had videotaped a twenty-minute version of her opening statement in the trial, and Bill Hodgman, play-acting the part of one of Simpson's lawyers, had taped a statement on behalf of the defense. The plan was to play both tapes for the "jurors" and listen to their reactions. (Skittish about the process, Clark thought the experiment might leak and asked that her tape not be played. Instead, while the mock jury waited, John Martel listened to Clark's tape and then paraphrased it for a camera, so the group actually heard Martel for the prosecution and Hodgman for the defense.)

Clark, Hodgman, and Garcetti watched the mock jurors from behind a pane of one-way glass, and what they heard astonished them. DecisionQuest had recruited a diverse panel—five men and five women; six whites and four blacks—and everyone expected some ethnic correlation to the results. But the racial divide, in this test at least, was stark and overwhelming: whites for conviction, blacks for acquittal. What was more, the partisans on both sides held their views passionately. Following the initial votes, Vinson spoke with the black panel members in an effort to learn what might change their minds about Simpson's guilt. As an experiment, he asked them to change several assumptions about the facts of the case: first, to assume that it was 100 percent certain the blood to the left of the shoe prints at Bundy was that of O. J. Simpson; second, that scientific tests on the glove at the crime scene positively identified the skin oils on the inside as Simpson's. This was practically a directed verdict of guilty. No matter. Three of the four blacks *still* said they would vote not guilty.

There was more. Vinson questioned the black women on the panel closely about the issue of domestic violence. He asked them to assume that Simpson had beaten Nicole and that he had threatened and stalked her. Their reactions were uniform:

"In every relationship, there's always a little trouble."

"People get slapped around. That just happens."

"It doesn't mean he killed her."

Clark didn't buy it—not the process, not the answers, and not Vinson. A doughy man with trim gray hair, a Ph.D. who liked being called "Doctor," Vinson spoke with a quiet assurance that his words were worth the millions that major corporations and law firms paid for them. Clark found him a condescending snob. Vinson thought little better of Clark, regarding her as a narrow-minded civil servant who preferred courthouse bromides to solid information. Neither was entirely wrong about the other, but Clark's failure to separate the message from the messenger would have disastrous consequences for her case.

Prodded by Garcetti, who remained a fan of Vinson's, Clark agreed to a more detailed follow-up to the July 23 focus group. Understanding Clark's fear of leaks in the frenzied atmosphere of Los Angeles, Vinson proposed that they move their next research session out of the city, to a place that was demographically comparable to the site of the trial. Phoenix seemed about right, he said. Vinson would even arrange for a private plane to whisk Hodgman and Clark out of the city secretly so they wouldn't have to worry about reporters learning of their trip. The prosecutors passed on the plane, but agreed to go to Phoenix and hear more about how prospective jurors might react to their case.

Clark and Hodgman met at the Burbank airport late on the afternoon of August 18 for the short flight to Phoenix. (Vinson and his colleagues flew from a different airport.) Rushing to catch the flight, Clark came to an abrupt stop in front of the metal detector.

"Oh my God," she said. "I've got my gun."

In light of her high public profile, the detectives on the Simpson case had prevailed upon Clark to start carrying a gun. At the airport, she had forgotten all about it until the last minute. Hodgman ran ahead to the gate to try to hold their flight. Airport security personnel were not amused at her oversight, and their representative told Clark she would have to fill out a federal form if she wanted to be allowed to travel by air. People at the airport scurried to find the right paperwork, but no one could find it in time for Clark and Hodgman to catch their flight. They stewed in an airport lounge, and when the official with the form arrived, he was followed by a reporter and photographer from the *National Enquirer*. By the time Clark and Hodgman were able to get on another flight and make it to their hotel in the suburb of Peoria, they were frazzled and exhausted, and now beset by a full squadron of journalists demanding to know what business they had in Phoenix.

What should we do? they asked themselves.

"Bag it," Clark said. "The press'll be all over this thing tomorrow. Let's just go home."

John Martel, who got along better with Clark than Vinson did, tried to talk to her. Perhaps they could salvage at least part of the project, he suggested. Instead of having the lawyers make presentations to the mock jurors, Vinson proposed that they should simply ask the participants questions about what they thought about the case so far. That way, there would be nothing to leak. It would just be a survey of the impact of the media on the case. Reluctantly, Clark agreed to listen.

The following day's session involved seventeen mock jurors again divided more or less evenly along gender and racial lines. As in the first focus group, the racial division of opinions was nearly absolute, with black women backing the defendant most intensely. Detailed questions revealed even more shocking results. Vinson asked the panel members to rate everyone in the case on a scale of 1 to 10 based on how much sympathy they felt for them. From the black women, O. J. Simpson received all 9's and 10's. Nicole Brown Simpson—a murder victim!—scored a 7, a 5, and a 3. Then the questions turned to the mock jurors' impressions of the lawyers. The black participants almost uniformly described Robert Shapiro as "smart" and "clever," while the reactions to Clark were scathing:

"Shifty."

"Strident."

"Bitch."

"Bitch."

"Bitch."

Marcia Clark had to sit in an adjacent conference room and listen, on a closed-circuit video feed, as black women—*her* jurors, she had thought—described her in these unflattering terms.

As if the situation could get any worse, several of these mock jurors spent much of the following week giving interviews—on the *Today* show, CNN, and a variety of other media outlets—and discoursing at length on how unpersuasive the prosecution's "evidence" had been. Martel was beside himself, desperate to respond in public that there hadn't even been any presentation of evidence by the prosecution at the focus group. But Garcetti's spokeswoman, Suzanne Childs, preferred to say nothing. Thus, the impression persisted that there had been some sort of prosecution failure in Phoenix.

With jury selection just a few weeks away, the prosecutors had to take stock. Between the two focus groups and a general telephone survey conducted in Los Angeles by DecisionQuest, there certainly had been no ambiguity in the results: African-Americans remained devoted to Simpson's innocence, with black women his strongest supporters. According to the telephone poll, black men were three times more likely than black women to believe that Simpson was guilty. Moreover, black women felt overwhelmingly that even if Simpson had engaged in a pattern of domestic violence against his ex-wife, that didn't make him appreciably more likely to have killed her. According to the telephone poll, a full 40 percent of black women felt that the use of physical force was appropriate in a marriage. And black women especially could not abide Marcia Clark.

Vinson asked why. Evaluating the data in social science terms, he came up with what he called a "psychosexual" reason for the results. He said that African-Americans viewed O. J. Simpson as a symbol of black male virility in a predominantly white world. He was handsome, masculine, likable, and charming. As a consequence, according to Vinson, black women in particular saw Clark as a "castrating bitch" who was attempting to demean this symbol of black masculinity. Everything about Clark was harsh—her demeanor, her clothes, even her rapid-fire speech, which Vinson felt intimidated those of lesser educational backgrounds. Vinson ran his theories by Clark, and the consultant even volunteered some personal advice for the prosecutor. Vinson said that Clark might want to soften up her appearance for the trial—with a new hairstyle, fewer business suits, more dresses.

On the eve of jury selection, Marcia Clark sat down and thought it over—the focus groups, the telephone survey, the jargon-filled demographic analyses, and even the fashion hints. Then she made up her mind: Don Vinson could go to hell. She was going with her gut.

|||||

Lance Ito forgot to turn on his microphone when he took the bench on Monday, September 26, 1994—a small sign that the usually meticulous judge had the jitters on the first day of jury selection. It had been a considerable accomplishment on his part to start jury selection on time, but he—like everyone else in the courtroom—knew that the decisions made now would dwarf all others in importance.

Ito had arranged for a huge pool of potential jurors—more than nine hundred—to be brought forward for the Simpson case. The prosecution had asked that the jury in this case be sequestered, a request that had become almost customary in recent years for the highest-profile cases. Sequestration would mean that the jurors and alternates would be almost entirely cut off from the outside world for the duration of the trial. They would live in near isolation, with all but their conjugal contacts monitored for exchanges of information about the case. Not surprisingly, many potential jurors refuse to sit in sequestered juries, especially for trials anticipated to be long. Because Los Angeles County pays jurors a stipend of just five dollars a day, only retirees or mid- or low-level employees of large institutions—the kind that continue to pay employees during jury service—were likely to agree to serve. Conventional wisdom among lawyers holds that a sequestered jury is a convicting jury, but this case, as ever, presented unusual complications. Sequestered juries also tend to scare off most people, leaving only those with a strong incentives—or big agendas—to serve. In this case, the most passionate partisans tended to favor the defense.

The prosecutors hoped the judge might signal to the potential jurors that for all the hoopla surrounding the Simpson trial, it was, in fact, just another criminal case. But Ito, carried away with the excitement of the moment, did just the opposite when the large group assembled before him. "I have never seen a case quite as unusual as this case," the judge said. "This is perhaps the most important decision you will make in your own personal life." Ito thought the candidates deserved fair warning of what might be in store for them. As the first group sat before him in the Criminal Courts Building's large jury-assembly room, Ito told them that the trial was expected to go "through the end of February of 1995." (He was off by more than seven months.)

The nine hundred potential jurors had filled out brief questionnaires for this first portion of jury selection, called the "hardship" phase. They provided basic demographic information about themselves and supplied reasons why service in the case would be a "hardship" to them. This initial group provided a fair approximation of the overall jury pool in the downtown Los Angeles area. They were roughly equal in men and women, 28.1 percent African-American, 37.9 percent Caucasian, with the remainder divided among Latinos, Asians, and others. (Overall, the downtown jury pool is about 31 percent African-American and 30 percent Caucasian.) The potential jurors were a fairly well educated group; nearly three quarters of them had some college or were college graduates.

The purpose of the hardship phase was to determine which jurors had irreconcilable personal conflicts with jury service and which ones would go on to the next round of inquiries. As it turned out, Ito was a soft touch: Anyone who wanted out got out. Of the 219 potential jurors who arrived on the first day, Ito excused 90 solely on the basis of their questionnaires. Most said that their employers would not pay them during long jury service or that their personal situations made such service impossible. Moving to the next phase, the judge and the lawyers retreated into a small anteroom to question those jurors whose hardship answers were ambiguous. Deirdre Robertson, Ito's clerk, drew the first juror number to be questioned.

"Number . . . thirty-two," she said.

Ito smiled, for this had been Simpson's number throughout his football career. "I don't know if this is an omen," the judge quipped, and the defendant eagerly nodded his head.

The hardship phase of jury selection took only four days, less than anyone had expected. To Ito's surprise, many jurors seemed downright anxious to be jurors on the case. By Thursday, September 29, the judge had assembled the pool of 304 willing citizens from which the 12 jurors and 12 alternates would be selected.

||||||

The lawyers on both sides spent the following ten days poring over the prospective jurors' answers to a much more elaborate questionnaire that Judge Ito had given them. He had asked both sides to submit questions to him, and in an ominous harbinger of how he would conduct the trial, the judge basically threw up his hands and let both sides ask pretty much anything they wanted. This laissez-faire approach yielded a monstrosity—an eighty-page list of 294 questions, to be answered in writing, many of them calling for essay-type responses. The questionnaire began with reasonable-sounding inquiries about prospective jurors' employment and prior jury service, but it quickly descended into an absurd and insulting fishing expedition: "Have you ever asked a celebrity for an autograph?" "Have you ever known anyone who had problems leaving an abusive relationship?" "What do you think is the main cause of domestic violence?" (Three lines were provided for an answer.) "Have you ever dated a person of a different race?" "How important would you say religion is in your life?" "Have you or anyone close to you undergone an amniocentesis?" "Have you ever written a letter to the editor of a newspaper or magazine?" "Are there any charities or organizations to which you make donations?" "If not currently a fan, have you in the past ever been a fan of the USC Trojans football team?" "Does playing sports build an individual's character?"

As the prosecutors digested the vast collection of answers, they learned one important thing: The hardship process had acted like a vacuum cleaner for educated, white, and male jurors—all groups that had showed a predisposition in favor of the prosecution. A little less than one third of the original pool of nine hundred consisted of African-Americans. In the group that remained in the process at the questionnaire stage, their number jumped to about one half. And three quarters of the black prospective jurors were female—the most pro-Simpson group of all.

The lawyers had their chance to meet the jurors face-to-face on October 12, when individual questioning of prospective jurors—that is, voir dire—began in Judge Ito's courtroom. According to Proposition 115, the law-and-order voter initiative passed in 1990, voir dire in criminal trials was supposed to be conducted principally by the judge, not the lawyers. This is the custom in American federal courts, and it not only speeds the process considerably, it also prevents the lawyers from using their questions to advertise the arguments they will be making during the trial. But in another disturbing preview of what was to come, Ito caved in and let the lawyers do the asking—and the puffing. Clark, for example, asked many jurors whether "the celebrity of the defendant would affect your ability to render a verdict."

One theme of the defense lawyers' stood out. In question after question, Robert Shapiro and Johnnie Cochran made sure that the jurors knew this was a case about race.

"Now, with regard to other aspects of answers that you gave us," Cochran said to a white candidate on the first day, "on the question of whether or not you felt the issue of discrimination against African-Americans, you said you felt it was a serious one, is that correct?"

"Yeah . . ." the man said.

"All right," Cochran went on. "Now, with regard to the whole question of race, interracial marriage, you felt you had no problems with that, is that correct?"

And so it went . . . day after day. Again, to Ito's surprise, many jurors seemed to be auditioning, rather than shrinking from the prospect of service on the case. Many seemed to be lying, too. In

Vinson's telephone survey, about 60 percent of the respondents had said they had more or less made up their minds about whether O. J. Simpson was guilty of the two murders. But among those who answered the questionnaires, only 23 percent said they had. Either the prospective jurors were an usually impartial group, or—more likely—they were playing coy in order to slip through the process.

In jury selection, as in the rest of the case, Simpson's lawyers coordinated their courtroom and public relations strategies. On October 27, for example, Hodgman sharply questioned an elderly black man whose answers demonstrated that he had a lengthy catalogue of grievances against the LAPD. Any responsible prosecutor would have used this juror's voir dire to lay the groundwork for a request to have him excused for cause. And that is what Hodgman did, although the process clearly irritated the juror, who said to the even-keeled prosecutor, "You are sort of riling me." The defense, however, launched a coordinated media attack on Hodgman. Immediately after the day's session, Cochran ventured from Ito's ninth-floor courtroom up to the media headquarters on the twelfth floor, where he held an impromptu news conference. "We're really concerned about the tenor of the questions and the way they go after certain jurors," Cochran said. As if the point could be missed, while Cochran was discoursing upstairs, Shapiro addressed the reporters who were assembled in the courthouse lobby. Of Hodgman's questioning, Shapiro said, "It implies an insidious effort to try to get black jurors removed for cause because they are black, because they have black heroes, and because O. J. Simpson is one of them. There's no other reason." The lawyers' salvos led the local news that evening, and they paid off as well in the front-page headline on the next day's *Los Angeles Times*: PROSECUTORS TARGETING BLACK JURORS, SIMPSON TEAM SAYS.

Still, the case was making progress of sorts, as the parties had a chance to question a few jurors each day. Then forward momentum came to an abrupt halt—and the case nearly collapsed altogether—thanks to the literary labors of one diminutive woman.

|||||

There is surely no single appropriate way to mourn the loss of a friend. It is fair to say that Faye Resnick coped with the death of

Nicole Brown Simpson in a way that reflected Resnick's bizarre and chaotic life. She chose to grieve with a psychic, who came up with some useful career advice as well as spiritual succor. Talking with me shortly before Simpson's trial began, Resnick said, "When I went to see a psychic after Nicole was murdered, the woman gave me a message from Nicole. . . . The psychic said, 'You will be writing a book. Nicole wants you to be faithful to your heart. She wants you to call it as you see it.' "

At the time of the trial, Faye Resnick was thirty-seven years old, a native Californian with a trim build and orange hair. When we met, she was wearing bangles on both arms and three rings on her left hand, including one on her thumb. As the ex-wife of Paul Resnick, a wealthy Los Angeles businessman, she dabbled in charity projects and worked hard on her appearance. Nicole's advice from beyond the grave actually fit well with Resnick's needs. Faced with a dwindling divorce settlement and an expensive lifestyle, Faye needed the money a book deal could provide. The milieu in which she and Nicole lived is neatly summarized in a brief sentence in the book she eventually did write: "Almost every woman I know has had breast implants."

Resnick and Nicole met in 1990. They became close friends after Faye separated from Paul Resnick in early 1991. Resnick became friendly with O.J., too, as he and Nicole pursued their on-again, off-again relationship in 1993 and 1994. After the murder, however, she became convinced that O.J. had killed Nicole, and she was scathing on the subject. According to Resnick, "You would go to his house, and the children were not able to play in the house." She added that the kids were not even allowed in the kitchen at certain times, because O.J. and his housekeeper couldn't stand the mess they would make. "O.J.'s a double Cancer, I'm a double Cancer," she said. "I get it—I don't like messes—but kids are kids." Resnick implicitly blamed the stress of mediating between O.J. and Nicole for the recurrence of her own drug problem. In the decade before the murders, she did two stints at the Betty Ford rehabilitation center, and in June 1994, the week before Nicole's murder, she checked into the Exodus Recovery Center, in Marina del Rey. Shortly after the murders, Resnick said, she began to fear that she would be killed by O.J.'s loyalists.

Within a week or so of the murders, Resnick reported her gathering fears to Arthur Barens, a lawyer she knew through fundraising efforts for the Beverly Hills school system. Barens helped Resnick through her first meetings with the prosecutors in the case, and as they talked further at other meetings, the idea of a book came to the surface. "The book idea got started because she wanted to do something to be of service to the Simpson children and battered women," Barens said. "She told me at the same time that she had maintained a diary about what was going on between O.J. and Nicole. She was afraid for her well-being. I told her, for her safety, to record on tape what she remembered." Resnick made some recordings and gave them to the lawyer. Barens might have protected Resnick's safety merely by placing her tapes in a safe-deposit box; instead, he turned to Warren Cowan, a public relations executive, for advice on how to make use of them.

Cowan put Barens in touch with his client Michael Viner, a former record company executive, who had founded Dove, a company devoted principally to audiobooks, a decade earlier with his wife, the actress Deborah Raffin.

Viner quickly signed Resnick to a six-figure advance and then looked for a collaborator for her. "I knew Mike Walker in passing, and I had seen him on *Nightline* and *Larry King Live*," Viner explained. "And I sought him out." Shortly after the contracts were signed, Viner sent Walker and Resnick to a ski chalet he owns in Stowe, Vermont, where he gave them three and a half weeks to produce a manuscript, in secrecy. The partnership had its strains. According to Walker, "At one point, I telephoned Viner and said, 'Look, this woman is driving me nuts. She wants cappuccino.' The next day, a cappuccino machine arrived by Federal Express."

Ultimately, however, the pair produced the manuscript of what became the book *Nicole Brown Simpson: The Private Diary of a Life Interrupted*. Resnick and Walker's portrait presented Nicole as a brainless, sex-obsessed young woman whose banality was exceeded only by that of her ex-husband. For example, Nicole was portrayed as having an enthusiasm for fellatio with virtual strangers—a practice Resnick called the "Brentwood hello." More significant as far as the trial was concerned, Resnick depicted Simpson as an insanely jealous former spouse who openly discussed his thoughts of murdering Nicole. In the book, Resnick quoted Simpson as saying such things as "I can't take this, Faye, I can't take this. I mean it. *I'll kill that bitch.*" (When I asked Resnick if she had any literary influences, she said, "I wasn't inspired by a book to do this. The movie that inspired me was *The Pelican Brief.*")

The irony of Resnick's book is that notwithstanding the accusations against O.J., it amounted to a generous gift to the defendant—and another example of the ill fortune of the prosecutors in this case. With her history of drug abuse, Resnick would have made a dicey prosecution witness in the best of circumstances. Still, if she had simply come forward after the murder and told her story to the police, the prosecutors probably would have called her to the stand. But the book made Resnick anathema to Clark and Hodgman; it represented the cash-for-trash problem writ large. Resnick undoubtedly had close ties to both O.J. and Nicole, and many, if not most, of her accusations had the ring of truth about them. But her conspicuous cashing in on her access to the principals would have given the defense too much ammunition in their cross-examination. Both during and after the trial, Resnick emerged as one of Simpson's most vocal public accusers. But in fact her greed—and that of her publisher—made her an accomplice to O.J.'s acquittal.

Aiming for maximum publicity, Viner and Resnick decided to release *Private Diary* in the middle of jury selection—on October 17. The news media reacted predictably, hyping Resnick's accusations against Simpson. On the day it came out, Resnick's book actually rated rather modestly on the Simpson-news Richter scale—bigger than my Fuhrman story but smaller, certainly, than the release of the tape of Nicole's plaintive calls to 911. What made this story different was that it broke when Lance Ito was in charge of the case—and his reaction to it revealed much about him and the future course of the trial.

||||||

Lance Ito thought a great deal about the news media. In a casual aside in court one day, Judge Ito remarked that he read five newspapers a day. In a later order to potential jurors about their television-watching habits, he specifically named, apparently off the top of his head, twenty-five different programs that were off limits, including *Marilu, Leeza, Jenny Jones, Sally Jessy Raphaël, Oprah, Donahue, Geraldo,* the news on MTV, and something called *Press Box* on a network called Prime Ticket. During his off hours, the judge wore a *Today* show baseball cap. In the middle of jury selection, Ito even gave a much-hyped interview to Tricia Toyota of KCBS television in Los Angeles. Though the judge said nothing sensational in his conversations with Toyota, Ito definitely complicated jurors' efforts to avoid news coverage of the trial; he even had to dismiss some potential jurors because they had seen parts of his TV interview. Throughout the trial, Ito would often delay court sessions so that he could usher well-known media figures, like Geraldo Rivera, and the occasional movie star, into his chambers for private chats.

As a result of Ito's media obsession, the import of the Resnick book eluded him. The sensible course would have been to ignore *Private Diary* and, if the subject came up at all, to remind the jurors that they were to rely only on evidence presented in court. Like every other sensation in the case, Resnick would have faded, too. But Ito couldn't leave Faye Resnick alone. On Tuesday morning, October 18—without even being asked by the parties—Ito suspended jury selection for forty-eight hours, he told the prospective jurors, because of "the publication of a book that has caused the Court great concerns about the ability of Mr. Simpson to get a fair trial. I need to look into the ramifications." The judge even wrote to the heads of the major news networks and asked them to cancel interviews they had scheduled with Resnick. (CNN complied, but Connie Chung's interview with Resnick on CBS went ahead.) Ito's decision to stop jury selection prompted a predictable reaction. It fueled intense curiosity about the book in the public—and probably in the prospective jurors as well. Thanks to the push from Ito, *Private Diary* rocketed to the number one spot on the *New York Times* best-seller list, passing Pope John Paul II's *Crossing the Threshold of Hope.* (As for Resnick's purported desire to help the Simpson children, Dove donated $10,000 to the foundation Nicole's parents established in her memory. This largesse amounted to about one cent for each of the one million or so copies of *Private Diary* that were sold.)

Surprised as anyone by Ito's reaction, the defense lawyers tried to use the Resnick crisis to provoke the judge into abandoning the case entirely. In a private conference in chambers on Wednesday morning, October 19, Shapiro made a rambling plea for Ito to do one or more of the following: dismiss all charges against Simpson; find Barens, Viner, and Dove Books guilty of obstruction of justice; sanction the district attorney's office for failing to prevent publication of the book; and/or delay the trial for a year and release the defendant on bail. With the exception of the request for a continuance, all of Shapiro's demands were absurd, but Ito patiently waited out Shapiro's harangue. As for bail, Shapiro said Simpson's attempt to flee on June 17 should not be held against him. "He has now had time to reflect upon this case, to reflect upon the evidence, and to be in a place where he wants to contest these charges in a court of law, and he wants to clear his name," Shapiro said.

Clark burned when she heard the defense lawyer complain about how his client was suffering from the pretrial publicity. "The defense has also leaked, as the Court is very well aware, in a very hideous and damaging way," Clark said in characteristic sputtering indignation. "They have attempted to speak of Mark Fuhrman with the most vicious of allegations concerning racism, one of the most inflammatory charges that could possibly be made. . . . They have attempted to capitalize on it . . . again in the questionnaire with every question posed concerning the issue of racial issues and racism. The defendant is again playing a race card while denying they're playing a race card, a very subtle game, but a very dangerous one for the People, because the officer who found the key piece of damaging evidence they have attempted to discredit in the most hideous of ways."

Shapiro hated being confronted with his own fingerprints on the racial controversies in the case. As always, he wanted things both ways. He wanted to use race to get Simpson acquitted, but he never wanted to admit that this was what he was doing. "Regarding the race issue," Shapiro said, "I have stood before you, I have stood before the American public, and said race is not and will not be an issue in this case. I still stand by that. Credibility will be an issue in this case. Regarding the article in *The New Yorker*," Shapiro went on, reacting to what Clark had said, "I was assured that it was going to be a photo essay . . . pictures only, no cap-tions." This was not true; I'd never said a word to Shapiro about how our interview might be illustrated. Shapiro went on before the judge: "Jeff Toobin's article came out, and I was shocked to find my picture there by innuendo suggesting that I had somehow made derogatory remarks toward Detective Fuhrman. That is not true. In fact, a careful reading of that article as well as an analysis by journalists have the article saying that was a theory that may possibly be explored by the defense."

This monologue by Shapiro was more than Cochran could take. He had been on the case for about four months at this point, and thus far he had carefully deferred to Shapiro as lead counsel. But Shapiro's desire to finesse the race issue—that is, to call Fuhrman a racist and then deny that race mattered in the case—appalled Cochran. Over these four months, Cochran had spent more time with Simpson than Shapiro had, and the black lawyer knew he would be taking a major, if not the lead, role when the trial began. Cochran wanted race front and center in the case, and he wanted to let Ito and the prosecutors know that he wasn't about to apologize for it, either.

"I just want to say something about this 'race card,'" Cochran interjected, beginning a monologue that could have served as a personal credo. "I've been trying cases for a very long time, both civil and criminal throughout this country, and anybody who doesn't believe that when you have a case like this, when you have a case of murder, that race plays a part in everything—We don't introduce that. . . . There are racial issues. These jurors know it. Everybody knows it. . . . Race plays a part in everything in America. . . .

"Every time people don't believe race plays an issue, they wait until every few years until a major riot comes along and then people say, 'Well, we are not going to take it anymore.' And that's very unfortunate, but that's brought about from people who are totally insensitive to the problems of race in America and the underclass."

For Johnnie Cochran the connections between his millionaire client and "the problems of race in America and the underclass" were so obvious as not to require elaboration.

|||||

But what was the point of all this conversation? Wasn't this supposed to be a legal argument about a motion in a criminal case? It was—

and yet Shapiro was carrying on about his controversies with the media, Clark was raging against Shapiro, and Cochran was discoursing about the black underclass. This was how Lance Ito conducted oral argument, as a sort of group therapy through collective stream of consciousness, a process in which lawyers could talk for as long as they wanted about whatever happened to pop into their heads.

The subject the lawyers were nominally discussing was whether Simpson should be released on bail. As part of a subtle campaign to win Simpson's confidence—in part by showing that he himself had confidence in Simpson—Cochran suggested that Ito speak to the defendant about whether he should be released on bail. So, seated on a chair in front of Ito's desk, Simpson said, "Well, I feel I've been attacked here today. I'm an innocent man. I want to get to a jury. I want to get it over with as soon as I can.

"I have two young kids out there. That's my only concern. In the beginning, when they told me we should slow down, maybe we should slow down. I've read Mr. Gerry Spence's book that you shouldn't rush the jury. I've got two young kids out there that don't have a mother. And I didn't do it. I want to get to the trial as soon as I can get to trial. I've been told by everybody that I know, everybody that I spoke to, it is impossible for me to get a fair trial at this point. They told me maybe we should wait, maybe we should put it off. I can't afford to be away from my kids any longer than I have to be away from my kids at this point.

"Mrs. Clark—Miss Clark said that I was trying to run. Everyone knows that I called my father-in-law. I was not in a frame of mind—I admit that I was not in the right frame of mind at the time I was trying to get to my wife—"

"Your Honor, excuse me," Shapiro broke in, trying to stop his client's increasingly meandering speech.

"I was headed back home," Simpson continued.

Shapiro turned to O.J. "Mr. Simpson, I am telling you that I will not allow you to speak, and I will resign as your lawyer if you continue to do so." This threat, contained in a transcript that the media-savvy Shapiro knew would be released to the public, was actually his way of taking at shot at his rival Howard Weitzman. Weitzman had been criticized for failing to make just this kind of effort to prevent O.J. from talking to the police on June 13. This time Simpson did stop talking.

As he would so often, Ito backed away from the precipice. His fury about the Resnick book cooled, and he agreed to resume jury selection the following day. Ito, of course, did not release Simpson on bail. He tinkered with the process only by stopping the questioning of jurors in front of one another, a change he hoped would encourage candor.

The Resnick controversy did provoke Ito into taking a hard line with the jurors on the question of their own habits of media consumption. After the Resnick book was published, the judge ordered the remaining candidates not to watch any television, read any newspapers or magazines, or set foot in any bookstore. Ito discharged one juror after she admitted to watching videotaped episodes of *Beverly Hills 90210* and *Melrose Place*—no matter that her husband had first deleted all the commercials. A man was excused because he had watched cartoons with his grandson, as was a woman who watched a Barbara Stanwyck movie on television. With each winnowing, the jury pool grew ever more African-American and female.

Finally, the day came when the parties were to exercise their peremptory challenges—which would allow them to remove jurors without having to offer reasons. Each side had twenty challenges. For the defense, Jo-Ellan Dimitrius consulted closely with Shapiro and Cochran; she had been in the courtroom for every moment of jury selection, and the lawyers huddled with her about each decision. Dimitrius had put the key findings from her research in a memorandum to the defense team, "General Considerations for Jury Selection." Under the heading "Most Preferred Jurors," Dimitrius listed the following attributes: "Young; Less Educated; Blue Collar; African-American; No Prior Jury Service; Lower Income." (These were, predictably, the mirror image of Vinson's findings.) Cochran and Shapiro hewed closely to her suggestions.

Marcia Clark had allowed Vinson to sit in court for a single day of jury selection, after which she banished him; she never consulted him again. On December 8, the parties exercised the last of their challenges and accepted a panel of twelve jurors and twelve alternates. Their ethnic profile represented a stunning divergence from the group that had originally reported for duty—or, even more so, from Los Angeles County as a whole. Of the twenty-four jurors, there were fifteen African-Americans, six whites, and three Hispanics—in a county that is just 11 percent black.

Over the many months to come, ten jurors would be replaced by alternates. (Curiously, no alternates were ever removed from the case.) Based on their answers to the questionnaires, the twelve jurors who ultimately decided the case against O. J. Simpson had the following characteristics:

- All twelve were Democrats.
- Two were college graduates.
- Not one juror read a newspaper regularly.
- Nine lived in rented homes; three owned homes.
- Two had supervisory or management responsibilities at work; ten did not.
- Eight regularly watched television-tabloid news shows like *Hard Copy*. (Vinson's polling data had found a predilection for the tabloids a reliable predictor of belief in Simpson's innocence.)
- Five said they or a family member had personally endured a negative experience with law enforcement.
- Five thought it was acceptable to use force on a family member.
- Nine—three quarters of the jury—thought O. J. Simpson was less likely to have murdered his wife because he had excelled at football.

The final group included one African-American man; one Hispanic man; two white women; and eight African-American women.

On the whole, Marcia Clark was pleased, especially with the alternates. She and Bill Hodgman didn't even exercise all twenty of their peremptory challenges.

John Tobin was seventy-two years old and ailing in 1960, but his reputation as a criminal defense lawyer still towered in Massachusetts. That year, as was customary, Tobin was retained in the headline murder case of the day—the killing of Betty Edgerly, a Lowell housewife. Her body had been scooped out of the Merrimack River in pieces, and her grisly demise had given the crime its nickname: the Torso Murder. Her husband, George, was charged with the crime.

The key evidence against George involved a polygraph examination, and John Tobin knew nothing about the new and evolving science of "lie detection." He asked around for an expert, and all he could come up with was the name of a recent law school graduate by the name of Francis Lee Bailey.

Bailey was just twenty-seven years old at the time, the son of a struggling advertising man and a nursery-school teacher. His parents had sent him to prep school and then on scholarship to Harvard, where he drifted on "gentleman's C's" until the United States Navy summoned him for active duty. Bailey trained as a fighter pilot, and developed a lifelong obsession with flying and owning his own planes. As a secondary assignment, Bailey joined his unit's legal office, which transformed his life even more than flight school. He worked as a sort of jack-of-all-trades in the military justice system—trading roles as prosecutor, defense lawyer, investigator, and judge. Bailey developed a specialty in the use of the polygraph, a machine that has always been more favored in the military than in civilian life. When he went to Boston University for law school, Bailey refined his expertise with the polygraph when he moonlighted as an investigator for lawyers preparing for trials. He was still running his little investigation business when he passed the bar examination in November 1960, just a few weeks before he heard from John Tobin.

Tobin confided to the young lawyer that he had been snookered. Polygraph results were generally inadmissible in criminal trials, but Tobin had blundered into allowing the jury to hear that his client had flunked a test administered by a novice examiner. It looked like the entire case would come down to whether the defense could discredit Augustine Lawlor, a local pharmacist who had volunteered his polygraphy services to the police. Tobin was tired and sick, and after speaking to Bailey briefly about the new technology, he had a question for the young lawyer:

"Lee," he said, "would you be willing to come into the case to cross-examine this guy Lawlor? I don't think there's another lawyer in Massachusetts who would recognize a lie detector if you dropped one on him. I think you could help us."

F. Lee Bailey had never before set foot in a courtroom, but he jumped at the chance.

Over the years Bailey has written a great deal about his own career and about criminal law generally; his specialty—in both theory and practice—has been the art of cross-examination. His first law is a simple one: "The cross-examiner's first task is to pin down all that the witness claims to know about the subject and all that he says he doesn't know," Bailey has written. "Until a witness is firmly committed to a definite statement or position, he can parry a question or sidestep it with some kind of explanation."

Bailey's task, thus, was to pin down Lawlor, the polygrapher. The young lawyer brought a whole stack of books about the polygraph to the courtroom and tried to get Lawlor to concede that one of them was authoritative—which would allow Bailey to show how this beginner had violated the book's commands. Lawlor was wise to this game and would not vouch for any of the books. But Bailey—meticulously prepared—had also found the instruction manual for the polygraph machine that Lawlor used, and the witness, trapped, had to admit that the manual did describe the appropriate procedures. Bailey promptly went on to show the jury how the witness had violated many of the manual's commands. The weight of Lawlor's testimony crumbled.

One successful cross-examination does not make a career, but in fitting storybook manner, the elderly Tobin suffered a seizure shortly before final arguments in the Edgerly case. From his sickbed, he asked Bailey to give the summation.

Bailey did, of course, and then went to a neighboring tavern to await the verdict. "I kept fidgeting and drinking Scotch," he wrote of the scene. "I had done little boozing in the service, and I couldn't afford liquor while I was in law school. But I drank like fourteen fishes while the Edgerly jury deliberated. Interestingly enough, the liquor had little effect on me. Perhaps it has something to do with tension. Or with adrenaline. All I know is that most trial lawyers drink. And the good ones can hold their booze."

The verdict came back in less than a day: not guilty. A career—and a legend—was launched.

||||||

When Bailey told the story of the Edgerly case—as he has done in a pair of memoirs and hundreds of conversations—he lingered on his favorite part: his humiliation of the hapless Lawlor. Bailey was only sixty-one during the Simpson trial, but his heavily lidded eyes, which bore the toll of decades of drink and overwork, twinkled as he told of Lawlor's abject surrender. Bailey didn't spend much time worrying about whether George Edgerly actually murdered his wife. That was not Bailey's concern. Proximity to murder can harden a conscience, and so it is with Lee Bailey. He is a consummately cynical man, with an eye only for the bottom line—legal and financial. The guilt or innocence of his clients means little to him. He once wrote, "I prefer cases that offer whopping fees and/or professional challenge." Regularly and rancorously, Bailey has rotated law partners and wives. (He has been married four times.)

For all his stormy and dissolute personal life, insatiable ego, and pervasive misanthropism, one fact stands out about Bailey: He invented the contemporary practice of criminal-defense law. Prior to his emergence into public view in the 1960s, criminal defense had been a vaguely disreputable (and mostly unprofitable) backwater of the legal profession. Bailey changed that. First, he understood the news media and how to manipulate the press for his ends. If Bailey did not invent the impromptu press conference on the courthouse steps, he made the practice his own. He recognized the general importance of appearance. His clothes were tailor-made, and so were his elevator shoes. His lust for the spotlight even led him into questionable ethical territory when, on some cases, he accepted as part of his fee the right to write a book about his work on a case. Bailey also engaged in the kind of exhaustive preparation for cases that, before him, had been the practice of only the best lawyers in the biggest firms. Bailey came of age when the term "superstar" first came into vogue, and he was, without question, the first legal superstar. Within a half dozen years of his debut in the Edgerly case, he had an estate south of Boston and a helicopter for commuting to work. Before he was forty years old, he boasted that he had charged a client a million dollars.

There was no shortage of clients, at any price. Two days after Bailey's first anniversary as a member of the bar, he met Dr. Samuel Sheppard, an osteopath from the Cleveland suburbs who had been charged, like Edgerly, with murdering his wife. It was an even more sensational case—the inspiration for the television series *The Fugitive*—and Bailey spent half a decade winning Sheppard his freedom. Along the way, Bailey traveled on both the high and low roads, as would be his custom. To publicize his attempt to give Sheppard a polygraph test in prison, Bailey went on *The Mike Douglas Show* and demonstrated the technique on a comedienne. In a more exalted setting, the United States Supreme Court, Bailey successfully argued that Sheppard's original conviction should be thrown out because of excessive pretrial publicity. While Sheppard's case was moving through the system, Bailey also represented Albert DeSalvo, the admitted "Boston Strangler." (The court in the DeSalvo case rejected Bailey's argument that DeSalvo should be committed to a mental hospital rather than a prison. DeSalvo was eventually murdered in prison in 1973.) Bailey also won an acquittal for Dr. Carl Coppolino when he was charged with poisoning his lover's husband in New Jersey—but even Bailey couldn't help this doctor when he was charged with, and convicted of, poisoning his wife in Florida.

Bailey's lust for the spotlight—and cash—led him astray in the years after his initial fame. In 1973, he was indicted in a federal mail fraud conspiracy case in Florida, along with his former client Glenn Turner, whose motivational business, known variously as Dare to be Great and Koscot Interplanetary, turned out to be little more than a Ponzi scheme. (Characteristically, Bailey was tempted into working with Turner because the entrepreneur promised the lawyer a new Learjet as his fee.) Thanks to the efforts of his lawyer, Alan Dershowitz, Bailey managed to have the case against him dismissed. After the Turner fiasco, Bailey represented Patricia Hearst, the newspaper heiress, in the case that arose out of her kidnapping by the Symbionese Liberation Army. Bailey's performance was much criticized, and Hearst was convicted of bank robbery. In 1982, Bailey was again charged with a crime, drunk driving, and his friend Robert Shapiro successfully represented him at his San Francisco trial. Not coincidentally, the abuse of alcohol has been a leitmotif of Bailey's professional life. The first line of Bailey's 1975 memoir reads, "Heavy trials make me thirsty." He has long dismissed friends' advice to cut back. "It's my fuel," Bailey has said.

For all his faults and traumas, Bailey continued to try cases throughout the 1980s and 1990s and, for the most part, try them very well. Indeed, of all the lawyers on either side of the Simpson case, Bailey not only had the most experience trying murder cases, he had conducted the most recent murder trial as well. In March 1994, Bailey won an acquittal for one Paul Tanso, charged with a double murder in Boston's North End. Bailey's bravura cross-examination of Tanso's ostensible accomplice marked the turning point in the case. His trademark had not changed since John Tobin summoned him from obscurity almost forty years earlier. For all his fame, Bailey has never been an especially theatrical courtroom performer. He is, rather, a master of preparation. Endlessly, meticulously, remorselessly, Bailey investigates the facts—or hires those who do.

|||||

Immediately after he was retained by O. J. Simpson the week after the murders, Shapiro called Bailey. He treated Bailey with a deference befitting the elder lawyer's exalted history as a defense attorney, but there were tensions from the outset, too. Shapiro couldn't help but enjoy the change in status between them. Twelve years earlier, Bailey had favored Shapiro with the assignment of defending him in the drunk-driving case. Now Shapiro had the kind of case that once would have gone to Bailey as a matter of course. When Bailey appeared on the Simpson case's quasi-official forum, *Larry King Live,* on June 24 to announce that he had joined the defense team, his choice of words reflected the possibility of future trouble between him and Shapiro. "We are close friends," Bailey said of Shapiro. "I'm the godfather of Bob's oldest child. . . . I also want to make perfectly plain the fact that he is the lead counsel in this case, and I am consulting with him."

King asked why Bailey had waited to announce that he was part of the defense team.

"Simply because my recommendation, with all the sniping that someone has been sponsoring, saying Bob Shapiro couldn't handle this case—which I think is silly, because, when I was in trouble, I hired him, and he won my case. And he is the only lawyer in the country allowed to have my name on his letterhead. I thought it would be best to let the case proceed down the road a little bit, until it was firmly established that he had control. He has. He's handled it brilliantly."

In fact, there had been very little sniping about Shapiro's abilities until Bailey raised the issue on the air that night. As for the purported drama about when to make Bailey's announcement, Bailey invented that issue as well. His entire presentation had the air of a man protesting too much; by defending Shapiro, Bailey demeaned him.

Still, Bailey had been giving Shapiro very specific advice since the day he was retained. From his days as a private investigator during law school, Bailey never lost faith in their value. He urged Shapiro to have his own investigators chase down any favorable leads in the case before they grew stale. In comparison, Shapiro had little experience with private eyes (besides Bill Pavelic, whom he had engaged earlier), so he deferred to Bailey on whom to hire and where to send them. Bailey didn't hesitate with his first suggestion: Hire Pat McKenna and send him to Chicago.

McKenna—an affable and hardworking native of that city—lived near Bailey's adopted home of West Palm Beach, Florida, and the two men had occasionally worked together on cases in the past. On hearing from Shapiro and then Bailey, McKenna got himself on the first flight to Chicago to learn what he could about Simpson's brief stay there in the hours after the murders.

McKenna found a chaotic scene at the O'Hare Plaza—Chicago cops, Los Angeles detectives, a swarm of reporters from around the world, not to mention agents from the United States Secret Service who were preparing for an imminent visit by President Clinton to the hotel. Working an old connection with the Chicago police, McKenna managed to find a couple of people who had seen Simpson when he arrived in the city on his red-eye flight from L.A. These witnesses reported that O.J. seemed in relatively good spirits. His demeanor, it seemed, was not that of a killer. It was from tiny threads like these that McKenna—and Bailey—believed reasonable doubt could be knit.

McKenna traveled on to Los Angeles, where the scene at Shapiro's office seemed peculiar in another way. After the intense activity of the prelim, Shapiro had resumed the more sporadic work habits that were his custom. He sent his colleagues cryptic memoranda. For example, on August 18, Shapiro dispatched the following message to all the investigators: "Goldman was fired, allegedly, from the California Pizza Kitchen for giving a customer a free Coke. I will follow up on this." When Shapiro was in his office, the investigators often found him autographing photographs of himself with a gold pen. Shapiro's on-again, off-again presence left his nineteenth-floor office suite, nominally the nerve center of the case, directionless. Part of the reason was friction among the personnel. Shapiro had hired his own investigators, chief among them Bill Pavelic, who had brought the Fuhrman file to the defense's attention. The prickly former LAPD detective did not enjoy outsiders like McKenna treading on his turf. The problems were exacerbated when Shapiro, again at Bailey's suggestion, hired another investigator, John McNally. A gruff ex–New York City cop, McNally had worked with Bailey for more than twenty years. McNally took an immediate dislike to Shapiro and his media-friendly ways. Shortly after McNally arrived, he was looking through some unopened boxes of discovery material when, to his astonishment, he saw a man wandering around the office taking pictures of everyone. It was Roger Sandler, the ubiquitous photographer for *Time* and *Life*. Confidential documents were everywhere, and McNally wanted to throw him out, but Shapiro had given Sandler free rein.

Not wishing to intrude, and preoccupied with his own cases, Bailey initially spent little time in Los Angeles and heard only the complaints of McKenna and McNally. Bailey's one-on-one relationship with Shapiro remained close, and when he was in L.A., Bailey stayed at the Beverly Hills home of Shapiro's best friend, Michael Klein. Bailey tried to mollify his investigators as best he could and brought in another protégé, Howard Harris, a database specialist whose mission was to computerize the voluminous files in the case. At one point, McKenna saw Shapiro only once over a period of several weeks, and that was when he went to Shapiro's house to install his son's computer. "Don't worry," Bailey told his investigators when they complained about Shapiro. "He just has a different style than we do. He's really very bright." For his part, Bailey mostly remained in Florida, although he did arrange for the first volume of his memoirs, *The Defense Never Rests,* to be reissued in paperback. A cheerful new blurb was added to the cover: "O. J. Simpson's Acclaimed Defense Attorney Re-Creates His Most Famous Wife-Murder Cases."

Through the summer, the tensions grew between the Shapiro camp (Pavelic and various part-timers) and the Bailey group (McKenna, McNally, and Harris). Their differences were partly philosophical. Bailey's team favored a minute dissection of the government's case. For example, McKenna and McNally—and sometimes even Bailey—repeatedly walked up and down Bundy Drive knocking on doors in an effort to locate witnesses who could contradict the prosecution's theory of when the dog started barking (and thus when the crime occurred). In this way, Bailey hoped, they could undermine the government's case piece by piece.

In contrast, Pavelic favored an all-or-nothing approach and accordingly spent much of his time chasing theories about the identity of "the real killer." Almost daily, Pavelic would return to Shapiro's office with a breathless new theory. On June 22, for example, Pavelic sent Shapiro a memo that stated, "Rumor has it that Ron's lover discovered his infidelity with Nicole Simpson . . . and killed them both." Pavelic had many other theories, however.

"A house burglar saw the guys who did it!" he announced one day. In his memorandum outlining this theory, Pavelic reported that he had spoken to the burglar, and he "distinctly recalled hearing one of the suspects saying, '**slit the Nigger fucking/lovin bitch.**' " (Unfortunately for the defense, this burglar also claimed that he had seen the murder of Polly Klaas and a hit by John Gotti.)

"Goldman had semen in his ass, and it was a gay hit!" (The autopsy showed no such evidence, and Goldman wasn't gay.)

"A marcher at a Gay Pride parade saw two men covered with blood at a phone booth yelling, 'O.J. is going to pay for what he did to us!' " (Too ridiculous even to consider. "You're a fucking Martian," McNally told Pavelic.)

It didn't matter to Pavelic that his theories usually conflicted with one another. His enthusiasm was boundless—as was his contempt for Bailey's investigators. Howard Harris spent a great deal of time setting up a computer program that was supposed to give the defense team access to virtually every address and phone number in the Los Angeles area. On the day it was completed, Pavelic typed in his own name, and he was delighted when nothing came up—even though he had lived in the same house for decades.

One day late in the summer, Shapiro invited all of the investigators to a screening of *Forrest Gump* held at the Beverly Hills mansion of his friend Robert Evans. Before the lights were lowered, Shapiro rose and addressed the group. "I know I haven't been too friendly. I've been accused of being too aloof," he said. "That's going to change."

McNally, who loved to twit Shapiro, spoke up in response: "That's not the problem, Bob. The problem is no one does any work out here." Shapiro ordered the movie to begin.

By the time jury selection was completed, McNally decided he had had enough. The last straw for him came when Shapiro told the investigators that Skip Taft, O.J.'s business manager, had told him there would have to be pay cuts all around. McNally was supposed to have received $22,500 for his work over the summer, and the bill hadn't yet been paid. Instead of taking a pay cut, John McNally returned to New York for good.

The tensions among the defense investigators only replicated those that had been simmering, albeit more decorously, among the defense lawyers. When Cochran had been hired, there was no question that he ranked behind Shapiro in the unspoken but real hierarchy of the defense team. Yet the issue of Cochran's role in the upcoming trial, which had been left conspicuously unsettled all through the fall, weighed heavily on Shapiro. At one level, he never had the illusion that he could try the case by himself, and he welcomed Cochran to the team. But Shapiro all along saw himself as a sort of master of ceremonies for the defense, a notion that became increasingly untenable over time. Throughout the fall, Cochran spent increasing amounts of time at the jail with O.J., and Simpson became ever more enamored of Cochran and alienated from Shapiro—who had always loathed having to visit prisoners. Race, too, assumed ever more importance in the defense strategy, and Shapiro—notwithstanding his having launched the issue in the first place—hated confronting its incendiary aftermath.

Simpson had hired Cochran as a trial lawyer, and the trial was fast approaching. How could Cochran remain number two? He couldn't—and the implications made Shapiro squirm. In a bid to forestall the inevitable, Shapiro made a final effort to keep control of the case in the only way he knew how.

One afternoon late in the jury selection process, Bailey and Kardashian were talking with Simpson in the tiny lockup beside Judge Ito's courtroom. Shapiro joined them and said he had just spoken to the prosecutors. He said that he now understood their theory of the case. "The prosecutors think that you were mad at Nicole because she didn't invite you to dinner at Mezzaluna with the kids," Shapiro told Simpson. "They think you sat around your house getting pissed off, then went over to Nicole's, probably with the idea of slashing the tires on her car. There was some sort of confrontation at the house, and you killed her. Then Goldman showed up."

The lawyers and their client listened to Shapiro's summary without comment.

"So," Shapiro went on, "that leaves room for manslaughter. And Bob [Kardashian] would have to account for the knife, but that's probably no more than five years for accessory after the fact."

There was stunned silence—incredulity that Shapiro would propose a plea bargain at this late date. But cutting deals was Shapiro's specialty, and making one now was the only way for him to remain in charge of the case. Simpson did not reject the proposal so much as ignore it. The conversation simply moved on to other topics.

With this final gambit, Shapiro ignored his own lessons about the importance of deference to celebrity clients. There was no logical reason to suggest a plea at that moment. The Fuhrman issue had poisoned the racial atmosphere surrounding the trial in a way that could only help the defense. Thanks to Cochran, jury selection seemed likely to produce a politicized, pro-defense panel. By proposing that Simpson agree to plead guilty to anything—at a time when O.J.'s outright acquittal was more likely than ever—Shapiro alienated his client beyond measure (likewise Kardashian, Simpson's most loyal courtier). Shapiro's prompt departure from leadership of the case became, at that moment, inevitable.

|||||

The impending end of his reign as lead defense counsel led Shapiro into increasingly erratic behavior. In early December, he sent several reporters who were covering the case (including me) a gift. It was a large bottle of men's cologne; the brand, D.N.A. News of the gift promptly leaked, of course, and virtually all the reports stressed the inappropriateness of the gesture. (Like many of the reporters, I sent mine back with a polite note.) Even Shapiro's friend Michael Klein was appalled. Klein told him, "Bob, don't you realize that two people are dead in this case?"

Klein also figured in another bizarre Shapiro episode. Later in December, Shapiro decided to take his wife and two sons to Hawaii for a brief vacation. Klein set up the trip through United Airlines, where he had high-level connections. The day before Shapiro's scheduled departure, the lawyer called Klein in a panic. He demanded that Klein change his reservations to a pseudonym: Tony DiMilo. Klein didn't understand the need for secrecy. All the while wondering about his friend's stability, he agreed to put through the change. It was a pointless formality, of course, for Shapiro was instantly recognized both on the plane and at his hotel. While in Hawaii, Shapiro also put in a strange phone call to

Bailey. Still hoping to salvage control of the case, Shapiro beseeched Bailey, "You gotta get Johnnie to back off."

Bailey was noncommittal to Shapiro, but he would tell Cochran no such thing. A savvy political creature himself, Bailey saw that Shapiro had at this point no chance of remaining in charge. Indeed, Bailey had spent much of the fall cultivating Cochran so that he, Bailey, would be able to carve out a significant role at the trial. Almost in passing during this long conversation from Hawaii, Shapiro mentioned Bailey's financial status in the case. This is always a prickly subject among lawyers, and Bailey's arrangement had been conspicuously vague for several months. But Bailey had had other business and his time commitment to Simpson had been modest, so he hadn't pressed for a resolution of the issue. Still, Bailey was not prepared for what Shapiro told him from Hawaii: "You know you're a volunteer, right?"

Bailey was, though he didn't know it. Shapiro's retainer agreement with Simpson was contained in a letter dated August 24, 1994. (Shapiro never showed this agreement to Bailey.) "Dear O.J.," the letter read. "You will compensate me for my personal legal services through the end of the . . . trial in the sum of $1,200,000, payable as soon as reasonably possible, but no later than in monthly installments of not less than $100,000." The letter went on to state, "You will not be responsible for any additional payment of fees for legal services performed by . . . F. Lee Bailey, which shall be my responsibility, if any." (Cochran's separate agreement called for a fee to him of $500,000.) Bailey knew none of this at the time. Nor could he know, of course, that once Shapiro's role in the trial was reduced, he would stop receiving the monthly checks, and that he would ultimately receive only about $700,000 from Simpson, plus expenses.

At the time of the phone call, Bailey was enraged by Shapiro's presumptuous reference to his status, not to mention the status itself. Bailey was in the Simpson case more for ego gratification than for money, but he found Shapiro's treatment of him demeaning. (Bailey later negotiated a modest retainer agreement of his own with Skip Taft, O.J.'s business manager.) In this phone call from Hawaii, Shapiro succeeded only in alienating Bailey, an erstwhile ally. It would soon become clear that Shapiro had no allies left.

As part of his effort to ingratiate himself with Cochran, on December 21 Bailey sent Cochran a thirteen-page single-spaced memorandum as "a preliminary effort—i.e. a 'first cut'—to bring the preferred trial strategies and tactics in the forthcoming trial into focus." The memo, which turned out to be remarkably prescient, laid out a number of defenses to be used at the trial. They included "Demeanor Evidence"—proof that Simpson was the usual "relaxed, happy, affable O.J." before his trip to Chicago; once he learns of the murder, "his affect reverses." There was also the "Time Line" defense, "to demonstrate that at no time is there a 'window' of fifteen or more minutes when O.J. could have snuck off and committed the crime." About the time line, Bailey wrote, "Properly orchestrated, this can be a powerful garden in which reasonable doubt can grow and flourish." There was also "Lack of Motive"—no reason why Simpson "would butcher the mother of the two small children he adored," especially "in light of his manifest equanimity when confronted . . . with Nicole's sexual expeditions."

In sum, Bailey wrote, the evidence in the case "warrant[s] a demeanor of controlled indignance. . . . This ought not to be a polite request to the jury, but a formal demand supported by a foundation of appropriate righteousness. . . . The manner in which the investigation in this case was botched from beginning to end—including protection and preservation of the crime scene, intervention of the medical team, letting the Bronco sit about for all to enter, delaying the blood testing unconscionably, and 'salting' the blood evidence to incriminate O.J.—will be described by historians as a blight on the face of justice." In a footnote to this peroration, Bailey showed just how well he understood the case. "None of the above will have much value," he wrote, "unless and until it is translated into the 'Downtown' dialect by our able colleague Cochran; given the makeup of the jury, he would probably be very effective at delivering his translation himself."

||||||

Pat McKenna had only the residue of an unpleasant divorce to return to in Florida so, unlike McNally, he decided to stay on in Los Angeles, even with a pay cut. He and Harris did take a brief Christmas vacation, and when they returned to Shapiro's office on January 4, 1995, they sensed a distinct chill from Shapiro's secretary, Bonnie Barron. McKenna gave her a hug, as was his custom, and Barron kept her hands at her sides. Harris and McKenna were still puzzling over Barron's reaction to them when, later that night, they were having a drink at the Bel Age Hotel. As they were chatting, Harris's cellular phone rang. The caller was Kristin Jeannette-Meyers, an energetic reporter who was covering the defense team for Court TV. Harris listened for a moment. A big grin spread across his face, and then he started repeating the same phrase over and over again:

"Oh my God. Oh my God. Oh my God."

When Harris handed the phone to McKenna and he heard what Jeannette-Meyers was saying, McKenna reacted the same way. *This* was why Barron was upset.

Jeannette-Meyers was reading them a column by Mike McAlary from that day's New York *Daily News* headlined VAIN SHAPIRO DE-SERVES HIS FATE. It began, "He has spent a year fooling the nation, this lawyer. He has made them all believers: that he is a heroic, hard-working lawyer in the hunt for a grand, fantastic verdict. Un-fortunately, Robert Shapiro is your typical Hollywood invention— a character only tan-deep in makeup and significance."

The column was filled with details known only to a handful of insiders. It mentioned how Shapiro had recently taken a vacation in Maui, to which he flew first-class and his kids traveled coach, and had registered at the Grand Wailea Hotel under the alias Tony DiMilo. "Unlike Venus," McAlary quipped, "this statue is head-less." McAlary observed that Shapiro "has amazed members of the defense team with his unfamiliarity with the facts." Shapiro thought, for example, that on the night of the murders Ron Gold-man had walked from his waiter's post at Mezzaluna to Nicole's house, when in fact he drove a borrowed car. The story went on to detail Shapiro's vanity, in particular how he had hired an extra secretary to clip stories about him out of newspapers. (The desig-nated clipper was actually Petra Brando, daughter of Marlon and sister of Shapiro's onetime client Christian.) McAlary's story con-cluded by explaining how Shapiro had recently decided to cut back on defense team expenses: "From his first-class plane seat, Shapiro phoned the office and fired one of the secretaries he hired with O.J.'s money to snip the name Robert Shapiro out of newspapers."

After hearing the column read to them, McKenna and Harris had no doubt about what to do next. Still using Harris's cellular phone, they dialed John McNally in New York. Chuckling, McKenna asked McNally, "You crazy fuck, how could you give that shit to the papers about Shapiro?"

McNally laughed right back at him. "Fuck him," McNally said. "He's an asshole anyway. And besides, he still owes me money."

McAlary's column prompted no laughter from Bob Shapiro. He had been stewing for weeks, torn by conflicting emotions about his role in the case. On the one hand, he loved his newfound social prominence, and he reveled in the attention he received at restaurants and public occasions. When, over the summer, the big-screen video projector at the Rose Bowl focused on him during a Rolling Stones concert, Shapiro waved his arms with delight and the crowd cheered. But it also galled Shapiro that the press sniped at his many public appearances. On December 25, 1994—just before McAlary's column ran—a gossip column in the *Los Angeles Times* sniffed that Shapiro "goes to the opening of every (bleep)-ing door." Simpson himself had taken note of Shapiro's high public profile and asked him to lower it. Shapiro complied, but the instruction irritated him and enraged his wife, Linell, who relished their nights out together.

The McAlary column attacked Shapiro's refined sense of his own dignity. Furious, he asked Bill Pavelic to conduct a secret investigation to see who had leaked the inside information, and Pavelic quickly came back with the predictable report that it was McNally. Rather than blame McNally, Shapiro fixated on Bailey, whom he held responsible for the investigator's hostility. So Shapiro decided to strike back in similar terms. He leaked word to *Newsweek*'s Mark Miller that he was no longer speaking to his old friend Bailey. In the issue that was released on Sunday, January 15, 1995, Miller broke word of the breach in the defense camp. The *Newsweek* report stated that an unnamed defense source (obviously Shapiro) believed that "Bailey-inspired 'saboteurs on our own team' have been working to destroy [Shapiro's] credibility and reputation through leaks to the media."

David Margolick, the *New York Times* reporter covering the case, followed up by calling Shapiro that Sunday. This time Shapiro agreed to go on the record. Margolick wrote on January 16 that "an extraordinary and apparently irreparable break has developed between" Shapiro and Bailey. Margolick quoted Shapiro as saying, "The landmark word to me is 'loyalty.' I felt a lifelong commitment to him because he gave me the opportunity to represent him when his professional reputation was at stake. But recent events have been so painful that we'll never be able to have a relationship again." Shapiro told Margolick that he hoped Bailey would leave the defense team. "His presence before this particular jury adds nothing that can't be done by Johnnie and others on the team." But as for the final word on whether Bailey stayed or went, "I'm leaving that decision to Mr. Cochran." When the *Los Angeles Times* joined in the next day, Shapiro was even more scathing. "We can't have snakes sleeping in the bed with us," he said.

Cases involving multiple defense lawyers invariably generate internal tensions, but Shapiro's public attack on a colleague was unprecedented. (Shapiro was on the warpath privately, too. He insisted that his friend Michael Klein evict Bailey as his houseguest, and Klein, with some embarrassment, did so.) As much as anyone on the defense team, Shapiro understood the importance of public relations. At this moment, on the eve of opening statements, the only priority should have been to stress Simpson's innocence, or at least the weaknesses in the government's case. Instead, with his client's freedom for the rest of his life on the line, Shapiro shifted the focus to his own complaints—to O.J.'s clear detriment. In times of crisis—as during his press conference after Simpson disappeared on June 17—Shapiro invariably placed his own interests above those of his client. Worse yet, his grievances with Bailey were largely unjustified. While McNally had indeed attacked Shapiro in the press, Bailey himself was innocent of this kind of chicanery. In response to Shapiro's tirades, Bailey knew that he had to take the high road. In a statement released through his office, Bailey said only that he "declined to disparage Mr. Shapiro in any way. This case is not about Mr. Shapiro or Mr. Bailey. It is about O. J. Simpson."

The controversy ended the only way it could: Simpson demanded that all his attorneys meet him at the jailhouse and end all public feuding. "I played football with plenty of guys I didn't like," Simpson told them, "but it was a team and we got along. Your job is to get along."

On the morning of Wednesday, January 18, the lawyers met at Cochran's office shortly after seven. Roosevelt Grier, the minister and former football star, was there, and he approached Shapiro. "I've looked into this situation, and I believe that Brother Bailey is innocent of what you think he did to you," Grier said. "I believe you should apologize to him." Now completely alone on the defense team, Shapiro had no choice but to utter a few perfunctory words of contrition to Bailey. Also in response to Grier's suggestion, Shapiro and Bailey arrived at the courthouse together. Press reports said that the two men had arrived "arm-in-arm," and that was, at some level, technically true. As they left Shapiro's car, Bailey placed his hand on Shapiro's wrist. For a moment, Shapiro regarded Bailey's hand as one might look upon a putrid fish. Shapiro did not exactly recoil, but he marched down the steps to the door with a cross between a smile and a grimace on his face.

After court that day, the lawyers returned to the lobby for a news conference. Cochran—now clearly the leader of the defense team—stood between Bailey and Shapiro, and he beamed while announcing that the defense was a united front. "The Dream Team is never going to break up," Cochran proclaimed. Shapiro, looking pained, nodded dutifully. Asked about the controversy, Bailey said simply, "That's history." The unity tableau was marred only by the presence—in the background, behind the first-string lawyers—of Cochran's young associate Shawn Chapman and Shapiro's junior colleague Sara Caplan. Every time the lawyers told the reporters that the feud was over, history, forgotten and unimportant . . . the two underlings, who had enjoyed front-row seats to the diatribes, started to laugh.

||||||

Shapiro sulked. In court, he sat at the opposite end of the defense table from Bailey, and for the next nine months the two men did not exchange a word. Outside the Criminal Courts Building, Shapiro's petulance took another form. Slowly but inexorably, he began broadening the circle of people to whom he told his true feelings about his client. From the start of Shapiro's representation, his wife, Linell, had never had any compunction about sharing her views at social gatherings: "Guilty, guilty, guilty." Both inside and outside the defense-team offices, particularly as the racial polarization about the case intensified, Shapiro decided to prove his kinship with the West Los Angeles world that meant so much to him. Their view of the case was his, too. "Of course he did it," Shapiro would say.

For his part, Bailey, who never worried too much about any client's guilt or innocence, just wanted to return to the big time. Indeed, one irony of Shapiro's attack on Bailey is that it was launched before Bailey had uttered a single word in Judge Ito's courtroom.

In the last legal argument before opening statements, Bailey would finally speak in that court for the first time. Prosecutors had urged Ito to let them introduce evidence of Simpson's pattern of domestic violence against Nicole as proof that he murdered her. This was an important controversy for Ito to resolve, but in a rather minor sideline to the main issue, prosecutors called to the stand a Canadian expert to testify about domestic violence in general. Late on a sleepy Thursday afternoon, Bailey rose to cross-examine Dr. Donald Dutton of Vancouver.

Nature has favored Bailey with a glorious voice, which summons a stream of Dewar's tumbling down a pebbly brook. His hands tremble a good deal, but with one in his pocket and the other on the lectern, Bailey can still command a moment. He speaks a language that has almost vanished from American courtrooms, a kind of British English that combines wry whimsy and baroque locution. When Dr. Dutton didn't understand a question, Bailey attributed it to "the vicissitudes of give-and-take," and when the Canadian witness was not clear on another matter, Bailey asked to "see if we can surmount the barrier of our common language."

In his redirect examination, prosecutor Scott Gordon at one point asked Dutton to explain a phrase he had used: "narcissistic personality."

"A narcissistic personality," the expert explained, "will be someone who has an exaggerated or a grandiose view of their own importance, who needed a constant kind of reinforcement, who over-reacted to any kind of slight criticisms, and was incapable of developing empathy with other people."

In the silence before the next question, Bailey took a long look at his colleagues on the defense team. Then he leaned over and whispered to Gerry Uelman: "Sounds like everyone at this table."

12. A VISIT FROM LARRY KING

The decision—the last roadblock to opening statements in the Simpson trial—was the most important of Lance Ito's career. At one level, the issue was a simple one: Would the prosecution be allowed to present to the jury evidence of Simpson's history of physical and emotional harassment of his former wife? At another level, however, the domestic-violence motion raised profound questions about the nature of criminal trials. Should any information about a defendant be kept from a jury, even if it is accurate? What evidence, if any, is *too* prejudicial to a defendant? If a husband abuses his wife, does that mean he is more likely to murder her? Does a defendant stand trial for what he did or for who he is?

On this and all issues raised in the Simpson case, Ito proceeded methodically. The judge came to work early, around seven every morning, when the traffic from his home in Pasadena was still light. The Criminal Courts Building was mostly empty when he slipped into his chambers on the ninth floor, just across a battered linoleum hallway from his courtroom, which was known as Department 103. A window at one end of his long, narrow office looked out over the *Los Angeles Times* building and beyond, to the many towers of downtown, but the vista was obscured by piles of papers on the windowsill. Ito decorated in Neo-Workaholic style. Just two personal touches stood out from stacks of files and computer wires: a handsome formal photographic portrait of Ito and his wife, Margaret York, who was one of the highest-ranking women in the Los Angeles Police Department, and a small stand of historic Japanese flags. As an adult, Ito had come to take his heritage seriously. A third-generation Californian, he grew up knowing that his mother and father had met in a Wyoming internment camp during the Second World War. Even Lance Allan Ito's name bore witness to the difficult days of the war: It honored a lawyer, Lance Smith, who helped protect the Ito family's property while they were interned, and a minister, Allan Hunter, who brought food and moral support to the inmates of the internment camp.

Shortly before the camera on the wall of his courtroom came to life, around nine o'clock, Ito would stroll from his office to his bench and check to see if the day's paperwork was in order. He wasn't wearing his robe then, so a pocket full of pens—his nerd pack—peeked out from the breast pocket of his shirt. When dressed in full judicial regalia, Ito tended to hunch over; his robe would blend into his black beard, giving him a soft, pudgy look. This was misleading. The forty-four-year-old judge was trim, almost wiry, and the veteran of a pair of marathons.

In contrast to the adversaries before him, Judge Ito worked with very little assistance. A handful of students from local law schools rotated through his chambers over the course of the trial, but Ito did all the writing—and the deciding—alone. He had a fear, almost a phobia, of appearing unprepared on the bench, so he read all the cases the lawyers cited to him. This meant long hours of work after court sessions, either in his chambers or at his home, which was electronically linked to his office computer network.

Ito, as much as anyone, understood the importance of the domestic-violence issue to the prosecution's case. The prosecution had asked him to rule on fifty-nine different "alleged significant events or incidents of misconduct by the defendant"—including Simpson's conviction in 1989 for beating Nicole, and Nicole's 911 call in 1993, when she begged for police assistance while O.J. bellowed at her in the background. Ito's decision would determine whether the prosecution's case would be a rather dry and technical one based exclusively on circumstantial and scientific evidence, or a melodrama of increasing domestic violence ending in death.

Ito agonized in a characteristically meticulous way. He asked the parties to make a chart for him listing each incident, along with a thumbnail argument for why this evidence should be admitted or excluded. As he would several times in the case, Ito asked the lawyers to give him the information on a computer disk, so that he could tinker with it himself. He read the cases, reread some of them, then began working his way through the domestic-violence incidents, one by one. In order to avoid delaying the trial, Ito had to issue his decision by January 18. Up to that point, he shared his conclusions with no one—or almost no one.

The judge did tell Larry King how he was going to rule.

||||||

Lance Ito was a paradoxical figure. Although he is a thoughtful jurist whose work reflects his earnest and rigorous approach, in the crucible of the Simpson trial, he displayed another facet of his character, too. Unfortunately, over the course of this long case the less appealing side of Lance Ito came increasingly to the fore. Frequently during the trial, Ito behaved like just another celebrity-crazed resident of Los Angeles, but the problem went deeper than a simple case of starry eyes. Ito suffered, in the end, from an undue eagerness to please, an unwillingness to offend—and a fatal lack of gravitas.

The outrageously inappropriate disclosure to King (which the talk-show host, fortunately for Ito, kept to himself at the time) was only one symptom of Ito's affliction. His extraordinary interview with KCBS—which came about because Tricia Toyota's husband, an old friend of Ito's, had asked him to do it—was another. A third example came when Ito heard arguments about whether cameras should remain in the courtroom.

At his core, Ito loved the attention that the cameras brought, and he never seriously entertained the possibility of exiling the viewing public from the trial, but the judge did love to tweak the news media. On the day the media lawyers were to appear before him, November 7, Ito decided to play to the courtroom camera in his own way. The judge directed that twenty-one boxes of mail he had received urging him to ban cameras be stacked up beside the bench. (A letter-writing campaign had been prompted by Chicago newspaperman Mike Royko.) Noting the mail, Ito asked Kelli Sager, the lawyer representing the various news operations, "When you say you speak for the public or that the public has an interest in knowing this, the public has overwhelmingly told me that they want me to pull the plug. How do you respond to that?"

Sager, who made regular (and highly distinguished) appearances before Ito throughout the trial, dismissed Ito's box-stacking stunt in a flash. "Certainly my clients would be happy to organize a letter-writing campaign if that were the way the Court was to decide issues in this case," she said. "But I would urge the Court not to make rulings . . . based on public opinion. If twenty thousand people wrote in and said, 'We think the DNA evidence should come in,' I'm sure the Court would not then make a decision based on the fact that the public has spoken." Ito quickly retreated. The cameras stayed in place, and the stacked boxes joined the KCBS interview as symbols of Ito's naïveté.

First-time visitors to Ito's courtroom who had previously seen it only on television always said the same thing: It's so small. The room was about the size of a tennis court, with only four rows of benches for spectators. In courtrooms, as in weddings, where you stand determines where you sit, so the prosecution and defense each marked its territory from the start of the case. Behind the prosecutors, on the side of the courtroom near the jury box, sat the victims' families. Ron Goldman's sister, Kim, came virtually every day, as did her stepmother, Patti. Ron's father, Fred, made it several times a week. The Browns came more sporadically—Nicole's mother, Juditha, most often; the three surviving sisters, Denise, Dominique, and Tanya, rarely. The press corps, sitting in their twenty-five tightly rationed seats, surrounded the victims' families. Behind the reporters stood three still photographers and a pair of technicians who ran the remote-controlled video camera on the wall.

The defense side featured a similarly consistent cast. O.J.'s two sisters, Carmelita Durio and Shirley Baker, along with Shirley's husband, Ben, came every day. They passionately believed in Simpson's innocence, yet they treated those who didn't—including the victims' families and many of the reporters—with consummate grace. Ito kept four seats on the defense side for his own friends, and in the back row, a half dozen winners of the daily lottery for public seats took their places. That was it—about fifty people. It was the kind of place where newcomers were quickly noticed, and on January 14 there was no way to miss the arrival of Larry King.

Larry King Live was among the shows on which Faye Resnick had been scheduled to speak after the release of her book in October, and Ito had written to CNN, along with the other networks, asking that their interviews be postponed. Unlike Connie Chung's program at CBS, King's show had canceled the interview, and Ito had written him a note of thanks and invited King to drop by his chambers. (It was a gracious gesture, but also one of a man who liked to have stars visit him.) So, during the mid-morning break in court on the fourteenth, King, his senior executive producer, Wendy Walker Whitworth, and King's daughter, Chaia, were ushered into Ito's chambers. Ito was thrilled by King's presence, and started rambling about the domestic-violence decision he had to make. "I know Nicole's call to the shelter is powerful evidence," Ito told his stunned guests, "but it's hearsay. I can't let it in." The talk meandered for about forty minutes on various topics—Ito's plans to work on the juvenile court someday, Chaia's course work at American University—until King finally asked, "Don't you have to get back to court?"

The break had been scheduled for only fifteen minutes, so Ito found a fidgety group before him when he returned to the bench. Incredibly, King and his entourage followed him through the rear door into the well of the courtroom. O.J. rose in deference to the visiting celebrity and reached out to shake hands. The bailiffs, however, hustled the defendant back into his seat. Chastened, O.J. said to King, "Thanks for being so fair." Next, King moved to Robert Shapiro, who gave him a bear hug. Then King shook hands with Lee Bailey. All this attention to the defense camp disturbed Suzanne Childs, Gil Garcetti's peripatetic director of communications (and a future romantic interest of King's). Childs rushed from her seat to the defense table and steered King over to the prosecutors. "I watch you all the time!" Marcia Clark told him.

At this point Wendy Walker Whitworth started to feel self-conscious about the commotion they had caused, and she hustled to leave. Unfortunately, she reached for the door to the holding cell where Simpson sat during breaks. A bailiff stopped her.

"Most people try to stay out of there," he observed dryly.

At last King and his entourage, having worked the courtroom like the deck of a cruise ship, left through the spectators' door. Judge Ito had observed the whole scene with a serene smile.

My own visit with the judge during the trial reflected this same puzzling longing for the favor of the well known. Late one morning early in the case, the superior court's director of public affairs, Jerrianne Hayslett, said that the judge wanted to meet me at lunchtime. (The judge met with many reporters over the course of the trial, even though most judges in high-profile cases feel it is preferable to never so much as say hello to journalists.) Hayslett took me back to Ito's chambers.

Mostly, Ito and I made small talk—the weather, my decision to give up law for journalism, his passion for the flea market at the Rose Bowl in Pasadena. At one point, I told him that I thought he had a very tough job in this case.

Ito paused, then smiled. "Want to see something?" he asked me.

Sure, I said.

"Want to see something great?"

I did.

Ito reached into his desk and pulled out an envelope that he cradled like a precious heirloom and handed to me. I opened it and found a letter that the sender had thoughtfully backed with cardboard, suitable for framing.

In the brief message, the author said he had been watching the Simpson case unfold on television, and he thought Ito was doing a terrific job under difficult circumstances. It was signed with a flourish: "Arsenio Hall."

I said it was a very nice letter. Ito beamed.

|||||

The contradictions—between the serious judge and the ditsy Angeleno—reflected Lance Ito's background. Of all the principals in the case, he was the only one born in Los Angeles, and he had deep roots there. The judge's grandfather had helped found the first interracial Methodist church in the city, and his father, James Ito, was raised in the solid middle class. James had graduated from college, started a truck farm on twenty-seven acres in West Covina, and even joined the California National Guard when World War II began. As it would for so many Japanese-Americans, the war turned James Ito's life upside down. He was ordered to resign from the Guard, sell his assets, and report to an internment camp—all within two weeks.

Lance was born in 1950, and his parents, who eventually became schoolteachers, settled in the middle-class district of Silver Lake, near Dodger Stadium. James Ito had once harbored hopes for a more exalted career for himself, but the war dashed those dreams, and instead he focused his hopes on young Lance, who had an almost stereotypically all-American boyhood. He became president of the student body at the racially mixed John Marshall High School and excelled in the Boy Scouts, earning the coveted Eagle Scout badge. His scoutmaster, a young lawyer named Delbert Wong, became a mentor and role model. (Wong would go on to become one of the first Asian-American superior court judges in California. He was retired from the bench when Ito chose him as the special master to examine the contents of the "mystery envelope" in the Simpson case.)

Ito's teenage rebellions were modest, limited mostly to his refusal to take the Japanese-language lessons his parents urged upon him. When he arrived at UCLA in 1968, he brought a first-rate mind and all the accoutrements of the good life in the Beach Boys era: a collection of *Playboy* centerfolds to decorate his room, a stereo system, an attractive girlfriend, and a Boss 302 Mustang with rear window slats, air intake on the hood, and chrome Magnum 500 wheels. He also had a less-than-reverential attitude toward the traumatic Japanese-American experience in the United States. Ito lived on campus in Sproul Hall—nicknamed Bacchus House, after the god of wine—and on Pearl Harbor Day, the future judge would put on a battered leather aviator's helmet and an improvised cape, and run through the halls yelling, "Banzai!"

Still, the roots of a judicial career were in place. As a college student, Ito served as the director of student parking at UCLA, a crucial mediating assignment in a car-crazy city. Ito also excelled in his studies, graduating cum laude in political science and earning admission to the University of California's eminent law school, Boalt Hall, in Berkeley. After graduating from Boalt in 1975, Ito spent two years at a law firm, and then became a deputy district attorney in Los Angeles.

Ito's experience as a prosecutor shaped his judicial outlook. He specialized in cases against violent Los Angeles gangs, and he was eventually assigned to a special unit dedicated to trying these large and complex cases. (As a fringe benefit of this kind of work, he first met his future wife, who was then a homicide detective, at a murder scene at four o'clock one morning.) It was in 1983 and 1984, during the tenure of Robert Philibosian, one of the few Republicans to serve as Los Angeles district attorney in recent years, that Ito's career took off.

According to Philibosian, "Lance was a Democrat, and I was a Republican, but he was very sympathetic to the things we were trying to do in those days." One of the most important things Philibosian did after he left the D.A.'s office was to help launch a revolution aimed at toppling the California Supreme Court, which at the time stood out as perhaps the most liberal court in the nation. Led by Chief Justice Rose E. Bird and other appointees from Jerry Brown's two terms as governor, the seven-member court fought a long and rancorous war with prosecutors, which ended only when voters recalled Bird and two colleagues in 1986—the fight Philibosian helped conduct. (The court is now solidly conservative.) "Lance was not crazy about Rose Bird," Perry Mocciaro, a law-school classmate of Ito's who is still a friend, said. "His feelings about her were no different from any other prosecutor's in the state." Ito didn't directly participate in the recall effort, but he made his feelings about the Bird court unusually plain. His car in those days bore a license-plate frame with the words CALIFORNIA'S SUPREME COURT; the young prosecutor's vanity plate read, in commentary, 7 BOZOS. In 1987, Philibosian recommended Ito to a fellow Republican, Governor George Deukmejian. The governor appointed Ito to the municipal court that year, and to the superior court, where he remains, in 1989. Once elevated to the bench, Ito changed his license plate but not, it seems, the sentiments behind it.

|||||

One of the most important buzzwords used in the attack on Justice Bird and other judicial liberals was "truth." Ito would also use it in one of his early written rulings in the Simpson case. "The Court must always remember this process is a search for truth," he wrote.

The observation that a trial is a search for truth might sound axiomatic to nonlawyers, but the idea is in fact the subject of intense ideological warfare in the legal community. An approach based on truth cuts across the traditional battle lines between government and defense. The "truth school," as it is sometimes known, asserts that the paramount value is protecting innocent defendants from being wrongly convicted. But it is not at all troubled by guilty defendants who are convicted, even if the police may have violated some provisions of the Constitution in collecting evidence against them. That, of course, is the rub.

For more than a generation, the judicial system's remedy for improper police work has been to exclude the evidence gathered by these means—and therefore sometimes the guilty go free. Truth-school adherents say that while they do not countenance unconstitutional action by the police, they believe that suppressing evidence is not necessarily the way to address such misbehavior. If the police violate someone's rights, they suggest, it might be better if that person sued the cops for money damages in a civil lawsuit—or, alternatively, if the offending officers were administratively sanctioned for their violations of the Constitution. But in any criminal case, according to the truth school, the jury should be able to hear all reliable evidence against the defendant, regardless of how the police behaved. As Akhil Reed Amar, a professor at Yale Law School and a leading truth-school adherent, puts it, "Criminal trials shouldn't be a sport or a game where judges just try to even the odds between the two sides. The point is that the jury should have all the facts available to it to make the right decision." When judges must decide whether or not to provide all available information to the jury—about a defendant's prior record, say—truth-school adherents generally believe that jurors should hear it and draw their own conclusions.

|||||

The day Lance Ito selected to hear argument on the admissibility of evidence about the domestic-violence incidents—January 11, 1995—turned out to be critical in the evolution of the Simpson case. It was the day he ordered the jury to report to a secret location—the Inter-Continental Hotel in downtown Los Angeles—for sequestration. The jurors were now officially twiddling their thumbs, with nothing to do. This personal imposition on these citizens, as well as the accompanying financial burden on the county's taxpayers, gave a new urgency to Ito's desire to get the trial started. Before January 11, reporters and other spectators were allowed in the courtroom on a more or less first-come, first-served basis. But on this day, for the first time the seats in the spectator section of Department 103 were marked with numbers, and the bailiffs admitted only those with passes for specific seats. Final preparations were nearly complete. A full complement of both victims' family members filled the seats. No one could mistake that the crucial moment had drawn near.

The defendant showed the strain. O. J. Simpson has long been a compulsive talker. His friends knew that when they were speaking with O.J. on the telephone, they could safely put down the receiver for minutes at a time and return to a flowing monologue. No subject moved him to speak more than his relationship with Nicole. Visitors to Simpson in jail found him nearly obsessed by the subject. "Nicole wanted to get back together with *me*," O.J. would say over and over again. "I wanted to get away from her. How can they say I killed her because I wanted her back?" Simpson even talked a lot in the courtroom. Every judge allows lawyers and clients some leeway in communicating in court, but Simpson always seemed to intimidate Ito to a certain extent, and throughout the trial the judge gave this defendant nearly free rein to jabber. This was never more true than on January 11. As the lawyers dissected O.J. and Nicole's relationship, O.J. offered his own audible commentary as well.

The defense was represented by Gerald Uelman. The slow-talking professor from Los Angeles had something of a tin ear for public relations, and he began by making a gesture that neither Cochran nor Shapiro would have attempted. Uelman asked that Judge Ito exclude from the courtroom members of the Brown family because they might be asked to testify about issues that would be discussed in court that day. In fact, Nicole's family had been exhaustively interviewed on this subject by police investigators; the defense had copies of all these reports. Uelman's request only invited the prosecutors to wave the banner of victims' rights. The Brown family, Christopher Darden said, "have an interest in hearing the truth and learning the circumstances surrounding and leading to the death of their daughter and sister. Having already suffered the death of a daughter and sister at the hands of the defendant, I doubt that there is anything that will occur in this court today . . . that can affect them any more than what has already happened." Ito agreed. The Browns stayed.

The defense position on the domestic-violence evidence was simple and well stated by Uelman at the outset. He quoted the prosecution brief, which had stated, "This is a domestic-violence case involving murder, not a murder case involving domestic violence." Uelman responded, "By attaching that label, by saying this case is a domestic-violence case, they seek to transform these proceedings from an inquiry into who killed Nicole Brown Simpson and Ronald Goldman on June 12, 1994, into a general inquiry into the character of O. J. Simpson, in which he will be called upon to explain every aspect of his life for seventeen years. And there is a fundamental problem with what the prosecution is trying to do here." The problem, Uelman said, quoting a well-known case, was that "it is fundamental to American jurisprudence that a defendant must be tried for what he did, not for who he is."

This was an unexceptional and entirely appropriate argument. But Uelman's ponderous manner and tony credentials hid a street fighter's soul. Uelman had his own "label" for this case. "None of the traditional earmarks of a domestic-violence or a relationship-violence homicide are present here," he said. "How many domestic-violence cases involve multiple victims?

"How many involve the commission of a murder with the use of a knife?

"How many involve a complete silence preceding the murder, suggesting that the murder was committed by stealth rather than being preceded by any sort of violent confrontation or argument?

"In fact, if we had to put a label on this case based on these factors, the label we would put on it is that it bears all of the earmarks of a drug-related homicide, in which the frequency of multiple victims, the use of knives, the use of stealth, is much more frequent than it is in the case of domestic violence."

As Uelman uttered the words "drug-related," there was an audible intake of breath in the courtroom. The suggestion was (and remains) preposterous, even on Uelman's own terms. First, by any theory, Nicole was the real target of the crime and Ron Goldman just happened on the scene—and his murder was entirely consistent with jealous rage from Simpson. Second, Uelman was simply wrong about knives. Drug dealers overwhelmingly prefer guns. Finally, most domestic-violence murders take place in or near homes, which means that frequently they are not overheard by others. Most important, neither Nicole nor Goldman had any ties to the drug world that would make them targets of a "drug-related homicide." Uelman's suggestion—a real calumny on the graves of these two dead people—marked the beginning of a new phase in the defense strategy. The red herring of the "drug hit" theory was the kind of move most characteristic of F. Lee Bailey, who, seated at counsel table beside the podium, gave Uelman a wide smile at the sheer deviousness of his gesture.

Uelman then proceeded to respond to the fifty-nine domestic-violence allegations one by one. He did so virtually in tandem with the defendant, who, seated between Shapiro and Cochran, provided a running commentary on each of the accusations against him. (Shapiro also recorded in a memo Simpson's responses to all of the domestic-violence allegations against him.)

The first incident was from 1977, when Simpson was alleged to have broken some picture frames during the course of a fight with Nicole. "*She* broke them," O.J. muttered to Cochran.

Uelman moved quickly to one of the most important incidents, the fight at their home on January 1, 1989, after which O.J. pleaded no contest to battering Nicole. "With respect to this incident," Uelman told Judge Ito, "we have police reports, we have accounts in the form of letters of explanation written by the defendant himself, interviews, and a good deal of information about what actually took place. And what apparently took place was that at the conclusion of a New Year's celebration in which both Mr. Simpson and Nicole Simpson had a lot to drink, they got into an argument in their bedroom. And the culmination of that argument was a physical assault in which Mr. Simpson admitted that he slapped and punched Nicole Brown Simpson."

Hearing this, O.J. nearly vaulted out of his chair. "I did not!" he told Cochran, who patted him on the shoulder and urged him to calm down. Both in conversations with friends and in several interviews following his criminal trial, Simpson had a precise, and narrow, view of his misdeeds in that New Year's Day fight. In a deposition in the civil case against him, he said, "Never once did I ever hit her with my fist, ever. . . . Never once have I ever slapped Nicole." As for what happened on that January day, he said, "I rassled her. . . . That means I had my hands on her, and I was trying to force her out of my bedroom. [A curious choice of pronoun, since she lived there, too.] She fell when she was outside." Uelman's description of the event—that O.J. "slapped and punched" Nicole—thus conflicted with Simpson's own interpretation of it.

The prosecution had alleged that O.J. also beat Nicole after a gay man kissed their son, Justin. In his memo on O.J.'s responses, Shapiro wrote, "O.J. says this took place in Hawaii with the entire Brown family. Nicole said to O.J., 'Lots of people think your daddy's gay.' O.J. got mad. Words were said, but there were no physical actions taken."

The list of incidents went on. In 1993, after the divorce, Simpson hid in the bushes outside Nicole's front window on Gretna Green and watched her have oral sex with Keith Zlomsowitch. O.J. to Cochran: "It was the sidewalk."—i.e., he watched from a public place, not from among the bushes.

After that incident, Simpson stared Nicole and Zlomsowitch down at a restaurant in Brentwood. O.J.: "I just said hello to her."

He stalked Nicole and sometimes wore disguises. O.J.: "Where does that come from?"

In the middle of the afternoon, during the course of the argument, a lawyer representing the Sojourn battered women's shelter in Santa Monica appeared in Ito's court and handed a thin envelope to the prosecutors. At the end of a long day in court, Lydia Bodin, one of the deputy district attorneys, disclosed the envelope's contents. "We have received information from Sojourn shelter that on the date of June the 7th, 1994, Nicole Brown Simpson made a contact with Sojourn. She complained that she was being stalked. She was afraid. She felt confused. She didn't know what to do, and she named the defendant as the person who was stalking her."

Again, many in the courtroom gasped: The date was just five days before the murder. On hearing the words "June the 7th," Cochran and Shapiro looked stricken.

It was a sad moment. By any measure, Nicole Brown Simpson was a wealthy woman, even after her divorce. Yet at her time of greatest fear, with her life literally on the line, she apparently felt unable to turn to the police, to her friends, or even to her family. She had nowhere to go except a public battered women's shelter—the very charity that her husband was forced to contribute to after he beat her in 1989. And even Nicole's final appeal to Sojourn, the courtroom recognized at once, did not manage to save her life. For once, not even O. J. Simpson had anything to say.

|||||

Uelman's opposite number on the prosecution team was Hank Goldberg, and he seemed, in some respects, a miniature version of the professor. Soft-spoken, with a paleness of skin and hair that seemed to render him nearly invisible at times, Goldberg gave the nearly perfect legal argument on the domestic-violence evidence—especially for a judge like Ito, who had a predisposition toward the truth school.

Goldberg began with a hypothetical question for Ito. "Let's imagine that we tried the case, Your Honor, without telling the jury that Nicole Brown Simpson was ever married to the defendant—was just a woman who was murdered," Goldberg said. "Ronald Goldman was just a man that was murdered, and we did not tell them of the existence of any relationship at all."

The proposal, Goldberg said, was self-evidently absurd. "It's almost unimaginable, because the jury would have to call into question all of our evidence, no matter how strong it was, pointing to the defendant as the murderer, because why on earth would Orenthal Simpson kill an entire stranger, just this woman named Nicole. . . . Why would he have killed them so brutally? It wouldn't make any sense, and it would undermine the prosecution's case, clearly.

"It is only when you understand the relationship, and you understand the jealousy, the possessiveness, that the killing and the brutality of the killing of Nicole makes sense."

Ultimately, in a scholarly ten-page single-spaced opinion issued on January 18, 1995, Ito allowed the prosecution to prove most, but not all, of the domestic-violence incidents it wanted to intro-

duce. The prosecution would be permitted to use the most powerful evidence—the 1989 beating, the 1993 call to 911—but not all
of it. With some apparent regret, Ito excluded Nicole's call to Sojourn on June 7 (this was the part of the ruling the judge had
shared with Larry King several days earlier). "To the man or
woman on the street," Ito wrote, "the relevance and probative
value of such evidence is both obvious and compelling, especially
those statements made just before the homicide." But Ito correctly
excluded Nicole's statement as inadmissible hearsay—as are all
"statements by a homicide victim expressing fear of the defendant,
even on the very day of the homicide."

Over all, Ito's domestic-violence ruling amounted to a paradigmatic, and admirable, example of his truth-oriented judicial philosophy in action—as well as a buoyant send-off to the prosecution
for opening statements. The judge's preference for truth in pack-
aging extended even to nomenclature. As Ito stated in his opinion,
Simpson's defense team had asked him to prohibit the prosecution
"from using such terms as 'battered wife,' 'battered spouse,'
'spousal abuse,' 'stalker,' and 'stalking' because they are unduly
prejudicial, inflammatory, and not supported by the evidence." Ito
dealt with this argument quickly. On the basis of what he had seen
of the prosecution's evidence, he noted dryly—and chillingly—
"such restriction is not warranted."

Christopher Darden paced in front of the jury box. As he walked, he kept his eyes on the floor, and his double-breasted jacket flopped open in front of him.

"Now, we're here today obviously to resolve an issue, to settle a question, a question that has been on the minds of people throughout the country these last seven months. It certainly has been on the minds of my people up in Richmond, California, and friends in Fayetteville, Georgia, and all across the country. Everybody wants to know, and everybody I know often poses a question to me: Did O. J. Simpson really kill Nicole Brown and Ronald Goldman?"

The phrase "my people up in Richmond" was not an accidental choice. Both the diction and the reference to the location came fraught with meaning. In general, white Americans do not refer to their relatives as "my people," nor do they, for the most part, live in Richmond, California. The overwhelmingly black city near Oakland was Darden's hometown, and his mention of it marked a small effort at solidarity with the African-American jurors who were arrayed before him.

Darden was nervous, as any person would be in his position. On arriving at the courthouse this morning, January 24, the lawyers had run a gauntlet of twenty-six video cameras and perhaps twice as many still photographers. Seven news helicopters had circled overhead. Even the core group of spectators—the reporters and family members who had seen each other almost daily for several months—took on a hushed, almost reverent attitude on this day.

There was an important new face among them, too. Eunice Simpson, the defendant's mother—tall and regal, even though wracked by arthritis—appeared in her wheelchair in the courtroom's center aisle. As soon as Eunice Simpson arrived, Juditha Brown—likewise a grandmother to Sydney and Justin Simpson—gave her a hug. Hands fluttering nervously on her lap just before Darden rose to begin his opening statement, Juditha Brown dropped her eyeglasses, and Kim Goldman casually leaned over from her nearby seat to pick them up. Retrieving Juditha's dropped glasses had cost Kim's brother his life.

That it was Chris Darden who began the case demonstrated how much the prosecution effort had evolved over the months leading up to the trial. Shortly after Simpson's arrest, Garcetti had asked Darden to conduct the grand-jury investigation into the Bronco chase. At the time, Darden was at loose ends; he had been named to run the D.A.'s Inglewood branch office, but he had not yet moved. Darden had an excellent reputation in the office as an investigator (less so as a trial lawyer), and Garcetti and Hodgman thought the grand-jury role made sense for him. But as the scale of the trial expanded, particularly in the scientific area, Clark and Hodgman realized they could not handle it all themselves. Clark, an old friend of Darden's, urged that he be invited to join the trial team. The racial tensions in the case made the logic of adding Darden even more compelling. The case needed a black prosecutor.

Darden's rise also reflected Don Vinson's fall. By late January, the results of Vinson's focus groups were a forgotten memory. The prosecutors had decided to make domestic-violence evidence a linchpin of their case. From an early date, Clark and Hodgman had divided the labor so that Clark would handle testimony about the events of June 12, 1994, and Hodgman would focus on the scientific evidence. That left the ever-expanding number of domestic-violence witnesses still to be assigned. Those went to Darden. And since the prosecution lawyers had decided they would attempt to prove that O.J. and Nicole's relationship provided the motive for the murders, it made sense for Darden to begin the prosecution presentation to the jury.

In his opening, Darden went right to the heart of the prosecution's theory. "The answer to the question is, Yes, O. J. Simpson murdered Nicole Brown and Ronald Goldman. And I'm sure you will be wondering why as the trial proceeds on, and I'm sure you are wondering why right now. . . . Why would he do it? Not O. J. Simpson. Not the O. J. Simpson we think we know. . . . But that is another question. . . . Do you know O. J. Simpson? . . .

"We watched him leap turnstiles and chairs and run to airplanes in the Hertz commercials, and we watched him with a fifteen-inch Afro in *Naked Gun 33 1/3*, and we've seen him time and time again, and we came to think that we know him." Here Darden paused.

"What we've been seeing, ladies and gentlemen, is the public face, the public persona, the face of the athlete, the face of the actor. It is not the actor who is on trial here today, ladies and gentlemen. It is not that public face. Like many public men . . . they have a private side, a private life, a private face. And that is the face we will expose to you in this trial, the other side of O. J. Simpson, the side you never met before. . . .

"When we look upon and look behind that public face . . . you'll see a different face. And the evidence will show that the face you will see and the man that you will see will be the face of a batterer, a wife beater, an abuser, a controller . . . the face of Ron's and Nicole's murderer." Darden recited the litany of abuse in their relationship: "domestic abuse, domestic violence, stalking, intimidation, physical abuse, wife beating, public humiliation." He said at one point, "Please keep in mind that all of these different kinds of abuse were all different methods to control her." And yet the list of incidents, on close analysis, was rather thin. In Simpson's trial, the prosecution could point to only a single example of "wife beating," the 1989 incident for which Simpson was arrested and then pleaded no contest. There were no other proved examples of physical violence between them. Nicole had referred to several more incidents in the diary she prepared in connection with her divorce proceeding, but Ito had ruled (correctly) that that document was inadmissible hearsay evidence. Here, the Simpson case illustrated one of the larger tragedies of domestic violence—that it usually takes place without witnesses.

Still, with the district attorney having made the Simpson trial into a domestic-violence showcase, Darden pressed on, even lapsing into a kind of California psychobabble at times. "He stripped her of her self-esteem," Darden said. "He was so controlling that he attempted to define her identity. He attempted to define who

BLAMING FAYE ||| 245

she was." Darden's theory even turned what others might call Simpson's generosity against him. Darden said with disdain that O.J. gave Nicole money. "By the time she was nineteen, she was driving a Porsche. He got it for her." That, too, according to Darden, was evidence of his desire for control.

Everything Darden said was probably true, but his opening could also be interpreted as a great edifice of rhetoric built on a foundation of little evidence. The prosecution's problem was exacerbated, of course, by the makeup of the jury, which was filled with people predisposed to admire Simpson and to discount evidence of domestic violence.

Darden finished with the story of Sydney's dance recital on the night of June 12. The prosecutor had picked up confidence as he spoke, and he now addressed the jury instead of his shoes. O.J. arrived late at the recital, bearing flowers for Sydney, Darden said, and he greeted everyone in the Brown family—"except Nicole." Simpson moved a chair to the corner of the auditorium, and "he sat there facing Nicole, and he just stared at her. He just sat there staring at her. . . . This was a menacing stare, a penetrating stare. It was an angry stare, and it made everyone very uncomfortable."

The Brown family, Darden said, had decided to have dinner at the Mezzaluna restaurant, and "as they left, they made it clear to the defendant that he was not invited, and he wasn't invited. And by not inviting him, it was a reaffirmation of what he had already been told, and that is that it was over. He was no longer being treated as a part of the family. He was no longer the central centerpiece of every family outing. Nicole was getting on with her own life.

"And as the Brown family left, they looked toward the defendant and they saw him, and he was angry and he was depressed, and they were concerned, and everyone wondered, What is he up to now?

"Ms. Clark," Darden muttered quietly, "will tell you exactly what the defendant was up to as the day proceeded on."

His conclusion was almost elegant in its simplicity: "She left him. She was no longer in his control. He could not stand to lose her, and so he murdered her."

|||||

Marcia Clark's style differed from her colleague's. Businesslike, almost chipper, she stood behind the podium and moved only when she had somewhere to go—as opposed to Darden's nervous pacing. She began by introducing all of the lawyers on the prosecution team, the traditional duty of the lead counsel. And that, in part, was her mission on this day. A good prosecutor commands the courtroom, orchestrates the case. She wanted to show the jury who was in charge.

Darden had spoken without exhibits; Clark employed a series of elegantly integrated photographs, slides, and charts in her presentation. This in itself was unusual. Most district attorney's offices cannot afford to give their prosecutors much more than a blackboard. But even though Clark had dismissed DecisionQuest from jury selection, the prosecution did continue to accept the company's pro bono assistance in making charts and other visual aids. DecisionQuest ultimately made hundreds of these state-of-the-art exhibits over the course of the trial, an effort that would have cost a paying client nearly $1 million.

Picking up the story on the evening of June 12, Clark introduced the jury to "Kato," whose last name would scarcely ever be uttered during the trial, and she told of his trip to McDonald's with Simpson, which ended with their parting around 9:40 P.M.

Her pace quickening, Clark turned to Nicole's movements in the hours before the murders. After the dance recital, Nicole and her family had dined at Mezzaluna. They returned home and then, also at 9:40 P.M., Juditha Brown called her daughter to say she had dropped her glasses on the sidewalk outside the restaurant. "That was the last time Juditha ever spoke to her daughter Nicole," Clark said. Nicole then called Mezzaluna and asked that her friend Ron Goldman, a waiter there, bring them to her house. He left for his home, and then Nicole's, at about 9:50 P.M.

It was a very specific opening statement, with a multitude of times and places identified for the jury. This is risky business for a prosecutor, for an opening is nothing more (and nothing less) than a promise to the jury of what the evidence will show. Broken promises, even on relatively innocuous subjects, can embarrass a prosecutor—or worse. There was, in fact, no real reason to lay the story out with such precision; no jury could be expected to remember such details over the many months to come. But it was a measure of Clark's confidence that she thought she had the story so thoroughly nailed down.

Clark's precision extended even to the animal world—that is, to the subject of barking dogs. "At approximately 10:15 P.M.," she said, "Pablo Fenjves, who lived diagonally across the alley behind Nicole's condominium, heard a dog begin to bark." A moment later, Clark even repeated the time, this time without the qualifying "approximately." The dog barked at "10:15." Clark thus committed the prosecution to a theory of the case that had the murders taking place shortly before 10:15 P.M. As Clark knew even before her opening statement, other credible evidence put the time of the murders about fifteen minutes later. Placing the murders at 10:30 or even shortly after—or, better yet, leaving the time somewhat vague at that early stage in the case—could still have served the prosecution's purposes. But again Clark's arrogance led her to an unwise commitment.

Speaking with few notes, Clark gracefully integrated the disparate strands of the story. O.J.'s whereabouts were unaccounted for after 9:40 P.M., when he and Kato parted, until Allan Park, the limousine driver, saw him at 10:55 P.M. hustling into the house. During that period, Kato heard loud thumps outside, near the air conditioner, which was precisely where the bloody glove was later found. (Never in her opening did Clark mention the name of the detective who had found the glove, Mark Fuhrman.) Even though it was a cool night, Clark noted that O.J. asked Park to turn up the limo's air conditioner as they raced to make Simpson's 11:45 P.M. flight to Chicago. She turned, at last, to the discovery of the bodies.

"Now I'm going to show you what Sukru Boztepe saw when Nicole's dog took him to 875 South Bundy," Clark said, and then she nodded toward Jonathan Fairtlough, a junior prosecutor whose role it would be throughout the trial to control the video and slide projections on the large screen that was bolted above the witness stand.

"P-7," said Fairtlough, calling out the exhibit number.

The photograph had been taken from the sidewalk, looking toward the stairway that led up to Nicole's front door. The young woman lay in a fetal position in a pool of blood. Clark had shown these photographs to the family members before so that they wouldn't have to see them for the first time in the courtroom. But Juditha and Lou Brown still shuddered, steeling themselves as they saw again the scene of their daughter's death.

Clark then described how Officer Riske crept up the walkway, trying not to disturb the trail of blood, "to a point where he was able to see . . . that it was not just Nicole, but also Ron."

"P-11," said Fairtlough.

The Browns—the parents and the three surviving sisters—heaved their shoulders as one when the photograph of Ronald Goldman came up on the screen. It was a far more gruesome image: his body wedged into the corner of the fence, his shirt pulled over his head, and his exposed torso—so muscular and young—marred by obvious knife wounds filled with congealed blood. Clark's words added to the horror: "He was literally backed into a cage where he had nowhere to run and that is how his murder was accomplished in a very short amount of time." A *cage*—the phrase was so awfully right for the place that Goldman had died. Clark next moved to a photograph of Nicole taken from the top of the stairs. Her body was curled, and no wounds were visible, but the quantity of blood was shocking.

Clark turned now to the last and most powerful portion of her opening statement: the story of the blood. She offered a brief, homey introduction to the subject of DNA testing—"Some of you talked about *Jurassic Park* and they used DNA to make dinosaurs"—and then she offered a preview of the results. Fairtlough put up the slides of the various blood spots:

By the left door handle in O.J.'s Bronco: "Matches the defendant," said Clark.

On the center console of the Bronco: "Consistent with a mixture of the defendant and Ron Goldman."

The socks in Simpson's bedroom: "The blood on one spot matched the defendant. The blood on another spot matched Nicole."

Each one of the blood drops to the left of the bloody size-twelve shoe prints leaving the murder scene:

"Matches the defendant."

"Matches the defendant."

"Matches the defendant."

"Matches the defendant."

"And the results of the analysis of that blood confirms what the rest of the evidence will show," Clark said, "that on June the 12th,

1994, after a violent relationship in which the defendant beat her, humiliated her, and controlled her, after he took her youth, her freedom, and her self-respect, just as she tried to break free, Orenthal James Simpson took her very life in what amounted to his final and his ultimate act of control." She then paused a beat.

"And in that final and terrible act, Ronald Goldman, an innocent bystander, was viciously and senselessly murdered."

||||||

Shortly after Clark finished her opening statement, a producer for Court TV, which ran the camera in Ito's courtroom, advised the judge that the camera had accidentally shown the face of an alternate juror for about a second. A furious Ito said categorically, "I'm going to terminate the television coverage as a result of that." But in what would become characteristic of his style throughout the trial, Ito cooled off and changed his mind the following morning. No one enjoyed the attention more than the judge; the cameras could stay. He even praised Court TV for its candid acknowledgment of the mistake. Then he called for Johnnie Cochran to begin his presentation for the defense.

Cochran wore a periwinkle suit. Vertical white stripes ran the entire length of his tie, and there were blue and white vertical stripes on his shirt, too, to go with a contrasting white collar. Somehow it looked right, all that exuberance in Cochran's dress. He stood before the same podium the prosecutors had used, but he radiated a confidence that they could not hope to equal. Cochran's chest looked like it was ready to burst out of his form-fitting double-breasted suit.

Anyone wondering what place race would play in the defense of O. J. Simpson had only to wait about one minute into Cochran's opening statement. The jurors, Cochran said, would hear a lot of talk about justice. Searching the jurors' faces, he went on, "I guess Dr. Martin Luther King said it best when he said that injustice anywhere is a threat to justice everywhere, and so we are now embarked upon this search for justice, this search for truth, this search for the facts." Cochran then paused to pay tribute to the jurors. "We are very, very pleased with the fact that you have agreed to serve as jurors, to give us your time, to leave your lives, to be sequestered as it were. That is a remarkable sacrifice," he continued. "Abraham Lincoln said it best when he said that the highest act of citizenship is jury service."

Having enlisted King and Lincoln in the cause, Cochran went on to discuss parts of the case that Clark and Darden "didn't talk about yesterday." He started with the tale of the maid who lived next door to Simpson on Rockingham: Rosa Lopez. On the night of the murders, according to Cochran, Lopez "heard something very strange. She heard a prowler." When Lopez came out to walk her dog at 10:15 P.M.—ostensibly the time of the murders—she saw the Bronco parked in the same place it had been earlier in the evening. From Lopez, Cochran moved on to Mary Anne Gerchas— "a very interesting lady"—who was apartment hunting on Bundy Drive on the night of the murders. Shortly after 10:30 that night, Cochran said, Gerchas was walking on Bundy, and "she sees four men who come within ten feet of her, two of which gentlemen appeared to be Hispanic, I think the others are Caucasians, several of which I believe have knit caps on their heads. The two who are behind apparently have something in their hands they are carrying."

Cochran charged that these witnesses had been ignored by the police and prosecution. Cochran noted with disdain that Lopez had been interviewed by one Mark Fuhrman. "Detective Mark Fuhrman will play an integral part in this case for a number of reasons. Now, it is very interesting that the prosecution never once mentioned his name yesterday. It is like they just want to hide him, but they can't hide him. He is very much a part of this case. We can only ask ourselves, Why didn't they mention him? I think that answer will become very clear to you as the case progresses." And as for Gerchas, Cochran said she had called the police hot line about the case and was told, " 'Excuse me, I'm talking to a psychic right now, and I will get back to you.' " Cochran shook his head at the lack of respect for the "very interesting" Mary Anne Gerchas.

But the treatment of these witnesses all fit into a larger pattern. "This case is about a rush to judgment," Cochran asserted, "an obsession to win at any cost and by any means necessary." Invoking Malcolm X's most famous phrase, "by any means necessary," Cochran declared war on the LAPD. The case against O. J. Simpson, in other words, was really about the conspiracy to convict him.

It was about something else, too. Like the prosecution's juror research, the defense focus groups had also found hostility among black women toward Nicole Brown Simpson. In his opening, Cochran gave the jurors every reason to reinforce their presumed predisposition to view O.J. as an icon and Nicole as a tramp. Cochran took issue with Darden's assertion that O.J. had "exercised all this control over her and picked her friends. . . . The evidence will show that Miss Nicole Brown Simpson is a very strong, independent woman," Cochran went on. "She picked and chose her own friends, [neither] O. J. Simpson or no one else could tell her who her friends were to be. She had whatever friends she wanted, she did whatever she wanted."

Cochran then regaled the jury with tales of Nicole's fast life. Though nominally aimed at refuting the charge of stalking, Cochran ran though a catalogue of her sexual exploits. Sex on a couch with Keith Zlomsowitch while the children slept upstairs . . . Sex with one of Simpson's best friends (Marcus Allen, though Cochran did not name him) . . . One man "sitting astride Miss Nicole Brown Simpson, giving her a massage or something in her shoulders" . . . "Miss Nicole Brown Simpson came over to the Rockingham house and said she had found a boyfriend, somebody different than Keith." But with these examples, Cochran was just warming up for his main point about Nicole's sordid personal life—that the sinister figure of Faye Resnick was at the center of it.

"Let me say this about Faye Resnick," Cochran said gravely. On June 3, 1994, her boyfriend, Christian Reichardt, had thrown her out of their house because she was freebasing cocaine. "They ran in this circle out there in Brentwood. And when she was put out on June third, . . . she then moved over and lived with Nicole Brown Simpson."

Cochran implied that Nicole and Faye were doing drugs together: "Because they were friends, they would go out at night. The evidence will be these ladies would go out two, three, four nights a week and stay out until five o'clock in the morning. Nobody was controlling these women . . . They go out dancing, they would do whatever they would do, and we know Faye Resnick was using drugs during this period of time." Cochran went on to say that Faye's drug problem got so bad that on June 8, her ex-boyfriend and ex-husband forced her to enter a drug treatment facility. Cochran then said Faye Resnick was "one of the people that called Miss Nicole Brown Simpson on the night of June 12, perhaps after nine o'clock, that particular night, from this drug treatment facility." After a pause, Cochran said darkly, "We will be talking about that and her role in this whole drama."

Cochran's opening statement represented a bold risk. Most defense attorneys use their opening statements to remind jurors of the presumption of innocence, to urge them to keep an open mind—and to make as few promises as possible. A defendant in a criminal case has no obligation to put forward any evidence, and few defense attorneys want to commit themselves at the beginning of a long trial to naming the witnesses they will call to the stand. So what Cochran did was all the more remarkable. He made scores of specific, factual claims about the evidence in the case, and described in detail some of the witnesses he would be calling. Cochran's supremely confident opening statement demonstrated how central a figure he was to the defense strategy. He became the very incarnation of O. J. Simpson, his voice for the jury. Cochran sought to transfer his enormous prestige in the middle-class black community to his client. On the defense team, only Cochran had the stature—and the race—to do that.

|||||

There was another new player in the courtroom during opening statements, and he took an amused interest in Cochran's tale of the nefarious Faye Resnick. Five and a half feet tall and nearly as wide, Lawrence Schiller would become a frequent presence in the corridors outside Department 103 and in the twelfth-floor media center. Bearded, balding, shoveling endless fistfuls of M&M's past his yellowing teeth, the fifty-eight-year-old Schiller represented an apotheosis of sorts for the O. J. Simpson spectacle: the perfectly amoral profiteer. Schiller bore a passing resemblance to the actor Zero Mostel, and he appeared in the Simpson case as the reincarnation of Mostel's character in the film *The Producers*—the man who tried to sell the public on a show called *Springtime for Hitler*.

A onetime photographer for *Life* and other magazines, Schiller operated on the fringes of show business for decades and left a trail of multiple divorces, embittered business associates, and bankruptcy. Schiller specialized in exploiting an arcane and odious corner of the literary marketplace: the purchase of book rights to murderers' life stories. He made deals with Jack Ruby, Susan Atkins (of the Manson family), and Gary Gilmore. It was, in fact, Larry Schiller's interviews with Gilmore and others that provided the raw material for Norman Mailer's masterpiece *The Executioner's Song*. The only real surprise about Schiller was that he took several months to surface in the Simpson affair. Schiller even had good entree: He was a longtime acquaintance of Robert Kardashian, and had lived near O.J. and his first wife many years before. Through Kardashian, Schiller inveigled an invitation to visit Simpson in jail. As he later described it to a friend, Schiller told O.J., "You are a literary resource. You need someone who can exploit it"—i.e., me.

Simpson agreed, and Schiller came up with the idea of a book of O.J.'s responses to the many thousands of letters he had received in jail. With Kardashian's help, Schiller contrived to have his name placed on the list of "material witnesses" who were allowed to visit Simpson in jail. (There were, ultimately, fifty-two people on this list, and many of them, like Paula Barbieri, were Simpson's friends more than potential witnesses in the trial; this arrangement is another example of Simpson's favorable treatment by law enforcement authorities.) Schiller acknowledged privately that it was preposterous to suggest that he was really a "material witness" in the case, but the jail guards never challenged him, even when he began to lug a large, high-quality tape recorder into his meetings with the defendant.

At his home in Studio City, Schiller used his personal computer to edit the letters and O.J.'s responses, and even to lay out the pages. As Schiller put it together, the book was almost comically sympathetic to O.J. In a chapter called "Spousal Abuse," for example, the first letter to Simpson began, "Mr. Simpson—One thing I wanted to say, everyone is focusing on the alleged abuse you inflicted on your ex-wife. No one has mentioned the abuse she inflicted on you. . . ." Simpson responded to these letters with a series of banal pieties, most of them focusing on his supposed great faith in God. (In fact, before his arrest, Simpson neither attended church nor showed any interest in spiritual matters in conversations with friends.) Speculating about his life after prison, Simpson wrote, "I know that I will raise my children differently in relationship to God. Without a doubt. I can visualize it. I have already visualized each Sunday. I won't play golf. Sunday we will go to church. . . ."

Wandering around the pressroom, Schiller chuckled at the notion that Simpson's protestations of innocence might be true. His interest in the matter was purely commercial. In concert with his publisher, Little, Brown, Schiller arranged for the book to be printed under false names at three plants around the country. Then, according to the plan, the trucks would roll up to bookstores just before Cochran was to begin his opening statement. In perhaps his greatest marketing coup, Schiller arranged for an audiotape of Simpson reading excerpts from the book to be sold at the same time. Schiller thought the tape itself might be profitable, but he knew that the news media would rush to give the public the opportunity to hear Simpson's voice—and thus give the book enormous free advertising.

Schiller's plan worked to perfection. The book, called *I Want to Tell You*, was released a few days early, on January 7, and it became an enormous success, selling more than 650,000 copies. As Don Vinson might have predicted, booksellers found that black women bought the book in especially large numbers.

It wasn't just Simpson's obvious guilt that Schiller found amusing. He also scoffed at the notion that Simpson actually wrote or said all that was attributed to him in the book. One of the most quoted passages in the book came on the very last page: "I know in my heart that the answer to the death of Nicole lies somewhere in the world that Faye Resnick inhabited." According to Schiller, "I put that in at the last minute."

It was all, thus, part of a coordinated attack on Nicole, her lifestyle, and especially her friends—Uelman's elliptical hints about drug dealers; one of Cochran's opening remarks about "these ladies [who] would go out two, three, four nights a week and stay out until five o'clock in the morning"; and finally, Schiller's book. Through all these allegations—indeed, through the entire trial and beyond—not a shred of evidence ever surfaced linking any individual except O. J. Simpson to the crime. The defense never ventured an explanation of why drug dealers linked in some way to Faye Resnick would have wanted to kill Nicole Brown Simpson (much less Ron Goldman). That wasn't the point of the defense strategy. The point was to muddy the character of the target of this homicide.

In the end, the reason for the defense's obsession with Resnick can be found in the focus groups—that is, in the overwhelming lack of sympathy that black women felt for Nicole Brown Simpson. The "Resnick card" was just another version of the "race card"—in this case, an outlet for the resentment of black women toward the blond temptress who had snared this black hero.

||||||

The remainder of Cochran's opening statement hewed predictably to the defense themes. He described what he called O.J.'s "circle of benevolence"—a phrase the lawyer used to describe the defendant's financial contributions to charity (which in fact were minimal) and to Nicole's family (which were considerable). He said that O.J. suffered from arthritis so severe that on the day of the murder, "he could not shuffle the cards when he played gin rummy at the country club." Cochran mentioned a dog walker by the name of Tom Lang (not the detective), who said he saw Nicole embracing a man on the street in front of her home on the night of the murder, as well as "a man that he described as Hispanic or Caucasian standing . . . there looking as though he was angry." Cochran disparaged the work of the LAPD employees who had collected and analyzed the evidence, and he offered a brief criticism of the DNA evidence. At the same time, Cochran asserted that DNA tests (presumably reliable ones) proved that blood found underneath Nicole's fingernails was inconsistent with her own, Goldman's, or Simpson's. Finally, Cochran returned again and again to Rosa Lopez—the next-door maid who would testify that O.J.'s Bronco was parked on Rockingham at the time that the prosecution asserted the murders were taking place. (In all, Cochran mentioned Lopez's name more than a dozen times.)

It was, on one level, a remarkable opening statement. Cochran cited any number of specific witnesses who would directly contradict the government's theory of the case. If the defense lawyers could back up Cochran's claims, the prosecution's case would be shattered. But as it turned out, they couldn't; indeed, they didn't even try. By the end of the trial, the defense would never back up *any* of Cochran's startling claims. It would never call dog walker Tom Lang to the witness stand. It would never call Faye Resnick. It would never even call Rosa Lopez (although she would indeed become a participant in the trial.) The blood under Nicole's fingernails turned out to be her own. The reason Simpson didn't shuffle the deck of cards was because his friend Alan Austin didn't let him: Austin knew O.J. always cheated when he dealt. And Cochran's star witness, Mary Anne Gerchas, turned out to be a pathological liar who spent her life dodging creditors and who, shortly after Cochran's opening statement, would plead guilty to defrauding the Marriott Hotel of more than $24,000. Before Gerchas pleaded guilty, she claimed that an impostor using her name had actually run up the bill at the hotel. The defense would never call Gerchas, either.

In his opening, Cochran built a Potemkin village of assertions. There was nothing beneath the rhetoric. No matter; the evidence mattered less than what Cochran said it would be. He had planted the seeds: The LAPD was corrupt; O.J. was virtuous; Nicole deserved what she got.

||||||

Cochran's opening statement was also an unethical piece of lawyering. California discovery law obligated each side to turn over to the other all statements by witnesses it planned to call over the course of the trial. As part of the discovery process, starting even before the preliminary hearing, the prosecution had given the defense tens of thousands of pages of material. The defense, in contrast, had given the prosecution next to nothing. This was not in itself highly unusual—the defense in a criminal case always generates far less investigatory material than does the prosecution. But as the prosecution continued to demand defense-witness statements throughout the summer and fall and into the winter, the defense lawyers responded that they understood their obligations but had nothing to share.

Then, during Cochran's opening statement to the jury, his major-domo, Carl Douglas, announced that he had found statements of twelve witnesses whom Cochran had suggested the defense was going to call. Many of these statements, including one by Mary Anne Gerchas, had been taken by the defense several months earlier. This discovery failure, as it is known, put the prosecutors at a real disadvantage—not so much because they couldn't prepare for Gerchas's testimony in the defense case, which would not begin for months, but because if Clark had known about Gerchas's claims, she could have addressed them in her opening statement. The news of the Gerchas statement blindsided Clark and her colleagues.

The next day, Carl Douglas addressed the issue of the discovery failures by the defense team. Douglas made his living by keeping track of Cochran's schedule and making sure Cochran had the right file in his hand at the right time. When the center of operations in the defense camp shifted from Shapiro's office to Cochran's after the first of the year, it was Douglas's thankless task to untangle the files.

Now, in his arch, almost archaic speaking style, he tried to explain that the withholding of the documents had just been an unfortunate mistake. "The Court is well aware that we have been working diligently in this matter," Douglas said. "The Court is equally aware that the work in this case has been divided among a couple of offices and investigators, et cetera. It perhaps is regrettable that I stand before this Court, that we have not coordinated all of our defense efforts as well as I would have liked before this point. I say that because, Your Honor, I have some documents that I do intend to give over to the people. . . . Your Honor, I acknowledge and I anticipate that there will be strenuous efforts to impugn both my personal integrity and the integrity of the defense team. I tell this Court, looking the Court straight in the eye with all seriousness, that it had been an oversight, and I am embarrassed by it and I take full responsibility."

Ito, who had been studying the prosecution table as Douglas spoke, observed, "I have to say, Mr. Douglas, I've had long experience with Mr. Hodgman. I've known him as a colleague, as a trial lawyer, and I've never seen the expressions on his face that I've seen today."

The judge turned to the bearded and usually stoic prosecutor and said, "Mr. Hodgman, why don't you take a few deep breaths, and we'll take a look at this."

Among his other responsibilities, Bill Hodgman supervised the discovery process for the prosecution. The disclosure about these twelve witness statements came on top of the defense's disclosure, one day earlier, that it had a list of thirty-four new witnesses it planned to call during the trial. These were appalling violations of the discovery laws, and Hodgman felt personally wounded by what he regarded as a dirty trick. In the Todd Bridges attempted-murder case, Hodgman had enjoyed a cordial relationship with Cochran; in a prosecution of financier Charles Keating before Judge Ito, Hodgman had likewise had the confidence of the court and his adversaries. As Ito observed, Hodgman now looked stricken.

Shapiro noticed, too. When Hodgman rose to speak, Jo-Ellan Dimitrius whispered to Shapiro at the defense table, "You know, Bill doesn't look too good." Shapiro agreed, then quipped, "Yeah, tomorrow they're going to take him out on a stretcher."

14. THANK YOU, CARL

It to broke for the day early on January 25 so that the prosecutors could regroup and decide what sanctions they would ask the judge to impose on the defense for its discovery violations. Hodgman trudged upstairs with his colleagues to weigh what they should do.

For Bill Hodgman, assignment to the Simpson case had paid few dividends. He did not escape all of his administrative responsibilities, yet he didn't have full control of the trial, either. Though Clark had recently served as Hodgman's assistant in the office, and though the two of them were nominally identified as co–lead counsel, the case remained fundamentally hers. Their temperaments were ill matched: Clark, mercurial, passionate, disorganized; Hodgman, methodical, contemplative, a little dull. He scheduled meetings at three-thirty, and Clark appeared at five. It wasn't that Clark was slacking off—she probably worked more total hours than her colleague—but she did it in an anarchic manner that drove Hodgman to distraction. Hodgman felt betrayed, too, by the discovery violations and other ethical lapses of Cochran and his colleagues. In all, the pressure was great, the rewards few.

As Hodgman and Clark were briefing Gil Garcetti on the day's events, Hodgman noticed a strange feeling in his chest. Not pain, exactly, but a tightening. He got up and walked around, but the sensation didn't go away. At Garcetti's suggestion paramedics were called, and at about 6:20 P.M., an ambulance took Hodgman to the California Medical Center. He was, at the time, forty-one years old. Doctors found an irregular pattern in his electrocardiogram and decided to keep him overnight. A senior member of Garcetti's staff called Ito at home to give him the news, and by morning word of Hodgman's hospitalization had leaked out to the news media. The hospital was promptly besieged by television satellite trucks, and white-jacketed doctors began conducting briefings in a manner usually associated with presidential illnesses. In the end, Hodgman was fine; his condition was temporary, seemingly the result of stress and overwork. Though he returned to the D.A.'s office after only a few days at home—and he continued to supervise the case—Hodgman had to yield his courtroom role. Henceforth, the case would be tried by Marcia Clark and Chris Darden.

Hodgman's departure would turn out to be one of the most important events of the trial. His absence deprived the prosecution of a day-to-day center of gravity, a voice of calm and maturity. Hodgman could tell the difference between an everyday dispute and a bona fide crisis. Clark and Darden, in contrast, tried cases in an atmosphere of perpetual turmoil, much of it self-generated.

The shift in mood was immediately apparent. Addressing Judge Ito about the discovery violations, Clark and Darden nearly became unhinged. True, the defense had engaged in rather cynical misconduct, but in the context of a long trial, the withholding of a few witness statements was probably not going to amount to much. What should have mattered more to the prosecution was simply getting the case under way and its witnesses on the stand. Instead, for several hours, Clark and Darden ranted.

Clark: "Unfortunately, because of the nature of this misconduct, which is egregious and flagrant and not the minor violation that [Cochran] attempts to represent to this court, he's attempting to sweep it under the rug, claim ignorance and use Mr. Douglas as a sacrificial lamb, and that is absolutely inappropriate. Counsel should bear the brunt of his own misconduct, which is willful and deliberate and intentional, and it is in effect a thumbing of his nose at this Court's order. . . ." And so on.

Darden's behavior was even stranger. Cochran's stature in L.A.'s black legal community was such that the relatively inexperienced Darden was, perhaps understandably, intimidated by his mere presence (and the older man would use this against the younger man time and again during the course of the trial). Cochran's hold over Darden bordered on the mystical—or, more precisely, the parental. This often led the prosecutor to behave like an adolescent, appearing alternately to disdain and beseech his elder. When Cochran spoke in court, Darden would often hunch over in his seat, hold his head in his hands, puff his cheeks, and pout theatrically.

On this day (and several others during the trial), Darden seemed to blurt out the first thing that came into his head. "Had we known about some of these witnesses," Darden said to Ito (and, quite obviously, the television camera), "we could have informed counsel that they are heroin addicts, thieves, felons, and that one of these witnesses, one of their so-called material witnesses, is the only person I have ever known to be a court-certified pathological liar." This was a scandalous remark to make about a dozen people who had done no more than have their names mentioned by a lawyer in a criminal trial. To be sure some of them, like Gerchas, were questionable characters, but others were upstanding, ordinary citizens who had cooperated with both sides and simply remembered events in a manner helpful to the defendant's case. Darden's group libel reflected his own immaturity more than the witnesses' true natures.

Rambling on, Darden turned to the subject of Cochran. "You know, as I sat there yesterday . . . watching Mr. Cochran, I noticed that his opening statement, most of it was typed. He had time to type it, to type out that opening statement, and it was a very fine opening statement. And I'm always proud of Mr. Cochran whenever I see him in court, Your Honor. I love him. I just don't like to go up against him. But if he had time to type his opening statement, then he had time to turn it over. And I'm disappointed in Mr. Cochran."

So it went—for hour after hour. Darden at one point requested that the trial be delayed for thirty days as a result of the defense misconduct—a patently absurd idea when a sequestered jury was waiting to hear testimony. Ito, characteristically, said nothing during the lengthy harangues by the lawyers, not even when Darden made his bizarre profession of love for Cochran. After only about fifteen minutes, the lawyers started repeating themselves, concentrating mainly on cranking up the invective. Ito froze. A stronger, more self-confident judge would have stopped the name-calling, limited debate, and focused on the jury, which had been sitting in a hotel room for two full weeks and had not even heard all of the opening statements.

In the end, Ito reached a reasonable resolution of the issue. He agreed to put off the conclusion of Cochran's opening statement until Monday, January 30, to advise the jury that defense misconduct had caused the delay, and to allow Clark to make a brief re-opening statement the following day.

|||||

It was 10:05 A.M. on January 31 when Lance Ito asked, "Mr. Darden, who is your first witness?" (During jury selection in the fall, Ito had told the panel that he expected the *entire trial* would be over by late February.)

Prosecutors know they have a jury's full attention at the beginning of a trial, so they like to start out with a dramatic, powerful witness who cannot be effectively cross-examined. Darden and Clark chose well.

"Sharyn Gilbert, Your Honor."

Gilbert, a rotund and good-natured black woman, was working as a 911 operator in downtown Los Angeles during the early morning hours of January 1, 1989. Her phone rang at 3:58 A.M.

This was not Nicole's famous 911 call from 1993. This was, in its way, far more chilling. When Darden played the tape of this call, there were no words, just a rumbly silence, as if a phone had been left hanging limp from a table. Then a woman screamed . . . and screamed some more. Next, unmistakably, flesh collided with flesh—the sound of slapping or hitting of some kind. After about three minutes, the line went dead.

Gilbert's computer had registered that the call came from 360 North Rockingham, so she urgently dispatched a police unit to the location. The assignment went to Officer John Edwards, who was working in a patrol car with a trainee, Patricia Milewski. Darden called Edwards as his next witness. Edwards told of finding Nicole, her face battered, staggering around the bushes in just sweatpants and a bra. He recalled her prophetic cries of "He's going to kill me! He's going to kill me!"

Cochran's cross-examination was more notable for what he didn't do than what he did. The lawyer poked a little fun at the detective, noting that he had languished as a patrol officer for nineteen long years. Continuing his effort to diminish Nicole in the eyes of the jury, Cochran also asked a whole series of questions that suggested (without any evidence) that Nicole had been drunk during the New Year's Day altercation. But Cochran had a grenade in his pocket that he declined to use. Cochran never pointed out for the jury that in 1991, John Edwards had been named one of only forty-four officers identified by the Christopher Commission as part of a "problem group" within the LAPD. The commission, formed to investigate the police in light of the Rodney King beating, found that these officers had received highly disproportionate numbers of complaints for use of excessive force, dishonesty, discourtesy, and other misdeeds. In the Los Angeles black community, following the release of the Christopher Commission's report the existence of "the Forty-four" became important symbols of the LAPD's malevolence. Yet Cochran passed on the chance to tie Edwards in to his favorite theme of police racism.

The reason for this uncharacteristic diffidence became apparent as Edwards was followed to the stand by other officers involved in the 1989 incident. What was remarkable about their testimony was not how hard they had been on O. J. Simpson but how easy. Faced with a badly beaten woman who had the red imprint of a human hand on her neck, Edwards did not arrest the man who admitted to causing her injuries, not even after learning from both O.J. and Nicole that police had been called out to the house repeatedly on domestic-violence calls. Rather, even after O.J. conceded that he had hurt Nicole, and even after Nicole told him that O.J. kept guns in the house, Edwards graciously allowed Simpson to return to his house by himself and change out of his bathrobe. And then Edwards stood by as O.J. leaped into his Bentley and drove off. In the course of his examination, Darden had asked Edwards why he didn't arrest Simpson on the spot.

"Because I knew that if I took O. J. Simpson, a person of that stature, to the station in his underwear that there would be repercussions because the media would show up and it would be blown out of proportion."

Edwards admitted he didn't even file a complete report of the incident; he omitted, he said, Simpson's statement that he had had sex with one of the women living in the house earlier that day. Why did Edwards leave it out? In part because he didn't think it was relevant, but also because "it would just be a sensationalism thing."

This deferential police attitude toward Simpson became even more obvious when the next witness, Mike Farrell, the detective in charge of the 1989 domestic-violence investigation, took the stand. Farrell's inquiry, such as it was, consisted of calling O.J. on the telephone and then calling Nicole. Farrell's conversation with Nicole appeared to have amounted to the detective's telling the crime victim how she could drop the case against the man who had beaten her. In a manner typical of domestic-violence victims, Nicole preferred to get on with her life rather than take her husband to court. Farrell testified, "She said if she could avoid it, she doesn't want to prosecute." As Farrell admitted on the stand, the only reason he referred the case to the city attorney's office for prosecution is that the California domestic-violence law required him to do so.

The coddling of O.J. by the police placed Clark and Darden in an uncomfortable position. In the murder case against Simpson, of course, they were joined with, and supportive of, the LAPD. But it was clear to all of the prosecutors that the police had horribly bungled the domestic-violence matter. In a remarkable footnote to their brief to Judge Ito on the domestic-violence issues, the prosecutors made clear their disdain for their ostensible allies. "Nicole's feelings of helplessness and belief that the police would not do anything to the defendant were well founded," they wrote. "Members of the [West Los Angeles] division of the LAPD frequented defendant's home, often utilizing the pool and tennis courts. When the officers required the appearance of a celebrity at the yearly Christmas party, [the] defendant eagerly agreed to appear. When the officers desired his autograph on footballs, he responded. In turn, the officers responded to Rockingham in response to Nicole's calls for help 7–8 times prior to the 1989 incident. Each time the defendant was not arrested."

However, the true measure of Nicole's isolation came only with the next witness.

||||||

The lawyers on both sides of the Simpson case often learned as much through the news media as from their own investigators. For example, during jury selection, the prosecutors found out about one witness in Sheila Weller's *Raging Heart*, one of the "instant books" that were published in the months after the murders. The opening scene of Weller's book described a conversation between Simpson and a man "whom we will call Leo" in Simpson's bedroom late on the night of June 13, after Simpson had returned from his trip to Chicago and had been interviewed by the detectives at Parker Center. Simpson told "Leo" that the police had told him they had found blood in his house. "How long does it take for DNA to come back?" Simpson asked. "Leo," who didn't know, guessed two months. "They asked me if I would take a lie detector test," Simpson continued, adding that he didn't want to take one. " 'Cause," Simpson added with a kind of a chuckle, "I have had some dreams of killing her."

It didn't take long for the prosecutors to identify "Leo" as Ron Shipp, a former LAPD officer and longtime friend of O.J.'s. Shipp was a rather typical, if revealing, figure in Simpson's circle of hangers-on. Simpson and Shipp were, on one level, peers—black men of about the same age and background. Shipp had first met Simpson in the 1960s, when his brother played high school football against Simpson. But Simpson became a major figure in Shipp's life in the late seventies, when he was a patrol officer assigned to West Los Angeles. During that period, Shipp would stop by O.J.'s house on Rockingham as often as twice a week, to use the tennis court or just shoot the breeze. In 1982, Shipp was transferred downtown, so he visited the Rockingham house less often, about once a month. (Shipp had also served as a kind of counselor for Jason Simpson, O.J.'s troubled son from his first marriage. He spoke to the boy once when O.J. found that Jason had used cocaine and again when Jason attacked the life-size statue of O.J. by the Rockingham pool with a baseball bat.) In more recent years, Shipp had not prospered. He had developed a

drinking problem, was suspended from the police force, accepted
early retirement in 1989, and then, a year later, tried and failed to
be reinstated as a cop. His efforts at an acting career met with little success, save one small part on a television program that O.J.
helped him get.

Even though California law prohibited the prosecution from
mentioning the polygraph issue in front of the jury, the prosecutors wanted to call on Shipp to testify about his conversation with
O.J. about his "dreams" of killing Nicole. According to prosecutor Hank Goldberg, the statement would illustrate "the defendant's mental state and show his intention at or around the time
of the murder." (In a later argument on the same issue, Marcia
Clark cited Hollywood authority in support of admitting the
dream testimony, telling the judge, "Walt Disney said it best, I
think, in *Sleeping Beauty:* 'A dream is a wish your heart makes.' ")
Because Cochran was distantly related to Shipp, Carl Douglas
handled the witness for the defense. He urged Ito to exclude
Shipp's testimony because, as Douglas put it, dreams "are not
predictive of events that may have occurred in the past or predictive of things in the future." Evidence about the dream would
prove very little, especially divorced from its context in the conversation about the polygraph. Ito weighed the decision whether
to allow the dream testimony—and blew it. For all his failings as
a judge, Ito handled the hundreds of legal rulings in the case with
considerable skill; but he missed on this one. The judge said the
dream was admissible. (Ito essentially acknowledged this mistake
at the end of the trial by instructing the jury to discount the testimony about the dream.)

Simpson had absorbed the first few days of the trial impassively,
occupying himself with doodling or whispering comments to
Shapiro on his left or Cochran on his right. When Shipp walked to
the witness stand, though, Simpson came alive. He shook his
head, muttered beneath his breath, and generally made his contempt unmistakable.

After he took the oath, Shipp tried to avoid Simpson's gaze. The
former cop appeared a genuinely tortured figure—beholden to
Simpson, still admiring of him in some ways, and yet conscience-
stricken about what he knew. One could tell how much he had en-

joyed the days when he could come and go freely through the electric gates at Rockingham, when he had entered a world of privilege and savored his proximity to celebrity.

"Did you take officers to the defendant's home . . . ?" Darden asked him.

"Yes, I did. If I was on patrol, sometimes I would take people over there. I used to get a kick out of not telling them where I was going and ringing the doorbell and have O.J. come out and greet them."

"How many other officers would you say you took to Rockingham?"

"Wow. I would have to say approximately maybe—maybe forty guys maybe."

Darden asked if he and Simpson remained friends.

"I still love the guy, but, um, I don't know. I mean, this is a weird situation I'm sitting here in."

Shipp had made his love for Simpson evident following the January 1, 1989, incident with Nicole. Two days after the beating, Nicole called Shipp, who had some training in domestic-violence situations, to talk about what had happened with Simpson. Nicole asked Shipp to talk with O.J. and impress upon him how seriously she regarded the incident. Shipp did talk to Simpson, who "was very upset because he thought that he was going to lose Hertz and his image was going to be tarnished." Instead of helping Nicole, Shipp went to his supervisors at the West L.A. station and asked that the case against Simpson be dropped.

It is possible, then, to summarize Nicole Brown Simpson's experience with the LAPD after her beating in 1989. The officers on the scene let O.J. run off into the night. The detective on the case told her how to drop the charges. Nicole sought help from one police officer she knew, Ron Shipp, and he ran right to O.J. Shipp then went to a supervisor to try to get the charges dropped and in the end returned to Nicole to implore her to leave O.J.'s precious "image" intact. In a trial that resounded with talk of conspiracies within the LAPD, this was, in reality, the *only* conspiracy: the one to help O. J. Simpson escape prosecution for beating his wife in 1989. Small wonder, then, that in the week before her death, Nicole called a battered women's shelter, not the police, to report that her ex-husband was stalking her.

|||||

An effective defense cross-examination of Ron Shipp might have consisted of a question or two: "Mr. Shipp, do you want to do in your real life everything that you dream about?" "Do you know— does anyone know—what any specific dream really means?" Such an exchange would have communicated quickly to the jury just how much this "dream" testimony appeared to be worth.

Carl Douglas chose another tack: war. In this, he was reflecting the wishes of his client. Simpson was appalled that this hanger-on had turned on him. It upset the natural order of relationships he had lived with, and ruled over, for decades. The Ron Shipps simply do not do this sort of thing. And if they do, they are punished. Unfortunately for him, Simpson had to deputize the punishment of this lackey to Carl Douglas, who was almost certainly the weakest of the lawyers who appeared regularly in front of this jury. The cross-examination of Ron Shipp turned out to be very different from what the defense had planned. It became a study of celebrity and of power—indeed, an explanation in microcosm of why O. J. Simpson had murdered his wife and why he thought he could get away with it.

Instead of dismissing the dream comment, Douglas built it up. He began his cross-examination of Shipp by asking a long series of questions to establish that the witness had not disclosed the dream conversation in a number of interviews—with the police, with defense investigators, with Douglas himself. Shipp had essentially admitted all of this on direct examination, but then Douglas made a cardinal error. He asked a "why" question, which allows a witness, in effect, to say anything he wants. Why didn't you tell these people about the "dream"?

Because, Shipp said, "I really did not want to be really involved in all of this, and I didn't want to be going down as a person to nail O.J."

Suddenly, the dream remark wasn't innocuous; it nailed O.J. Unhappy with this answer, Douglas shot back, "Well, you're not. So don't worry about that." Clark objected, and Ito scolded Douglas. "Counsel, you know better," the judge said. "The jury is to disregard counsel's remark."

Clark smiled at Douglas's blunder and scribbled a note to Darden: *Thank you, Carl.*

Douglas then set off on another series of questions aimed at proving that Shipp had made up the story about the dream. Why didn't he tell the police earlier? Wasn't he just trying to enhance his acting career? Was he acting now? Trying to make himself famous?

Shipp replied with quiet dignity as the attacks grew harsher. "Mr. Douglas," he said at one point, "I put all my faith in God and my conscience. Since Nicole's been dead, I've felt nothing but guilt, my own personal guilt, that I didn't do as much as I probably should have."

Clark wrote it again. *Thank you, Carl.*

There was some irony in this line of attack, because Douglas—and all the other lawyers—knew that Shipp was almost certainly telling the truth about what he had heard Simpson say. Shipp asserted that his conversation with Simpson took place late on Monday night, June 13. Just a few hours earlier that day, Simpson had been interviewed by Vannatter and Lange. In the course of that conversation, Lange had asked Simpson whether Weitzman had talked about his taking a polygraph examination. "What are your thoughts on that?" Lange asked.

"Should I talk about my thoughts on that?" Simpson mused to the detectives. "I'm sure eventually I'll do it, but it's like I've got some weird thoughts now. I've had weird thoughts . . . You know when you've been with a person for seventeen years, you think everything. I've got to understand what this thing is. If it's true blue, I don't mind."

When Shipp spoke to Weller, he had no way of knowing what Simpson had said to the police on June 13. Yet Simpson's comments in the two conversations—to the detectives in the afternoon and to Shipp at night—bore a striking resemblance to one another. The police interview represented strong independent corroboration of Shipp's account.

Still, Douglas continued to flog Shipp. He suggested that Simpson in fact went to bed at 8:00 or 8:15 on the night of June 13. Shipp denied it. Douglas said other family members would confirm the early bedtime.

Shipp did something extraordinary at that point. Instead of answering Douglas, he started directing his testimony directly to the
defendant. "Is that what they are going testify to?" he implored his
former patron. As Douglas continued to press the issue, Shipp
started shaking his head. After a long pause, he stared again at
Simpson and said simply, "This is sad, O.J."

Simpson wasn't used to this kind of confrontation from the likes
of Ron Shipp. O.J. looked shaken, rubbing his hands nervously.
Shapiro noticed this and put his arm around him, as if in protection.

Douglas moved to his big finish for the day. "Were you and he
close friends?"

"I would say we were pretty good friends," Shipp said. "We
didn't—never went out to dinner like on a regular basis and stuff
like that."

Douglas seized on the phrase "regular basis." He pointed out
that Shipp and O.J. almost *never* ate meals together. Shipp readily
agreed. In contrast to Douglas's insinuations, Shipp was not trying
to project any false intimacy with O.J. The power of his testimony
came from the fact that Shipp knew what a toady he was. He knew
he adored and looked up to O.J., and he knew—ultimately—that
O.J. couldn't have cared less about him.

"O. J. Simpson is a football fan, isn't he?" Douglas asked.

"Yeah, he loves football, yes, he does."

"He goes to games a lot."

"Yes, he does," Shipp replied.

"You and O. J. Simpson have never attended a football game together—"

"Never."

"—in the twenty-six years that he's been your supposed friend,
have you?"

"Not one."

"You and your wife have never gone on a double date with Nicole
and O. J. Simpson in the entire time that you've known them, have
you?" Douglas sneered.

"You're absolutely correct. . . ." said Shipp.

"All the times that you claim that you were over his house playing tennis, you have never in your entire life played tennis on the
same court with O. J. Simpson, have you?"

"Never."

Then, finally, with disgust: "You're not really this man's friend, are you, sir?"

Shipp sighed. "Well, okay. All right. If you want me to explain it, I guess you can say I was like everybody else, one of his servants. I did police stuff for him all the time. I ran license plates. That's what I was. I mean, like I said, I loved the guy."

Thank you, Carl.

The voice of a victim from beyond the grave, lawyers always say, never loses its emotional power. Nicole calling 911 on October 25, 1993: "He's back. Please. . . . He's O. J. Simpson. I think you know his record. Could you just send somebody over here?" Weeping: "Could you please send somebody over?"

When Darden played the tape for the jury, the courtroom went absolutely still. Most people who listened to it on that day, including several jurors, had heard portions of the tape at one time or another, so many of Nicole's words had a familiar sound to them. Yet the playing of the tape in its entirety gave it a fresh meaning—and horror. Nicole could not have feigned the terror in her voice, the trembling, the weeping, as she alternated between beseeching the dispatcher and pacifying her ex-husband.

"Okay, just stay on the line," the dispatcher said.

"I don't want to stay on the line. He's going to beat the shit out of me," Nicole said, then she drew a long breath to try to calm herself.

There was a simple barometer of Simpson's reaction to testimony during his trial: The more it hurt, the more he talked. During innocuous testimony, O.J. would sit quietly, doodling or listening in a casual way. But incriminating testimony set him to responding, although he only had Shapiro to his left and Cochran to his right to lobby. Though ultimately unpersuasive to the jury, the domestic-violence evidence particularly set Simpson off. It hit him in the ego, and he played his favorite themes in response: But she wanted to get back together with me. The backdoor to Nicole's house on

Gretna Green, which Simpson damaged during his October 1993 tirade, was already broken. Simpson yammered through almost the entire playing of the tape. Cochran nodded vacantly at his client; Shapiro winced and tried to ignore him. O.J., oblivious to either reaction, talked on.

It was almost impossible to make out most of what O.J. was saying on the tape, but his voice conveyed astonishing rage, in both the intensity of his tirade and its duration. For the full thirteen and a half minutes of the telephone call, Simpson's screaming just went on and on, with no diminishment of fury.

Nicole pleaded, "O.J., O.J. The kids. O.J., O.J., the kids are sleeping." O.J.'s response was one of the few times his words could be made out clearly: "You didn't give a shit about the kids when you was sucking his dick in the living room. They were here. Didn't care about the kids then."

The dispatcher jumped in: "Is he upset with something that you did?"

"A long time ago," Nicole sighed. "It always comes back." The reference was to Nicole's encounter with Keith Zlomsowitch in 1992, which O.J. had observed from his stalking post outside her front windows.

Nicole: "Could you just please, O.J., O.J., O.J., O.J. Could you please leave? Please leave. Please leave."

"I'm leaving with my two fists is when I'm leaving."

For all the power of the tape, the next two witnesses demonstrated the limits of Darden's domestic-violence presentation. Carl Colby and Catherine Boe, husband and wife, had lived next door to Nicole on Gretna Green. They testified that they sometimes saw Simpson standing on the sidewalk looking into Nicole's house. But it was all pretty vague, especially because O.J.'s children lived there and their father had a right to visit them. Boe was especially spacey. At a sidebar conference, after Darden said, chuckling, "You just never really know what you are going to get from Mrs. Colby," Cochran chimed in, "She is an alien from another planet." At one point, when Boe began an exegesis on which varieties of trees around her house shed berries and why O.J. might not have wanted to park his white car beneath them, Darden had to turn his face away from the jury box because he was laughing so hard.

|||||

Denise Brown was supposed to be different. She had extensive firsthand exposure to O.J. and Nicole's relationship, including its darker sides. Since the moment Detective Tom Lange called her parents' home on the morning after the murders, Denise was convinced that O.J. had murdered her sister. If anyone could explain how this had happened, it would be Nicole's older sister. When Denise walked to the witness stand on Friday afternoon, February 3, she did not so much as glance at her former brother-in-law.

The four Brown sisters all looked and sounded alike, and they reflected the values of their moneyed Orange County upbringing. All four had breast implants, but not one had a college degree. The two oldest sisters, Denise and Nicole, the brunette and the blonde, came closest to embodying a certain California ideal: lithe, athletic, out for a good time, each a homecoming princess at Dana Point High School. Denise graduated in 1975 and became, briefly, a New York model. Nicole graduated on May 20, 1977, and met O. J. Simpson three weeks later.

Denise circulated on the periphery of Nicole's life for many years, alternately competitive and supportive, combative and loving. She dated many of Simpson's friends, including Al Cowlings, boutique owner Alan Austin, and advertising executive Ed McCabe. Married briefly in 1984, Denise had a child with another man several years later. In 1994, she and her son were living in her parents' home. The month before Nicole's murder, Denise spent eight days—from May 9 to May 17, 1994—as an inmate in the Huntington Beach jail, after pleading guilty for the second time to drunk-driving charges. (She had pleaded guilty to the same crime in 1992 but was not sentenced to jail.)

Though still beautiful, Denise Brown had an unmistakable hard edge. Taking the stand in a black pantsuit and a large gold cross, she obviously wanted this jury to convict.

"Miss Brown," Darden began. "You are Nicole Brown's oldest— older sister?"

"Yes. . . ."

"Do you have other sisters?"

"Yes. . . ."

"How many?"

"There's Dominique and Tanya and of course Nicole."

Darden began by asking when Denise first met "the defendant." She said that Nicole had invited her to travel to Buffalo in 1977, to see a Bills game with her. She said that at the game, "a friend of O.J.'s was there. He came over and said hello to us, and Nicole said hello, kissed him on both cheeks."

Darden asked if anything unusual then happened.

"Yeah," Denise said. "O.J. got real upset and he started screaming at Nicole."

This was less than five minutes into her testimony, and it brought both Shapiro and Cochran flying out of their seats to object. When the lawyers approached Ito at the sidebar, Ito wondered what was going on. "Mr. Darden," the judge said, "I thought we were just going to do a few more foundational things, not incidents, and my ruling on domestic violence doesn't include anything in this era. What are we doing here?"

"I'm not about to allege or solicit any testimony that the defendant beat Nicole in 1977, Your Honor," Darden said. "I'm just trying to define and explain the nature of their relationship, how it developed over the years." The judge didn't even have to hear from the defense lawyers to reject Darden's argument. The prosecutor was trying to pile on additional misdeeds by O.J. in front of the jury without having allowed the judge to rule on them first. Of course, the defense lawyers were wise to this game as soon as Darden started playing it, and Ito shut him down immediately.

It was an amateurish mistake by Darden, and bad strategy to boot, putting Denise on the stand and immediately eliciting tales of O.J.'s misbehavior from her. Properly prepared, Denise could have given the jury some real understanding of Nicole and O.J.'s relationship, the good times as well as the bad. She could have helped explain why Nicole was so attracted to O.J., indeed why she loved him so much and why she stayed with him even though he abused her. An honest summary of their relationship would have given Denise that much more credibility when she started describing O.J.'s bad acts. Instead, Darden tried to present O.J. as simply a domestic-violence machine, which was untrue and, in any event, unlikely to be believed by a jury already sympathetic to him.

Darden walked back to the podium still miffed at Ito's ruling and said to the witness, "Miss Brown, we're not going to talk about anything that occurred between 1977 and December 31, 1984, you understand that?" In other words, no context: Darden would just head straight to the first of the domestic-violence incidents. With just a question or two of introduction, Denise recalled a scene in 1987 at the Red Onion restaurant in Santa Ana. "At one point," Denise said, "O.J. grabbed Nicole's crotch and said, 'This is where babies come from and this belongs to me.' And Nicole just sort of wrote it off as if it was nothing, like—you know, like she was used to that kind of treatment and he was like—I thought it was really humiliating, if you ask me."

It was obvious that Denise was trying her best to bury O.J.—volunteering the additional (and inadmissible) details that Nicole was "used to" this treatment and that Denise found it "humiliating." Cochran understood what was going on. Back at the sidebar, Cochran implored Ito, "Now, we may look back on this and smile when the jury verdict comes in May or June [sic]. But for right now, we can't allow this to take place. I just don't think it's right."

Ito invited Darden's response.

"Your Honor," said the prosecutor, "I don't know what Mr. Cochran means by 'we can't allow.' Is he wearing the robe in this courtroom today?" Cochran so flummoxed Darden that the prosecutor thought he could use personal attack in lieu of legal argument.

Cochran responded as if he were speaking to a child: "I said we can't allow this without objection. That's all I said, Counsel."

Again, Ito directed Darden to take better control of his witness. Once more, with barely any introduction, Darden moved to another domestic-violence incident, a fight between O.J. and Nicole at the Rockingham house sometime in the mid-1980s. It started, Denise said, when she told O.J. he took Nicole for granted.

"Why did you tell him that?"

Shapiro objected, and Ito sustained it for the obvious reason: "Why this witness thinks that Miss Brown Simpson was taken for granted is not relevant."

Darden asked what happened next.

"He started yelling at me, 'I don't take her for granted. I do everything for her. I give her everything.' And he continued, and then a whole fight broke out, and pictures started flying off the walls, clothes started flying." Denise seemed on the verge of tears at this point. "He ran upstairs, got clothes, started flying down the stairs, and grabbed Nicole, told her to get out of his house, wanted us all out of his house, picked her up, threw her against the wall, picked her up, threw her out of the house. She ended up on her— she ended up falling. She ended up on her elbows and on her butt. . . . We were all sitting there screaming and crying, and then he grabbed me and threw me out of the house."

"Are you okay, Miss Brown?" Darden asked.

"Yeah," said Denise, pausing between tears. "It's just so hard. I'll be fine."

Darden turned to the judge. "Your Honor, if it pleases the Court, can we adjourn and continue this Monday morning?"

It is classic courtroom strategy to end with a dramatic moment on Friday afternoon—something for the jury to think about all weekend—and Darden had chosen this closing with care. As usual, however, Cochran was about three steps in front of him. In a heated sidebar conference before they broke for the weekend, Cochran lectured Darden for staging Denise's crying stunt at the end of a Friday. "They're not fooling anybody with this stuff," Cochran said. "I mean, I'm telling them it's going to backfire on them. They keep doing it, and it's not right."

Darden protested his innocence. "Mr. Cochran," he lectured his counterpart, "how else do you expect her to react, especially given these circumstances, given her relationship to the defendant, given how long she's known him? She is grieving, Mr. Cochran. It happens when people lose their loved ones. And I can't control that. I can't stop that. I didn't wield the knife. I didn't kill her. . . . Frankly, I'm touched by it. I feel bad about it. Maybe I'm a little slow to stop her, but I will attempt to do better. I will say, however, that Mr. Cochran has been my mentor for years, and I've learned—"

His "mentor" cut him off.

"Well, he's going to see what effect it has on the jury," Cochran said. "I don't think it's going to have the effect you think you are having." Cochran was going with the focus groups—and his gut. "Watch them," the defense lawyer urged. "See if they're manipulated or not. You guys keep trying this and see how it ends up. . . .

I'll remind you about it." (Cochran was right. Several jurors said after the trial that they were offended by Denise's obvious bias and had discounted much of what she had to say.)

||||||

Monday morning started with another Darden fiasco. Shortly after he started examining Denise Brown again, Darden placed a photograph of a battered Nicole on the courtroom overhead projector, which was known throughout the trial by its brand name: the Elmo. The prosecution had already shown the photographs taken by the police following the incident on January 1, 1989. This one showed similar, but not identical, bruises.

Denise said she had seen this photograph in Nicole's bathroom drawer. "Did you and she discuss the photograph?" Darden asked.

"Yes, we did."

"What did she tell you about the photograph?"

"Objection," said Shapiro. "Hearsay, Your Honor."

Ito called the parties to the sidebar. Darden's question, quite obviously, did call for hearsay evidence in response. But that was not the worst of it. The judge asked Darden which incident of domestic violence this photograph involved.

"I don't know what the incident is that relates directly to this photograph," Darden said.

Ito sighed, asked the jury to return to the jury room, and demanded that Darden explain how this photograph might be admissible. Darden said only that it had been found in Nicole's safe-deposit box after her death, with the photographs from the 1989 beating.

"Counsel," Ito said with mounting impatience, "you can't just show horrible photographs without tying it to something relevant to this case."

For once, the defense histrionics that followed were justified. "I have been practicing for a long time," said Shapiro, "and I have never seen anything quite this extraordinary where a photograph that is clearly inadmissible is just thrown up on a giant-screen television for the jury to see . . ."

In legal terms, Darden had failed to establish the photograph's "foundation"—this is, the time and place it was taken, along with the relevant surrounding circumstances. By showing the photograph to the jurors, Darden obviously intended for them to draw the inference that O.J. had caused the wounds. But he had no way of proving it. In shorter, less-publicized cases, this is the kind of error that results in convictions being overturned on appeal. As Ito put it, with characteristic restraint, "What concerns me is the rather inflammatory nature of that photograph, and to show it to the jury, without any foundation for it, is more than inappropriate."

Ito levied less of a sanction than some judges might have. He simply instructed the jury to disregard the photograph and asked Darden to move on. From there, Darden wrapped it up with Denise pretty quickly. He brought out that O.J. had called Nicole a "fat pig" when she was pregnant—loathsome behavior, to be sure, but not exactly wife beating, either. She concluded her testimony with a description of O.J.'s behavior at Sydney's dance recital in the early evening of June 12, 1994.

Darden asked about O.J.'s demeanor that night.

"Um," said Denise, "he had a very bizarre look in his eyes. It was a very faraway look. . . . It wasn't like O.J., just walking into a place and being, you know—'Hey, here I am'—you know, kind of sure of himself type of attitude. It was more of a—of a—like a glazed over, kind of frightening, dark eyes. It just didn't look like the O.J. that we knew."

Perhaps Denise really did see O.J. this way. But Cochran had these jurors pegged; unmoved by her tears, they regarded Denise with cold, hard stares.

||||||

Denise Brown's testimony essentially closed the domestic-violence part of the prosecution's case. To a jury predisposed to believe such evidence—or one inclined toward hostility for the defendant—the presentation might have had considerable impact. After all, O.J. had been convicted of beating his wife, and there had been a handful more of incidents of violence, at least according to her sister. The 911 tape from 1993 suggested that O.J. was certainly capable at least of violent anger toward his wife, and the stalking evidence, even if ambiguous, suggested a continuing obsession on his part. Overall, however, the domestic-violence evidence was just short enough of overwhelming that the defense could continue to ignore it. Shapiro, for example, barely cross-examined Denise Brown. Cochran's mantra from his opening—this is a murder case, not a domestic-violence case—remained the core of the defense strategy.

So the prosecution, at this point, set out to prove its murder case. Marcia Clark called a series of witnesses who had testified at the preliminary hearing: the waiters at Mezzaluna who had served Nicole and her family on June 12; the bartender who took the call from Juditha Brown at about 9:40 P.M. and then ran out to the sidewalk to locate her dropped glasses; the dog walkers who tended to Nicole's bereaved Akita and then located the bodies. The defense lawyers mostly gave these early witnesses a pass—until the police officers started taking the stand.

Cochran's entire demeanor changed when he rose to cross-examine Robert Riske. A uniformed patrol officer, Riske had been the first member of the LAPD on the crime scene at Bundy, arriving at 12:13 A.M. on June 13. Under Clark's questioning, Riske had testified about being directed to the bodies by Sukru Boztepe and his wife, Bettina Rasmussen. Riske had actually done very little. After briefly inspecting the bodies, he had walked through the house, collected Justin and Sydney from their upstairs bedrooms, and called for reinforcements. (Racial antennae were high even during this innocuous testimony. Riske mentioned that a sergeant named Coon arrived on the scene, prompting Clark to ask, "That Sergeant Coon, is he any relation to another one?" As this jury surely knew, Stacy Koon was one of the officers who had beaten Rodney King. There was no relation.)

Two themes stood out in Cochran's cross-examination. First, he asked any number of questions about the cup of Ben & Jerry's ice cream that Riske had discovered on a back stairway. Riske had said the dessert was "melting," not "melted." To Cochran's way of thinking, that meant that the time of the murder must have been at 11:00 P.M. or even later; otherwise the ice cream would have been completely "melted." What kind of ice cream was it? Did you take any pictures of it? Where exactly did you find this ice cream? Why didn't you photograph the ice cream, preserve it, analyze it? Incredibly, Cochran spent several hours on this trivia with Riske and the officers who followed him.

The other theme was the coroner, who had not arrived on the scene to remove the bodies until 9:10 A.M. Again, according to Cochran's suggestions to the jury, if the coroner had arrived on the scene earlier, he might have been able to pinpoint the time of death. Many more hours of cross-examination were devoted to this subject as well.

These two subjects had another common thread: As defense arguments, they were absurd. The police had no way of knowing for sure how melted the ice cream was when it was first placed by the stairs, presumably by Nicole. Thus, examining or photographing the ice cream later would have yielded no relevant information. Likewise, even if the coroner's representatives had come to the murder scene within minutes of Riske's arrival, they could not have made a relevant finding on the time of death. The prosecution asserted that the murder took place starting at about 10:15 P.M.; the defense claimed 10:35 P.M. or later. Forensic pathology is simply not capable of narrowing down with such precision a time of death. However, these arguments over the ice cream and the coroner still served Cochran's purposes. As the questions were raised over and over again—to Riske; to his boss, Sergeant David Rossi; then to Detectives Ron Phillips and Tom Lange—Cochran put the officers on the defensive. By sheer force of repetition, Cochran made it sound like there had been some major police lapse at the crime scene. The focus thus shifted from O. J. Simpson to the deficiencies of the LAPD.

Cochran spent four days cross-examining Lange, the co–lead detective with his partner, Vannatter. Lange would not be riled. In fact, sometimes it seemed the detective was having trouble staying awake. Bald, with a bushy mustache that seemed to camouflage any change in expression, Lange met each of Cochran's sallies with a phlegmatic reply. No, he didn't call the coroner right away; no, he didn't preserve the ice cream. In some respects, Cochran broke the rules of cross-examination. He didn't ask closed-ended questions—that is, questions that can be answered only yes or no. Cochran's attention wandered, and he let his witnesses wander, too. But what Cochran did very effectively was tell stories. The answers to his questions almost didn't matter. Cochran was talking to the jury.

Telling a story is precisely what Cochran was doing when, early in the cross-examination of Lange, he asked about the detective's arrival at the murder scene. "And then you drove from your home in Simi Valley down to the location, is that right?"

"Yes."

"And how long did it take you to get from Simi Valley to the location in Brentwood?"

"Perhaps fifty minutes . . ."

The incantation of the fact that Lange lived in Simi Valley was anything but accidental. The place—even just the words "Simi Valley"—was anathema to black (and many white) Angelenos because it was the site of the notorious acquittal, on state charges, of the police officers who beat Rodney King. Overwhelmingly white, highly conservative, and not coincidentally the home of many Los Angeles police officers, Simi Valley had a reputation as the paradigmatic racist Southern California community. Cochran wanted the jury to know that Lange lived there.

The reference had actually been long planned. Bill Pavelic, the ex-LAPD renegade working for the defense team, had run the detectives' names through several directories and never learned where they lived. But one time when Pavelic and the detectives were standing around during a search at Simpson's property, Pavelic decided to make conversation with Lange. It was all very casual.

"Did you get much damage in the earthquake?" Pavelic asked.

"Not too bad," said Lange.

"Oh, where do you live?"

"Simi Valley."

Knowing he could use it, Pavelic filed the information away, and eventually he passed it along to Cochran.

During the cross-examination, shortly after the first two references to Lange's home in Simi Valley, Cochran asked another question about some evidence the detective had found at Simpson's home.

"You took those shoes home to Simi Valley with you?"

"That is correct," Lange said.

Cochran used the early part of his cross-examination of Lange to expand on his theme of Nicole-as-sexual-predator. He asked pointedly if Lange had requested that Nicole's body be tested with a rape kit. Since there was no evidence that she had been sexually assaulted—no removal of her clothing, for example—the only purpose of such a test would be to see if she had recently had intercourse. Cochran dwelled lovingly on the number of candles burning in the house when Lange arrived. In the living room? Yes. In the bedroom? Even in the bathroom? Yes. And, of course, the large bathtub was full of water.

"So would you say there were at least nine candles altogether burning at this point?"

"Yes."

There was even music playing. "What kind of music did you hear?" Cochran asked.

"It seemed to me to be a new-wave-type music, instrumentals," Lange said, apparently searching for the term New Age.

Cochran asked: "Kind of soft, romantic kind of thing?"

Lange said he couldn't be sure, but the answer to a question like that one doesn't matter.

Cochran interspersed a series of questions about frequent visitors to Nicole's home, pointing out that Marcus Allen, the football star, seemed to be among the regular guests. He let linger the issue of what Allen was doing with Nicole.

"Did you know whether or not Miss Nicole Brown Simpson had a visitor that evening after 10:00, a male visitor? Do you know that?"

Ito overruled an objection and let Lange answer: "The only male visitor I'm aware of is the other victim."

As if the point could be missed, Cochran followed up with "But in your investigative capacity, you decided not to order this rape kit which you could have ordered. Isn't that correct, sir?"

It was correct, and Cochran wasn't asking about rape. It was as if he had heard every argument made by Don Vinson, the prosecution's ignored jury consultant. The questions reinforced the jury's picture of Nicole as a slut who pursued men in general and craved black men in particular.

Chris Darden suffered as he watched Cochran push these buttons, and he took out his frustration in a particularly inappropriate way. On the night of February 22, the first day of Lange's cross-examination, Darden was working in his office when he saw the daily discussion of the trial on *Rivera Live,* on the CNBC cable network. Darden called in to the station to add his own analysis (although, implausibly, he later asserted that he did not know his comments were being broadcast). Speaking with Geraldo Rivera, Darden laid into Lange's performance as a witness. "I would like the officers to be a bit more aggressive," Darden said. "They are answering the questions being put to them, and I think some of the questions, I think, are a bit ridiculous. And I wish that they would point that out to the jury on occasion." Speaking of Cochran, Darden added, "I am sure he is scoring some points."

Darden's ill-advised phone call did nothing but make trouble for him. For starters, it was unseemly for a prosecutor in the middle of a murder trial to shoot the breeze with a talk-show personality. That alone violated the D.A.'s office policy. More important, Darden was publicly criticizing an ostensible ally, Lange, and implicitly chastising all of the officers who had testified. On Thursday morning, February 23, Darden's colleagues made it clear to him that he should cease his role as a TV trial analyst. Lange and Vannatter—who stewed throughout the trial about a perceived lack of support from Clark and Darden—were furious.

Cochran sensed this prickly atmosphere and sought to exploit it. His suggestions on his second day of cross-examining Lange were even more outlandish, especially when he returned to his favorite project, dirtying up Nicole.

"Now," Cochran began, "during the course of your investigation, do you know who Faye Resnick is?"

"Yes."

"And how did you become aware of the name Faye Resnick during the course of your investigation?"

"When I learned that Faye Resnick was a friend of victim Nicole Brown Simpson," the detective explained.

Cochran wanted his Faye Resnick theory in front of the jury—the idea, which never had any evidence to support it, that the murders had been committed by drug dealers looking for Resnick. To that end, Cochran needed to establish that Resnick had lived with Nicole for a few days in the beginning of June. But Cochran did not want to call Resnick as a defense witness. She loathed Simpson, thought he was guilty, and asserted that O.J. had told her he wanted to kill Nicole. Under the rules of evidence, Cochran couldn't call her as a witness to tell some things (that she had moved in with Nicole) but not others (that O.J. had told her he wanted to kill Nicole). So Cochran tried to get his desired sliver of the story in through Lange.

"Did you learn," Cochran asked Lange, "whether or not Faye Resnick moved in with Nicole Brown Simpson on Friday, June 3, 1994?"

Clark objected. The answer called for hearsay—i.e., what someone had told Lange. Ito sustained it.

Cochran tried another tack. "Did you ever ascertain whether or not Miss Nicole Brown Simpson had anyone who lived with her in the month before June 12, other than the children?"

Yes, said Lange.

"Did you find out . . . that Faye Resnick moved in with Nicole Brown Simpson on or about June 3, 1994?"

Clark objected, but this time Ito let Lange answer, and the detective said he had heard that Resnick had moved in on that date.

When Cochran asked another question about Resnick, Judge Ito called the lawyers to the sidebar. He posed a question that revealed much about his judicial philosophy, asking Clark if Resnick really had lived with Nicole. "Is this a disputed fact?" As always, Ito cared more about getting accurate information to the jury than about some of the finer points of evidence law. Clark was so angry she could barely speak. "I'm not—" Clark sputtered, "I'm not sure when Faye Resnick lived with her, if they ever lived there on any kind of a permanent basis. . . . It doesn't matter whether it is a disputed fact or not. . . . We have all kinds of slop in the record now that has been thrown in front of this jury through counsel's method of cross-examination by saying, 'Have you heard this,' 'Do you know about that.' " Clark said Cochran should call a witness who could testify from firsthand knowledge that Resnick lived there.

Hearing this, Cochran decided to twit his adversaries. "I can choose the witness that I want," Cochran said. "They obviously haven't tried any cases in a long time, and obviously don't know how, but this is cross-examination."

Darden rose to Cochran's taunting, saying in a voice loud enough to be heard across the courtroom: "Who is he talking about, doesn't know how to try the case?"

"Wait, Mr. Darden," Ito instructed. In an effort to keep some semblance of order, the judge had made a rule that only one lawyer per side could speak on any issue. This was Clark's issue—and besides, Darden was just sparring with Cochran.

But Darden didn't wait—he couldn't control himself where Cochran was concerned, and he kept on talking against the judge's orders. "Is he the only lawyer that knows how to try the case?" Darden blurted out.

Ito was appalled at Darden's direct violation of his order: "I'm going to hold you in contempt," the judge threatened.

Darden couldn't stop. "I should be held in contempt. I have sat here and listened to—"

"Mr. Darden," Ito continued, "I'm warning you right now."

"This cross-examination is out of order," Darden shot back.

Ito moved from his position by the sidebar back to the bench. Sighing, he excused the jury. The lawyers returned to their respective tables. The brief pause should have broken the tension and given Darden a moment to compose himself.

After the jury left, Ito turned to Darden. "Mr. Darden, let me give you a piece of advice. Take about three deep breaths, as I am going to do, and then contemplate what you are going to say next. Do you want to take a recess now for a moment?"

"I don't require a recess," Darden said.

"I will hear your comments at this point. I have cited you. Do you have any response?"

"I would like counsel, Your Honor," said Darden. (It is not a good sign when a prosecutor feels the need to have his own lawyer in the middle of a murder trial.)

"You can have counsel," Ito said coolly.

It was so simple. All Ito wanted was an apology. Every trial lawyer knows that judges sometimes act irrationally, rule incorrectly, act impetuously. Here Ito had arguably made a mistake by letting in hearsay evidence, and Darden had exploded. His job, his obligation as a prosecutor, was to apologize and get on with the case. Gracious and tolerant to a fault, Ito could not have been clearer about what he wanted, saying, "I invite counsel to . . . think very carefully about what they are going to say to the Court next. That is an opportunity to get up and say, 'Gee, I'm sorry, I lost my head there, I apologize to the Court, I apologize to counsel.' When I get that response, then we move on."

Ito gave Darden a moment to confer with Clark. They stepped aside, and Darden shook his head. When Ito asked what they had decided, Clark said again that Darden wanted a lawyer for the contempt proceeding. Ito gave Darden more time to think it over. Once again, Clark said that Darden wanted to be represented by counsel. He would not apologize. Darden stood alone by the jury box, head down, arms crossed in front of him, agonizing.

Ito would be pushed no farther. "I've offered you now three times an opportunity to end this right now. This is very simple." More silence.

Gerry Spence, the Wyoming attorney, was seated in the press section of the courtroom. (He was doing commentary on the trial for CNBC and other television stations.) Spence was so frustrated by Darden's intransigence that he slammed a pad down on his thigh and said, "Jesus Christ!"

"Mr. Spence, your comments aren't necessary," Ito said.

Still, Darden said nothing.

||||||

Christopher Darden was no fool. He knew he should have learned to ignore Johnnie Cochran. Yet Darden's feelings were so intense that he couldn't help himself.

In some respects, Darden's family story bore an uncanny resemblance to Cochran's. Both their families had come from the South, and both had arrived on the West Coast as part of the great migration of African-Americans drawn by the prospect of work in factories during World War II. The Cochrans came from Louisiana and settled first in Oakland; Chris Darden's father came from outside Tyler, Texas, and settled in Richmond, the city next door to Oakland. While Johnnie Cochran, Sr., had found work building troop ships for Bethlehem Steel, Eddie Darden welded submarines for the navy.

Despite these similarities, the two black families were separated by a gap that is no less real for being mostly invisible to white

Americans, who tend to regard African-Americans as a single struggling social unit. To be sure, the Cochrans were no aristocrats and the Dardens no paupers, but still, the difference between them was class. Johnnie Cochran, Sr., bolted the blue-collar world as soon as Japan surrendered. His first son came of age with not just a hope but an expectation that he would surpass the considerable success of his father. Eddie Darden, in contrast, had a blowtorch in his hand until the day he retired, decades later. His son Chris, the third of eight children, had no family guide in the hunt for entree into the professional world.

Richmond itself conferred few advantages. A sleepy community of 21,000 at the outbreak of the war, it became a veritable metropolis of 100,000 within a year. Kaiser, Southern Pacific Railways, and Bethlehem Steel—not to mention the great military shipyards of Port Chicago and Mare Island—inhaled new workers as quickly as they could settle into the flimsy shacks that were being thrown up along treeless streets every day. But unlike Oakland, where black folks eventually gained political power comparable to their numbers, Richmond remained for years under the control of a small white elite. Services were poor. Richmond had no superior court, no county hospital. "It was a plantation," according to one of the few prominent black lawyers in Richmond, "the Mississippi of the West."

In Eddie Darden's case, that racism extended to the workplace as well. He toiled as a civilian employee in the vast naval shipyard at Mare Island, in nearby Valeo. The better-paying and higher-skilled positions at Mare Island were called journeymen jobs; they were for welders, pipefitters, sandblasters, and the like. Those jobs went overwhelmingly to whites. For many years, the black workers, like Chris's father, were allowed to work only as helpers, the lower-paid assistants to the journeymen. It was only with the birth of affirmative-action practices in the 1960s and 1970s that blacks like Eddie Darden became journeymen in any significant numbers. In addition to raising her eight children, Chris's mother, Marie, worked in a school cafeteria—another typical dead-end occupation traditionally filled by the African-Americans of Richmond.

The Dardens had enough money to buy a small, two-story frame house in the working-class south side of Richmond, but there was no money for luxuries, or even such basic necessities as dentist visits for all the children. An absence of early care sentenced Chris to a lifetime of dental miseries.

The Darden family did have, however, similar attitudes about education to the Cochrans'. Mr. and Mrs. Darden believed that only schools with significant numbers of white children received adequate resources, so those would be the schools for their children. Here the Dardens were fortunate, because John F. Kennedy High School opened within a few blocks of their home just as their first children were coming of age. A modern building, with a pool and several athletic fields and a fully integrated student body of about two thousand, Kennedy High drew the city's most motivated students. Edna, the oldest Darden child, served as student body president in 1972; Chris's beloved older brother, Michael, came next and was a standout on the track team, though he later succumbed to a life of drug addiction. Never the favored son like Johnnie Cochran, Chris Darden took his place in the Kennedy High class of '74 with something to prove.

A quiet kid, with a temper that heated and cooled quickly, Darden worked hard in school, made a mark as both a student and an athlete, and held down a job in a liquor store besides. His passion was football, where he played wide receiver. (He neither wore number 32 nor especially idealized O. J. Simpson; like most people in Richmond, Darden rooted for the Oakland Raiders.) Darden never had much of a chance to shine on the football field because he played behind Robert "Spider" Gaines, who went on to the University of Washington, where he would win the most valuable player award in the Rose Bowl. More dogged than especially talented, Darden shifted his energies to track, where he ran the quarter mile and served as captain of the cross-country team. A National Honor Society student, he scraped together the money for junior college and then, a year later, for San Jose State.

The mid-1970s were a dramatic time to be a young track athlete at San Jose State. In the 1968 Olympic games in Mexico City, Tommie Smith and John Carlos—who were students at San Jose State—won the gold and bronze medals in the 200-meter dash. During the awards ceremony, the two young men shocked the world by giving black power salutes during the playing of the national anthem. Smith and Carlos had left the university by the time Darden arrived, but their fiery spirit still resonated on the track team and, indeed, among black students there in general. Yet even more than the track team, the formative experience of Darden's college years came from his membership in the Alpha Psi Alpha fraternity.

Predominantly black fraternities play an important role in African-American life. Denied access to many of the networks that whites take for granted, many black college men form lifelong attachments to these institutions, whose influence stretches well beyond campus walls. It is a far cry from the *Animal House* model of many white frats, especially at Alpha Psi Alpha, the oldest and most prestigious black fraternity (Martin Luther King, Jr., and Thurgood Marshall were members). Alphas at San Jose State had an activist, even militant, cast. (In a characteristic difference, Johnnie Cochran belonged to the UCLA chapter of Kappa Alpha Psi, which was known as the "playboys," the most social of the black frats.) The Alphas didn't even have a building on the San Jose State campus, so they met in classrooms, where they devoted themselves to organizing projects like a tutoring program for kids in the city's poorer neighborhoods.

Darden's frat name was Sugar D—because, it is said, he was sweet. He led quietly, more by example than exhortation, but his passionate commitment to his fellow African-Americans stood out even in that politicized era. At the stylized interrogation sessions for prospective Alphas, Darden always had the same question for pledges: "What are you going to do for your people?" Even before Chris Darden became famous in the Simpson case, a younger Alpha had saved for many years a note that Darden had written to him upon his joining the fraternity: "It matters not who you are, where you come from, or how you think—what matters is whatever the hell you do with it." Signed, Sugar D.

He quit track suddenly. A history professor in Afro-American studies, Gloria Alibaruho, had become a mentor to him. Darden later wrote that when he studied the world of his ancestors, "my eyes opened like slipped blinds and all of a sudden my own life was explained to me. Martin Luther King had taught me what was fair; the Black Panther newspapers screamed at me what was unjust;

but it was Gloria Alibaruho who taught me who I was. It was like discovering gravity. It explained the universe to me. So, this is why people treat me the way they do. This is why women grab their handbags when I get on an elevator."

Alibaruho sat Darden down and appealed to his growing political consciousness. Speaking both metaphorically and literally, she asked him, "When are you going to stop running in circles?" He did just that and, soon after, applied to law school. He took an apartment in Richmond and commuted across the Bay Bridge to Hastings law school, in San Francisco. His passage was anything but smooth. As Darden later admitted, he shoplifted regularly through college, and he fathered a child out of wedlock while a student at Hastings. He graduated in 1980 and took a job with the National Labor Relations Board for $17,000 a year. A few months later, he moved to Los Angeles and the district attorney's office. The money was better—$24,000 a year—and, as he said at the time, "I want people like me making the decisions."

||||||

Darden had come farther and overcome more than any of the principal lawyers in the Simpson trial, and probably bore the best intentions as well. But he was also different from Cochran, Shapiro, and Marcia Clark in another way. Chris Darden was not, alas, an especially talented trial lawyer.

For one thing, Darden had tried relatively few cases. After the customary few years of working minor cases, Darden spent the bulk of his fifteen years as a prosecutor in the Special Investigations Division of the district attorney's office. SID has the most politically sensitive duty on the D.A.'s staff: the investigation of public officials, most notably officers in the LAPD. The lawyers at SID, including Darden, approached their work meticulously. In light of the difficulties of prosecuting the D.A.'s usual ally, the cops, the lawyers in SID filed charges only in the strongest cases. It was not unusual, for example, that Darden had only one major trial at SID during his tenure there. As it turned out, though, he was the prosecutor in one of the most notorious episodes in the modern history of the LAPD, the 1988 police raid on apartments at Thirty-ninth Street and Dalton Avenue. It was supposed to be a rather minor drug bust, but the eighty LAPD officers who went to the scene wreaked havoc that had lasting repercussions. The raid eventually cost the city more than $3 million in civil settlements to the victims, and Darden investigated and prosecuted the three top police officials responsible. "Chris felt very strongly that we needed to hold the command level responsible, and at that point Daryl Gates got involved," Ira Reiner, who was the district attorney at the time, said later. The police chief wrote Reiner a letter claiming that Darden was pushing too hard, being too aggressive. "Anyone else would have laughed it off," Reiner continued, "but not Chris. He wanted to fire back a letter. This was a classic case of police misconduct, and of course we went ahead with it. Chris handled it with commitment and emotion. That's just the way he operates." In the case Darden tried, all three officers were acquitted.

Darden's first important moment in the Simpson trial came shortly before opening statements, when Ito was weighing whether to allow the defense to cross-examine Mark Fuhrman about his prior use of the word "nigger." Other prosecutors had conducted the bulk of the legal argument on the issue, but Darden rose on January 13 as a sort of expert witness on the subject.

"It is a dirty, filthy word," Darden said. "It is not a word that I allow people to use in my household. I'm sure Mr. Cochran doesn't. And the reason we don't is because it is an extremely derogatory and denigrating term, because it is so prejudicial and so extremely inflammatory that to use that word in any situation will evoke some type of emotional response from any African-American within earshot of that word."

Darden said allowing use of the word "will do one thing. It will upset the black jurors. It will issue a test . . . and the test will be, Whose side are you on? The side of the white prosecutors and the white policemen, or on the side of the black defendant and his very prominent black lawyer? That is what it is going to do: Either you are with the Man or you are with the Brothers. That is what it does. That is exactly what it does."

Darden's speech was about evenly divided between text and subtext. In part, he simply meant what he said; "nigger" is a uniquely offensive epithet, and Darden thought Ito should exercise caution before he allowed anyone to utter it in court. But Darden's words also reflected his frustration at how the defense had seized the racial high ground in the trial from the beginning. The strategy Shapiro advocated from practically the day Simpson was arrested—which Cochran embellished even beyond the original conception—called for placing race at the center of the defense. That strategy started with Fuhrman and went on to include the focus on race in jury selection, the defense obsession with police misconduct, and the trashing of Nicole. As a prosecutor who had devoted his career to ferreting out genuine police racism, Darden seethed to see O. J. Simpson—who had done precisely nothing for his fellow African-Americans over the course of his lifetime—capitalizing on his race. In his frustration, Darden started to ramble.

"Mr. Cochran and the defense, they have a purpose in going into that area, and the purpose is to inflame the passions of the jury and to ask them to pick sides not on the basis of the evidence in this case. And the evidence in this case against this defendant is overwhelming," he went on. "I don't have to educate the Court on this point, but we have a right to a fair trial just like the defendant has. We are not running around or talking about or seeking to introduce to the jury the notion that this defendant has a fetish for blond-haired white women. That would be inappropriate. That would inflame the passions of the jury. It would be outrageous."

It was Darden at this point who was outrageous, in floating the white-women obsession for the benefit of the television cameras. After nearly twenty minutes of stream-of-consciousness babbling, Darden finally sat down.

Johnnie Cochran had planned to leave court early that day, but he remained to respond to Darden's monologue on the "n-word." Cochran walked slowly to the podium. Bigger, older, stronger, wiser, Cochran dominated Darden in both physical and intellectual terms. "I have a funeral to attend today, [and] there are few things in life more important than attending the funeral . . . where you have been asked to speak, but I would be remiss were I not at this time to take this opportunity to respond to my good friend Mr. Chris Darden."

"Good friend"—that was a tip-off to the assault to come.

"His remarks this morning are perhaps the most incredible remarks I've heard in a court of law in the thirty-two years I have been practicing law. His remarks are demeaning to African-Americans as a group. And so I want, before I go to this funeral, to apologize to African-Americans across this country. Not every African-American feels that way. It is demeaning to our jurors to say that African-Americans who have lived under oppression for 200-plus years in this country cannot work within the mainstream, cannot hear these offensive words. . . . I am ashamed that Mr. Darden would allow himself to become an apologist for this man [Fuhrman]."

Darden was beside himself. He stood up and walked in a tiny circle behind his chair, as if he were weighing whether to walk out. Finally, he sat down and swiveled his chair away from the podium in symbolic, if rather childish, protest.

By overstating his own case about the "n-word" so dramatically, Darden had opened the door for Cochran's righteous indignation. "All across America today, believe me, black people are offended at this very moment," Cochran went on, "and so I have to say this was uncalled for, it is unwarranted, and most unfortunate for somebody that I have a lot of respect for—and perhaps he has become too emotional about this." Which Darden certainly had.

When Cochran finally finished this peroration, he pushed to an even greater theatrical height, emotionally embracing Simpson and all the other lawyers at the defense table. Leaving at last for the funeral, he had time only to whisper a brief word to Darden—the classic rebuke: "Nigger, *please* . . ."

|||||

Darden never really recovered his composure. In repartee among the lawyers at the sidebar, he often revealed an astonishing lack of professionalism. One day early in the trial, Darden suggested that Ito should make an instruction clearer to a witness, then added, "I'm not criticizing you, Judge. You're my bud." A shocked Cochran interrupted: "It's not a question of him being your *bud*. I move to strike that." Sometimes Darden's humor misfired. On another occasion at the sidebar, he protested that Cochran "has stepped on my shined Ferragamos. You know, I think he should have to buy me another pair of Ferragamos." The ever tolerant Ito answered, "Come on, guys." More seriously, Darden wore his emotions on his sleeve in front of the jury, alternately mugging and scowling to tele-graph his reactions to the testimony. Sometimes he jangled his keys in irritation. Whatever the message Darden intended to send with these gestures, the jury only picked up on his nervousness and immaturity.

Of course, the jury had been excused when Darden had his show-down with Ito on February 23, during Lange's cross-examination. After a third invitation to apologize—and several more agonizing moments of silence—Darden broke down and offered the most grudging words of conciliation.

"Your Honor," he said. "Thank you for the opportunity to review the transcript of the sidebar. It appears that the Court is correct, that perhaps my comments may have been or are somewhat inap-propriate. I apologize to the Court. I meant no disrespect."

Ito, in contrast, was far more gracious than Darden had any right to expect. "Mr. Darden," the judge said, "I accept your apol-ogy. I apologize to you for my reaction as well. You and I have known each other for a number of years, and I know that your re-sponse was out of character, and I'll note it as such."

Ito then invited the jury back to the courtroom, and Cochran re-sumed his cross-examination of Detective Lange. It didn't last long, however, because a new and even more bizarre crisis erupted. The star of Johnnie Cochran's opening statement—Rosa Lopez, the maid in the house next door to O.J.'s—was threatening to re-turn to her native El Salvador.

In her opening statement, Marcia Clark had surprised Johnnie Cochran by declaring so emphatically that the murders had occurred at precisely 10:15 P.M. Talking with his colleagues on the defense team, Cochran learned from investigator Bill Pavelic that he had a witness who said she saw Simpson's Bronco outside his house at 10:15 P.M. That was Rosa Lopez, the maid at 348 North Rockingham, next door to O.J.'s house. Responding to Clark in his own opening statement, Cochran leaned heavily on Lopez's expected testimony, though he himself had never spoken to Lopez. Cochran made the point repeatedly that if the murder took place at 10:15 and the Bronco was still at Rockingham at 10:15, O.J. could not have done it.

No one was more surprised to hear this than Rosa Lopez. From her base with the Salinger family just south of Simpson's estate, the fifty-seven-year-old maid followed the case closely on television, and even told several friends and family members in Los Angeles of her memories of the night in question. What Lopez told them, however, was that she had seen the Bronco at around *10:00* P.M., not 10:15. When Cochran said her name in his opening on January 25, reporters quickly learned where she lived and began staking out her home. That was nerve-racking enough for Lopez, but it was the disparity between her memories and Cochran's characterization of them that caused her real dread. As she well knew, a 10:00 sighting was neutral at best and incriminating at worst for O.J., because the murder scene was only a five-minute drive from his house. Lopez had told several other maids in the neighborhood that she remembered seeing the Bronco at 10:00. Word began circulating in the neighborhood that Rosa was lying or had been paid off or was otherwise in thrall to the defense camp. Lopez had also told her daughter, who lived in the Los Feliz neighborhood of Los Angeles, about seeing O.J.'s car at 10:00. The reporters, the rumors, the scolding looks from her friends and family—they all combined to turn her misery to panic.

The defense lawyers learned of Lopez's dismay and, as they did so often when confronted with a delicate task, turned to investigator Pat McKenna. Outgoing and friendly, McKenna was the obvious choice to mollify Lopez and keep her from fleeing before she could testify. He did what he could. McKenna and Cochran arranged for Lopez to have her own lawyer. Unappeased, Lopez quit her job with the Salingers on February 10 and went into hiding with her daughter in Los Feliz. The press found her there, and she called McKenna to help her escape. The next day, McKenna picked her up and led a fleet of local television vans on a brief eighty-mile-per-hour chase through the streets of Los Angeles until he lost them. Still, Lopez fretted. A few days later she disappeared altogether. She spent the night of Wednesday, February 22, in her car, and then drove aimlessly until she wound up in New Mexico. From there she called her lawyer, who, on Cochran's behalf, begged her to return. She agreed to fly back to L.A.—but only, she said, for a single day. She would come to court on Friday, February 24, but she vowed to leave for her native El Salvador the following morning. After nearly thirty years in the United States, she had decided to leave—tomorrow.

Lopez's flight from New Mexico landed in Los Angeles at 1:30 A.M. on February 24, and when she appeared in court at 9:00 that morning, she looked haggard and bewildered. Seated in the back row of the courtroom, waiting to be called to the witness stand, she wore a purple velour jumpsuit and a dazed expression.

Born and raised in rural El Salvador, Rosa Lopez led a life of extraordinary hardship until she came to the United States. One of ten children, she dropped out of school at age nine to help her parents harvest their small crop of corn, beans, and rice. She married young and had seven children, but only four survived childbirth. Two more died in the course of her country's long civil war: a fifteen-year-old daughter, who was kidnapped and killed, and a son, a government pilot whose helicopter was shot down by guerrillas. The two survivors came with her to Los Angeles, where she had worked as a maid for about thirty years. Rosa Lopez brought a survivor's instincts to the witness stand in the Simpson case, as well as a considerable reservoir of street smarts.

When Ito called Lopez to the witness stand, she revealed a quirky stage presence. Ito had called in a Spanish interpreter, but Lopez obviously understood all the English that was spoken around her. The purpose of the hearing this day was to allow Ito to decide whether he was going to interrupt the prosecution's case and allow Lopez to testify. Was she actually going to leave for El Salvador the following day, and, if so, was she important enough for the defense to be allowed to call her as a witness out of the usual order?

"Why were you living in another state over the course of the last several days?" Cochran asked Lopez during direct examination, which lasted only about ten minutes.

"Because the reporters won't leave me alone. I'm tired of looking at them. They have been harassing me." Lopez's style was cryptic, dismissive, and oddly grand.

Lopez said she had reservations to fly to San Salvador on Saturday, and hoped to be on her way.

Rising to cross-examine, Darden first made sure of one point that Cochran had already covered. Lopez had said she had a reservation but no ticket for the February 25 flight to San Salvador on Taca airlines.

"You just made the reservation, didn't you?"

"Yes."

"You made that today?"

"Yes."

"Prior to coming to court this morning?"

"Yes."

At that moment, Cheri Lewis, a prosecutor who was sitting next to Darden at their table, rose to go to the telephone in the courtroom. What she was doing was obvious: checking to see if Lopez really had made the reservation. Moments later, Darden had his answer.

"Miss Lopez," he said, "we just called the airline. They don't show a reservation for you. Can you explain to the Court why it is that you just told us you have a reservation?"

No matter how many times she was contradicted by the facts—and this was the first of many—Lopez was never rattled. She serenely adjusted her story, but never her supercilious demeanor. "Because I am going to reserve it, sir. As soon as I leave here, I will buy my ticket and I will leave. If you want to, the cameras can follow me."

Darden pursued her. "You lied to us, didn't you? Yes or no?"

"Because—because the agencies are closed. They open at 10:00 in the morning, and I was brought here very early, sir."

"You don't have any plans to leave Los Angeles at all, do you?"

Suddenly, Lopez answered in English: "Of course, sir. My bags are packed. Everything is ready."

And so it went—for hour after hour. Lopez remained unflappable even as her story crumbled around her. It turned out she had bought a *round-trip* ticket to El Salvador a few weeks earlier; she had looked into receiving unemployment benefits—not the act of someone planning to leave the United States permanently; she said she was anxious to see her ill sister in El Salvador—but she then admitted that they hadn't spoken in many weeks.

The exchanges between Darden and Lopez sometimes had a surreal quality.

"You've been here twenty-seven years, correct?" Darden asked.

"I came in '69. You figure it out."

"Okay, why don't you tell me how long you've been here?"

"Let's say thirty-four years."

Even Lopez's supposed loathing for the press seemed questionable. She had actually given several television interviews, including one with a Spanish-language station just a week earlier—when she had said nothing about wanting to flee the country. During one break in the testimony, as she was leaving the courtroom, Lopez stopped to chat with Kristin Jeannette-Meyers, a reporter covering the trial for Court TV. Darden asked Lopez if she said, "I love you on TV," to Jeannette-Meyers.

"Yes. Because I see her on TV."

"You weren't terrified of that TV reporter, were you?"

"No, because she doesn't have a camera in front of my face."

At the end of Lopez's long day of testimony, Ito gave the defense a break. He conceded that Lopez had contradicted herself any number of times, but he thought she was sincere in her determination to leave the country. Based on Cochran's representation that she would say she saw the Bronco at 10:15 P.M. on June 12, Ito thought she was important enough to delay the trial. It was already after 5:00 P.M., but Ito ordered the bailiffs to bring the jurors from their hotel to the courtroom. Ito was ready to sit until midnight if necessary.

At 5:49 P.M., Marcia Clark stood at the podium and, her voice husky with emotion, made a request. "I have informed the Court that I cannot be present tonight because I do have to take care of my children, and I don't have anyone who can do that for me. And I do not want proceedings to go before a jury when I can't be here." She said she had thought that Ito was going to order Lopez's testimony for Monday, not this very day.

Nearly crying, Clark added, "I can't be here, Your Honor."

The situation placed Ito, in effect, squarely between two women: Rosa Lopez, who said she was planning on leaving the country the following day, and Marcia Clark, who had to care for her children.

Ito backed Clark, putting off Lopez's testimony until Monday and betting that the maid could add one more weekend to the decades she had already lived in the United States. The judge called Lopez to the podium where the lawyers usually held forth. Ito said he would put her up in a hotel for the weekend. Elbows propped on the podium, Lopez wailed, in English, "I don't want to be here any longer. All these reporters have destroyed my life."

"Ms. Lopez," the judge continued solicitously, "the planes fly, as you know, to El Salvador on a regular basis. I will start your case, your testimony in front of the jury, the first thing we do with the jury Monday at 9:00."

Suddenly almost coquettish, Lopez said to the judge, "I will do it for you, Your Honor."

|||||

Marcia Clark's problem was not so easily solved. She had been separated from her second husband, Gordon Clark, for a little more than a year. On June 9, 1994—just three days before the murders on Bundy Drive—she had filed for divorce. As the months passed, their relations grew more strained. Clark's sudden celebrity, combined with the extraordinary demands on her time generated by the Simpson case, increased the tensions between them.

The events of February 24 were typical of their problems. Marcia and Gordon Clark had two boys, aged three and five at the time. According to the interim custody-sharing agreement they had worked out, Gordon would have the boys every other weekend, starting at seven o'clock Fridays. Two weeks earlier, Marcia had arranged for Gordon to pick up the kids at Marcia's home at seven. However, according to Marcia, the boys preferred for her to take them to Gordon's rather than for their father to pick them up. During the court day on February 24, she had told Ito several times that she had to be home in time to take the kids to her husband's by seven. She lived in Glendale, not far from downtown, but when Ito shut down court shortly before six, Clark barely had time to make the seven o'clock limit.

Gordon Clark wasn't watching the trial on February 24—he made it a point never to watch—but when he found out what Marcia had said to Ito about her child-care obligations, he and his lawyers were aghast. According to their understanding of the custody arrangements, Gordon could easily have picked up the kids himself. In their view, Marcia was lying to the court to gain a tactical advantage for the prosecution—that is, additional time to prepare for cross-examination of Rosa Lopez—and public sympathy for herself as a working mother. Thus did a private and, alas, fairly typical divorce become part of the communal narrative of the Simpson case—with, of course, the public nature of the dispute racheting up the rancor between the parties.

Spurred by Garcetti's PR director, Suzanne Childs, the media took Marcia's side with a vengeance. The Clarks' divorce was promptly elevated to the cover of *Newsweek*, where the headline declared, "Marcia Clark Fights for Her Kids. Are Mothers Penalized for Working?" The stories inside included a full-page of instructions to Gordon Clark, written by a New York book editor who had never met anyone in his family, about how he should behave during the divorce proceedings. Based on a single courtroom exchange and a few snatches of information from her divorce file, Marcia became an overnight female icon—the heroine of working women everywhere. There was some truth in this cardboard-cutout portrayal of the prosecutor. However, real life was considerably more complicated, too.

|||||

A young Russian émigré named Pinchas Kleks arrived on the shores of what was known as Palestine in 1918. At the beginning, he made his living delivering kerosene by donkey. From that modest start, Kleks came to open a gas station, and then he devoted his professional life to running a modest chain of service stations in what would become the nation of Israel. In 1930, Pinchas and his wife had a son, Abraham.

A tall and strapping sabra, Abraham Kleks came of age with the young nation. He graduated from high school and went straight into the Israeli army, where he served as a seventeen-year-old lieutenant in the War for Independence. Shortly after that war was won in 1948, Abraham decided to see the world a little and followed some friends to the University of California at Berkeley. At the Jewish Community Center of San Francisco, Abraham met and fell in love with a girl from Brooklyn. Abraham and Roslyn married, settled in the United States, and a year later, on August 31, 1953, had their first child, Marcia.

Abraham was promptly drafted into the U.S. Army for the Korean War. Thus began nearly two decades of extraordinarily peripatetic family life. Abraham had studied microbiology at Berkeley, and he pursued this interest in assignments at army medical laboratories in Texas and later Washington State. From the army, Abraham joined the Food and Drug Administration, where he moved up the career ladder with jobs across the nation: five years in Los Angeles, four near San Francisco, one in Detroit, one near Washington, D.C., and two in New York City. During that last tour, young Marcia completed her high school requirements at Susan Wagner High School in Staten Island. By this point she also had a brother, Jonathan, six years her junior.

Marcia was a quick-minded, good-natured girl with an extraordinary talent for languages. She mastered Spanish and, after just two months in Israel one summer, gained a fluent command of Hebrew as well. Notwithstanding the frequent moves (or perhaps because of them), she became a great joiner of activities—cheerleading, school plays, and the like. Her home life was neither especially contentious nor highly religious. To her mother, at least, it seemed that they quarreled no more than most adolescent children and their parents.

A rift between Marcia and her parents began when they moved from New York back to Los Angeles—their final relocation—in 1970. The family bought a house in the San Fernando Valley, and Abraham served as the district director of the FDA until he retired in 1985, while Roslyn worked for a county supervisor. Marcia had little to do in that first year back west. The local high schools required a year's residency before they would give her a degree, but she had already fulfilled all her course requirements. Marcia wanted badly to get out of the house, but she couldn't go to college without a high school degree. Amid the tension at home and frustration about school, Marcia developed bulimia, an affliction she would battle on and off for more than twenty years.

At last Marcia escaped to UCLA. She was still an undergraduate when she met her first husband, a dashing and handsome young man, Gaby Horowitz, like her father an immigrant from Israel. As Gaby used to tell the story, he was driving his Mercedes around the campus when he saw this gorgeous woman—Marcia—and decided then and there he had to meet her. The courtship was brief but intense, and they married shortly after she graduated, without even telling Marcia's parents first.

Gaby Horowitz made his living as a professional backgammon player while Marcia started law school. The late 1970s were boom years for the game, and for a while Horowitz thrived in the epicenter of the craze. He played occasionally at Pips, a glitzy club founded by Hugh Hefner and frequented by many modest celebrities of the era (including, now and then, O. J. Simpson). But mostly Horowitz frequented the Cavendish West, a haven for serious backgammon and bridge players on the Sunset Strip. Marcia Horowitz became an unlikely regular at the Cavendish, too. She rarely played the game, and instead studied her law books at unoccupied gaming tables. "She was around all the time, a quiet girl,"

Buddy Berke, a Cavendish regular, said later. "She was attractive, she was sweet, always very cordial, a lot better with the social graces than Gaby was."

Gaby was, in fact, a controversial figure in the backgammon world. According to Danny Kleinman, who self-publishes books about backgammon and bridge in Los Angeles, "Gaby was a fine player but, more importantly, a flashy, spectacular player. He looked like Jean-Claude Van Damme, about six-three, and he kept himself in good shape. He was a health-food nut.

"He was a very good player, but he used to cheat. In one case, I saw him move pieces on the board when his opponent's head was turned. I walked out of the club with him and asked him why he had done it. He gave me his rationale. He said he was a much better player than his opponent, and the only way he might lose was through luck. So he felt he had a right to win and a right to cheat."

Though Marcia was often present at the club, no one ever suspected her of being involved in Gaby's cheating. "Everything that I know about Marcia is that she was honest and straightforward," Kleinman said.

Marcia prodded Gaby to develop a career interest beyond backgammon, and he decided to learn about real estate. He didn't have much confidence in his English in a professional setting, so a friend of his—a backgammon-playing dentist named Bruce Roman—asked Gaby to join him at Scientology meetings. Marcia never joined the church herself, but she did tag along with Gaby and Bruce on occasion. In 1979, she told her parents she was divorcing Gaby. About a month later, she announced she was marrying Gordon Clark, whom she had met at the Scientology meetings. At twenty-two, he was five years her junior, and an administrator with the Church of Scientology in Los Angeles. Bruce Roman, who was also a lay minister in the church, performed their Scientology wedding ceremony. (Marcia didn't invite her parents to that wedding, either.)

Gaby's fortunes went south with the end of both his marriage and the backgammon craze. According to Kleinman, "His cheating became much more extensive and elaborate. He used a variety of methods—manipulation of dice, magnetic dice, electromagnetic boards." In the spring of 1989, Gaby Horowitz was accidentally shot in the head while he and a friend were examining a gun. In a bizarre coincidence, the friend was Bruce Roman. In the investigation of the shooting, which ended without any charges being filed, Roman's lawyer was Robert Shapiro. Several people who have seen Gaby Horowitz since his accident say he can no longer walk or talk. Shortly before the Simpson trial, Horowitz moved to Israel. (The Cavendish did not prosper, either. In 1987, the police raided it as part of an investigation for illegal gambling; however, no charges were ever filed against its owner, who was also represented by Robert Shapiro. Nevertheless, the club closed for good in 1994.)

The years Marcia and Gordon Clark lived together were the time that Marcia came of age as a prosecutor. Gordon stopped working for the Church of Scientology, returned to college, and became a modestly successful computer programmer. They had two sons. One day, a few years before the Simpson case, Marcia's grandfather, Pinchas Kleks, who was visiting from Israel, spent an afternoon on a spectator bench in one of Marcia's trials. Though he spoke little English and thus could not understand precisely what was going on, the experience of watching Marcia in court ranked as one of the great thrills of Pinchas's long life.

At the end of 1993, a few months after her fortieth birthday, Marcia Clark made several dramatic changes in her life. She told Bill Hodgman that she didn't like her administrative job and wanted to return to the courtroom, even if it meant a cut in pay. In December, during a long drive north to the Bay Area to visit friends, Marcia told Gordon that she wanted a divorce. To both Gordon and her parents, she was cryptic about her reasons. "He's not for me," she told her father in Hebrew. And then about a month after she split with Gordon, Marcia told her parents that she never wanted to speak to them again. She said they had been icy and unsupportive, and she wanted nothing more to do with them. At just about the same time, Jonathan Kleks, an engineer in Northern California, told his parents that he, too, wished never to speak to them again.

The Kleks were thunderstruck, heartbroken. They had become very close to Marcia and Gordon's older child, who was four at the time his parents separated. They had less of a chance to know the

Clark's second boy, who was just a baby. They figured the crisis—whatever its mysterious origin—would blow over. It never did. Abraham took to making surreptitious visits to the older boy's nursery school to spend a little time with him. Once he brought Roslyn with him. When Marcia learned of it, she denounced the school director in front of a roomful of people. Abraham called Marcia to tell her that her mother was undergoing major surgery in September 1994, the time of jury selection in the Simpson case. Marcia never called back.

Gordon was shocked and bitter about the separation. When the Simpson trial began, Marcia's sudden celebrity gave Gordon the opportunity to take a very public form of revenge. By coincidence, on February 24, the same day Marcia said she had to leave court during Rosa Lopez's testimony, Gordon filed a motion in their divorce case to change their custody arrangements. The actual adjustment he sought was rather minor and reasonable: increased visitation while Marcia was working late on the case. But in his accompanying affidavit, Gordon portrayed Marcia as a workaholic and a neglectful parent. "I have personal knowledge that on most nights she does not arrive home until 10 P.M. and even when she is home, she is working," Gordon wrote in the document, which his lawyers knew would quickly become public. In contrast to Marcia, Gordon said, he always made it home by 6:15 P.M. "While I commend [Marcia's] brilliance, her legal ability and her tremendous competence as an attorney, I do not want our children to suffer because she is never home and never has any time to be with them." It was this affidavit—made public just after she said she had to leave court to be with her children during Lopez's testimony—that made Marcia's personal life a matter of public controversy.

Professionally powerful, Marcia was personally fragile. Gordon thought she drank too much. She smoked more than she wanted to—long greedy pulls on strong European cigarettes. The years of bulimia had exacted a painful price. Extreme tooth decay is a common side effect of bulimia, and in her original divorce petition with Gordon, Marcia said, "Within the last two years I have suffered a medical/dental catastrophe for which I initially borrowed $16,000.00, $14,000.00 of which is still unpaid. In addition, it was necessary to withdraw $26,000 from my pension plan, in order to finish my dental work." Money stresses compounded the ugliness of the divorce. At the time of their separation, Gordon's earnings amounted to a little more than half of Marcia's $96,829 yearly salary, so he could not be counted on for major support.

The shattered relationship with her parents caused Marcia additional worry. She knew that her parents were actually supporting their son-in-law's efforts to obtain more time with their grandchildren. (Since the spring of 1994, all of the Kleks' contact with the children had been through Gordon.) An acute student of public relations, Marcia knew that a public disavowal by her own parents would greatly compromise her image as a heroic working mother. Throughout the trial, in addition to all her other anxieties, she feared above all a public denunciation from her parents.

At times, the compounded stresses of ending a long marriage, trying the Simpson case, and enduring the indignities of unsought celebrity nearly drove Clark to the breaking point. At the supermarket one day, as she bought some Tampax, the grocery bagger quipped, "I guess the defense is really in for it this week." At another time, during Denise Brown's testimony, the *National Enquirer* published topless photographs of Clark from when she had been on vacation years earlier with Gaby Horowitz. She was so humiliated that one day she actually began sobbing quietly at the counsel table in Judge Ito's court. She scribbled a note to Scott Gordon, the prosecutor who was seated next to her. "I'm losing it," Clark wrote. Darden noticed her distress and subtly shifted his position so that the courtroom camera would be directed away from Marcia. Thinking fast, the roly-poly Gordon jotted Clark a response: "The *Enquirer* was going to run the same pictures of me, but Greenpeace wouldn't let them do it." Clark smiled, and that crisis, at least, passed unnoticed by the public.

||||||

Judge Ito had seriously considered ordering Rosa Lopez to jail for the weekend before she was to testify. Ultimately, however, the judge accepted her promise that she would appear on Monday, so he directed that the county put her up at a downtown hotel, the Checkers. Fearful of more surprises, Johnnie Cochran directed Pat

McKenna to book the room next to hers and never let the house-keeper out of his sight until she appeared for court on February 27.

They made an unlikely pair, the tiny El Salvadoran woman and the big, bluff Irishman, yet they became fast friends, after a fashion. McKenna would try to buy Lopez some food or a drink, but Rosa seemed scarcely to eat and never drank a thing. Trying to think of something that might cheer her up, McKenna remembered her room at the Salingers' house. Like many Latin American women of her generation, Lopez liked to keep a little shrine of small candles, known as *veladoras,* on her dresser. McKenna had learned his Catholicism in Chicago, so he was unfamiliar with the custom. Still, just before they were to return to court, the investigator decided to improvise a gift to his charge. He went to a local drugstore and bought Rosa a few candles that she might use for her worship. Deeply touched, she invited McKenna to join her in prayer. A little rusty in this department, the investigator agreed to keep Rosa company and have a drink from the mini-bar while she prayed to God.

Unfortunately, the candles McKenna had bought were somewhat larger than the usual *veladoras.* After a few moments of her devotions, the smoke detector in Lopez's room went off. Rosa began crying. McKenna tried smothering the candles and covering the smoke detector with a laundry bag. Nothing worked. Their problems were compounded because this was the week of the Grammy Awards in Los Angeles, and the Checkers served as the unofficial headquarters of the country-music contingent. The alarm wouldn't stop ringing, so in a few moments the lobby of the hotel was packed with evacuees, mostly women in big hair, men in cowboy boots—and Rosa Lopez and Pat McKenna.

The comedy of errors grew worse when court convened on Monday morning. Marcia Clark opened the session with a passionate appeal for Lopez's testimony to be taken on videotape, not in front of the jury. The defense could play it later if it chose to do so; that way, defense evidence would not be deposited right in the middle of the government's case. Ito agreed. Cochran, for his part, accused Clark of staging her child-care crisis of the previous Friday so she could reargue the issue of Lopez's testimony. In response, Clark rose in righteous indignation. "I'm offended as a woman, as a single parent, and as a prosecutor and an officer of the court to hear an argument posed by counsel like that of Mr. Cochran today," she said. "Some of us have child-care issues, and they are serious and they are paramount. Obviously, Mr. Cochran cannot understand that, but he should not come before this court and impugn the integrity of someone who does have those considerations." It was that sort of telegenic off-the-cuff eloquence that made Clark so impressive in court—even if, as was the case here, Cochran may have been right on the merits.

Ito sent the jury back to the hotel and ordered that a video camera be brought into court to record Lopez's testimony. Then he had to ask for a new interpreter because several television viewers had called or written and said that the woman on Friday had used a Mexican dialect rather than El Salvadoran. Then the defense admitted it had found a statement that investigator Bill Pavelic had taken from Lopez shortly after the murders. This was the kind of late disclosure that had caused such a tumult during opening statements. Clark had a chance to vent some more outrage on this score, and it wasn't until the middle of the afternoon that Rosa Lopez returned to the witness stand.

She wore a new purple dress with a beaded collar and shiny black pumps. They had come as gifts from a defense-team supporter in Las Vegas who used to call McKenna now and then. Questioning her through her now appropriately Central American interpreter, Cochran finally began walking Lopez through the events of June 12, 1994. At one point, Cochran put up a map of the area around Rockingham on the video monitor next to the witness stand. Amid all her recent moves, Lopez had lost her eyeglasses. Cochran began canvassing the courtroom for glasses. "How about somebody near her age?" Cochran quipped. "I'm looking for Mr. Bailey." After sampling several pairs, Lopez narrowed her choices to Bailey's aviator model and a bright-green pair donated by a spectator. For several long minutes, Lopez, Cochran, Bailey, and the interpreter were all huddled around the witness stand—giving it the look of the stateroom scene in A Night at the Opera.

When Lopez reached the critical moment in her testimony—what she saw at around 10:00 on the night of the murders—she hedged. She said she took her dog for a walk and saw O.J.'s Bronco sometime after 10:00, but it clearly could have been anywhere from two to fifteen minutes after the hour. What was clear from the outset, then, was that Rosa Lopez was simply not a very important witness. She didn't help or hurt either side very much. Yet because of her, Ito had allowed the trial to come to a crashing halt.

At the end of the day, Cochran confessed that the defense team had found *another* previous statement by Lopez, this one a taped interview with Pavelic. Ito devoted the bulk of the following day to a hearing on why the defense had failed to turn this statement over to the prosecution. The answer, it became clear, was that chaos had reigned while the case was in Shapiro's hands, and no one knew where anything was. (Shapiro did not even attend an important conference in Ito's chambers on this subject on Tuesday; he remained in the courtroom to chat with Barbara Walters.) Ito finally resumed Lopez's testimony late Tuesday afternoon, saying, "We will finish the questioning by Mr. Cochran, and then I'll order you to come back on Thursday to complete this."

But the housekeeper, recognizing her newfound clout, decided she was through for the day. She informed Ito, in English, "I am very tired. I want to go rest, sir. I don't want any more questions. Thank you." And then she just walked out the courtroom door.

Ito appeared incapable of putting the Lopez issue to rest. The judge devoted all of Wednesday, March 1, to the subject of sanctions on the defense for its failure to turn over Lopez's previous statements. One after another, Douglas, Uelman, and Shapiro offered their apologies, which Clark spurned with acid contempt. (Ito ultimately imposed some modest fines on the lawyers and told the jury, in a rather convoluted way, that the defense had misbehaved.) On Thursday Lopez finally returned to the stand, and she completed her testimony on Friday. Her singsong voice saying "*no me recuerdo*"—"I don't remember"—and references to Cochran as "Mr. Johnnie" briefly became national touchstones. Darden made many points in his cross-examination, but it, too, wandered all over the map, from the important (Lopez admitted she had never really looked at a clock on June 12) to such irrelevancies as her taste in food ("I love tamales!").

In the end, the jurors did not return to the courtroom until Monday, March 6—*nine days* after they had last heard testimony.

The Lopez interlude amounted to another example of the prosecution's bad luck and the defense's good fortune. Cochran had been livid when Ito ruled that Lopez's testimony would not be presented live to the jury. But if the jurors had been present, they would have seen this witness implode on cross-examination. As a result of this defense "loss," Cochran could decide later whether he wanted to show the tape of her testimony to the jury. (In a characteristic show of defense-team harmony, Shapiro told reporters after Lopez stepped down that the defense would decide later whether the jury would see her testimony; that same night, F. Lee Bailey went on *Larry King Live* to declare that the defense would definitely be playing the Lopez tape to the jury.) Ultimately, of course, the defense would decide not to play the tape.

The real loser in the Lopez episode was Lance Ito. The handling of Lopez's testimony represented an appalling piece of judicial mismanagement. At great expense to Los Angeles County, Ito forced the sequestered jurors to sit in their hotel for all that time—just so the defense could call a witness who didn't help either side very much. Not once over those nine days did the judge hurry the lawyers along. As so often happened in moments of stress for the judge, he simply froze.

When her testimony concluded, Rosa Lopez did indeed return to her remote hometown of Sensuntepeque, El Salvador. There was one fitting postscript. In April 1995, a comedian from Baltimore named Mike Gabriel traveled to El Salvador hoping, on a lark, to meet Rosa. He managed to find her, and they took a few photographs together. When Gabriel—who performs as a "sensei" mystic, teaching yoga to cats—returned to the States, he announced that he and Rosa were engaged to be married. The hoax succeeded beyond Gabriel's greatest hopes. For many months, the pending nuptials were reported deadpan in any number of newspaper reports, magazines, and television shows. Rosa Lopez, still single, has never returned to the United States.

17. "IN THE PAST TEN YEARS, DETECTIVE FUHRMAN . . ."

After the conclusion of Detective Lange's long-delayed testimony just before lunch on March 9, the trial reached a critical juncture.

"The People call Detective Mark Fuhrman," said Marcia Clark.

Neither side made even a pretense of treating Fuhrman as just another witness. His arrival was timed with military precision. Before most witnesses in the trial were summoned to Ito's courtroom, they waited in the ninth-floor hallway, chatting nervously with passersby. Not Fuhrman. The D.A.'s office had gone to extraordinary lengths to insulate him from any unplanned encounters. Unlike any other witness in the case, Fuhrman came down from the district attorney's headquarters on the eighteenth floor on the freight elevator—the same one used by the jurors. Even the prosecutors crammed into the passenger elevators along with all the other courthouse denizens, but the D.A.'s office didn't want to take that chance with Fuhrman. And unlike other witnesses, Fuhrman walked into court surrounded by a quartet of beefy bodyguards, investigators assigned to the district attorney. Clark's examination promptly bore out the metaphor implicit in Fuhrman's arrival: She—and her office—were protecting him.

In the flesh, Mark Fuhrman was an imposing figure, a muscular six foot three inches, the first man in the courtroom who appeared a physical match for the defendant. He fit perfectly into his blue suit, and his white shirt and red-print tie made a handsome match to his freshly cut dirty-blond hair. The room perked up when

Fuhrman walked in, and even O. J. Simpson looked a touch startled by the detective's commanding physical presence.

Marcia Clark stepped to the podium, cocked her head to one
side, and asked her first question as if it had just popped into her
head. (It was, in fact, carefully planned.)

"Detective Fuhrman, can you tell us how you feel about testifying today?"

"Nervous," Fuhrman said, not at all nervously.

"Okay," Clark prompted.

"Reluctant," Fuhrman continued.

"Can you tell us why?" she asked.

"Throughout—since June thirteenth, it seems that I have seen a
lot of the evidence ignored and a lot of personal issues come to the
forefront. I think that is too bad."

"Okay," Clark said. "Heard a lot about yourself in the press,
have you?"

"Daily," Fuhrman said gravely.

"In light of that fact, sir, you have indicated that you feel nervous
about testifying," Clark went on. "Have you gone over your testimony in the presence of several district attorneys in order to prepare yourself for court and the allegations that you may hear from
the defense?"

"Yes."

Clark asked if this preparation session concerned the events at
Bundy and Rockingham.

"No," said Fuhrman.

"It dealt with side issues, sir?"

"Yes, it was. . . . It seems that the issues we were concerned with
weren't evidentiary in nature or about the crime; mostly of a personal nature."

Clark paused, soaking up the answers from her witness, and
then turned to her pad and the beginning of the conventional portion of her direct examination. "Can you tell us how you are employed right now? . . ."

Seen on its own terms, Clark's unorthodox introduction of
Fuhrman to the jury succeeded. Under her sympathetic questioning, Mark Fuhrman presented himself as an earnest civil servant
who tried to do his job in the face of unwarranted and irrelevant

personal attacks. Clark's message to the jury could not have been clearer: Here before you is a good man.

Seen in retrospect—indeed, even in light of what Clark knew at the time—her examination of Fuhrman stands as her biggest miscalculation of the trial.

|||||

This critical set piece in the Simpson trial—the testimony of Mark Fuhrman—represented another illustration, in microcosm, of why the trial ended the way it did. The prosecution's arrogance led it to disaster. The defense's obsession with race led it to victory.

There was no mystery in the nature of the defense's line of attack on Fuhrman. More than seven months before he took the stand, my story in *The New Yorker* had shown that the defense would attempt to portray the detective as first and foremost a racist but also, more speculatively, as the man who had planted the right-hand glove on Simpson's property. But that story was only the beginning. As often happened in the Simpson case, a disclosure in the media flushed out additional people with similar stories to tell. In the case of Mark Fuhrman, my story provoked several people to come forward with tales of his racist behavior—a reaction that should have served as a warning to the prosecution.

After "An Incendiary Defense" hit the newsstands on Monday, July 18, 1994, one person who saw a television report about it was Kathleen Bell. The report so startled her that she was moved to write a letter to Simpson's attorneys.

"I'm writing to you in regards to a story I saw on the news last night," Bell wrote to Johnnie Cochran on July 19, 1994. "I thought it was ridiculous that the Simpson defense team would even suggest that their [*sic*] might be racial motivation in the trial against Mr. Simpson. I then glanced up at the television and was quite shocked to see that Officer Ferman [*sic*] was a man that I had the misfortune of meeting. You may have received a message from your answering service last night that I called to say that Mr. Ferman may be more of a racist than you can even imagine."

Bell went on to write that she had worked as a real estate agent in Redondo Beach in 1985 and 1986. Her office was above a marine recruiting station where Fuhrman sometimes visited friends. "I remember him distinctly because of his height and build," Bell wrote. Talking about his police work one day, "Officer Ferman said that when he sees a 'nigger' (as he called it) driving with a white woman, he would pull them over. I asked would if [sic] he didn't have a reason, and he said that he would find one. I looked at the two Marines to see if they knew he was joking, but it became obvious to me that he was very serious. Officer Ferman went on to say that he would like nothing more than to see all 'niggers' gathered together and killed. He said something about burning them or bombing them. I was too shaken to remember the exact words he used. . . ." Bell gave Cochran her name and number, and her story surfaced in the news media as well, several months before the trial began.

On that same day—July 19, 1994—a deputy district attorney named Lucienne Coleman was going about her business in the Criminal Courts Building when she happened to run into LAPD detective Andy Purdy. Having seen the same reports Bell had seen, Coleman mentioned in passing that she thought it was absurd that the defense was alleging Fuhrman had planted evidence. "I don't think it's ridiculous at all," Purdy answered. "I wouldn't put it past him." Purdy went on to say that shortly after he married a Jewish woman a few years before, Fuhrman had painted swastikas on Purdy's locker. A few weeks after receiving this news, Coleman ran into some other officers who said they had heard Fuhrman making remarks about Nicole Brown Simpson's "boob job." Coleman did the responsible thing. In early August 1994, she brought these remarks to the attention of Marcia Clark and Bill Hodgman.

Coleman had once been among Clark's closest friends in the office. The two women and their husbands had socialized together for several years. But as often happens in divorces, the Clarks' friends had taken sides in their divorce, and Lucienne had taken Gordon's. That, inevitably, cooled her relationship with Marcia, so Lucienne Coleman was a messenger Clark was only too pleased to shoot.

"This is bullshit!" Clark cried when Coleman mentioned the reports about Fuhrman. "This is bullshit being put out by the defense!" Hodgman reacted less passionately, but he also appeared to pay Coleman's report little mind. Clark told Coleman to take her complaints to the LAPD's Internal Affairs Division.

In fact, Fuhrman's reputation was such that it almost reached into my own family. On the Friday after my story about Fuhrman came out, my wife called me from her office at the large corporation in Manhattan where she worked. One of her colleagues, a young African-American business-school graduate named Jarvis Bowers, had noticed the publicity about my story and sought advice about reporters who were now calling him about his link to Fuhrman. Jarvis had grown up in Los Angeles, and one day in 1984, when he was eighteen, he and his father had gone to a movie in Westwood. Officer Mark Fuhrman stopped Jarvis for jaywalking, put him in a choke hold, and threatened to kill him. Bowers was so outraged that he filed an official complaint against Fuhrman, which was sustained; the officer was docked one day's pay.

Clearly, then, there was not just smoke but fire in Fuhrman's past. Clark, though, had her own method of determining whether Fuhrman was telling the truth: She simply asked him about the charges. He confessed that the psychiatric reports revealed in *The New Yorker* were genuine, but he said those problems were long in the past. Kathleen Bell? A liar. Swastikas? Never happened. Fuhrman even had an impressive character witness within the district attorney's office. In recent years, the detective had worked closely with a prosecutor based in Santa Monica named Danette Meyers, a black woman. (Fuhrman had actually called Meyers to warn her that the *New Yorker* story was coming out and to make the case that he was a changed man.) Meyers told the Simpson prosecutors that Mark Fuhrman had never showed her the slightest hint of racism, and she gave him high marks as a detective and as a person.

There were several ways the prosecution could have taken the middle ground with respect to Mark Fuhrman. Clark could simply have avoided calling him. She could have introduced the glove found at Rockingham through Lange or Vannatter, who had both seen it in its untouched state on the path behind Kaelin's room. That strategy would have prompted some mockery from the defense—"They're hiding him!"—but such criticism wouldn't have amounted to much, because Simpson's attorneys could always have called Fuhrman themselves. Similarly, Clark could have called Fuhrman but shown the jury—through both verbal and nonverbal signals—that the prosecution was not embracing the detective. A brief, chilly direct examination would have sufficed.

But it was not in Marcia Clark's nature to equivocate. It was, after all, her job to tell the good guys from bad guys, and she had no doubts about her ability to do it. Faced with a problematic witness like Fuhrman, many prosecutors would insist at a minimum that he undergo many hours of grueling mock cross-examination. Such an approach both tests the witness's veracity and prepares him for what is to come. Clark and her team decided not to bother. Their preparation amounted to about a half an hour of Fuhrman fielding questions while he ate a sandwich. He spent much of the time complaining about the press. The prosecutors commiserated. They stood by their man.

||||||

In court, Clark took Fuhrman briefly through his background and then had him tell the jury about the time he responded to a domestic-violence call at Simpson's home in 1985, when O.J. shattered a Mercedes-Benz window with a baseball bat. Then she moved to a new topic.

"Now, back in 1985 and 1986, sir, can you tell us whether you knew someone or met someone by the name of Kathleen Bell?"

"Yes, I can tell you," Fuhrman said evenly. "I did not."

Clark displayed Bell's original letter to Cochran on the overhead projector. The jurors had the opportunity to study the precise, awful words that Bell said Fuhrman had uttered: that, among other things, Fuhrman wanted "all 'niggers' gathered together and killed." It was one thing for Fuhrman to issue a general denial, but Clark pushed these ugly sentiments right in the jurors' faces. This gesture was a measure of her confidence in her witness.

Clark then established that Fuhrman had been instructed to watch (what else?) *Larry King Live* when Bell had appeared on the program about a month earlier.

"Did you recognize her?" Clark asked.

"No, I did not."

Clark continued, "Did the conversation Kathleen Bell describes in this letter occur?"

"No, it did not."

This entire exchange was little short of madness on Clark's part. Bell was a credible witness. She had no ax to grind with the defense or the prosecution; indeed, as she had told Larry King, she thought Simpson was guilty. More important, Clark knew that the defense could corroborate Bell's story with people she had told of Fuhrman's comments at the time he made them. The psychiatric records established that at least at one time Fuhrman had claimed to harbor similar sentiments. Clark thus had to know that Kathleen Bell was almost certainly telling the truth. Yet still Clark went with her gut—and Fuhrman.

The remainder of her direct examination was uneventful, underlining how minor a role Fuhrman had played in the overall investigation. As Clark intended, Fuhrman's testimony mostly repeated what the jurors had already heard from Lange and the officers who discovered the bodies. Ultimately, a half dozen police officers made the same point: There was only one glove at the murder scene on Bundy Drive. With Fuhrman, the idea was to show (correctly) that there never was a second glove to move to Rockingham and, furthermore, that even if he had wanted to, Fuhrman never had the opportunity to move or plant any evidence. Clark also had the opportunity to finish the week with a flourish. Fuhrman testified that while he was examining the Bronco on the sidewalk outside Simpson's home, he saw through a window a large heavy-duty plastic bag and a shovel. With great ceremony, Clark presented Fuhrman with a package wrapped in brown paper and police-evidence tape. She asked Fuhrman to unseal it, and he ripped the bag open and described what he saw.

"It appears to be a bag that's approximately three foot by four or five feet," Fuhrman said.

"And is that the plastic that you recall seeing in the rear cargo area?" Clark asked.

"Yes, it is."

Fuhrman held it up. No one needed to point out that it looked like a human being could fit right inside—a sinister image for the jurors to savor all weekend long.

Over that weekend, thanks to the televised broadcast of the trial, Bronco owners arose. They made telephone calls to the prosecution, the defense, even to the judge. Clark's demonstration had suggested quite a bit more than the facts allowed. She had to begin the following week with a rather important, and sheepish, clarification.

"Now, that plastic," Clark said. "Do you happen to know whether it belongs in a Bronco or anything about it?"

"Well, now I do," Fuhrman replied.

"And what is that?"

"The spare-tire bag"—standard equipment that comes with all Ford Broncos. (And O.J. generally used the shovel as a pooper-scooper for his dog.)

On that anticlimactic note, Clark turned over Mark Fuhrman to F. Lee Bailey.

|||||

"Good cross-examination," Bailey once wrote, "suffers at the hands of public misunderstanding. This achieves serious proportions because it is the public that fills our jury boxes. Too many jurors are waiting for Perry Mason; they expect the lawyer to bring the witness to the point where he cries out that the defendant is innocent, that *he's* the one who killed the go-go dancer. Well, it happens—on television."

There was just such a public expectation when Bailey rose to cross-examine Fuhrman, but it was largely Bailey's own fault. He was so hungry for the spotlight—and so embarrassed by his meager role to date in the trial—that he held a series of press conferences in the courthouse lobby during Fuhrman's direct examination to announce how much he was looking forward to cross-examination. "Any lawyer in his right mind who would not be looking forward to cross-examining Mark Fuhrman is an idiot," Bailey said, adding that he thought Fuhrman was comparable to Hitler. Bailey built expectations so high that even Perry Mason himself couldn't have matched them.

In a display of brooding courtroom machismo, Bailey had not objected a single time during Clark's direct examination, preferring instead to smirk silently as Fuhrman told his story. But when his turn came, Bailey rushed to the podium in a burst of manic energy. He bounced on the balls of his feet as he asked questions.

He began by driving home Clark's folly with the plastic sheet. "After nine months of investigation, you discovered on Saturday that this important piece of evidence was perfectly innocuous, is that right?"

Clark objected, but the point was made.

Bailey, however, was so pumped with adrenaline that he couldn't focus on any subject for more than a few moments. He talked about Fuhrman's educational background—a high school dropout, Fuhrman later received an equivalency degree—and then the lawyer jumped to the domestic-violence incident at the Rockingham house in 1985. Bailey returned to Fuhrman's activities on the night of the murder, and then he was off to the marine recruiting station where Kathleen Bell used to visit. As Bailey meandered on, Fuhrman grew confident enough to venture a little joke. Asked about Bell, the detective said, "The name Bell does not ring a bell."

Bailey grew frustrated, and by the end of the day, he was ready for a desperate lunge.

"Did you wipe a glove in the Bronco, Detective Fuhrman?"

This surprised the witness. Since Fuhrman did not know whether O. J. Simpson was even in the United States at the time of the murders, it was preposterous enough to suggest that he would take a bloody glove to plant at his house. But the idea that Fuhrman, or anyone for that matter, would use the glove as a sort of paintbrush to spread incriminating evidence—well, it was actually kind of amusing. (In the age of AIDS, the health risks alone to the glove planter would seem to render the suggestion absurd.) Yet there was an insidious cleverness to Bailey's conjecture. If Fuhrman had wiped the glove in the Bronco, it would explain how Goldman's blood wound up there. (In fact, after the trial, several jurors mentioned this as a possibility.)

Fuhrman gave a small smile, a faint chuckle of perverse admiration. But all he said was, "No."

"You did not?" Bailey asked again.

"No."

Bailey made no progress that day in budging Fuhrman from his story about his activities on the night of the murders; indeed, he never would. So the following morning, Bailey sought greener pastures: Fuhrman's racial views. In a pretrial ruling, Judge Ito had held that the defense could question Fuhrman about his alleged statements to Kathleen Bell but not his comments to the psychiatrists in his disability case; those remarks, Ito ruled, were too remote in time to be relevant. On the morning of March 14, however, Bailey asked Ito to allow him to cross-examine Fuhrman about additional examples of his hostility to blacks. Bailey was willing to plumb the most obscure corners of Fuhrman's life to shift the focus away from the bloody corpses at Bundy. Using Kathleen Bell as his wedge, Bailey sought to turn the Simpson trial into an examination of the social life at a marine recruiting station ten years earlier. Bailey wanted to ask about a statement that Fuhrman allegedly made in the presence of Andrea Terry, a friend of Kathleen Bell's, at a bar in Redondo Beach. Terry said Fuhrman had asserted that for a black man and a white woman to be together was a "crime against nature." According to Bailey, another witness, a former marine named Maximo Cordoba, would testify that at the recruiting station, Fuhrman had called him a nigger.

Clark couldn't refute the Terry remark, and Ito let Bailey ask about it. But the prosecutor professed amazement at the Cordoba request. "We have interviewed Max Cordoba a long time ago," Clark said. "He never made such a statement, and he never alleged that Mark Fuhrman ever made such a statement."

Bailey loved twitting Clark, and he spoke in a near shout when he rose to refute her. Cordoba, Bailey vowed, would indeed say that Fuhrman had called him a nigger. "Your Honor," Bailey said gravely, "I have spoken with him on the phone personally, marine to marine. I haven't the slightest doubt that he will march up to that witness stand and tell the world what Fuhrman called him on no provocation whatsoever." In light of this disagreement about what Cordoba would say, Ito ruled that Bailey could ask Fuhrman about it only after the prosecution had had a chance to interview Cordoba again.

Another fruitless day of cross-examination followed. Bailey tried to impeach Fuhrman with his testimony from the preliminary hearing. At one point in that testimony, Fuhrman had appeared to refer to more than one glove at the murder scene, using the plural "them." But Fuhrman easily turned aside this line of questioning, pointing out that he was referring to the glove and cap as "them."

Bailey asked about Bell's friend Andrea Terry, whom the height-obsessed Bailey referred to as "attractive but tall." Fuhrman claimed never to have met her. But she's "over six feet high"? Still Fuhrman claimed no memory—and still Bailey made no progress.

That night, March 14, the NBC program *Dateline* broadcast an interview with Max Cordoba in which the ex-marine asserted that Fuhrman had called him a nigger ten years ago. It was all so ludicrously distant from the issues at hand, like a situation comedy playing on another channel: Max and the wacky crew of a beach-front marine recruiting station meet the flirty real estate agent from upstairs, Kathleen, who tries to fix up the handsome cop, Mark, with her excessively tall friend, Andrea. (Bailey even wanted the man who ran "the ladies' wear shop next door" to testify.) Curiously, Cordoba also asserted on *Dateline* that he had never spoken to Bailey—marine to marine, or otherwise. Clark played that excerpt from the broadcast the first thing the next morning in court.

Bailey was even more red-faced than usual, furious. He said that he *had* spoken to Cordoba, he just hadn't discussed the facts of the case with him; Bailey had left that to Pat McKenna. In a phone call late the previous night, Bailey said, Cordoba had acknowledged to him that he had been mistaken on *Dateline*.

Now it was Clark who had the spring in her step when she took to the podium. She wasn't buying Bailey's subtle distinctions. "This is the kind of nonsense that gives lawyers a bad name, Your Honor," she said. "He was intending to convey to the court that he had personal knowledge of what this man said because this man said it to him personally"—and here Clark puffed up her chest and parodied Bailey—" 'marine to marine,' and now he is standing up and hairsplitting with us."

Bailey looked as if he might expire right there in the courtroom. His hands shaking, his face a map of tiny blood vessels, he kept trying to edge Clark off the podium. Clark noticed and didn't give an inch. She pointedly turned her back on Bailey and told Ito, "Mr. Bailey—you can see how agitated he is—has been caught in a lie, and you know something? Not in this case. You don't get away with that. There are just too many people watching."

Clark started to play more from *Dateline*, and Bailey stood up with his hand on the podium. "I object to that, Your Honor," he said, "and I ask that you put a stop to it." Her face inches from his,

Clark chastised Bailey as if he were a naughty child. "Excuse me, Mr. Bailey. Stand up and speak when it is your turn." Bailey looked like he might take a swing at her—but he restrained himself, and this confrontation, like so many during the trial, burned itself out without a clear resolution.

Bailey had one more request before he resumed his cross-examination. He wanted to use a brown leather glove, which he had placed in a Ziploc bag, in questioning Fuhrman. "Detectives frequently, as we have seen in this case, collect evidence in plastic bags," Bailey explained. "Marines tend to carry things in their socks, the same way some detectives carry an ankle holster for a backup weapon. This package could easily have been kept in a man's sock, short or tall. . . . I think it fair to ask Detective Fuhrman if it would have been possible for him to put a glove in a plastic bag to which he had access and to stick it in his sock and to later pull it out and dispose of the plastic bag." This speculation (outside the presence of the jury) was as close as the defense ever came to articulating a theory for how Fuhrman might have transported a second glove from Bundy to Rockingham.

Clark again was outraged by this suggestion, which had not a shred of evidentiary support. "With respect to this plastic bag, this is ridiculous," she said. "There is no connection to this case. A leather glove of a different size, a different color, a different make, a different style, that has no relevance to this case either. . . . This has no part in any search for the truth. This is a fantasy woven by the defense for which there is no evidentiary basis, no logical or factual connection to this case."

Rising from his torpor, Ito asked to examine the glove Bailey proposed to use, then handed it back to Clark.

"Let me ask you this," the judge said. "What is the glove size that is on the glove that was recovered at Bundy?"

"Extra-large," said Clark.

"The glove there is a Brooks Brothers size small," Ito observed.

"Right," said Clark.

"They are out of extra-large," Bailey interjected. (Pat McKenna had done the shopping.)

"Not only that," Clark continued, "but the glove in issue is an Aris, and it is not a Brooks Brothers. I can't even tell if it is a man's or woman's glove."

Clark fondled the glove for a moment in silence. Then she said, "Size small—I guess it is Mr. Bailey's."

There was a slight pause as everyone in the courtroom registered that Marcia Clark was referring to the folklore about the inferences to be drawn from the dimensions of a man's hand. At one level, Clark's comment was a pretty funny line; but it was a nadir of sorts, too—a symbol of just how out of control Ito had allowed the proceedings to get. The judge said nothing, though he did slip his own hands under his desk when Clark made her quip.

Bailey didn't pick up on what Clark had implied until a few moments later. Then, out of the blue, he held up his right hand for the court (and the camera) to see. "Let me state very clearly, and I should point out," Bailey said, "that if Miss Clark thinks that hand and this glove would ever work together, her eyesight is as bad as her memory."

That is the kind of courtroom it was: one where there was not just a stray comment, but actual repartee, about the size of F. Lee Bailey's penis.

|||||

Bailey had failed to budge Fuhrman on his story about his role in the investigation. All he wanted now was to leave the sound of the word "nigger" ringing in the ears of the jurors.

Bailey knew better than most lawyers the power that word exerted over a jury, especially one that included African-Americans. When Bailey had defended himself against fraud charges in Florida in 1973, the government's first witness in the trial was a man named Jimmie James. A former executive at Glenn Turner's Koscot Interplanetary company, James testified that the operation was little more than a Ponzi scheme. Though all of Bailey's fellow defendants were white, Bailey knew a surefire way to inject race into the case. During his cross-examination of James, Bailey asked him if he had ever said, "I hate niggers." James denied it.

Recalling the scene in his book *For the Defense,* Bailey wrote that the atmosphere in the courtroom "changed noticeably when I used the word 'niggers.' I had barked out the word, trying to give it as much meanness and venom as I could. It hung in the air, an all but palpable accusation."

Continuing, Bailey had asked James, "You say that you did not. You do not use that word at all, do you?"

Bailey knew it was the perfect question on cross-examination. As he explained in the book, "I knew that if James denied using the word, I could put the investigator on the stand to refute him, thereby impeaching that statement and casting doubt on the rest of his testimony as well." James tried to wiggle out of a firm commitment on the issue, but Bailey never forgot the reaction of a black woman juror on hearing the "nigger" testimony. "The juror next to her, another woman, kept patting her on the knee the whole time, saying what even an amateur lip reader could recognize as 'Calm down now, calm down.'"

Moments after his confrontation with Clark on March 15, Bailey sought to re-create almost word-for-word his cross-examination of Jimmie James with Mark Fuhrman. "Do you use the word 'nigger' in describing people?"

"No, sir," said Fuhrman.

"Have you used that word in the past ten years?"

"Not that I recall, no."

Bailey was too clever to let Fuhrman plead a failure of recollection. "You mean if you called someone a nigger you have forgotten it?"

"I'm not sure I can answer the question the way you phrased it, sir."

Bailey was going to make sure he had Fuhrman's denial down cold. What followed was perhaps the most quoted exchange in the entire trial. "Are you therefore saying that you have not used that word in the past ten years, Detective Fuhrman?"

"Yes," Fuhrman said with just a touch of nervousness, "that is what I'm saying."

"And you say under oath that you have not addressed any black person as a nigger or spoken about black people as niggers in the past ten years, Detective Fuhrman?"

"That's what I'm saying, sir."

"So that anyone who comes to this court and quotes you as using that word in dealing with African-Americans would be a liar, would they not, Detective Fuhrman?"

"Yes, they would."

326 ||| THE RUN OF HIS LIFE

"All of them, correct?"

"All of them."

"All right," said Bailey. "Thank you."

Bailey had closed every possible escape hatch.

Marcia Clark could have cried in frustration. She knew without *knowing*—knew without being told—that Fuhrman had probably said "nigger" in the past decade. At that point, there was nothing she could do. After embracing Fuhrman during his direct testimony, there was no way she could distance herself from him at this point. When it came time to conduct a redirect examination, she tried—with a growing sense of futility—to focus the jury on what mattered in his testimony.

"The first time you walked out to the south pathway at 360 South [sic] Rockingham, did you know the time of death for Ron Goldman and Nicole Brown?"

"No," said Fuhrman.

"Did you know whether Mr. Simpson had an alibi for the time of their murders?"

"No."

"Did you know whether there were any eyewitnesses to their murders?"

"No."

"Did you know whether anyone had heard voices or any sounds or any words spoken at the crime scene at the time of their murders?"

"No."

"Did you know whether Kato had already gone up the south walkway before you got there?"

"No."

"Did you know whether any fibers from the Bronco would be found on that glove that you ultimately found at Rockingham?"

"No."

"And did you know the cause of death?"

"No."

That was Clark's entire redirect examination of Fuhrman—seven questions. Brevity is bravery in a courtroom, and Clark made her point as strongly as she could. Whatever Mark Fuhrman's character defects, it would have been sheer irrationality for him to plant that glove.

||||||

With the Fuhrman testimony behind them, Shapiro and Bailey were free to return to their top priorities: themselves.

Bailey, who for many years had lived by the sword of public acclaim, was now dying by the sword of "expert" condemnation of his cross-examination of Fuhrman. Despite his public mask of bravado, this criticism wounded Bailey, and he set off on a rather desperate attempt to pump up his reputation. Like an actor promoting a movie, Bailey did the rounds of interviews to praise his own performance. Bailey hosted an elegant dinner party on Friday, March 17, at the Beverly Hills home of a friend. At the appropriate hour, television sets were wheeled before the guests so Bailey could watch himself being interviewed on ABC's 20/20. Correspondent Cynthia McFadden asked Bailey if O.J. had been pleased with his cross-examination of Fuhrman. "He was extremely pleased," Bailey said. "And the reason was that Carl Douglas and Johnnie Cochran and O.J. himself all felt that it was very successful from the perspective of jury reaction. They did not feel that Mark Fuhrman had been bought by this jury, and that was the only issue. They really didn't care what you people thought."

Bailey was so desperate for approval that he even invoked his nemesis Marcia Clark as a witness in his own behalf. Bailey told David Margolick of The New York Times that he "received a very nice compliment from Ms. Clark" about his cross. To Bryant Gumbel, on Today, Bailey said, "We met the objectives that we set out to meet. But we dug [Fuhrman] in the hole that we wanted to dig and he jumped into it." To Time magazine, Bailey boasted, "Johnnie Cochran and O. J. Simpson understand that jury the way no white lawyer will. Days 2 and 3 of Fuhrman's cross, we got very good vibes. . . . Norman Mailer called me and said it was flawless. So I feel good."

Shapiro had his own strategy for reputation overhaul. After Fuhrman left the stand on March 16, Shapiro issued an extraordinary public statement from the steps of the courthouse, in which he essentially denounced his colleague's cross-examination of the detective. "My preference," Shapiro told a flock of cameras, "was that race was not an issue in this case and should not be an issue in this case, and I'm sorry from my personal point of view that it has become an issue in this case." This was an especially shameless display by Shapiro, considering that he had launched the race-based defense onslaught against Fuhrman in the first place. But times had changed. With Simpson's defense in other hands, Shapiro now cared more about ingratiating himself with West Los Angeles (i.e., white) society. This statement was a public step in that direction.

After court broke the following day, March 17, Shapiro spent the rest of the afternoon hanging around Larry King's room at the Beverly Wilshire Hotel. (Of course, the Shapiros were pointedly not invited to Bailey's soirée that evening.) Shapiro and King had become friends over the course of the case, and Shapiro confided that he was miserable. He told King that he loathed both Bailey and Cochran and wanted nothing more than to get off the case. Shapiro tagged along when King went to the CNN studio on Sunset Boulevard to do his show. King's guests that night were Alan Dershowitz and Dennis Zine, the head of the Los Angeles police union. Dershowitz had caused a minor storm the previous week when he asserted that many cops were trained to lie on the witness stand, and the professor reiterated his attacks on police in general, and the LAPD in particular, over the course of the broadcast. At the end of the show, which he watched from just off camera, Shapiro greeted Dershowitz with a single observation that summed up his alienation from his colleagues on the defense team.

"You're going crazy, Alan," Shapiro said.

Shapiro brought his petulance into the courtroom the following week. He made only his second appearance of the case (questioning Denise Brown was the first) when he cross-examined Philip Vannatter. Under direct examination by Darden, Lange's partner and the co—lead detective on the case did little more than corroborate what Phillips, Lange, and Fuhrman had told the jury earlier. Shapiro did a competent job of cross-examining Vannatter, focusing on his false statements in the search-warrant affidavit for Simpson's home and the detective's decision to carry O.J.'s blood sample all the way from Parker Center to Simpson's house in Brentwood. (Rather than reflecting conspiratorial behavior, Vannatter's delivery of the blood merely illustrated his own laziness; by giving the blood to Dennis Fung at O.J.'s house, Vannatter spared himself the headache of stopping at another location and doing the paperwork on the evidence.)

What was striking about Shapiro that day was his appearance. The lawyer conducted the questioning while wearing a blue ribbon on his lapel. The chief of the LAPD, Willie Williams, had started a campaign for citizens to wear these lapel pins in support of the police. Williams had very explicitly stated that the pins stood for defending police officers against the accusations leveled at them by O. J. Simpson's lawyers. Shapiro never made clear just why—other than perhaps sheer perversity—he had decided to wear one. (To mock Shapiro around Cochran's office, investigator Pat McKenna also took to wearing a blue pin—on the fly of his pants.)

Shapiro's blue-pin gesture nearly drove his client over the top. Coming right after Shapiro attacked Bailey's cross-examination of Fuhrman, the lapel pin was too much. Simpson gave Shapiro an ultimatum: One more stunt and you're off the team.

This would have been Shapiro's opportunity to flee—that is, if he had really wanted off. But in his heart Shapiro loved the attention that came to him as a result of the Simpson case—the knowing winks from celebrities, the autograph seekers. Shapiro also knew even before the trial had started that he wanted to write a book about it. He couldn't give it all up now. Better, he decided, to spend the remainder of the trial as a guest at the Thanksgiving from hell: stuck at a table with people you can neither abide nor escape.

|||||

Marcia Clark was suffering, too. Bad enough that she was beset by the tabloids and a vengeful ex-husband; worse yet, she was watching the Simpson case become more racial morality play than murder trial. Clark had a gift for surviving on very little sleep, but so, alas, did her two sons, and they did not always choose the same five hours as each other or as their mother. Red-eyed, she would complain in the morning, "I got double-teamed again last night." All of that, plus her incessant smoking, gave her a cold marked by a persistent, hacking cough and watery, bulging eyes. She was sick for weeks.

And then she had to deal with Kato Kaelin. His life was the antithesis of Clark's—carefree, aimless, without plan or responsibility. In fact, Kaelin's cuddly image obscured a darker personal history. He may have looked and acted like a teenage slacker, but he was a lot closer to forty than twenty, and his perpetual freeloading was viewed with scorn by his ex-wife, the mother of their daughter, whom Kaelin intermittently supported. For that and any number of other reasons, Marcia Clark loathed him. But she needed him. Whatever else he did, Kaelin circumscribed O.J.'s alibi; the two men had arrived home from their famous trip to McDonald's at about 9:40 P.M. on June 12. Kaelin had also heard the thumps near the air conditioner, which had prompted Fuhrman's expedition to the pathway behind the house. Clark needed Kaelin to place those facts in front of the jury.

When Kaelin took the stand—twitching, tieless, in black jeans and, of course, his unruly mop of greasy blond hair—everyone, including the usually deadpan jury, had to smile at his bravura goofiness. On the night of the murders, the jury learned, Kaelin spent from 7:45 to 8:30 P.M. in O.J.'s Jacuzzi—a marination of almost superhuman duration. At one point, Clark asked him about the clock in Simpson's Bentley, the vehicle they drove to McDonald's.

"Was this a digital clock?"

"No," Kaelin said, and he then began waving his arms in a sort of cretinous attempt to act out the hands of a watch. "It was a numbered clock. Well, I mean numerals." He stumbled along. "A digit would be that, too, but you know what I'm saying."

Ito finally ended the agony. "Analog," he said.

Clark did get an interesting new fact out of the witness. It was always the prosecution's theory that Simpson, while planning the murder, had tried to use Kaelin to set up his alibi. After Simpson returned from Sydney's dance recital, he did something he had never done before—knocked on Kaelin's door and said he only had hundred-dollar bills on him and needed a five to tip the skycap at the airport later that night. Kaelin didn't have a five either, but he did give Simpson a twenty-dollar bill. Also during that visit, Simpson told Kaelin he was going to get something to eat. Had all gone according to Simpson's plan, Kaelin would have reported this conversation to the police later. However, to Simpson's surprise, Kaelin invited himself along. They had never gone to dinner together previously. Simpson agreed to take Kaelin, and the two men made a quick trip together to McDonald's—a time when, according to Kaelin, Simpson was brooding about Nicole's inappropriately sexy attire at the recital.

The key new testimony concerned payment at the drive-through window. Kaelin had handed Simpson a twenty-dollar bill with which to pay, and after paying, Simpson had handed *all* of the change back to Kaelin. So, even though Simpson went to Kaelin's room with the stated purpose of getting a five-dollar bill from him, he never took it even when he had the chance at McDonald's—interesting circumstantial evidence that Simpson had tried to use Kaelin to set up an alibi for a premeditated murder.

Simpson had dictated a memo from jail advising Shapiro how to cross-examine Kaelin, urging the lawyer to establish that on the night of the murders his attitude was "just kicking back, was tired, and that was his frame of mind." Shapiro followed his client's advice, and Kaelin did portray Simpson's demeanor as more matter-of-fact than tense. In the prelim, Kaelin had suggested Simpson was in a dark mood that evening, and the shift in his testimony enraged Clark. She displayed great impatience with Kaelin during his redirect testimony and even had Ito declare him a "hostile witness," which entitled her to ask him leading questions. Ultimately, Clark did get the bare minimum she needed out of him, but her hostility, combined with Kaelin's vapidity, made this witness ultimately a lost opportunity for the prosecution.

Not so Allan Park, who represented one of the rare occasions when fortune smiled on the prosecutors. Poised, intelligent, with a record of cellular telephone calls to corroborate his story about the night in question, the man who drove Simpson to the airport in a limousine proved a devastatingly incriminating witness.

Nervous about picking up a celebrity for the first time, Park had arrived for his 10:45 P.M. pickup about twenty minutes early. He drove up Rockingham at about 10:25 P.M, and—this was crucial—*Simpson's Bronco was not there*. He made a right turn onto Ashford and waited. He rang Simpson's bell at about 10:40 P.M. No answer. He went around the corner to the Rockingham gate. No signs of life—and still no Bronco parked there. Park began to panic. He didn't want Simpson to miss his 11:45 P.M. flight to Chicago. Using the limo's cell phone, Park called his boss. He even called his mother. He kept ringing the bell to the house. Peering through the gate, he saw that the house was dark, except for a single light upstairs. At 10:52 P.M., Park's boss called him in the limo. A minute or two later, two sights caught the driver's eye. First, a man (Kaelin) emerged briefly from the shadows near the back of the house. Second, in front of the house, a 6-foot, 200-pound black person walked into the front door of the house from outside. Park buzzed again. For the first time, the lights went on downstairs, and O. J. Simpson answered the intercom, then opened the gate by remote control.

"I overslept," Simpson said. "I just got out of the shower, and I'll be down in a minute."

Clark knew how to milk a moment in the courtroom, so she asked Simpson to rise from his seat at the defense table. "Can you tell us," she asked Park, "if that appears to be the size of the person that you saw enter the front entrance of the house at Rockingham?"

Cochran objected. Ito overruled him. Simpson winced as if in physical pain.

"Yes, around the size," said Park.

Simpson spent about five minutes rooting around in the now fully lit house and rushed downstairs with a few bags, Park said. Kaelin and Park helped him load them into the car, although Simpson insisted that only he touch a small black duffel bag. (Prosecutors argued that this bag held the clothes Simpson wore during the murders.) When Park drove his limo down the driveway and made a left onto Rockingham, he noticed something that was different from when he had arrived. The Rockingham curb had been empty at 10:25, but at this point, shortly after 11:00, "something was obstructing my view" on the right—apparently, the Bronco. In other words, O. J. Simpson's Bronco was *not* parked by his house at the time of the murders, but it *was* there after Simpson materialized back at his house. It was startling evidence of Simpson's guilt. Cochran made scarcely a whit of progress on cross-examination.

James Williams was the skycap who had checked Simpson's bags through to Chicago at Los Angeles International Airport. In brief testimony after Park's, Clark had Williams explain that there was a big trash can on the sidewalk in the area where Simpson got out of Park's limousine. The implication, which Clark never stated directly before the jury, was that Simpson might have discarded, in that trash can, the small black duffel bag he had insisted on handling back at his house.

Carl Douglas rose to cross-examine, full of bluster. Clark's insinuations about the trash can were so vague that a more confident lawyer might simply have ignored them. But Douglas would not be deterred.

"Mr. Williams," Douglas barked out, "you don't recall ever seeing Mr. Simpson anywhere near that trash on June the twelfth, do you, sir?"

Williams didn't hesitate. "Yes, he was standing near the trash can."

Douglas looked like he had been clubbed with a two-by-four. Clark stifled a smile.

Williams stepped down on the afternoon of March 29, and on that rare happy note for her in Department 103, Marcia Clark effectively disappeared from the case. She did not examine another witness for nearly three full months, until June 21. Preoccupied with her divorce case, she rarely even made it to court on time. Over the following weeks, it was often 9:30 A.M. or later when Clark burst through the courtroom double doors and, juggling purse, files, and food, settled noisily into her seat. The jurors, who as near prisoners had to rise daily at 5:30 A.M. and thus had no choice about being on time, regarded Clark's entrances with long, cold stares.

18. THE BEST TRIAL LAWYER

Barry Scheck looked different and sounded different. His entire wardrobe of ill-fitting double-breasted suits probably cost less than just one of Cochran's or Shapiro's buttery ensembles. In more ways than one, Scheck spoke in a language that few in the courtroom understood. There was his accent for starters—a New York honk that never blended into the beige California soundscape—but there was also his vocabulary: the language of forensic DNA technology, with its "alleles," "autorads" and "daughter ions." When Scheck first turned up in the case at a handful of hearings during the summer of 1994, he and his partner, Peter Neufeld, seemed rarely even to talk to their colleagues at the defense table.

But the courtroom camera never caught the most important difference between Scheck and the other defense lawyers.

Scheck worked. Cochran left the detail work to Carl Douglas. Shapiro enjoyed a nap after a day in court. When Scheck left Ito's courtroom, he would bend his pudgy frame over a table in Cochran's office suite and examine the scientific evidence against O. J. Simpson the way no criminal prosecution case had been scrutinized before. When Shapiro had hired him the week after the murders, it wasn't even clear what Scheck's role would be. The vague idea was that Scheck and Neufeld would brief Shapiro for the hearing on the admissibility of DNA evidence. At that point, the idea that Barry Scheck would deliver one of the closing jury arguments in the case would have been laughable. But by dint of the sheer quality and quantity of his effort, Scheck emerged, after

Cochran, as the most important trial lawyer in the case—and, in terms of courtroom skills, the single best trial lawyer as well.

What Scheck did in those endless sessions at the table in Cochran's office was construct a brilliant defense. The genius of it was that it merged perfectly with the cruder race-based strategy Shapiro and Cochran had orchestrated from the beginning. As with the race defense, Scheck's efforts had little to do with establishing that someone other than Simpson had murdered Ron and Nicole. Far from it. Scheck's work had everything to do with undermining the integrity and competence of the LAPD. The results of the LAPD's work, Scheck told the jury, could not be trusted. Cochran attacked the hearts of the policemen; Scheck, their minds. Scheck's goal epitomized the nihilistic function of a defense lawyer—to establish that the mountain of forensic evidence against his client means nothing.

The most remarkable thing was that Scheck actually accomplished this goal. By the end of the case, he had a plausible scientific basis for arguing away every piece of physical evidence against Simpson. To be sure, many of these explanations were fanciful, and some were silly. They were, in part, contradictory to one another, positing a police department that was both totally inept and brilliantly sinister. Scheck's arguments presupposed a conspiracy so immense within the LAPD that, analyzed objectively, it seemed a practical impossibility. But Scheck's passion and skill made his theories real for the jury. And for that reason, he as much as any other person in that courtroom was responsible for the verdict that came out of it.

|||||

With a shift of about a half dozen years, Barry Scheck might have been Marcia Clark (and she, him). Both came from upwardly mobile middle-class Jewish families that stressed education and liberal politics. Both were smart, verbal kids who did well in school. Both seemed destined to be lawyers. But Scheck, born in 1949, came of age at a time when the highest goal for a liberal lawyer was to fight the system—as a criminal defense lawyer at least and a Legal Aid lawyer at best. A few years later, kids like him would become prosecutors.

Besides, Barry couldn't dance. His father, George Scheck, had been born into a poor family of eight children on Manhattan's Lower East Side. George dropped out of elementary school and started hanging around a bank, where the janitor taught him to tap-dance. George became so skilled that he was one of the few white men of his generation to play the Apollo in Harlem. During World War II, George started a local radio revue called *Swing Shift Follies*, which aimed to discover musical talent among the Rosie-the-Riveters on the assembly lines. After the war, George became a musical-talent manager, and he nurtured the early careers of such stars as Bobby Darin, Connie Francis, and Hazel Scott. Thriving, the Schecks and their two children moved from Queens to a big house on Long Island.

In 1959, when Barry was ten, the big house burned down. His sister, then seven, died in the fire. The family moved to an apartment in Manhattan. The ordeal may have quite literally broken his father's heart: George couldn't work full-time because of ill health, and he ultimately suffered twelve heart attacks before he died in 1987. Barry's mother was forced into work at an office-supply business. They focused their hopes on their one precocious surviving child.

Scheck had a *Doonesbury*-esque experience at Yale in the 1960s, which was not entirely surprising, because his room was across the hall from Garry Trudeau's. When Scheck arrived as a freshman, he wore ties and cast his lot with Yale's Young Democrats; by the time he graduated, he could only enter the Yale Club in New York through a side door, because his political convictions demanded that he wear work shirts. Along the way, Scheck presented his draft card to the famous Yale chaplain William Sloane Coffin for delivery to the Pentagon, in protest of the Vietnam War. Scheck campaigned for Norman Mailer when he ran for mayor of New York City. Still, he did go to law school, at Boalt Hall in Berkeley, and after graduating went to work for Legal Aid in the Bronx.

Scheck spent about five years in that combative, unionized, highly political office (where Neufeld also worked), until he took a job as a clinical law professor at the Benjamin N. Cardozo School of Law in lower Manhattan. The position allowed Scheck both to teach and to defend criminal cases, and in 1987 a fellow lawyer called him with a plea for help. The lawyer's client, Joseph Castro, had been charged with murder, and the case against him was based principally on the infant science known as DNA fingerprinting. Scheck and Neufeld agreed to help out.

What struck the two lawyers was the hypnotizing power of DNA technology. As they steeped themselves in this new science, they realized that the best way to attack it was from the ground up—that is, through the evidence collection and preservation techniques of the police. The tests themselves were close to unassailable, but they were sensitive, too, geared more to laboratory conditions than to the chaos of crime scenes. Garbage in; garbage out—that was the theory. After protracted hearings in the Castro case, Scheck and Neufeld persuaded the judge to exclude the DNA evidence as unreliable. (It wasn't wrong, though—Castro himself ultimately pleaded guilty in the case.)

The power of the technology pricked the two men's social consciences as well. Scheck and Neufeld realized that DNA testing on blood or semen could free the unjustly convicted, and they began representing prisoners they believed were innocent. They recruited Scheck's students at Cardozo to help, and called their efforts the Innocence Project. Tracking down forgotten evidence—sometimes many years after the trials that sent their clients to jail—Scheck's team subjected it to DNA testing. In just a few years, they helped more than fifteen convicted prison inmates go free.

At one level, though, Scheck and Neufeld weren't so different from their more cynical colleagues on the Simpson defense team. There was a conflict in Scheck and Neufeld's two approaches to DNA: They trashed it when it implicated their clients and embraced it when it excluded them. The pair dealt with this state of affairs by resolutely refusing to acknowledge it, asserting instead that DNA "matches" were simply less reliable than exclusions. But even Scheck's and Neufeld's admirers in the scientific community—and there are many of them—found this position difficult to swallow. According to Richard Lewontin, a professor of population genetics at Harvard, "Unlike most lawyers, Barry and Peter really know what they're talking about when it comes to the technology. When they've defended clients, they've done brilliant work in showing the problems with the DNA labs. On the other hand, I have to say, they have no compunction about supporting the technology when it's useful for the defense. They are defense attorneys—and they're not always consistent, because they're defense attorneys."

||||||

The forensic-evidence portion of the Simpson case began with the testimony of Dennis Fung, the diminutive, soft-spoken thirty-four-year-old criminalist who had collected evidence from both Bundy and Rockingham on the morning after the murders. The prosecutor was Hank Goldberg, a skilled appellate advocate, but a trial lawyer with the stage presence of a voice-mail attendant. Prodded gently by Goldberg, Fung told the story of how he had collected the various tiny drops and hairs into plastic bags for transportation back to police headquarters.

Scheck began cross-examination on the afternoon of April 4. A junior colleague of Fung's, Andrea Mazzola, had actually assisted the criminalist in processing both crime scenes. It was only Mazzola's third crime scene, and her inexperience proved a matter of some embarrassment to the prosecution. Scheck began exploring whether, in earlier testimony, Fung had exaggerated his own activities in order to play down the role of his novice accomplice. In a pattern that would recur throughout this long cross-examination, Fung at first denied that he had ever before given misleading testimony, but then, pummeled by Scheck, he admitted defeat.

"So you didn't tell the grand jury that Andrea Mazzola was actually the one that swatched that red stain off the handle of the Bronco, right?"

"At the time—" Fung stumbled.

"Did you tell them that?"

"No."

"You said *you* did it."

"Yes," said Fung.

"And you said the same thing about stain four [at Rockingham]?"

"Yes."

"Five?"

"Yes."

"Six?"

"I don't recall," Fung said, sighing, "but yes."

Scheck thus began by establishing that Fung had made repeated misstatements about the evidence during previous sworn testimony. In Fung's direct testimony, Goldberg could have previewed these problems—fronted them, as lawyers say—but he left Fung to fend for himself against Scheck's meticulously prepared onslaught.

Having decimated Fung's credibility, Scheck then went after his competence. Using both police and news media photographs of the crime scene to make his point, Scheck established that Fung had neglected to pick up a piece of paper near Goldman's feet; that a blanket covering Nicole's body could have transferred evidence fibers from inside the house; that the glove and the envelope holding Juditha Brown's glasses had been collected after Ron Goldman's body was dragged over them by the coroner.

This went on for days—a medley of Fung's mistakes, some trivial, some not. Large purple blotches that looked like bruises began to appear under Fung's eyes. First Fung said he was sure that he never collected evidence with his bare hands; then he wasn't sure. First he was positive that he hadn't collected any evidence until the coroner's representatives had left the scene; then, after seeing a video, Fung conceded that he had. No, he probably didn't change his rubber gloves as often as he should have. No, he hadn't seen any soil inside Simpson's home at Rockingham. Yes, he should have taken larger samples of blood from O.J.'s Bronco. No, he hadn't noticed any blood on Simpson's socks when he first picked them up at the foot of O.J.'s bed at Rockingham. At least some of these flaws could be attributed to the LAPD's underfunding of its Scientific Investigative Division (and undertraining of its personnel), but whatever the reasons, the failures reflected on the prosecution's case against O. J. Simpson. It was a brilliant—and devastating—cross-examination.

|||||

These efforts served a larger goal than merely embarrassing Dennis Fung; Scheck used them to offer a comprehensive view of the evidence. His dissection of the blood evidence on the back gate at Bundy was a classic demonstration of the Scheck method. Through sheer intellectual calisthenics, Scheck not only neutralized some of the most powerful evidence in the case against Simpson but turned it into arguable proof of a police conspiracy against him.

On first blush, it was devastating evidence. Many of the first cops on the scene noticed the bloody smudge on the back gate; the blood was located just where an intruder might put his left hand to open the gate and leave the pathway that ran along the side of Nicole's house. Fuhrman referred to the blood on the back gate in three separate entries in his contemporaneous notes from the crime scene. The DNA tests on the bloody smudge came back as virtually conclusive. There was only a 1 in 57 billion chance that the blood belonged to someone other than O. J. Simpson—who, of course, had a cut on his left hand on the morning after the murders. There are men on death row with far less persuasive evidence against them.

So Scheck went to work. He noticed first that Fung had not collected the blood on the gate until July 3, 1994—three weeks after the killings. Fung had explained in his direct examination that he had simply missed this blood when he took samples at the scene on the morning after the murders. Revisiting the scene with Detective Lange later, Fung realized he had to check to see if the blood was still on the back gate. It was, and Fung took it in for testing.

Scheck then noticed something curious in the test results. For many of the stains that Fung collected from the walkway outside Nicole's home, the DNA had substantially degraded. As a result, these stains could only be subjected to the PCR type of DNA testing, which yields less precise results than the RFLP method. But the blood on the back gate was scarcely degraded at all. It was so rich in DNA that the police could, and did, do RFLP testing on it. Scheck found this paradoxical. Why would blood that had sat outside for three weeks be *less* degraded than blood that was collected within a few hours of the crime? Scheck saw conspiracy. If the blood had been planted on the rear gate after that first day—and, of course, after Simpson had given his reference sample to the police—that would explain why it was so rich in DNA.

Scheck didn't stop there. He examined photographs of the crime scene. On the morning after the murders, Fung had worked closely with the photographer at the crime scene, but because Fung didn't focus on the rear gate, neither did the photographer. There was no clear photograph of the back gate from those taken on the morning of June 13. The only head-on pictures of that stain were taken when Fung finally did remove a sample, on July 3. But Scheck did find one photo from June 13 that revealed a distant view of the back gate. He had it blown up many times. Though the photo was blurry and somewhat ambiguous, Scheck could argue that the blood was simply not there on June 13. In a dramatic moment in his cross-examination of Fung, Scheck showed Fung the July 3 photo, where the blood is clearly visible, and then the earlier photo, where it is not.

"Where is it, Mr. Fung?" Scheck asked with a sneer in his voice. Fung couldn't say. This exchange ended the court day on April 11. When Scheck returned to the defense table, Shapiro told him, "Perfect!"—which it was. (Shapiro's only other contribution to the Fung cross-examination was to joke, during a break, that he was eating fortune cookies from the "Hang Fung Restaurant." He later offered an oleaginous public apology to Fung and "all my friends in the Asian-American community" for the remark.)

But Scheck wasn't finished. He focused on the preliminary-hearing testimony of Thano Peratis, the police nurse who took Simpson's blood sample on the afternoon of June 13 at Parker Center. Peratis had testified on cross-examination at the preliminary hearing that he had taken about 8 milliliters of blood as a sample—a standard amount. Using this fact, Scheck then did something that had probably never been done before in a criminal case: He reviewed the records to see how much of Simpson's blood sample had been used up in all the subsequent testing. Again, Scheck found something peculiar. The subsequent tests accounted for only about 6.5 milliliters of blood. Scheck thus concluded that some of Simpson's blood was "missing." Scheck also found an expert to say that the blood on the gate contained EDTA, a preservative used in the test tube where Simpson's blood sample had been stored.

Thus, Scheck had the raw material for his counternarrative of the blood on the back gate. The story went like this: On June 13,

Fung did not collect the blood on the back gate because it wasn't there; the photos were proof of that. Between June 13 and July 3, someone—probably Vannatter—planted O.J.'s blood on the back gate. (After all, Vannatter, curiously, had brought O.J.'s blood sample all the way back to Brentwood from downtown Los Angeles to hand to Fung.) If the photos themselves were not enough proof that the blood was planted after the fact, the DNA tests themselves were. The DNA of the blood left at the actual crime scene had degraded, but because the blood on the gate came from Simpson's fresh sample, it yielded definitive results. Someone had planted some of Simpson's "missing" blood on that back gate: Q.E.D.

Now, the prosecution had a response to this story, but it was a complicated one—and it depended, in significant part, on the jurors' believing in the incompetence of the LAPD, which was not a message the government otherwise wanted the jury to accept. First of all, the prosecutors asserted, Fung did simply miss the blood on that first morning. On that day, he collected dozens of stains at Rockingham and Bundy, and this one just fell through the cracks. The fact that many police officers saw the blood on the back gate established that it was not planted at some later date. As for the good quality of the back-gate blood several weeks later, that too related to a flaw in Fung's work. After Fung collected the samples on June 13, he placed them in plastic bags and then stored them for several hours in an unair-conditioned truck. In retrospect, it was clear he shouldn't have done that, because heat and humidity degrade DNA. But the blood on the gate spent three weeks resting on a clean, painted surface in the cool Brentwood air. Naturally, the DNA in it did not degrade. The photographs proved nothing, establishing only that neither Fung nor the photographer had paid attention to the back-gate stains on June 13. A government expert also challenged Scheck's claim about the presence of the preservative in the blood. In some of the most highly technical evidence in the case, an FBI expert said the blood from the gate contained no EDTA.

As for "missing" blood, that was a figment of Scheck's imagination. Peratis had testified without thinking at the preliminary hearing; he said he took 8 milliliters, but that was just a standard amount. When it comes to such small differences as 1 or 2 milliliters, nurses generally pay little attention to the amount of blood they take from living people. It doesn't make any difference; if more blood is needed, the person can simply give more at another time. And Peratis, who was in poor health, gave a videotaped statement at the trial in which he confessed that he had been too categorical when he testified at the preliminary hearing that he took 8 milliliters from Simpson. It might have been as little as 6.5 milliliters. (This important conflict over Peratis's testimony at the prelim showed just how important it was that Dershowitz had succeeded in stopping the grand jury. If prosecutors had indicted Simpson before a grand jury, Peratis never would have been cross-examined before the trial.) As for Vannatter's delivery of the blood to Fung in Brentwood, that took place at O.J.'s home on Rockingham. A news video showed Fung placing the vial in his truck outside O.J.'s house. Thus, that blood couldn't have been planted at Nicole's condo on Bundy.

More fundamentally, though, the prosecutors wanted the jury to believe that the police did not plant blood on Nicole's back gate because they would not do such a thing. Vannatter, Lange, Fung—they all gave their word that they did not do it. That, the prosecutors believed, should have counted for something. But with a jury predisposed toward sympathy for the defendant and hostility to the police, Scheck's counternarrative found a receptive audience.

|||||

Scheck's theories covered far more than just the bloody smudge on the back gate. He argued that the blood drops to the left of the shoe prints at Bundy had been cross-contaminated with Simpson's reference sample; he contended that some nefarious police officer—never named—splashed some of Nicole Brown Simpson's blood on O. J. Simpson's socks, which were recovered from the foot of his bed. Scheck asserted that Mark Fuhrman had planted Ron Goldman's blood in O.J.'s Bronco—though not the way Bailey had contended. Unlike Bailey, who had asserted Fuhrman used the second glove like a paintbrush in the car, Scheck suggested that Goldman's blood simply rubbed off as Fuhrman was illegally rooting around inside Simpson's car while it was parked outside Rockingham in the early morning hours of June 13. As with the blood on the rear gate at Bundy, Scheck was able to tease some evidentiary support for each of these hypotheses. With the exception of Fuhrman, Scheck never named the perpetrators of these misdeeds, nor did he explain how or why so many disparate people—which would include, at a minimum, Fuhrman, Vannatter, Lange, Fung, Mazzola, and two other LAPD criminalists, Collin Yamauchi and Michele Kestler—undertook this massive conspiracy. Still, Scheck's arguments amounted to more than mere conjecture, and he made them earnestly and with zeal.

Fung ultimately spent nine days on the witness stand, and his departure from it prompted one of the more bizarre scenes of the trial. By the end of his ordeal, Fung's pitiful appearance served as the best argument that he was no conspirator. Even if Fung had wanted to frame Simpson, he was clearly so hapless that he didn't seem up to the task. As Fung was ready to step down, Scheck thanked him twice. Fung walked by the prosecution table, where Darden gave him a halfhearted handshake. When he reached the defense table, Fung was greeted like a hero. Johnnie Cochran grasped his hand. Shapiro enveloped Fung in a bear hug. Then O. J. Simpson reached out and gave Fung a big smile and a handshake—all this for a man who, Scheck contended, had lied to cover up his involvement in a scheme to frame a man for murder. (Courtroom-security rules prohibit defendants from making such gestures, but the bailiffs, like everyone else, were too stunned to intervene.)

In its way, the defense team's hearty farewell to Fung displayed a kind of sportsmanship to a vanquished adversary. It is possible to read something more sinister, however. At a minimum, Shapiro, Cochran, and Simpson himself knew how absurd the idea was that Simpson had been framed for this crime. But because of Fung's abysmal performance (and Goldberg's inferior preparation of him), that idea had achieved some currency in front of the jury. No wonder the defense wanted to thank him.

|||||

Andrea Mazzola followed her boss to the stand, and endured a similar—though not so disastrous—ordeal. A shy and ingenuous young woman with an apparently sincere passion for forensics, Mazzola did admit making a few minor errors in handling the evidence—not changing gloves frequently enough and things like that. But Peter

Neufeld's sneering cross-examination made no progress in portraying her as a member of some grand conspiracy. Mazzola lingered on the stand for more than a week, which meant that the prosecution presented only two witnesses—Fung and Mazzola—in the entire month of April.

What followed should have been the highlight of the prosecution's case—the presentation of the results of the DNA testing. Garcetti had recruited two of the top DNA prosecutors in the state to present this portion of the evidence, Rockne Harmon from Oakland, and Woody Clarke from San Diego. Earlier in the case, these two had offered to step aside and let one of the local prosecutors handle the evidence in front of the jury. But, facing too many witnesses in too little time and also wanting to share the limelight, Marcia Clark had let Rockne and Woody handle it. The result, probably inevitably, was that this part of the case expanded. When Woody Clarke put on Robin Cotton, the laboratory director at Cellmark, the private DNA operation in Maryland that did much of the testing in the case, Clarke spent a full day and a half just on introducing the technology to the jury. (In a subsequent trial, shortly after Simpson's, Cotton began giving DNA results after just one hour of preliminaries.) Attempting to be thorough, Woody Clarke made the subject boring and incomprehensible, especially to an uneducated jury.

Still, the results of the more precise RFLP type of DNA testing were striking. For one of the blood drops on the path at Bundy, the odds were 1 in 170 million that it came from anyone other than Simpson. For the blood on the socks found in Simpson's bedroom, the odds were 1 in 6.8 billion that they came from anyone other than Nicole Brown Simpson. (There are about 5 billion people on earth.) The results from the less exact PCR tests were less impressive only because of the overwhelming numbers from the RFLP testing. (The PCR odds in the blood evidence mostly came back as one in several thousand.)

In every one of several dozen tests, the DNA results matched the prosecution's theory of the case: O.J.'s blood to the left of the bloody shoe prints at Bundy; Ron Goldman's blood in the Bronco and on the bloody glove found at Rockingham; O.J.'s blood again in the foyer of his home on Rockingham. In the case on which Marcia

Clark and Phil Vannatter had first worked together, they had won a conviction based on a single fingernail-size drop of blood found in a car truck. The Simpson case, in contrast, probably featured more DNA evidence than any criminal trial in American history.

But the possibility of evidence planting cast a pall over all of these prosecution numbers, impressive as they were. If police had swabbed Simpson's and the victims' blood at the crime scenes, then of course the numbers would be overwhelming. It was Barry Scheck who succeeded in undermining the significance of this evidence for the jury.

Whatever the jury may have thought, the DNA testimony had a shattering impact among O. J. Simpson's wealthy friends in West Los Angeles. At this stage of the trial, his most prized supporters melted away—among them Allen Schwartz, a clothing wholesaler and probably O.J.'s closest friend in Brentwood, and Alan Austin, a boutique owner and O.J.'s most frequent golfing partner. Now they finally knew what they didn't want to know—that O.J. had killed Nicole, whom many of these men had grown to care for over the years. The DNA testimony shrank Simpson's coterie of white friends to a lonely pair: Don Ohlmeyer, president of NBC's West Coast operations, and Craig Baumgarten, a movie producer.

It was perhaps because of this abandonment that O. J. Simpson, seemingly the only person in the courtroom to do so, took the DNA evidence so hard. As Robin Cotton or Gary Sims, the California Department of Justice DNA expert, gave their reports, Simpson greeted them with nervous monologues to Cochran or Shapiro or whoever happened to be seated next to him at the defense table. Usually impassive, Simpson greeted the enormous DNA numbers with scowls of derision. Though the jury had yet to speak, at this point Simpson knew with certainty that his former life was over. The friends, the hangers-on, the world of "being O.J.," was now, clearly, gone forever.

|||||

The length and complexity of the DNA testimony pushed the trial toward a kind of giddy exhaustion. Though Ito had originally told jurors the case might end in February, the marathon now appeared headed well into the summer. The principals coped. During Fung's testimony, Marcia Clark changed her perm to a more natural hair-style—a much-admired transformation that landed her hairdresser on *Oprah*. Darden meanwhile seethed in quiet frustration, his distress compounded because his beloved older brother, Michael, a former drug addict, lay dying of AIDS near their hometown of Richmond. Every hour in court was time that could have been spent with him. Cochran, cheerful as always, read his office mail as the other lawyers droned.

Ito floundered. Courtroom discipline fluctuated according to the judge's press clippings. When, as happened periodically, a big story in the *Los Angeles Times* or on one of the networks chided him for letting the case drag on, the judge would snap to attention for a day or two, refusing to hold sidebars and generally pushing things along. His resolve would then fade until the next critical story. After *Newsweek* put Ito's picture on the cover under the headline WHAT A MESS, the judge lashed back at the press by permanently evicting two reporters from the courtroom, ostensibly for talking. Gale Holland of *USA Today* and Kristin Jeannette-Meyers of Court TV paid the price for Ito's pique. When *The New York Times* published a hostile editorial entitled "Bankers' Hours for the O.J. Case?" Ito lengthened the court day. Fundamentally, though, nothing much changed.

The families of the victims dealt with the stress in strikingly different manners. For many months, the Goldman family simply bore witness at the trial and said little in public. Denise Brown used the occasion of the trial to embrace the cause of domestic violence. She and her family created the Nicole Brown Simpson Charitable Foundation, devoted to the issue of spousal abuse. It was launched at a press conference at the Rainbow Room in New York, sponsored by No Excuses sportswear, best known previously for some scandal-scarred spokeswomen, among them Donna Rice, Marla Maples, and Paula Jones. As the first president of the foundation, the Brown family named Jeff C. Noebel, a forty-year-old Dallas businessman who was awaiting sentencing for lying to federal authorities in a savings-and-loan scam and who had been named in a domestic-violence restraining order for posing a "clear and present danger" to his estranged wife and two children. (Noebel stepped down when these facts about his past became public.)

19. STOCKHOLM SYNDROME

Their greatest humiliation, the jurors remembered later, came right before bed. At 11:00 every night, one of the deputy sheriffs would walk around the fifth floor of the Inter-Continental Hotel, knock on the jurors' doors, and demand their room keys. This ceremony went on every night for months before anyone even asked about it. This was how the jurors behaved—trusting, accepting, even passive about the many embarrassments of their quasi-custodial living arrangements. Finally, someone worked up the nerve to ask why they had to surrender their keys for the six and a half hours until the deputies returned to wake them up.

"It's so you don't go into each others' rooms," the sheriff's spokesman replied.

That was that. The jurors were to be trusted to decide whether O. J. Simpson murdered two human beings but not to sleep with the keys to their own rooms. As usual, there was no protest, and the jurors continued to yield the keys until their last night in confinement. As with so many petty insults, the jurors lived with this one, too.

By summer, they were struggling. Twelve jurors and twelve alternates had reported for sequestration under the twenty-four-hour-a-day supervision of the Los Angeles Sheriff's Department on January 11. With the exception of occasional weekend outings—a much-enjoyed group ride on a blimp, a disastrous boat ride to Catalina Island, on which almost everyone got seasick—the jurors' world was circumscribed by the courthouse and the Inter-

Continental, about a mile away. Their rooms had no telephones or televisions. Deputy sheriffs dialed and monitored all telephone calls from a central "telephone room," and screened newspapers for references to the case, clipping them out. Blockbuster supplied an unending stream of movies for the pair of "video rooms," dubbed Cinema 1 and Cinema 2 by Judge Ito. The jurors ate their meals as a group. One night a week, from 7:00 to midnight, the jurors were allowed unsupervised conjugal visits with their spouses or significant others.

Not surprisingly, these arrangements produced immediate and lasting stresses on the jurors. The strain showed itself in trivial ways. Like summer campers (or, more relevant, prisoners) everywhere, the jurors complained about the food. As Armanda Cooley, who eventually became foreperson, once put it in a meeting with the judge, "Same thing, repetitious, too many particles walking, crawling, talking in the food." Movie selection produced enduring tensions, as did movie-watching behavior. Ito devoted a great deal of time to mediating between jurors who wanted to talk and those who preferred silence during the videos. The alleged foot odor of one juror, Tracy Kennedy, was another problem. There was also what Judge Ito bemusedly referred to as the "famous Target/Ross shopping incident," which involved one juror's complaint that one group of jurors had an hour to shop at the Ross discount store and thirty minutes at a Target emporium, whereas other jurors had only a half hour at each.

The aggrieved shopper was Jeanette Harris, a thirty-eight-year-old African-American employment interviewer and a divisive force on the jury from the first day. In light of Harris's answers during voir dire, it was bewildering that the prosecutors had left her on the jury at all. When Clark asked Harris about the low-speed Bronco chase on June 17, Harris said, "My family is comprised mostly of males, so I know that females have this real desire, you know, to protect their young men. . . . My heart just went out." Asked about Simpson's plea of no contest to domestic-violence charges in 1989, Harris said, "I guess if I was a celebrity, there probably would be times when I would say no contest . . . because the media is so vicious." Less than a month after the jurors were sequestered, Harris put Ito and the lawyers on notice that tensions were brewing among the jurors over something much more important than videos. In a secret closed-door session on February 7, just a few days into the taking of testimony, Harris told them that the jury was splintering along racial lines.

Harris had requested the meeting ostensibly to complain about the "famous" shopping incident and her difficulties with another juror. She said the deputies had intentionally given the white jurors the extra half hour to shop at Ross while hurrying the black jurors through the store. Harris also asserted, improbably enough, that she had been pushed by Catherine Murdoch, a sixty-three-year-old white legal secretary and only the first of several jurors Harris would accuse of striking her. "In the last week or so there has been like a major division," Harris said in the judge's chambers. Meal tables had become segregated by race, with Murdoch at a table with "all the white jurors and anybody that is not African-American." Shocked by the accusation, Murdoch denied any malign intent, and Ito believed her. Nevertheless, the very existence of the accusation put everyone on notice about just how fragile the jury was.

A full-fledged crisis was averted because Murdoch was removed from the jury on February 7 for an unrelated reason: Her arthitis doctor, who also treated Simpson, had been listed as a defense witness (though he never testified). Several other jurors also left the case in the early weeks, one because she was found to have covered up a history of domestic violence, another because he worked for Hertz and had apparently met Simpson. After Murdoch, Michael Knox was dismissed on March 1 for failing to report that he had been arrested for kidnapping a former girlfriend. Next came Tracy Kennedy, who was removed on March 17 because Ito believed he was keeping notes for a book. (Both Knox and Kennedy did manage to parlay their brief tenure as jurors into books.)

But it was Jeanette Harris who continued to absorb the attention of the lawyers on both sides. In March, the judge received an anonymous letter suggesting that Harris had been a long-term victim of domestic violence. Sheriff's deputies followed up on the lead, and they learned that in 1988 Harris had sought a restraining order against her husband. In voir dire and in her questionnaire, Harris had specifically denied any personal involvement with domestic violence. The prosecutors wanted her off the jury, asserting that she had lied during the course of jury selection. The defense lawyers wanted Harris to remain, arguing that her answers during voir dire amounted only to innocent mistakes. In the argument over Harris, Ito made a revealing observation: "The one thing that's interesting to me is that, were one to look at this case in the abstract and what we have here, it would seem to me that the defense would want her off in the worst way, that the prosecution would want to keep her. And I see the diametrically opposed position."

Ito was probably being coy, for by this point in the trial he knew how much race had trumped gender. The defense wanted to keep a black juror even if she had been abused by her husband. Through all the jury controversies, the one constant was the prosecution wanting to shed black jurors, the defense seeking to evict whites. In any event, on April 5, Ito dismissed Harris for her lack of candor about the domestic violence in her past—and she, in turn, promptly created an uproar in the case.

||||||

Pat Harvey, an anchorwoman at KCAL, a local television station in Los Angeles, had a dentist who had been teasing her with some tantalizing information during the first several months of the trial. He said he had a patient who was a juror in the Simpson case, but he wouldn't tell Harvey her name. When Harris was dismissed, the dentist confided that she was the patient, and he arranged for the ex-juror to sit for an interview with Harvey. In the conversation, conducted on April 5 just hours after Harris was dismissed, Jeanette Harris sat with Harvey in the co-anchor's chair and shared her impressions of the trial so far.

Jeanette Harris was, it turned out, the prosecution's worst nightmare. "From day one, I didn't see it as being a fair trial," Harris told Harvey. Prosecutors, she asserted, were "saying a whole lot of nothing." She accused Denise Brown of "acting" on the witness stand (just as Johnnie Cochran had predicted the black jurors would react). Harris said she believed that Mark Fuhrman was "capable of probably anything," including planting evidence. As for the defendant himself, Harris said that she was "quite impressed" with Simpson and his ability to handle his grief: "It amazes me; it totally amazes me that he handles things as well as he does."

Even worse than her pro-defense interpretation of the evidence was Harris's suggestion that the racial tensions surrounding the case might influence jurors' votes. "There is maybe a person that, say one of the Caucasians, will say, 'I can't vote him not guilty because when I walk out of here, I want to walk back into a life,' " Harris told Harvey. "Or an African-American might say, 'I can't say he's guilty because I want to walk out of here.' You know, those things cross your mind." In other words, jurors might vote to please their racial group. In addition, there was no doubt in Harris's mind that the sheriff's department was promoting racial divisions on the jury. "There are racial problems, and the deputies, some of them, not to bad-mouth the sheriff's department, but some of them are promoting it." Worst of all, as Harris told a reporter for KCAL off camera, jurors were discussing the facts of the case among themselves—in clear violation of Judge Ito's orders to them.

Harris's conduct was reprehensible. She had lied about her past to get on the jury. Once seated, she viewed the evidence with a completely biased eye in favor of the defense. (How, after all, could this have been an unfair trial "from day one"?) She admitted to being influenced by outside political pressures, and then she either lied about jurors' discussing the case or failed to bring this misconduct to Ito's attention when the violation of his orders was occurring. In retrospect, it is hard to imagine how Harris could have done more to betray her oath as a juror.

Yet Cochran knew just how to spin Harris's removal from the jury and her subsequent statements. The day after Harris's interview with Harvey, Cochran held an indignant news conference on the ground floor of the courthouse. But Cochran did not direct his indignation at Harris's misconduct. Rather, he asserted that the prosecution had undertaken "a concerted effort" to pick off jurors favorable to the defense. In a sound bite that was played repeatedly over the next few days, Cochran said, "We think that Big Brother is doing more than watching us. . . . We're very concerned about this obsession to win." Cochran had once again posed the Simpson case as a contest between the black community and the white establishment. "If Mr. Simpson can't get a fair trial," Cochran told the reporters gravely, "then all of us would be in trouble."

Faced with specific, unsolicited information about a juror, the sheriffs had investigated in an unobstrusive way—by examining a court file. This inquiry had produced information establishing beyond doubt that Harris had lied on a critical issue in jury selection. She was, accordingly, dismissed as a juror. This, to Cochran, was evidence of a racist conspiracy against O. J. Simpson. That Cochran would make this absurd claim in an environment in which, according to Harris, information from the press was leaking through to jurors shows just how calculated a gesture it was. From the Todd Bridges trial to the Michael Jackson investigation—from the O. J. Simpson case to the civil suit filed by the white trucker Reginald Denny—Cochran found a handy white vendetta to denounce in every case. Dreading, as always, the ordeal endured by *Time* magazine when it ran its darkened photo of Simpson on the cover—that is, being called racist—the mainstream press mostly reported Cochran's denunciations without comment.

||||||

Jeanette Harris also dumped a major dilemma in Ito's lap. By asserting that jurors were discussing the case, Harris raised the troubling prospect of additional misconduct by the jury and the removal of more jurors. With only six alternates remaining (and likely months of testimony to go), this was a disheartening possibility for the judge, to say the least. But Ito felt he had to follow up, so after bringing Harris back in to flesh out her allegations, he decided to interview the remaining jurors in his chambers, one by one. For the lawyers, this was an extraordinary (and rare) opportunity to get a glimpse of the jurors and their state of mind in the middle of a trial.

Merely conducting these inquiries unsettled the prosecution, because the judge's questions might raise the racial issue to jurors who may not have been affected by it. But as the jurors trooped through Ito's chambers during the third week in April, it was clear that they had done plenty of thinking about race without Ito's help.

The white jurors reacted to the racial issues with some hesitancy. Asked about racial tensions, Anise Aschenbach, a sixty-year-old white woman, said, "Well, I don't know. Nothing has been said that I could pinpoint where that really is a problem, so

I don't know." And several black jurors detected no animosity from anyone. (Cochran never let up on his charm offensive, though, especially in the intimate setting of Ito's small office. One black juror took the opportunity in chambers to ask if the judge could get the jurors a copy of the movie *Bad Boys,* a thriller starring a pair of handsome young black actors. "Good movie," Cochran volunteered.)

The real news of these sessions was that several African-American jurors were furious, especially the men. That the black men were suffering was hardly surprising. Though it was not well known outside of Southern California, the Los Angeles sheriffs had a reputation for racism that matched that of the LAPD. Worse, the training for all deputy sheriffs involved a peculiar procedure that required new recruits, as their first assignment, to spend two years as guards at the L.A. county jail. According to a widespread belief in Los Angeles, the sheriffs then spent the rest of their careers treating civilians like inmates. Since African-American men were disproportionately represented among the residents of the county jail, it is probably understandable that the black men on the jury chafed at the deputies' attitude at the hotel. Willie Cravin, one of the black jurors, told Ito simply that "some of the black jurors are treated like convicts."

But Cravin was a happy camper compared to Lon Cryer, a forty-three-year-old black telephone company employee. Cryer said he had been enraged one time when a female deputy had told him to get off the patio of the hotel when she allowed several white jurors to remain. As a result, Cryer said, "I'm to the point where I don't really trust anybody involved here. I mean, no disrespect to you, Your Honor, I don't even trust you, sir. I mean, I don't trust anybody." The experience with the deputy, Cryer said, reminded him of some other things.

"Tell me about that," Ito prompted.

"About police and—well, I—you know, I have no problems with police officers myself, but it kind of reminds me of why so many black men in America have such a problem with being confronted with white police officers in situations like when they are operating their cars, and they become very defensive about it, and it just kind of made me realize that those situations do exist, and you don't really have to be doing anything for them to take it upon themself to be harassing toward you."

One can scarcely imagine a monologue more likely to alienate the prosecutors in the case. But Clark and Darden made no effort to remove Cryer, and Ito completed his examination of the jurors without finding reason to dismiss any more of them. In the end, the notion of a prosecution conspiracy to eliminate hostile jurors was absurd. If anything, the prosecution probably should have been more aggressive in ferreting out the biases of potential and sitting jurors in the case. (After all, several months later, on the day the verdict came in, it was Lon Cryer who showed his support for the defendant in the most dramatic way.)

Ito did make one change as a result of his interviews with the jurors. Responding to the complaints of Cryer and a black twenty-five-year-old flight attendant, Tracy Hampton, the judge transferred three of the deputies who had been guarding the jurors at the hotel. The jurors noticed their absence on the night of Thursday, April 20, and several of them were outraged. They had formed attachments to some of the deputies and felt that the deputies had been treated unfairly. Thirteen jurors decided to write a letter of protest to Ito—and to back it up with an even more conspicuous display.

The following morning, Friday, April 21, began with one of the more curious public spectacles in the history of American jurisprudence. Every morning, the jurors would be taken from their bus to a lounge on the eleventh floor of the courthouse. A few minutes before testimony began, they would go down a freight elevator to the ninth floor, where they would walk single file past the reporters and spectators assembled for the day. On this Friday, the thirteen protesting jurors all wore black outfits to court, as in an ersatz funeral procession. The rest of the jurors, the remnants of the Jeanette Harris clique—including Lon Cryer, Tracy Hampton, and Sheila Woods—defiantly wore bright colors in counterprotest. To a certain extent, the protest crossed racial boundaries; all of the white and Hispanic jurors, plus seven African-Americans, wore black, but all of the counterprotesters were African-Americans, including both of the remaining black men. But even this signal was muddled, because the two black men on the jury, Cravin and

Cryer, couldn't abide one another. (The protest provided a vivid demonstration of the Stockholm syndrome, which holds that captives come to identify with their keepers: The one thing that stirred the jurors from their usual passivity was a perceived attack on the deputies who "protected" them.)

In short, the jury was in chaos, leaving the trial on the verge of collapse. Ito canceled testimony for the day, explained to the jurors that the deputies had been transferred, not fired, and generally gave everyone a weekend to cool off. It worked for a while, and the following week the judge eased tensions on the jury somewhat when he finally dismissed Tracy Hampton. She had looked almost catatonic through the entire trial, rarely directing her glance away from her feet during testimony, and she had asked several times to be excused from the case. On May 1, without objection from either side, Ito agreed. (A few months later, Hampton recovered sufficiently to pose for a *Playboy* pictorial.)

|||||

It was clear, as the DNA testimony droned on in the courtroom, which juror most troubled Cochran and the defense team: Francine Florio-Bunten, a thirty-eight-year-old white telephone-company employee, who was following the prosecution's case with keen interest. She was probably the most educated and worldly juror, the only one who complained about not being allowed to browse in bookstores. Jeanette Harris, the defense's biggest known partisan, despised Florio-Bunten. During the jury protest in April, Florio-Bunten wore a defiant expression and a long, flowing black gown.

On May 25, Ito called the lawyers to chambers to say that he had received a letter in the mail the previous day. He read it out loud to them. "Dear Judge Ito," it began.

> I have been debating over and over what to do with this information. But after seeing you last night on the news telling the pain your family went through during the war and what my family in Germany endured, it touched my heart and I felt so grateful to live in a country with very strong civil rights and a strong constitution. I guess that's why I feel so ashamed for the information I have.

I work for a literary agent. I'm only a receptionist. It is true I am very young, but I am aware of what is happening with this office and one of your jurors on the Simpson trial. It has been kept very secret, but I know for a fact that my boss has entered an agreement with a juror and her husband. The working title for the book proposal is, 'Standing Alone: A Verdict for Nicole.' It is obvious to me that the woman and her husband came to the conclusion of Mr. Simpson's guilt and sold the book with that agreement. I have not come to you sooner because I too feel Mr. Simpson is guilty. But after seeing you last evening on television, and seeing how what happened to your family and mine made you open your heart to the public, it affected me greatly. . . .

I am in a moral dilemma that a 20-year-old receptionist should not be in. I can only identify the juror as female, once an alternate, husband became ill, about 40 years old, a white woman. She did not want to be on the jury, but her husband is the one driving this. She is very apprehensive and is worried this will become public. The husband wants her to stay on, but she wants off.

My boss has met with the husband at the Intercontinental Hotel, which I assume is where the jury is staying. I know you are a very fair and decent man and judge. So I know and have faith that you will use this information in a way that you know best. . . .

The letter, which was postmarked Los Angeles, was signed "Anonymous." There was no mystery to anyone about the subject of the letter. Florio-Bunten was thirty-eight years old, and in late April she had asked to be removed from the jury because her husband was suffering from pneumonia. (At that time Ito talked her into remaining on the case.) Still, attempting to be thorough, Ito decided to undertake the by now familiar ritual of bringing the jurors into chambers one by one and asking them about the letter. Were they writing books? Had they spoken to a literary agent? All the jurors—including Florio-Bunten—said no.

Just in passing, in the course of these interviews in his chambers on May 25, Ito told each juror not to discuss the subject of his questions with the jurors who had yet to be interviewed. But Yolanda Crawford, a twenty-five-year-old black woman, told Ito that she thought two jurors had violated that instruction. She said that when Farron Chavarria, a twenty-nine-year-old Hispanic woman, returned to the jury room from Ito's office, she "wrote on a newspaper" and called Florio-Bunten over to read the note. "Just looked like they were trying, you know, to be secretive about it," Crawford said.

Ito sent his clerk into the jury room to collect all the newspapers, and sure enough, she found a copy of *The Wall Street Journal* on which was scribbled, "They asked me about a juror writing a book." Ito brought Chavarria back into his chambers. At first she denied writing a note, but when the judge confronted her with it, she broke down in tears and confessed that she had written it to Florio-Bunten. Jury service had obviously been a rough ordeal for Chavarria. Her skin had become blotchy and irritated, apparently because of the stress, and she had complained to Ito that Willie Cravin had stared at her and intimidated her several times. She read one self-help book after another—*The Dance of Intimacy*, then *The Dance of Anger*, and any number of others. Chavarria told Ito that she wrote the note to Florio-Bunten to remind her about an incident where another juror's girlfriend had made a remark about writing a book. Ito then called Florio-Bunten into his chambers.

"Did another juror before you came in here write you a note about our discussions in here?"

"No," said Florio-Bunten.

The judge then showed her the note. "Was that note shown to you, scribbled out by another juror?"

"No."

"You're sure?"

"I'm positive."

"Any reason why two other jurors would say that note was shown to you?" Ito asked.

"I have no idea," Florio-Bunten replied.

Everyone in the judge's chambers—Ito, the defense lawyers, even Marcia Clark—thought Florio-Bunten was lying about seeing the note. Ito brought Florio-Bunten back another time and confronted her with the anonymous letter about the book. Florio-Bunten was indignant. "This is ridiculous," she said. "I am here for one purpose, to be a juror." Plainly disgusted at the entire line of questioning, Florio-Bunten finally said, "I mean, you know, Jesus.

I want out. Just let me go. This is absolutely ridiculous." With Marcia Clark's consent, Ito did just that, dismissing Florio-Bunten for lying about the note from Chavarria, not specifically for the underlying accusations in the anonymous letter. Only four alternates remained.

The origin of the anonymous letter to Ito about Florio-Bunten remained (and remains) a considerable mystery. The author had a good deal of accurate inside knowledge, including Florio-Bunten's approximate age, her husband's medical condition, and the name of the jurors' hotel. Yet Florio-Bunten and her husband continued to deny that they had ever discussed a book project with anyone, and she ultimately did not write a book. A survey of all Los Angeles–based book agents by *60 Minutes* in March 1996 found no one who matched the self-description offered in the letter—which further corroborates Florio-Bunten's claim that no such conversations took place. Members of the defense team, who had a motive to want Florio-Bunten removed, have categorically denied any role in the letter, and no evidence has surfaced tying them to it. In the end it was probably either a freelance effort by an insider to help Simpson's cause, or part of a personal vendetta against Florio-Bunten.

In keeping with the obsessive media interest in the case, Florio-Bunten became a paid consultant to NBC's *Today* show in the late stages of the trial, analyzing developments in the trial from her unique status as a former juror. As it turned out, the judge's anonymous correspondent did O. J. Simpson a great favor, for Florio-Bunten said later that she definitely would have voted to convict him.

|||||

Both in the courtroom and in what passed for their private lives, several jurors showed signs of depression. One juror, Tracy Kennedy, tried to kill himself after he was dismissed, and another, Tracy Hampton, was rushed to the hospital with an apparent anxiety attack on the day after she left the jury. The jurors were further shaken when they learned that on July 19, one of the deputies who guarded them in the courtroom, Antranik Geuvjehizian, was murdered while trying to stop a burglary at a neighbor's house. The isolation from friends and family, the endless waits as Ito listened to the lawyers haggle, and the mind-numbing testimony about arcane scientific matters all gave the jurors more than adequate reason to be miserable. Watching one after another of their colleagues summoned to Ito's chambers and then dismissed—without being allowed so much as a goodbye to their fellow jurors or an explanation for the dismissal from the judge—added to the strain. Denied access to alcohol by the sheriffs, several jurors took solace in food. Family members, struggling to find some common ground with their increasingly estranged loved ones, began bringing gargantuan feasts to the hotel during visits—mostly cookies, cakes, and desserts of every description. The remaining jurors gained weight at a fantastic pace, which only compounded their despair.

Though Ito did not dismiss Farron Chavarria immediately after he caught her passing the note to Florio-Bunten, her days on the jury were numbered. On June 5, Ito decided to let her go because she had violated his order in tipping off her friend about the judge's inquiry. Ito's other action on that day came as more of a surprise. He dismissed Willie Cravin because "the Court has received numerous reports of personal conflict between [him] and other jurors," including Cravin's "deliberate and offensive physical contact and the threat of physical contact." Yet Ito provided a less than overwhelming list of Cravin's misdeeds—principally, a couple of purported shoves in the elevator and a pair of complaints from jurors that Cravin had stared at them.

In short, it appears that the judge, too, was monitoring the racial makeup of the jury. Upon reflection, Ito may have recognized that he had dismissed Florio-Bunten too precipitously, but having done so, he realized he had to dismiss Chavarria for essentially the same offense. That meant he was dropping consecutively two non-African-Americans. It is difficult not to conclude that Ito then pulled Cravin—a black man—as a sop to the prosecution. (Lawyers on both sides saw it this way.) The trial had become so swept up in race that, regrettably, the judge seemed also to be party to the bean-counting. The unexpected dismissal of Cravin sent Marcia Clark literally skipping with joy out of the courtroom.

The fourteen survivors—twelve jurors and now just two alternates—did not get much of a reward. After Chavarria and Cravin were ousted, they heard from Dr. Lakshmanan Sathyavagiswaran, the Los Angeles county coroner. He had not actually examined the two victims, but the pathologist who did, Irwin Golden, had made so many errors and testified so poorly at the preliminary hearing that the prosecution decided to call his boss instead. Dr. Lakshmanan, as he was addressed, couldn't do much more than guess how the murders had occurred, but he did so in dramatic fashion.

Lakshmanan said that he believed a single killer with a single knife could have inflicted all the wounds on both victims. In his scenario, Nicole was first knocked out by a blow to the back of the head. The killer then leaned over her unconscious body, pulled her hair back, and slit her throat. Prosecutor Brian Kelberg had Lakshmanan demonstrate the movement by standing behind Kelberg and using a ruler to simulate a knife. Jurors and spectators alike recoiled at the grisly spectacle.

This method of execution had drawn prosecutors' attention at an early stage in their investigation. Those with military experience recognized that the killing bore great similarity to the way U.S. Navy SEALs are trained to dispatch their adversaries. In the weeks before the murders, Simpson had been filming an NBC pilot, *Frogman,* where several ex-SEALs had served as technical advisers. Had O.J. been trained to kill this way? The prosecutors made a halfhearted effort to make the connection, but the technical advisers weren't very cooperative and the issue faded amid the press of other business.

There were, in fact, relatively few coroner-related issues in dispute in the trial, yet Kelberg kept Lakshmanan on the witness stand through eight excruciating days of direct testimony. A former medical student who switched to law, Kelberg had a sophisticated understanding of pathology, but he hadn't tried many cases in recent years. The examination amounted to a display of self-indulgence, with the jurors forced to stare at horrible autopsy photographs for days on end: Nicole's neck wound propped open, as big as a baseball, her eyes open in hazy comprehension; Goldman's savaged torso, pockmarked by knife wounds. Kelberg's extravaganza also cost the prosecution the high ground on the issue of the length of the trial. Previously, most of the delays had come from long and meandering cross-examinations. Now, defense lawyers could (and did) blame this prosecution excess.

The truth was, Kelberg's fellow prosecutors did not know when he was going to finish this marathon, so when he did, they were caught by surprise. Late on the afternoon of Tuesday, June 13, Richard Rubin received a frantic call in New York saying he had to be on a plane to Los Angeles the following morning. Rubin didn't even know precisely why he was being called to testify. He was, after all, only an expert on gloves.

In a trial that showcased a good deal of shoddy detective work, the investigators also scored some brilliant successes. One of them involved the famous pair of brown leather gloves—the left hand recovered from the murder scene, the right from the narrow pathway behind Kato Kaelin's room at Simpson's Rockingham estate.

The detectives set out to learn where and when—and, if possible, by whom—the gloves had been purchased, and they started with only one clue: the gloves themselves. Each glove bore a tag with the trade name Aris, the size (extra-large), and the style number (70263). A phone call to the Aris Isotoner company revealed that the prosecution had caught a break. Even though Aris was the biggest glove company in the world—selling about 4 million pairs a year—this particular style number constituted only a tiny part of its inventory. Even better, as far as the prosecutors were concerned, this style was sold only at one chain of stores in the United States: Bloomingdale's. When Phil Vannatter tracked down Richard Rubin, who had been the general manager of the Aris Isotoner glove business in the early 1990s, Rubin told him, "You have no idea how rare those gloves are."

So the investigators took it a step further. They asked Nicole Brown Simpson's parents if they could locate her old credit card bills. The Browns turned them over, and Vannatter and Lange carefully looked through them to see if there might be a charge for a glove purchase at Bloomingdale's. To their astonishment and delight, there was—right around Christmas 1990.

The detectives then enlisted the assistance of the FBI, which sent agents to Bloomingdale's in New York to locate the actual sales receipt. They were lucky again. According to a receipt, on December 18, 1990, Nicole Brown Simpson bought two pairs of "Aris Lights" leather gloves at the Bloomingdale's flagship store in New York. Researching further, the detectives found that while Bloomingdale's had received about twelve thousand pairs of Aris Lights in 1990, only three hundred were brown and size extra-large—and just two hundred of those had been sold.

Besides the DNA evidence, this sales receipt may have been the most incriminating evidence in the entire case. Who else in Los Angeles except O. J. Simpson would have had access to these extremely rare gloves? Who else except O. J. Simpson would have used them to murder his ex-wife? Even if one accepted the defense theory that Fuhrman had planted one glove at Rockingham, the record of Nicole's purchase of the gloves amounted to devastating evidence of her ex-husband's guilt in her murder. It is therefore all the more astonishing that the day prosecutors presented this evidence to the jury turned out to be the single best day of the trial—for their adversaries.

||||

The conclusion of Lakshmanan's horrific (and interminable) testimony left the participants in the case with an almost giddy sense of exhaustion. Even the defense team welcomed the glove evidence as a respite from Lakshmanan's catalogue of severed arteries and transected jugulars. When the doctor finished his testimony just before lunch on Thursday, June 15, the defense lawyers spent much of the break examining—and goofing around with—the gloves. Just about every lawyer tried them on. When Richard Rubin, the prosecution's glove expert, came to court and subjected the gloves to an almost comically meticulous examination, defense investigator Pat McKenna quipped, "Who is this guy—the Dr. Lee of Bloomingdale's?"

The lunchtime hijinks did have one important ramification. Shapiro and Cochran noticed that the gloves, even though size extra-large, were not very big—and Simpson's hands were. In the L.A. county jail, the defense lawyers had spent months greeting

Simpson with the customary jailhouse handshake, palm-to-palm contact against bullet-proof glass. They had seen his hands every day. The gloves, they suddenly realized, might not fit.

The subject of the gloves' fit was also on the prosecutors' minds that afternoon. Bill Hodgman was in his office preparing material for the cross-examination of Simpson, if he decided to take the stand. Sometime earlier, the prosecutors had examined the gloves and found just how tight they were. Phil Vannatter, who has a big, meaty fist, had put the gloves on and had noticed the snugness. This was intentional on the part of the maker, for the Aris Light was a very unusual model. Made from extremely thin leather, more like a woman's style, it was meant to feel very light for a cashmere-lined man's glove. It was designed to fit closely, almost like a racing glove.

At lunch, Clark and Hodgman discussed whether they should put the evidence gloves on Simpson's hands. They decided it wasn't worth the risk. These gloves were several years old, had been through extensive DNA testing, and had several small samples of the leather cut out. The two lawyers figured that all the wear and tear might have made them shrink. Worse, Simpson would have to wear latex gloves underneath the evidence gloves, which would almost certainly alter the fit. Especially when the latex gloves were taken into account, there were simply too many variables to risk a demonstration. Mostly, though, they feared that Simpson himself would control the experiment. Clark passed the word to Darden just after lunch.

"Don't do it."

Darden nodded agreement. Even though he'd had the eight-day duration of Lakshmanan's testimony to prepare his next witness, Darden had never spoken to Richard Rubin before the former glove-company executive arrived in Los Angeles the day before his testimony. When they did speak, Darden never asked Rubin a single question about the size of the gloves, their fit, or their condition. In other words, Darden called Rubin to the stand virtually cold.

Earlier that day, Darden had called Brenda Vemich, who had been the Bloomingdale's glove buyer, to testify about the receipt from Nicole's purchase of the gloves in 1990. Cochran couldn't do much with Vemich on cross-examination, so Darden was feeling pretty confident when Rubin followed her to the stand.

Rubin's direct testimony was actually very brief—no more than ten minutes—and had nothing to do with the size of the gloves. He testified solely to explain that Aris had delivered only about three hundred pairs of brown extra-large Aris Lights to Bloomingdale's in 1990. After a rather aimless cross-examination by Cochran, Rubin was about to be excused.

Just then, though, a paralegal arrived in the courtroom with a pair of gloves—a new pair—from the prosecution headquarters on the eighteenth floor. When Darden looked like he was going to use them for a demonstration as part of Rubin's redirect testimony, Cochran asked to approach the bench. There Darden whispered to Ito, "I would like to lay the foundation to show they are the exact same size, similar make and model so that perhaps we can have Mr. Simpson try them on at some point to determine whether or not the gloves found at the scene and at his home will fit him."

Cochran objected, and Ito had an understandable reaction: "I think it would be more appropriate for him to try the other gloves on . . . I mean, the real gloves that were found."

Clark had a ready (and appropriate) response, the same one she had discussed with Hodgman and Darden earlier: "The only problem is," she told Ito, "he has to wear latex gloves underneath, because they're a biohazard, and they're going to alter the fit."

Ito decided to excuse the jury for a moment to let Rubin examine the new gloves and determine if they were the same model as those in evidence. As the jury was filing out, F. Lee Bailey sidled over to Darden. Almost as much as Cochran, Bailey knew how to push Darden's buttons. "You have the balls of a stud field mouse," Bailey whispered to Darden. "If you don't have O.J. try them on, I will." With that, Bailey had baited the hook. When the jury was out, Rubin said that the new pair was not the same model as the evidence gloves, so Ito disallowed their use. (Darden, of course, had discussed none of this with Rubin in advance.) Flustered, Darden told Ito, "Before the jury returns"—that is, *outside* the presence of the jury—"we would like to have Mr. Simpson try on the original evidence items."

But Ito was momentarily distracted by another subject, and he invited the jury back in before Darden could conduct the demonstration with the evidence gloves. Embarrassed by his own lack of preparation, and goaded by Bailey, Darden barreled ahead—now in front of the jury.

"Your Honor," Darden said, "at this time the People would ask that Mr. Simpson step forward and try on the glove recovered at Bundy as well as the glove recovered at Rockingham." Seated beside Darden, Marcia Clark widened her eyes in astonishment. They had discussed this very subject. Darden had said he was not going to do this. Barely a minute before, Darden had said he was only going to do it outside the presence of the jury. Clark thought about saying something, risking the humiliation of her colleague by saying, "No! Stop!" But she kept her seat.

Ito's clerk passed a box of latex gloves to the defense table. For several agonizing minutes, Simpson struggled to get the thin rubber over his hands—and plainly failed to get the latex gloves on all the way. Light shined through the gloves between each of Simpson's fingers. Thus, even before Darden handed the evidence gloves to the defendant, it was clear that they could not fit over the latex.

Darden walked over to Simpson and said, "I'm handing Mr. Simpson the left glove, Rockingham." (This, too, was wrong—the left glove came from Bundy, the right from Rockingham.)

Darden asked Simpson to walk toward him and the jury, and both Cochran and one of the sheriff's deputies came with the defendant, creating a traffic jam in front of the jury box. As Simpson walked, he began trying to put on the left glove.

At all times, Simpson kept his thumb bent outward at a right angle to his wrist. That, too, made it impossible for the gloves to fit properly. O.J. grimaced and said more or less to Cochran, but really to the jury, "Too tight."

"Your Honor," Darden said, his voice now trembling, "apparently Mr. Simpson seems to be having a problem putting the glove on his hand."

Johnnie Cochran, stifling a smile, properly objected to Darden's narration of the event. Simpson struggled with the right-hand glove, and then began pounding between his fingers as if he were actually trying to make the gloves fit. But the bunched latex limited how far the gloves could go, and Simpson never pushed between his thumb and forefinger, where the angle was really preventing the gloves from going all the way onto his hands.

Darden noticed Simpson's cocked thumb and said, "Can we ask him to straighten his fingers and extend them into the glove as one normally might put a glove on?"

Ito said yes, but Cochran burst in again: "Your Honor, object to this statement by counsel." Still, because the demonstration was completely under Simpson's control, the defendant simply ignored the request to straighten his fingers.

Recognizing the catasphrophe he had wrought, Darden tried to salvage something. "Could we ask him to grasp an object in his hand, a marker perhaps, Your Honor?" Simpson took a marker and held it in his fist the way a baby would, with his thumb still splayed out. Panicking even more, Darden asked Simpson to simulate a stabbing motion, but Cochran scotched that idea with an indignant objection.

Ito sent Simpson back to his seat. O.J. slipped the gloves off in a flash, which would not have been possible if they were really too tight.

Floundering, Darden asked to approach the bench. As he did, Alan Dershowitz, who was making a rare appearance in the courtroom, had to cover his mouth to keep from laughing out loud at the fiasco. Darden secured permission for Rubin to place his hand against Simpson's to determine if the gloves should have fit. Ito approved, and Rubin placed his palm against the defendant's.

Back at the podium, Darden asked Rubin, "Should the gloves shown to you here in court today have fit Mr. Simpson's hand in your opinion?"

"At one point in time," Rubin replied, "those gloves would be actually, I think, large on Mr. Simpson's hand."

Prodded by Clark, Darden asked, "Could you tell whether or not he was intentionally holding his thumb in a certain position so that he couldn't put the gloves on?"

It was an argumentative and speculative question, and Ito prohibited it. Then the judge called it a day.

Back on the eighteenth floor, Darden—shell-shocked by the experience—sank into his office chair. Hodgman sought him out and said, "C'mon, Chris, we're trial lawyers. There's a way out of this." In the book he wrote later, Darden gave a self-pitying account of the aftermath of the demonstration—"I passed my colleagues in the hallway and they were silent"—but others on the team remembered that several people approached him to offer support. It was certainly true that Hodgman invited Rubin into Darden's office, and within minutes of the end of the court day, they were all planning how to undo the mess.

It was also true, however, that Clark did not speak to Darden. As she was driving home from the courthouse that day, she called her friend Lynn Reed Baragona on her car phone. "Do you think this is it?" Clark asked, not really wanting an answer. "Do you think it's over now?"

|||||

The glove demonstration provided the classic example of Darden's shortcomings as a trial lawyer—his impetuousness, his immaturity, his failure to prepare either himself or his witnesses adequately. Though some jurors thought Simpson was mugging and making a conscious effort to ensure that the gloves would not fit, several others viewed it as the turning point in the case. For good reason, then, the prosecutors sought to control the damage to their case.

Darden asked Rubin to stay in Los Angeles over the weekend, and on Monday asked him a series of tortured questions in court, attempting to undo the harm from the demonstration. Could the gloves have shrunk? Yes—something that would have been more obvious to a jury in a cold-weather region. Could the latex glove have affected the fit? Of course. Rubin had brought to court an unworn pair of the precise make and model of the evidence gloves and those—placed on Simpson's hand without a latex barrier—clearly did fit. The damage-control operation succeeded mostly in underlining that the prosecutors themselves regarded the previous week's stunt as a disaster. Cochran's smirking re-cross-examination of Rubin focused mainly on how distraught the prosecution was after the previous week's testimony.

Once again, the prosecution's distress overshadowed some highly incriminating evidence that came next. William Bodziak was the anti-Fung—the unassailable government forensic expert. He had devoted more than twenty years to the study of foot and shoe impressions, and he conducted a remarkably detailed analysis of the prints leading away from the murder scene to the side of Nicole

Brown Simpson's house. Bodziak said the shoe prints had been made by a size-twelve Bruno Magli shoe known both as the Lyon and the Lorenzo—a model that retailed for about $160. Based on the lengths of the strides and the size of the shoes, Bodziak said the individual who made the impressions was probably a little more than six feet tall. (Simpson stood six foot two inches, and, like only 9 percent of the population, wore a size-twelve shoe.) What was more, Bodziak found a slight impression of this Bruno Magli type of shoe on the rug of Simpson's Bronco, the presumed getaway vehicle. And perhaps most important of all, Bodziak's analysis of the crime scene photographs showed only one set of shoe prints at the scene—the most compelling evidence that there had been just one killer.

Finally, in the grisly if speculative conclusion of his testimony, Bodziak said that impressions on Nicole's back and on her dress were also consistent with the size-twelve Bruno Maglis. In other words, completing the picture from Lakshmanan's testimony, Bodziak suggested that Simpson had planted his foot on the unconcious Nicole's back, grabbed her hair with his left hand, and cut her throat with his right—an image of startling savagery.

Bodziak testified on Monday, June 19, and F. Lee Bailey had spent the previous weekend conducting, with characteristic gusto, a week-late celebration of his sixty-second birthday. In a bizarre and rambling cross-examination, Bailey actually suggested that two murderers might have conspired to wear the same shoes to throw off the police:

"Would it be possible for two people to arrange, knowing that footwear—particularly if you're in the business of crime—can be almost as dangerous as a fingerprint, would it be possible for two people to arrange to arrive at a crime scene in the same footwear, make and model?"

An incredulous Bodziak told him, "I don't believe, in my opinion, that that could possibly happen."

Pursuing this novel theory, Bailey first called Bodziak by the wrong name, then asked, "Do you think these fellows chat together at all once they get in the hoosegow?"

"I'm sure they do."

"And most of them are acutely aware of the mistakes they made? . . ."

"Yes."

Bailey went on, "Professional assassins frequently do not get caught, true?"

Hank Goldberg objected to this odd query, and Bailey staggered to another subject. During the break, Cochran followed Bailey into the lockup with Simpson and told his colleague to pull himself together. "Stay on point," Cochran scolded. "You're trying to show how smart you are, and all you're doing is showing how smart *he* is."

Later that day, Simpson himself was angry at Bailey's rambling about the "hoosegow" and other irrelevancies. Simpson never made up his mind about Bailey; he admired his roguish aggressiveness but feared his personal instability. "That's it," O.J. said after court on this June day. "I don't want to see him in court again. The man will do no more witnesses."

||||||

After her nearly three months without examining a witness, Marcia Clark returned to the trial nearly incoherent with indignation at the defense's racial appeals but at a loss for an effective response. When Dershowitz made a formal motion charging the prosecution with "targeting" certain black jurors for removal—a rather frivolous claim, to be sure—Clark replied with a bona fide courtroom rant. "Of all the motions made by the defense, I find this one the most offensive, groundless, and baseless," she said, by way of introduction. "This was a motion filed deliberately for inflammatory effect. It has no law in its support. It has no facts in its support. This is a scurrilous attempt to inflame the community, if not the very jury itself. It may be constitutionally protected speech, Your Honor, but constitutionally protected does not mean moral, does not mean ethical, and does not mean truthful. And the groundless, baseless, inflammatory allegations contained in this motion are the lowest tactics I have seen yet in this case." Ito rejected the defense motion, but it wasn't hard to catch the edge of desperation in Clark. (These tirades contributed to the impression that Clark had a larger role in the trial than she actually did. Her denunciations of the defense team made good television, and they often served as the trial's nightly sound bite even when Clark was not examining any witnesses.)

The prosecution never really rallied after the glove incident. Shortly after Bodziak completed his testimony, Peter Neufeld showed that a prosecution DNA expert witness named Bruce Weir had made errors in calculating some of the odds of the genetic matches in the case. The changes themselves did not amount to much, but they further damaged the air of incontrovertibility with which the prosecution had attempted to surround the DNA evidence. Clark had just one more important witness to present to the jury, Douglas Deedrick, an FBI hair-and-fiber expert, and that experience, too, began with a prosecution botch.

Though Clark had had nearly three months to prepare Deedrick's testimony, she did not turn over to the defense all the photographs Deedrick would be relying on until the night before he took the stand. Not surprisingly, and with some justification, the defense complained to Ito about being sandbagged by this late disclosure. When Ito gave the defense lawyers an extra night to examine the photographs and interview Deedrick, they found something else that the prosecution appeared to have withheld—an extensive written report on the evidence by Deedrick. (Clark said she had never seen the report.) Again, as Simpson's lawyers were only too willing to point out, the prosecutors had committed the kind of lapse in discovery for which they had so often denounced the defense. "This is more than a mistake," Cochran said. "This was calculated. . . . This egregious violation comes as our jury waits, as the [prosecution] case whimpers to a conclusion."

As a sanction against the prosecution, the defense asked the judge to exclude Deedrick's entire testimony—or at least a good part of it—and Clark nearly wept with frustration as she pleaded with Ito to let her proceed. "To preclude evidence that is important to the proof of the elements of the crime would unfairly punish not just the victims but the people of the state of California—and, I do point out to the Court, the families of Ronald Goldman and Nicole Brown Simpson," Clark told the judge. "If the Court feels that we have been remiss, then I would urge the Court to penalize us personally, or myself personally. But please don't—please don't penalize the proof of the case."

This speech by Clark—in particular the way she played the "victim card"—represented a considerable gamble. Many judges would have taken offense at Clark's attempt to make Ito feel guilty about hurting the prosecution's case. A crueler jurist than Lance Ito would have invited Marcia Clark to explain to the victims' families herself why her own mistakes (not the judge's) had jeopardized the case against O. J. Simpson. But Ito, placid to a fault, let Clark go without the reprimand she deserved. He also steered a middle ground in his ruling, one consistent with his truth-school inclinations. He allowed Deedrick to give the bulk of his testimony but precluded him from discussing some of the matters that had been mentioned in his belatedly discovered report.

|||||

And so, once again, devastating evidence against Simpson came after a disheartening preamble for the prosecution. Still, Deedrick did present a stunning catalogue of the evidence tying Simpson to the murders. Among his findings:

· Hair in the blue-knit watch cap found near Goldman's feet matched Simpson's hair;
· Hair found on Ron Goldman's shirt matched Simpson's hair—which was likely deposited by "direct contact," possibly when Simpson grabbed Goldman by the throat from behind;
· Hair matching Nicole's was found on the bloody right-hand glove at Rockingham—consistent with Lakshmanan's and Bodziak's testimony that Simpson had yanked her by the hair before he slit her throat;
· Blue-black cotton fibers—the color of Simpson's outfit when he went to McDonald's with Kaelin—were found on the Rockingham glove, the socks in Simpson's bedroom, and Goldman's shirt;
· Fibers from Goldman's shirt matched those found on each of the gloves;
· Carpet fibers like those from Simpson's Bronco matched those found on the knit hat and on the Rockingham glove.

It was on this last category that Clark paid the price for her discovery dereliction. In fact, Deedrick had written in his report that these rare synthetic fibers could have come only from a 1993 or

1994 Ford Bronco. (Simpson's was a 1994 model.) But under Ito's ruling on what Deedrick could testify about, the jurors could hear only that the fibers were consistent, not that they were so unusual.

Bailey, who had worked his way back into Simpson's good graces, made the point on cross-examination that hair and fiber matches do not yield results as conclusive as fingerprints or DNA tests. Still, analyzed objectively, the hair and fiber matches should have been close to conclusive evidence of Simpson's guilt—or, at the very least, a clear indication that Fuhrman did not plant evidence. How, for example, could Fuhrman have arranged for fibers from the Bronco to be on the Rockingham glove? Or Bronco fibers to be in the hat found at the crime scene? How could he have put Simpson's hair on Goldman's shirt?

In a perverse way, it almost hurt the prosecution that it had so much incriminating evidence against Simpson. In many murder cases, even a single hair or fiber match is unusual. Here the sheer number of associations between Simpson and the evidence made the evidence seem too complex when in fact it merely showed just how guilty Simpson was.

In the end, the hair and fiber evidence seemed to have had virtually no impact on the exhausted jurors. It was not even mentioned during jury deliberations. It did not help that Clark's rustiness showed during her examination of Deedrick. Rattled by Bailey's frequent objections, she provided a halting and convoluted presentation of this highly significant evidence.

Deedrick completed his testimony on July 5, almost one year to the day after the end of the preliminary hearing before Judge Kennedy-Powell. Scott Gordon, the prosecution's domestic-violence expert, never tired of arguing that the team should flesh out the story of Simpson's abuse of Nicole with a few more witnesses. With just two alternates remaining on the fragile jury—and no witness waiting in the wings to testify about physical altercations between O.J. and Nicole—Clark, Hodgman, and Darden decided that new witnesses weren't worth the consumption of time.

|||||

The prosecutors had long since decided to forgo presenting any evidence relating to Simpson's flight in Cowlings's Bronco on June

17, 1994. True, the low-speed chase amounted to evidence of flight—and the money and disguise in the car suggested a premeditated plan for escape. But Cowlings had said the cash was his own, and the detectives precipitately returned the money to him after the surrender on June 17. As for the disguise, Simpson had witnesses who would say that it was so he could take his children to an amusement park in peace. Even if Simpson's explanation sounded far-fetched, the prosecutors weren't positive that Simpson had really been trying to escape. All in all, as Hodgman said, the chase evidence was "a can of worms." It would require calling a number of witnesses—including Simpson's secretary, Cathy Randa, and of course his friend Al Cowlings—who were sure to shade their testimony in Simpson's favor. These witnesses would tell the jury a great deal about Simpson's grief over the death of his ex-wife. Worse, the full story of the chase might require several more weeks of testimony. After a nearly six-month-long prosecution case, the prosecutors didn't have the will for more—and it is difficult to blame them. "If the jury wasn't persuaded by the domestic violence and the DNA," Hodgman said later, "I don't think there was anything in the chase that would change their minds."

And so on July 6, 1995, after 92 days of testimony, 58 witnesses, 488 exhibits, and 34,500 pages of transcript, Marcia Clark told Judge Ito and the jury, "The People rest."

The prosecutors had no monopoly on arrogance in Judge Ito's courtroom. Forced for months to respond to whatever the prosecution threw at them, the defense lawyers hungered for the opportunity to make their own case to the jury. As always, their egos played a big part in their considerations. Each member of the defense team had researched a part of the planned defense case, and each one longed to present "his" evidence to the jury. Cochran had Simpson's family; Bailey (with Pat McKenna) had found the witnesses who could testify about the time of the murders and about Simpson's demeanor on June 12; Shapiro had Simpson's doctor, Robert Huizenga, and pathologist Michael Baden; Scheck had forensic expert Henry Lee. All wanted their moments onstage.

Simpson egged his lawyers on. Not surprisingly, he saw the trial in football metaphors. For months, in conversations with friends, Simpson had asked them to wait for the defense case: that's when his team would have the ball; that's when they would score their points. In fact, the football analogy was not apt. It is often best for defendants in criminal cases to do nothing. With no burden of proof, defendants (and their lawyers) often serve themselves best by poking holes in the prosecution's case and putting on no evidence at all. Taking the initiative to prove something carries risks. In a murder case, for example, a defendant who presents evidence at least implicitly suggests to the jurors that he will unveil the real killer to them.

But in responding to the entreaties of their client—and to the needs of their own vanity—the defense lawyers forgot something very important: that their client was guilty. And so to the extent that it concerned the events of June 12, 1994—as opposed to the police investigation of those events—the evidence the defense presented made Simpson look more guilty, not less. And yet, incredibly, the prosecution's arrogance and clumsiness during the course of the defense case managed even here to trump the folly of O. J. Simpson's lawyers.

||||||

Cochran wisely played it safe to start. He called to the stand three Simpson women: O.J.'s daughter Arnelle; his sister Carmelita Durio; and most dramatically, his mother, Eunice. All poised, all dressed in yellow, and all conspicuously loyal to O.J., the three women served more as exhibits than witnesses, with nothing of substance to say about the evidence. (Oddly, and irrelevantly, they all suggested that Ron Shipp was drunk on the night he said he had spoken with O.J. about his "dreams" of killing Nicole.) Cochran tried throughout the trial to separate O.J.—here portrayed as a loving father, brother, and son—from the "wild" world of white women like Nicole and Faye Resnick; the verbal and nonverbal testimony of these three appealing African-American women marked another way of reaching out to the eight middle-class black women on the jury.

Cochran followed Simpson's relatives with a number of people who saw O.J. in the days before the murders: a fellow guest at a fund-raising dinner on June 11, an interior decorator who met with him on June 6, and a man who played golf with Simpson on June 8, at a Hertz event in Virginia. All of them testified that Simpson had behaved appropriately, in a friendly and cordial manner. One can scarcely imagine less provocative (or relevant) testimony. So Simpson was nice to these people—so what? But with them, again, Clark's frustration surfaced. She went after these witnesses as if they were gangsters. Clark snarled at the golfer, Jack McKay, the mousy chief financial officer of the American Psychological Association: "After the two hours you spent with him, you don't know what he looked like, do you?" McKay said he didn't.

"You did not see him on June the ninth, 1994, correct?"

"Correct."

"The tenth?"

"No."

"The eleventh?"

"No."

"The twelfth?"

"No," the plainly terrified McKay conceded. Clark's hostility had, perversely, elevated the importance of a witness she should have dispatched with just a question or two. And with the hapless McKay, Clark was just sharpening her knives for the rest of the defense witnesses.

Moving through witnesses quickly—twelve in two days—Cochran turned next to Ellen Aaronson and Danny Mandel. On the night of the murders, this young couple had gone out on their first (and only) date, dinner at Mezzaluna. Aaronson lived near Nicole's condominium, and after their meal, she and Mandel strolled right by the murder scene. The key issue in their testimony was the time they passed Nicole's front door.

It would be difficult to imagine two more upstanding witnesses. Aaronson produced videos for children, and Mandel had a job in finance at Sony Pictures. They were educated and articulate; neither had an axe to grind or a lust for publicity; they had behaved responsibly since the night of the murders, calling the police immediately to report what they remembered. The computer receipt of their restaurant bill showed that it had been printed at 9:55 P.M. They had chatted for a while after Mandel paid the bill, and estimated that they left the restaurant at about 10:15. This would mean that, in Aaronson's words, they passed by Nicole's residence at "a little after 10:25." In their testimony, both Mandel and Aaronson remembered nothing out of the ordinary on Bundy Drive—no barking dogs and certainly no dead bodies.

For Marcia Clark, this was a problem. In her opening statement and through the testimony of Pablo Fenjves, Clark had committed herself to the murders having taken place at 10:15, the time that Fenjves asserted he heard the "plaintive wail" of the dog. But if the couple on the date saw or heard nothing at 10:25, what of Clark's theory? That was why the defense wanted Mandel and Aaronson on the stand.

In fact, Clark had several options for dealing with their testimony. Fenjves lived behind Nicole's house, while the couple had walked in front of it. Perhaps, Clark could have suggested, they simply didn't hear the same sounds. Likewise, perhaps they were simply a little off in their time estimates. Or—most likely of all—Fenjves may have been slightly mistaken and the murders did not take place—and Kato-the-Akita did not start barking—until around 10:30. That still would have given Simpson plenty of time to make the five-minute drive to his own house and appear in front of Allan Park, the limousine driver, at 10:55. All in all, then, Aaronson and Mandel's testimony was in no sense exculpatory for Simpson. Clark should have had no trouble integrating their version of events into the general prosecution outline of how the murders took place.

But Clark took a different approach to the couple's testimony. The prosecutor's explanation for Aaronson and Mandel's account? They were liars—and *drunken* liars to boot.

"I just have to ask you one question," Clark began her frosty cross-examination of Aaronson. "That credit card receipt in the amount of $47.50. . . . You guys didn't have anything to drink?"

"No," said Aaronson.

"You just had dinner?"

"No alcohol," the witness replied firmly—just as Mandel had said.

"Did that seem like a large amount to pay for just two dinners and a cappuccino?"

Cochran objected to this digression, but Clark kept pursuing Aaronson, forcing her to account precisely for what they ate and how it could possibly have added up to forty-seven dollars. In fact, if Clark had called Mezzaluna—or any of the other overpriced boîtes that dot Brentwood—she would have learned that it was easy to spend fifty dollars on practically no food at all. But Clark didn't. Instead, she just accused Aaronson of conducting a boozy debauch in preparation for her walk home. Practically spitting her words at Aaronson, Clark demanded to know how many people were in the restaurant, exactly the route she had walked, everyone she had talked to about the incident, when she had first called the police, even what Aaronson had been wearing.

"And you are not sitting here trying to tell us there was no body lying at the foot of the steps at 875 South Bundy?" Clark growled.

Ito asked her to rephrase the question.

"Ms. Aaronson," Clark said with no less hostility, "are you telling the jury that there was no one lying at the foot of the steps at 875 South Bundy when you passed by?"

"I have no idea," said Aaronson, who at this point was looking at Clark as if the prosecutor were insane.

Three more women from the neighborhood testified that the scene near Bundy was silent at 10:15, and one of them said that the dog didn't start barking until about 10:35. Again, it was all consistent with Simpson's guilt—but not with the prosecution's theory of the case.

||||||

The fact that Robert Heidstra lived up the block from Nicole demonstrated just how different Nicole's new neighborhood was from her old one, where she lived when married to O.J. Heidstra earned his living in a distinctively Southern California occupation—he was a "car detailer." Heidstra traveled to the homes of wealthy people and cleaned their automobiles in a particularly meticulous way. He used toothbrushes and Q-tips as the tools of his trade. He supplied, in other words, a kind of meta–car wash for this car-obsessed culture. (Among his clients were the Salingers, Simpson's next door neighbors and the employers of Rosa Lopez.) It was not especially lucrative work, and Heidstra, a middle-aged immigrant from France, lived in a single room in a small apartment house off Bundy Drive.

Cochran called Heidstra to testify about what he had heard while walking his dogs on the night of the murders. On direct examination, he said that he was walking on an alleyway parallel to Bundy at about 10:40 P.M. on June 12, 1994. At that time, he said, he heard a commotion in the area of Nicole Brown Simpson's condominium—two voices, one clear, saying, "Hey, hey, hey!" and the other indistinct. In this respect, Heidstra bolstered the defense theory that the murders took place around 10:30. (In a sobering reminder that this case involved actual human beings, Patti Gold-man, Ron Goldman's stepmother, told me at a break in Heidstra's testimony that she could tell this witness was indeed describing Ron's voice. "That's just what Ron would say if he came on a scene like this," Patti said. " 'Hey, *hey*, HEY!' ")

The defense's "time line" witnesses had been identified and cul-tivated by Bailey, McKenna, and Peter Neufeld. Cochran, who rarely did much preparation of witnesses, had only a general idea of what Heidstra was going to say. The prosecution, in contrast, knew a good deal about Heidstra. He had been interviewed several times, and the prosecutors nearly decided to call him as a witness in their own case (dropping him only because he conflicted with Clark's desire to place the murders at 10:15). But as Darden began his cross-examination, it became clear that Heidstra had a good deal to say that helped the government's case. For starters, Heid-stra admitted that he usually walked his dogs at 10:00, which, if he had done so on the night of the murders, would have put the killings at precisely the time the prosecution claimed. Heidstra also said that he saw a white vehicle that could have been a Bronco leaving the scene—another fact that was consistent with the gov-ernment's case. Twitching at the defense table, Cochran was losing his customary sang-froid as Darden converted Heidstra into a pow-erful prosecution witness. Continuing, Darden asked Heidstra, "The second voice that you heard sounded like the voice of a black man, is that correct?"

Cochran nearly jumped out of his chair. "Objected to, Your Honor," he sputtered. "I object." The defense caused such a com-motion that Judge Ito excused the jury and told Heidstra to step outside for a moment. Darden patiently recounted to the judge that an acquaintance of Heidstra's, Patricia Baret, had told Detec-tive Tom Lange that Heidstra told her that "he heard the very angry screaming of an older man who sounded black." Thus, Darden ex-plained to Ito, he had every right to ask the question.

But Cochran was not to be mollified. "I resent that statement," he thundered. "You can't tell by someone's voice when they're black. I don't know who's made that statement, Baret or Lange. That's racist." Cochran continued his tirade: "This statement about whether somebody sounds black or white is racist, and I resent it, and that's why I stood and objected to it. I think it's totally improper in America, at this time in 1995, just to hear this and endure this."

Darden looked stricken. The physical contrast between the two men had never looked greater—Cochran, eyes ablaze, full of blustering vitality; Darden, eyes down, looking skinny in his flopping double-breasted jacket, pacing splay-footed behind the podium. When Cochran finished, Darden replied evenly that he was simply questioning Heidstra about a statement the witness himself had allegedly made earlier. Then he came as close as he ever would to lashing back, and he addressed Cochran with quiet dignity: "That's created a lot of problems for my family and myself, statements that you make about me and race, Mr. Cochran." Ito called a recess, and tempers cooled.

Cochran's outrageous behavior revealed much about him and the way he approached his role as a defense attorney. In the first place, he was simply wrong. Many African-Americans do have distinctive accents and speech patterns. But Cochran's cynicism ran deep. His outburst came just as one of his witnesses was blowing up in his face. How better to stop an effective cross-examination than by throwing a stink bomb of racial grievance into the middle of the courtroom? When the facts went against them, Simpson's lawyers turned, as they always did, to race.

IIIII

Shapiro had not entirely disappeared from the case, and though he had little to do, he maintained his sullen vigil at the defense table to the end. When the time came for Michael Baden to testify, Barry Scheck made like a ventriloquist and fed Shapiro the substantive questions he should ask. With Baden's testimony, Shapiro could not resist playing the race card in his own clumsy, if genial, way.

Formerly the chief medical examiner of New York City, the curly-haired and loquacious Michael Baden practically ran to the familiar blue witness chair when Shapiro summoned him. As with any expert witness, Shapiro began by eliciting Baden's qualifications, which were considerable. The jury learned that Baden had graduated from the City College of New York in 1955 and the New York

University School of Medicine in 1959. Shapiro asked Baden what awards he had received at City College. Senior-class president, Phi Beta Kappa, and valedictorian, Baden replied.

"And where," Shapiro continued seamlessly, "was that college located?"

Baden was suddenly struck dumb, clearly puzzled by how the location of City College might edify these jurors on any issue relevant to the guilt or innocence of Shapiro's client. Baden stumbled as he began his answer. "It's located in upper Manhattan, New York City," he said. Then he caught on, and hastily completed his response: "Harlem area of New York City."

Having informed the nine African-American jurors that this white defense expert came of age in the unofficial capital of black America, Shapiro was off and running.

In example after shameless example, Shapiro sought to turn Baden into an Abraham Lincoln of the autopsy table. Did he serve on any state commissions? "Yes," Baden replied, "the New York State commission that investigates all deaths that occur in prisons and police custody in New York State"—an entity that, Baden said, had been set up "after the Attica deaths." Had he served on any federal commissions? Yes, he said, "on the congressional committee formed to investigate the deaths of President John F. Kennedy and Dr. Martin Luther King." Shapiro then elicited from Baden a lengthy exegesis on "the purpose of the examination of the death of Dr. Martin Luther King." Asked for any "highlights" of his efforts on behalf of prosecutors over the years, Baden replied, "I was recently a witness for the . . . prosecutor of Jackson, Mississippi, in the reinvestigation of the death of Medgar Evers, who had been a civil-rights leader who had been killed in 1963." Had he ever investigated cases for the Los Angeles District Attorney's Office? Indeed he had. "I was involved in the investigation—and re-autopsy—of the death of a young athlete, a football player in Los Angeles County, Ron Settles, who died in a police precinct in Signal Hill." Baden then hastened to add, "Initially, I was called by the attorney for the family, Mr. Cochran, Johnnie Cochran." As for the substance of the Simpson case, Baden had little to add other than that he thought Dr. Lakshmanan used too much guesswork in reconstructing the crime. As for the detectives' failure to call the coroner immediately after discovering the bodies—which was a subject the defense lawyers had dwelled on for many hours with the police witnesses—Baden had the integrity to admit under cross-examination that it would not have made any difference in determining the time of death.

The story was much the same, several witnesses later, with Henry Lee, another defense expert long on impressive qualifications but short on relevant evidence in the case. Under Scheck's questioning, the centerpiece of Lee's testimony was his claim that the LAPD criminalists might have missed a single non–Bruno Magli shoe print at the murder scene. Thus, according to Scheck, there was a second killer at the scene. Yet on close inspection this claim evaporated. There were more than a dozen shoe prints from the size-twelve Bruno Magli shoes—all arranged in a logical progression along the path at Nicole's condominium. The only evidence of a second killer was this possible—not definite—single shoe print. Did the second killer hop into the murder scene, remain on one foot in one place during the entire struggle, then hop away? The idea that this evidence truly suggested the involvement of a second killer was preposterous. Lee did, however, bestow one gift on the defense. When asked whether his review of the evidence revealed the possibility of tampering, Lee muttered darkly, if vaguely, "Something is wrong."

||||||

Robert Huizenga was more than simply another defense witness whose testimony backfired. The three days on the witness stand of this Beverly Hills internist turned out, surprisingly, to be one of the more profound moments of the trial. Not since Ron Shipp's pathetic visit to the stand was there so vivid a reminder of the empty world of O. J. Simpson.

At Shapiro's request, Huizenga had examined Simpson on June 15, 1994, just two days after he returned home from Chicago following the murders. The defense's (and especially the defendant's) idea was for Huizenga to testify about Simpson's various ailments, in an effort to persuade the jury that O.J. lacked the physical ability to commit the crimes. As even a layman could tell, such a claim was absurd. Despite his lingering football injuries, Simpson was bigger, stronger, and fitter than most people in the United States. What Huizenga's testimony did demonstrate was the extraordinary extent of Simpson's self-pity. The same side of his character that drove him to complain in his "suicide" note of being a battered husband drove Simpson, during his trial, to embrace Huizenga as a witness. Regardless of the facts, Simpson never saw himself as anything other than a victim. So, overcoming the skepticism of Cochran and other members of the defense team, Simpson and Shapiro (who wanted the airtime) prevailed and called Huizenga to the stand.

To call the forty-two-year-old Huizenga boyish does not do justice to the curiously unlived-in look of his face. He could have passed for a college student. Blandly handsome, blond, and fit, he seemed like a West Coast Dan Quayle. Huizenga had impeccable credentials—summa cum laude graduate of the University of Michigan; degree from Harvard Medical School; former chief resident at Cedars-Sinai Medical Center in Los Angeles; former team physician for the Los Angeles Raiders football team—yet it was precisely because of his eminent qualifications that his testimony and demeanor seemed so shocking. For it became clear, as soon as Shapiro called him to the stand, that Huizenga was completely in O. J. Simpson's thrall. In Los Angeles, it seemed, it wasn't just the Ron Shipps of the world—the hangers-on, the wannabes—who worshipped the local celebrities. Even Rob Huizenga, with all his fancy credentials, was willing to sacrifice his objectivity, his probity, and even his dignity to ingratiate himself with a famous man, even one accused of murder.

Huizenga was so eager to testify that he frequently cut off Shapiro before he could even finish his question. According to Huizenga's examinations of Simpson on June 15 and June 17 (at Kardashian's house, just before O.J. and Cowlings disappeared), Simpson suffered, the doctor said, from a "whole array of the typical post-NFL injury syndromes." He had a pair of bad knees, a bum right ankle, and a case of arthritis. "On the day I saw him, he had significantly limited mobility," Huizenga said. "Fast walking, certainly in terms of slow jogging, it would be very difficult if not impossible." Huizenga also showed the jury the photographs of Simpson taken during the examination of June 17: His torso was massive and hugely muscled, but Shapiro pointed out that he had no abrasions to suggest he had just fought a life-or-death struggle less than a week earlier.

In his breezy way, Shapiro asked whether the photographs didn't show "a man to be in pretty good shape."

Huizenga helpfully disagreed. "Curiously, some people have these phenomenal builds and really aren't in all that great aerobic shape. And I think that, based on my history, he hadn't really been doing much exercise, if any, and there are some very lucky people that looks can be deceiving and certainly in his case, although he looks like Tarzan, you know, he was walking more like Tarzan's grandfather."

Brian Kelberg, the former medical student who had examined Lakshmanan at such length, conducted what was possibly the best cross-examination of the entire trial. Kelberg began by exploring the question of bias. Huizenga had agreed that he had been hired by Shapiro under highly unusual circumstances, and Kelberg asked whether the doctor had viewed his role as "to start preparing a possible defense in the event Mr. Simpson was charged."

Huizenga pouted and disagreed. "I took it to address his mental problems, insomnia, and difficulty handling this incredible stress that maybe no other human being, short of Job, has endured."

There was a pause in the courtroom as lawyers on both sides did double takes, as if to assure themselves that Huizenga had really said what they thought he said. (Even the somnolent jurors perked up at the reference to Job.)

Kelberg knew just how to follow up. "I want to be clear in your answer," he said. "Is it your characterization that Mr. Simpson is in a situation which, to your knowledge, only Job has suffered more?"

"I think the pressure that was on him, for whatever reason, was a tremendous weight, the change in his life status that very few, if any, people have experienced in my opinion," Huizenga answered.

"And if he had murdered two human beings, Nicole Brown Simpson and her friend Ronald Goldman, would that be the kind of thing that would cause a great weight to be on a man's shoulders?"

Shapiro objected in vain, and Huizenga had to say, "If someone hypothetically killed someone, they certainly would have a great weight on their shoulders."

As Kelberg continued, Huizenga strained to spin every answer in Simpson's favor. Kelberg brought out that Huizenga had written Shapiro a series of letters in which he, a nominally independent expert, had helped Simpson's lawyer plot legal strategy. Kelberg showcased Huizenga's preening ego for the jury, showing how the doctor larded up his résumé with his talk-show appearances. In answer after answer, Huizenga struggled to shade his answers to help the defense. It was an astonishing, and appalling, performance.

Even on the substance of the case, Kelberg used Huizenga to his advantage. The prosecutor meticulously went over the photographs of Simpson's hands that were taken on June 17, and revealed to the jury that Simpson actually had *seven* separate abrasions on his left hand and three different cuts. His right hand was unmarked. (This fit with the prosecution's theory that Simpson lost his left glove during the struggle at Bundy, cut his left hand, and did not lose his right glove until he returned to Rockingham.)

But Kelberg was just warming up. He showed a video clip from a motivational speech Simpson had given on March 31, 1994—a little more than two months before the murders—for an arthritis-relief product called Juice Plus. (Among other things, this demonstrated just how low Simpson had sunk in the entertainment world; once he had made Hertz commercials for national television, now he was pitching for a questionable medical remedy at a shabby convention in Dallas.) Mugging for the cheering distributors, Simpson said, "I started taking regularly Juice Plus and started feeling—I don't know if it was mind over matter, if it was a mental thing—but almost immediately I started feeling better all of a sudden. I was starting to get another ten yards on my drive!" Confronted with the tape, Huizenga had no choice but to speculate that Simpson was either lying to push the product or in fact had enjoyed some relief from his arthritis symptoms.

But the climax of Kelberg's cross-examination came when he played seventy minutes of raw footage from an exercise video that was later released as *O. J. Simpson Minimum Maintenance for Men*. Simpson had taped the routine—in which he looked fit and healthy in a T-shirt and Lycra shorts—at the end of May 1994, just two weeks before the murders. Trading inane patter with the coach who was directing the exercises, Simpson looked like a model of middle-aged fitness. Simpson stretched; he marched, bent his knees, did push-ups and sit-ups. The tape alone scotched the notion that Simpson did not have the physical ability to murder his ex-wife and her friend.

The most remarkable part of the tape came so fast that it was possible to miss it the first time through. One of the routines involved the participants simulating a punching motion—right jab, left jab, right jab, left jab. As the coach on the videotape later testified, Simpson ad-libbed a narration to the punching portion of the exercise. "Get your space in if you're working out with the wife," Simpson said to the camera, still punching at the air with his thick, muscled arms. Then he chuckled and added, "If you know what I mean, you can always blame it on workin' out." Meaning, if you punch your wife, you can always blame it on working out.

A convicted wife beater jokes about beating his wife. Could there have been a more chilling glimpse into O. J. Simpson's subconscious? (The jurors, it turned out from later conversations, never paid any attention to this. Indeed, they said little about the defense case at all, so exhausted and numb were they by the summer months. By this point, it appears, they had already made up their minds.)

The defense case, then, ranged from poignant (Simpson's family) to pathetic (Huizenga) to irrelevant (Baden and Lee) to downright incriminating (Heidstra and the exercise video). What many of the witnesses had in common was that their testimony pained them, embarrassed them, or otherwise diminished them.

Indeed, though Nicole Brown Simpson and Ronald Goldman were the first and most important casualties of this case, they were not the only ones. There was Simpson's family, those decent and loyal women in yellow who endured this long trial for a man they loved, and of course those two children, who would grow up without a mother. There were Simpson's friends, many of whom came to realize how blind they had been to O.J.'s narcissism and brutality. There were the peripheral figures, like Shipp and Huizenga, who degraded themselves on the altar of celebrity. (Shipp, at least, came to realize what he had done.) And there was even the public at large, whose passions and biases were inflamed by the events

Simpson had set in motion. None of this mattered to O. J. Simpson, because, as he had done his entire life, he cared only about himself.

Huizenga and Heidstra gave the prosecution a brief but undeniable lift. So the defense lawyers retreated to the safe harbor they sought whenever the evidence turned against them: race.

Shortly after three in the afternoon on July 7—the day after the prosecution rested its case—a secretary in Johnnie Cochran's office said she had a phone call to patch through to Pat McKenna's cubicle. The caller, the secretary said, did not want to give his name.

McKenna, as the lead private investigator for the defense, rarely came to the courthouse. Instead, he worked out of Cochran's office, chasing down witnesses, following up leads, and handling the endless number of tipsters who called with purported information about the case. McKenna's notes from most of these telephone calls wound up in a thick manila folder that bore the heading LOONIES.

The caller on this day sounded saner than most of the others, and he offered unusually specific information. He said he was a lawyer from San Francisco and he had a client who had a friend named Laura. The caller said that Laura had in her possession about a dozen audiotapes of Mark Fuhrman talking about his police work. Scribbling as the caller talked, McKenna noted what the caller said Fuhrman had discussed on the tapes:

>—*Plant Evidence*
>—*Get Niggers*
>—*So. Africa—Niggers—Apartheid*

The caller gave McKenna a phone number for Laura with a 910 area code—North Carolina. McKenna, as he sometimes did with the more credible tipsters, gave this one a code name, in case he wanted to get back in touch. "You're Brian," McKenna told the voice on the phone.

McKenna put down the phone with "Brian" and dialed Laura. A man answered; he said Laura was out but would be returning in about fifteen minutes. McKenna left his name and number—but not his affiliation—and Laura called him back in about thirty minutes.

"This is Laura Hart McKinny," she said.

"I'm a private investigator working for O. J. Simpson," McKenna told her, with an edge of nervous pleading in his voice. "We really believe our client is innocent, and we understand you have some tapes of Mark Fuhrman that we think could help us very much." Polite but noncommittal, McKinny told McKenna her lawyer would give him a call. Fifteen minutes later, a lawyer named Matthew Schwartz, who was based in Los Angeles, rang McKenna. Schwartz confirmed that the tapes existed and that they were authentic. He said that McKinny had interviewed Fuhrman for a screenwriting project. Schwartz said he thought if the defense subpoenaed the tapes, they could probably work out a way for them to be turned over.

At 5:08 P.M., less than two hours after he first heard of the tapes, McKenna faxed Schwartz a letter formally requesting them. It was only then that McKenna realized that, as he had been talking on the phone, he had traced and retraced the same words from his original notes:

—*Plant Evidence*
—*Get Niggers*

||||||

In the struggle over the Fuhrman tapes, the last great drama of the Simpson trial, it was as if the id of the case had been unleashed. All the smoldering passion, anger, and resentment shot directly to the surface. The Fuhrman tapes gave the defense the opportunity it had sought since the day of the murders to change the subject from the culpability of its client to the sins of the LAPD. But this time there was a twist. Of course, Cochran and company went about their work of exploiting racial tensions with their usual shady cynicism, but the tapes controversy gave the defense something it never had in earlier battles: the truth. About Mark Fuhrman's character, the defense was right and the prosecution wrong. The tapes thus forced the prosecutors to confront squarely the cost of their arrogance. Having had full warning about Fuhrman's twisted soul, Clark had embraced him nonetheless. With McKinny's tapes, Clark and her colleagues paid the price.

The roots of the final crisis went back more than a decade. Laura Hart McKinny had met Mark Fuhrman on a pleasant late morning in February 1985, at an outdoor café in Westwood. McKinny was sipping a drink and typing on a laptop computer, a novelty in those days, and Fuhrman came over to inquire about it. The two of them, both good-looking and in their mid-thirties, sat down to chat. Fuhrman asked what she was working on. She said it was a screenplay about female police officers. Funny, he said. He was an LAPD officer himself.

In the early 1980s, under political and legal pressure, the LAPD had dramatically expanded the number of women on the force. McKinny said she was writing about the stresses these women faced. Fuhrman smiled. He could be a charming man, especially around an attractive woman, so he decided to taunt McKinny a little bit and, at the same time, flirt with her. He said he didn't think women belonged as police officers, that they couldn't handle the job, and that the recruitment efforts for them were going to lead to disaster. In fact, Fuhrman told her, he belonged to a clandestine organization within the LAPD known as Men Against Women, or MAW, which was dedicated to resisting the encroachment of women onto this traditionally male turf. McKinny immediately recognized Fuhrman as a potential resource—an insider who could give her the perspective of the hostile, sexist LAPD traditionalist. Perhaps, they agreed that first day, they could talk some more about the subject.

That first meeting set the tone for a relationship that would last almost a decade. Their story was, in its way, a paradigmatic tale of modern Los Angeles, a city with an unproduced screenplay in many a desk drawer. Fuhrman and McKinny met again on

April 2, 1985, and this time she brought her tape recorder so she could preserve his sexist (and, secondarily, racist) rants. They agreed that McKinny would give Fuhrman a $10,000 fee as a technical consultant if the movie was ever produced. Because McKinny was obviously working on a fictional screenplay, she and Fuhrman never really dealt with the question of whether everything he told her—all of his opinions, all of his war stories— was literally true. He was obviously drawing on his own experiences, but he was also trying to jazz them up for her cinematic purposes. There was a personal dimension to their relationship as well. A dreamy 1960s throwback with a taste for liberal politics and natural foods, McKinny was a perfect foil for the right-wing Fuhrman. He delighted in shocking her with his preening, even exaggerated, bigoted braggadocio.

McKinny worked hard. She would carefully transcribe the text of their meetings, send copies to Fuhrman, and then arrive at their next encounter with a list of new questions. Ultimately, they had twelve sessions together, yielding about twelve hours of interviews. McKinny also went on drive-arounds with female police officers, and interviewed them as well. According to a producer who knew her, "Laura did everything a writer was supposed to do. She really got to know her subject, really did her homework. There was just one problem: She didn't write a very good screenplay."

McKinny produced the first draft of her screenplay in the late 1980s. She called it *Men Against Women*, after the organization Fuhrman had discussed with her. McKinny's tale concerned a rookie female officer who falls in love with her partner, who turns out to be a member of MAW. Shopped around to various studios, McKinny's work, like most screenplays, found no takers. Over the years, McKinny would serve as a rather extreme example of the difficulties of entering the screenwriting industry. In her entire career, she had never sold a single movie script, yet she continued to plug away. She taught part-time at UCLA and in the Malibu school district, all the while pursuing her research on the police project. However, she didn't meet with Fuhrman at all between 1988 and 1993, when she took time off to raise her two small children.

It was during this fallow period that her screenplay nearly came to life as a commercial project. McKinny's children attended a progressive school in Santa Monica called PS 1—short for "Pluralistic School number one." Her children played with the kids of another parent at the school, a producer named John Flynn, who took an interest in McKinny's project. Obviously, after all these years, there were no competing bidders, so in 1992 Flynn paid McKinny a token $1,000 for a two-year option on selling the script to a production company.

The early 1990s were a difficult period in McKinny's life. Her husband, Daniel, was a cinematographer who sometimes found work as a grip on movie sets. Laura worked part-time tutoring UCLA athletes. In 1993, owing $80,000 in credit card bills and back taxes, the McKinnys declared bankruptcy. They decided to pick up stakes and sign up as professors at the fledging North Carolina School of the Arts. Notwithstanding her own lack of success in the field, Laura taught screenwriting. Still, she never gave up on *Men Against Women*. In the middle of 1994, with the option about to expire, Flynn had a nibble on the project. He had spoken to a representative of Fred Dryer, the handsome ex–football star who had starred in the archetypical LAPD television series *Hunter*. Flynn was going to meet with Dryer, so he called on McKinny and Fuhrman to join him in a strategy session to prepare the pitch.

The date of their meeting was July 28, 1994—six weeks after the murders and ten days after my *New Yorker* story about Fuhrman appeared. At the meeting, which McKinny taped, Fuhrman was still fuming about the story, vowing to sue Shapiro, who he assumed had leaked it. Fuhrman said he had even talked with an attorney who might represent him. "Well, the funny thing about it is," Fuhrman told his colleagues, "just like the attorney said, 'For the rest of your life, this is you: You're Bloody Glove Fuhrman, that's it.' . . . He says, 'You might as well make it pay off; all you're doing is going through this heartache for nothing. Go for Shapiro, he's an asshole.' " In the end, though, Fuhrman felt confident that the LAPD would stand behind him in the growing controversy about his racial views. "I'm the key witness in the biggest case of the century," Fuhrman boasted. "And if I go down, they lose the case. The glove is everything. Without the glove— bye-bye."

|||||

Dryer passed on the project. But in anticipation of the negotiations with Dryer's company, McKinny had hired an agent, Jim Preminger, the son of the famed director Otto Preminger, as well as another parent at PS 1. Preminger never heard the tapes, but he had a general idea of what was on them. When the trial heated up the following spring, he called McKinny and told her she probably should get a lawyer. McKinny asked a colleague in North Carolina for a recommendation, and he suggested Matt Schwartz, a young lawyer with whom the colleague had recently attended UCLA film school. (In Los Angeles, everyone writes screenplays, but what they really want to do—even the lawyers—is direct.) In late May 1995, McKinny called Schwartz and explained what the tapes were and how she and Fuhrman had come to make them.

McKinny was in a quandary. Her fondest hope was that some company would finally buy and produce *Men Against Women*, but Schwartz recognized that the tapes with Fuhrman's voice were the more valuable commodity. Schwartz proposed—and McKinny agreed—that he "test the waters," to check out the market for the tapes. In June, Schwartz contacted several outlets in the cash-for-trash industry—London newspapers, supermarket and television tabloids, and Faye Resnick's publisher, Dove Books. Several expressed interest, and Schwartz faxed them nondisclosure agreements—documents that said the media outlets could examine the tapes, but only for the purpose of determining what to pay for them. Schwartz said later that he received a bid of $250,000 for the tapes, but McKinny turned it down.

Not surprisingly, Schwartz's testing of the waters started the rumor mill working—and set off another feud within Simpson's defense team. In early July, right around the time McKenna received the call from "Brian," McKenna's rival fellow investigator from the Shapiro camp in the defense team, Bill Pavelic, also heard about the tapes from a friend. This friend, a disbarred lawyer from near Oakland, told Pavelic that Schwartz was shopping the Fuhrman tapes to the tabloids, asking them to pay $10,000 just to listen to excerpts. (Schwartz later denied this.) Thus, Pavelic and McKenna both claimed to have "discovered" the tapes. In truth,

McKenna had located the first direct route to McKinny, but Shapiro (who loathed McKenna, along with his allies Bailey and Cochran) wanted his own fingerprints on the discovery. Shapiro later went so far as to arrange for Skip Taft, Simpson's business manager, to send the disbarred lawyer $1,500 (of O.J.'s money) for "your remarkable services in connection with the discovery of the Fuhrman tapes"—just to establish that Shapiro had played a role in tracking them down.

It was, in all likelihood, Schwartz's proto-auction that prompted the call from "Brian" to Pat McKenna as well as the tip to Pavelic. In any event, when word of the tapes' existence spread around the defense team during the second week in July, there was outright jubilation. "If this is real," Barry Scheck said at a defense meeting, "it could mean an acquittal—flat out." Gerry Uelman told McKenna, "This is manna from heaven."

But it was Cochran who was moved the most deeply. He took an almost mystical joy in the subject of the McKinny tapes. Though nominally appalled by their contents, Cochran at one point told Judge Ito that the tapes were "like Lay's potato chips—you can't put them down, and you can't eat just one." Cochran had spent his entire professional career both fighting and exploiting racism in the LAPD. Now there was, it appeared, tangible proof of that racism, and it had surfaced in the most important case of Cochran's career. Cochran could be bawdy, irreverent, and profane, but he displayed an unfeigned spiritual side in private as well. In all sincerity, Cochran told at least one colleague on the defense team that he believed God had brought the McKinny tapes to him. Cochran talked about, and seemingly thought about, the tapes all the time.

But Cochran had yet to get his hands on them. On July 12, the day of Cochran's "sounds black" outburst during Robert Heidstra's testimony, Cochran and Shapiro went to Matthew Schwartz's office to try to get a commitment that they could have access to the tapes. In the meeting, Schwartz put them off. McKinny was on vacation at the time, and Schwartz wanted to play out his "testing the waters" project. (Later, both Schwartz and McKinny ascribed a great deal of significance to the semantic, and possibly meaningless, distinction between "testing the waters" and actually trying to sell the tapes.) Schwartz did at least promise Simpson's lawyers that McKinny would not destroy the tapes. A week passed, and Schwartz finally said that McKinny would not surrender the tapes voluntarily. Schwartz now said McKinny regarded herself as a "journalist" in her meetings with Fuhrman, and she did not wish to share the fruits of her reporting. Frustrated, Cochran sent Carl Douglas to appear in secret before Judge Ito on July 20 and explain the situation to him. Ito agreed that the tapes were material to the Simpson case and signed a subpoena—which the defense team would now have to enforce in McKinny's home state of North Carolina.

||||||

All the defense lawyers, of course, wanted to be the ones to travel to North Carolina to argue that the tapes should be turned over. Cochran would go—that much was settled. Shapiro wanted Gerry Uelman to handle the legal issues. Bailey said that Uelman was a nice guy but he always lost his arguments. Bailey wanted . . . Bailey to go. In the end, Cochran decided to take Bailey. Usually, in the many briefs the defense filed over the course of the case, a secretary in Cochran's office signed the lawyers' names. But in a bizarre measure of how seriously the defense team took the McKinny issue, all the lawyers insisted on signing their own names to the North Carolina brief. (It was thus especially ironic that the true authors of that brief, Bailey's law partners in Boston, Ken Fishman and Dan Leonard, preferred to remain behind the scenes and did not have their names on it.)

So on Friday, July 28, Cochran and Bailey appeared before Judge William Z. Wood, Jr., in Forsyth County, North Carolina, to ask him to enforce the subpoena to McKinny. Since Ito, the trial judge in the case, had ruled that the material was relevant, Wood's approval should have been just a formality. In his chambers, Judge Wood let Cochran see transcripts of the tapes for the first time. They were worse (and, thus, from Cochran's perspective, better) than even he had imagined. Fuhrman used the crudest slurs imaginable, and "nigger" repeatedly. When McKinny took the stand in front of the North Carolina judge (and the waiting press corps), Cochran couldn't wait to work a few quotes from the tapes into his questions. For example, Cochran asked McKinny, "Did Detective

Fuhrman say to you during this first interview, when you were getting his attitude—quote—that 'we've got females and dumb niggers and all your Mexicans that can't even write the name of the car they drive. And you think I'm kidding? We have people who aren't even citizens on the department.' Did he say that to you?" McKinny said he did.

Yet Judge Wood—unaccountably—ruled against Cochran and Bailey, asserting that the tapes were not material to the Simpson defense case. This was a shattering blow, and Bailey immediately set his law partners in Boston to work on an emergency appeal. But as devastated as Cochran was by the ruling, he knew he had accomplished something important in getting at least a few of Fuhrman's words out via the North Carolina court hearing. The public quickly became more interested in the Fuhrman-tapes sideshow to the Simpson spectacle, especially since the trial itself had degenerated into a droning series of defense experts. In light of the growing public obsession with the tapes, Cochran changed his approach to the Simpson case. For the final month of the case, Johnnie Cochran would campaign for acquittal not just in the courtroom but in the country at large—and not just as a lawyer, but as a self-appointed civil rights leader.

|||||

After an extraordinary effort by Bailey's law partners, the North Carolina Court of Appeals overturned Judge Wood's plainly incorrect ruling on August 7. The McKinny tapes arrived at last in Cochran's office on August 9. Media interest in their contents grew even more fevered.

The loss in North Carolina, even though it was later rectified, rattled Cochran. Confident from the beginning that he could win a hung jury for his client, Cochran felt the tapes represented the ammunition he needed to push the jurors toward an outright acquittal. At the most basic level, of course, the tapes proved that Fuhrman had lied in answering Bailey's carefully phrased questions about whether the detective had used the word "nigger" in the previous ten years. But more than that, the tapes allowed Cochran to make Fuhrman's irrefutable bigotry stand as a proxy for the racism of the LAPD as a whole. The choice in the case would come down to exactly the one Darden had predicted seven months earlier in his original debate with Cochran over what became known in the trial as the "n-word": "Whose side are you on? . . . Either you are with the Man or you are with the Brothers."

But Cochran couldn't trust that Ito wouldn't, like Judge Wood, thwart him at the last moment. Like most of the lawyers on both sides, Cochran assumed that some news about the trial was filtering back to the sequestered jurors. He also thought that general public agitation about the tapes fed the prosecution's insecurity and growing sense of panic. All in all, then, Cochran needed a public airing of the tapes. In other words, he needed their contents leaked to the press.

The prosecutors, for their part, could tell what Cochran was thinking, and they tried to counter his strategy. If they could confine the McKinny controversy and limit public exposure of the tapes, they had a chance of preventing the case from evolving into a referendum on police racism. Therefore, the prosecutors were only too happy when Schwartz, McKinny's attorney, insisted before Ito that the tapes be governed by a tightly worded protective order. (Schwartz still entertained hopes of selling them.) On August 10, Ito directed that the audiotapes should "remain under seal" until he ordered otherwise. Ito's order permitted only the lawyers on the case and their direct assistants access to the tapes and the transcripts. Ito's order built a wall of secrecy around the tapes—until or unless the judge himself ordered them to be played in court.

In light of the protective order, Cochran couldn't simply hand the transcripts over to a friendly reporter. Same with the other defense lawyers—the risk of exposure was simply too great. The question thus became who on the defense team could do it. Who wouldn't mind taking the chance of directly violating a court order? Who had contacts among the reporters on the press corps? Whose ethics permitted him to do a job like that? All signs pointed to one man:

Larry Schiller.

O. J. Simpson's literary amanuensis, the coauthor of *I Want to Tell You*, had spent the entire trial ingratiating himself with reporters as well as gathering material from inside the defense camp for his next, still inchoate, ghostwritten version of Simpson's story. Schiller loved being at the center of the action, so he was only too happy to share the McKinny largesse with his journalist friends, and they were likewise pleased with their scoops. For the next week or so, Schiller leaked hate-filled tidbits to reporters. (Schiller denies doing this.) The ensuing outcry from the public against Fuhrman added immeasurably to the pressure on Ito to admit the tapes into evidence, just as Cochran knew it would.

||||||

When lawyers from both sides finally sat down to listen to the tapes, they were struck by something besides Fuhrman's bigotry. Everyone also noticed the references to Margaret York, who was Fuhrman's onetime commander in the West Los Angeles division and Lance Ito's wife. York had been one of the early female recruits to the LAPD (and, in true Los Angeles fashion, a model for the television series *Cagney and Lacey*). In keeping with his role in McKinny's project, Fuhrman had excoriated women police officers in general but also, it turned out, York in particular. Among other things, Fuhrman said on the tape that the judge's wife had "sucked and fucked her way to the top."

The lawyers brought this to Ito's attention in chambers on August 14. The issue was further clouded by the fact that earlier in the case, York had filed a declaration in the Simpson trial saying that she remembered little about Fuhrman except that he was once one of the officers under her command. As Cochran put it gently to Ito, "This is a very delicate issue. . . . It is going to have to do with credibility, because you know, her declaration—this guy, unless he is absolutely lying—and Marcia will back me up on this—the contacts he has with Lieutenant York are the kind that are very hard to forget him." In other words, as some lawyers on both sides came to believe, York may have lied in her sworn statement that she didn't remember Fuhrman.

The tapes issue thus quickly became one of daunting complexity—as were the parties' motives. The judge went right to the heart of the issue when he asked, in chambers, "Is there a conflict for me to hear this issue?"

"Right," said Clark.

"Which is a significant legal issue," Ito continued, "because we may be talking mistrial."

With the tapes in hand, the defense felt the best thing it could do was press on for a verdict in front of this judge and this jury. The prosecutors did not want to prompt a mistrial that might potentially, under the double-jeopardy clause of the Constitution, prevent a retrial, but Clark in particular had come to loathe Ito with a passion. By coincidence, right around this time Clark and I were chatting in the hallway and she launched into a lengthy tirade about the judge: "The worst judge I've ever been in front of—and the worst possible judge for this case. Totally intimidated by Johnnie, a total starfucker. . . ." But she and the other prosecutors also realized that it was almost impossible to bring a new judge into such a complex case at this late date.

And then there was Ito. A decent man, he mostly wanted to do the right thing under the law (though it was far from clear what that was). He had come to have an almost schizophrenic reaction to the media attention that the case had brought him. True, at times he reveled in it. But at the same time Ito suffered at the many (and ever increasing) critiques of his performance. Now his wife was being dragged into the mess. The pressure nearly drove him to snap.

After devoting nearly the entire next morning, August 15, to listening in silence to Clark and Cochran's rancorous arguments about how to handle the issue of his wife's involvement, Ito made up his mind. Staring at his notes, he said, "When a concern is raised regarding a Court's ability to be fair and impartial, it is not the actual existence of impartiality or partiality that is the issue. It's the appearance." Ito paused, gathering himself, the silence a reminder of how wrenching the experience had become for him. When he resumed, his voice was thick with emotion. "I love my wife dearly." He struggled to collect himself. "And I am wounded by criticism of her, as any spouse would be. And I think it is reasonable to assume that that could have some impact. As I mentioned, women in male-dominated professions learn to deal with this. And those who are successful, I think we all observe, are tougher than most." (Ito implied, winningly, that they are tougher than their husbands, too.) Ito did not recuse himself from the case—at least not yet. He said, in effect, that another judge should review the tapes and determine if Ito could still preside.

The entire courtroom then picked up and moved in a motley caravan up two flights to the courtroom of Judge James Bascue, the chief criminal judge of the superior court. Bascue assigned the case to Judge John Reid, in the courtroom next door. (There was a revealing moment in Bascue's brief tenure on the case. Though famously tough on crime in ordinary circumstances, Judge Bascue couldn't resist trying to banter a little with Simpson about football—striking, and distasteful, evidence of the effect of sports celebrity on middle-aged men.) Judge Reid, in turn, agreed to examine the tapes, and then sent the case back to Ito to continue the trial. This extraordinary merry-go-round—three judges in an hour, with the jury all the while sitting around and doing nothing—underlined just how anarchic the case had become.

The following morning, in an off-the-record session in Judge Ito's chambers, the prosecution's frustrations surfaced. Sitting around Ito's desk with the defense attorneys, Darden said, "Judge, I haven't vented in a long time, and I'd like to vent." He complained that the judge had interrupted and embarrassed prosecution lawyers in front of the jury. "We don't like that," Darden said. With the issue of Ito's recusal still hanging in the air, it looked like Darden was trying to intimidate the judge. After Darden's tirade, the defense lawyers bolted out of chambers and asked to go on the record in open court. There, Shapiro recounted the episode and said he was going to complain to the state bar. Such a remedy might have been excessive, but Shapiro's complaint about Darden certainly did have merit.

Now it was Darden's turn to become nearly unhinged. "Your Honor," Darden said, voice quavering, "I'm so offended at Mr. Shapiro's remarks—remarks that I'm sure are being fed to him by Mr. Cochran—I'm so offended by those remarks that I would rather not stand at the same podium at which he stood a few moments ago." Like a child fearing cooties, Darden kept his distance from the wooden stand. "Now, if Mr. Shapiro or Mr. Cochran want to refer me to the state bar, fine. Because when this case is over, I'm going to be referring the defense attorneys to the United States

Attorney's Office." Cochran laughed audibly at this preposterous suggestion. "And he chuckles now," Darden went on, "but will he be chuckling later on? It won't be so funny later on. They don't know everything that I know."

One can scarcely imagine more reckless behavior by a law enforcement official than Darden's empty threats (based on secret information) to report an adversary for a crime. Yet the defense did not even complain, because Darden was so obviously just posturing. (Needless to say, Darden never reported anything to the U.S. Attorney's Office. Notwithstanding the questions about the ethics of the defense lawyers in this case, no one could say that they had committed any federal crimes.) And all this distress for the prosecution came even before the judge decided when, or if, to play the tapes in public.

|||||

Cochran kept the pressure on. His experience told him that organized political pressure to release the tapes had to accompany general public outrage about them. When Cochran's client Michael Jackson was under investigation in February 1994, the lawyer had orchestrated a news conference of black ministers to call on Gil Garcetti to conclude his investigation of the singer. On August 28, 1995, much the same coalition was reassembled—this time to call for Judge Ito to release the Fuhrman tapes to the public. The heavily attended media event was spearheaded by Danny Bakewell, head of the Los Angeles civil rights organization known as Brotherhood Crusade. (This was the same Bakewell who had, less than a year earlier, bestowed on Cochran his organization's annual award, hailing the lawyer as "a tireless warrior against those who would deny justice for all.") Commenting on the Fuhrman tapes, Bakewell predicted dire results if the tapes were not released. "This community is a powder keg," Bakewell said, "capable of repeating the actions of 1992"—that is, the riots that had followed the acquittal of the LAPD officers who beat Rodney King. Bakewell's rhetoric was pure racial extortion: Release the tapes— or else.

The political maelstrom left Ito little choice when the issue was finally posed to him the next day, August 29. The prosecution had entertained a vain hope that Ito would at least decide the tapes issue without first playing them in public. But when weighing that decision, Ito addressed the general outcry about the tapes directly. "I think that there is an overriding public interest in the nature of the offer that you are making," Ito told the defense in a hearing before the television cameras but outside the presence of the jury, "and I don't want this Court to ever be in a position where there is any indication that this Court would participate in suppressing information that is of vital public interest." The judge allowed the defense to play the portions of the tapes they wanted the jury to hear. With that decision by Ito, all of the defense work—from Schiller's leaks to Bakewell's threats—had paid off.

In the courtroom that day, the first few examples from the tapes were fairly straightforward—brief sentence fragments of Fuhrman's familiar voice: "You do what you're told, understand, nigger?" Female officers, he said, "don't do anything. They don't go out there and initiate a contact with a six-foot-five nigger that's been in prison for seven years pumping weights." And: "These niggers, they run like rabbits." Of course, these snippets were bad enough, but then, late in the morning session, Uelman began to play the tape of what appeared to be Fuhrman's recounting of an incident that had happened to him in the field. It was, according to Fuhrman on the tape, "a real heavy investigation . . . sixty-six allegations of brutality . . . assault and battery under color of authority. Torture, all kinds of stuff." Then Fuhrman's disembodied voice described for the silent courtroom what had happened.

> Two of my buddies were shot and ambushed, policemen. Both alive, and I was the first unit on the scene. Four suspects ran into a second story in an apartment project—apartment. We kicked the door down. We grabbed a girl that lived there, one of their girlfriends. Grabbed her by the hair and stuck a gun to her head and used her as a barricade. Walked up and told them: "I've got this girl; I'll blow her fucking brains out if you come out with a gun." Held her like this—threw the bitch down the stairs—deadbolted the door. "Let's play, boys."

On the tape, McKinny interrupted to ask whether she could use this incident in the movie.

"It hasn't been seven years, statute of limitations," Fuhrman cautioned. "I have 300 and something pages of Internal Affairs investigation just on that one incident. I got several other ones. I must have about 3,000 or 4,000 pages Internal Affairs investigations out there." Then Fuhrman resumed his narration of the event.

Anyway, we basically tortured them. There was four policemen, four guys. We broke 'em. Numerous bones in each one of them. Their faces were just mush. They had pictures on the walls, there was blood all the way to the ceiling with finger marks like they were trying to crawl out of the room. They showed us pictures of the room. It was unbelievable, there was blood everywhere. All the walls, all the furniture, all the floor. It was just everywhere. These guys, they had to shave so much hair off, one guy they shaved it all off. Like seventy stitches in his head. You know, knees cracked, oh, it was just— We had 'em begging that they'd never be gang members again, begging us. So with sixty-six allegations, I had a demonstration in front of Hollenbeck station, chanting my name. Captain had to take them all into roll call, and that's where the Internal Affairs investigation started. It lasted eighteen months. I was on a photo lineup, suspect lineup. I was picked out by twelve people. So I was pretty proud of that. I was the last one interviewed. The prime suspect is always the last one interviewed. They didn't get any of our unit—thirty-eight guys—they didn't get one day [of docked pay]. I didn't get one day. The custodian, the jailer of the sheriff's department, got five days, since he beat one of the guys at the very end. . . .

Immediately after we beat those guys, we went downstairs to the garden hose in the back of the place. We washed our hands. We had blood all over our legs, everything. With a dark blue uniform, you know, and in the dark, you can't see it. But when you get in the light and it looks like somebody took red paint and painted it all over you. We had to clean our badges off with water; there was blood all over 'em. Our faces had blood on them. We had to clean all that. We checked each other, then we went out, we were directing traffic. And the chiefs and everything were coming down because two officers were shot—"Where are the suspects?" . . . And they took them to the station. Somehow nobody knows who arrested them. We handcuffed them and threw them down two flights of stairs, you know. That's how they came. That's where a lot of people saw, you know, "Look out! Here comes one! Oh my God, look out, he's falling!" I mean, you don't shoot a policeman. That's all there is to it. . . .

When this taped excerpt ended, Lance Ito's courtroom was as quiet as it had ever been over the previous year. Then there was a sound: Kim Goldman started to cry.

At last Gerry Uelman asked McKinny, "Do you have a particularly vivid memory of that account?"

"Of course," she said.

"Why is that?"

"It's, um, it's vividly described."

Judge Ito broke for lunch.

|||||

Cochran's colleagues had never seen him behave the way he did when Lance Ito's ten-page ruling slipped out of the fax machine on August 31. Cochran was distraught, speechless, despairing. In what seemed to be a shocking blow to the defense, Ito ruled that he would allow only two brief excerpts of the Fuhrman tapes to be played: "We have no niggers where I grew up," and "That's where niggers live." In lieu of playing the tapes, he would allow McKinny to tell the jury that Fuhrman had said "nigger" forty-one times on the tapes. Ito found that everything else on the tapes was either irrelevant to the Simpson case or unduly prejudicial to the prosecution.

Cochran proceeded to an impromptu news conference on the ground floor of his office building on Wilshire Boulevard. Wearing an electric-blue sports jacket over a black shirt buttoned at the neck with a jeweled clasp, Cochran denounced Ito in a most personal way. Surrounded by nearly a dozen colleagues on the defense team (but not Shapiro), Cochran called Ito's ruling "perhaps one of the cruelest, unfairest decisions ever rendered in a criminal court." He declared, "The cover-up continues. . . . This inexplicable, indefensible ruling lends credence to all those who say the criminal justice system is corrupt." And in a lightly veiled reference to Bakewell's incendiary threats of earlier in the week, Cochran said, "So all of the citizens in Los Angeles, they should remain calm."

Having stung Cochran in print, Ito still could not stand up to him in person. The next day in court, Friday, September 1, Cochran essentially went on strike. The defense was supposed to continue to call witnesses, but Cochran simply refused to continue the trial, in protest against the judge's ruling on the tapes. A tougher judge might simply have declared the defense case concluded and moved on to the prosecution rebuttal. But Cochran intimidated Ito too much for that. The judge simply and meekly informed the jury, which had heard scarcely any evidence in a week because of the tapes controversy, that the trial was breaking early for Labor Day weekend.

By this point, Fuhrman had retained a criminal defense lawyer, who wisely advised him to take the Fifth Amendment rather than answer any more questions in the case. The tapes had raised a real possibility that he might be prosecuted for perjury—or even for the crimes he had told McKinny he committed. When Fuhrman returned to the courthouse to take the witness stand once again, he answered each of Uelman's queries with invocations of his right to remain silent. (As was customary, Ito did not allow the jury to see Fuhrman take the Fifth.) Darden and his student clerks, the only African-Americans on the prosecution team, were not present when Fuhrman returned to appear before Judge Ito.

At long last, on September 6, the jury heard McKinny and the two short excerpts from the tapes. Ironically, the highlight of the day for the defense was not the playing of the tapes—which the jurors absorbed impassively—but rather Darden's inept cross-examination of McKinny. Darden belittled McKinny's credentials, questioned her motives, and generally treated her as if it were she—and not prosecution witness Fuhrman—who had done something wrong. Stung by Darden's hostility, McKinny blurted out at one point, "Why are we having this adversarial relationship?" Several jurors nodded, apparently wondering the same thing.

After the trial, most of the jurors said that the McKinny tapes had had little impact on their verdict. Even if one accepts this at face value, the tapes still had an enormous influence on the trial. The entire gestalt of the case was transformed. Because the tapes established definitively that Fuhrman had lied about using the word "nigger," the prosecution had to abandon its categorical de-

408 ||| THE RUN OF HIS LIFE

fense of him. This was true even after Ito's unduly restrictive ruling regarding playing the tapes in front of the jury. Fuhrman's damaged credibility, in turn, made it that much harder for the
prosecution to argue that all the other LAPD officers were telling
the truth. In terms of the courtroom chess match, the damage to
the prosecution from the tapes was probably as great as from Darden's glove demonstration.

The tapes also loom as an important historical artifact beyond
the give-and-take of this trial. It may never be possible to sort out
how much of Fuhrman's narrative was literally true. In the aftermath of the case, the LAPD and the United States attorney in Los
Angeles launched investigations based on the tapes. Fuhrman's extraordinary account of the beating of suspects following the shooting of two police officers did appear to be loosely based on a real
event that occurred in 1978, but his version had fictional aspects
as well. However, the tapes also pointed to larger truths. MAW existed. Mark Fuhrman—and others like him—thrived in the LAPD.
Ultimately, it is not surprising that black jurors decided to punish
the police for its sorry past and that, alas, O. J. Simpson turned out
to be the undeserving beneficiary of this ignoble tale.

|||||

After McKinny's brief turn on the stand, the defense closed its
case with three more witnesses who testified that they had heard
Fuhrman use the word "nigger." As if this were not enough, the
defense team decided to send one final nonverbal message. When
Ito said he would not tell the jury that Fuhrman had refused to
testify further, Cochran arranged for the entire defense team to
wear ties made from African kente cloth in protest—in front of
the jury, no less.

Ito could have stopped them. Very early in the trial, the judge
had told the prosecutors that they could not wear angel pins in solidarity with the victims of the case, even though, unlike the kente-
cloth ties, the pins bore no provocative message. But on the day
the defense team wore the ties, Judge Ito had only this to say to the
first defense lawyer to appear before him:

"Nice tie."

One night toward the end of the Fuhrman-tapes controversy, many leading figures of the African-American community in Los Angeles filled the vast Santa Monica Civic Auditorium for the annual Soul Train Lady of Soul Awards. Gladys Knight hosted this annual salute to black women in show business, and at the climax of the nationally televised broadcast of the ceremony, she said she had a special announcement. "To present the Lena Horne Award for outstanding career achievements," Knight said, "here is a man who has been a wonderful friend to all of us . . . a longtime supporter of everything good and positive that takes place in our community—Mr. Johnnie Cochran!"

Cochran appeared from behind a curtain, splendidly turned out in a perfect tuxedo and bright red cummerbund. The audience of three thousand burst into loud cheers when Cochran stepped forward, a greeting that quickly turned into a standing ovation, the warmest greeting any celebrity received at the event that evening. A handful of spectators started a chant, which spread in a few seconds to the entire crowd:

"Free O.J.!"
"Free O.J.!"
"Free O.J.!"

Standing at center stage, Cochran acknowledged the cheer with a pontifical wave. "I promise I'll work hard to do that," he said.

Then he turned to introduce a brief highlight film of the life of the career-achievement winner, actress and dancer Debbie Allen. These highlights, Cochran told the group with a knowing smile, amounted to "what *I* would call *concrete* visual evidence." This was real evidence as opposed to that which Cochran spent his work-week examining.

By the end of the trial, Cochran had become his client's surrogate, and the lawyer took every opportunity to promote the Simpson cause outside the courtroom. After court nearly every Friday during the last weeks of the trial, Cochran headed for the airport en route to speaking engagements around the country—including journeys to Florida, South Carolina, Louisiana, Pennsylvania, and Washington and around California. In his remarks, he invariably seized on the Simpson case as the paradigmatic civil rights issue of the day. On August 20 in Philadelphia, for example, Cochran urged the National Association of Black Journalists to "take on the forces of this country. If you do that, you are using journalism for good . . . and if you duck this fight, you'll leave a gaping hole, and the battle for civil rights is lost." Cochran charged that coverage of the Simpson trial had been too oriented toward the victims. "Even Simpson himself was a victim," he told the audience of fifteen hundred. "We believe he is wrongfully charged, and he, too, became a victim, but there has been no talk about that." Paraphrasing the novelist Richard Wright, Cochran told the gathered reporters, "We black folk are history. We are cast in the familiar role as America's conscience."

Cochran was even more explicit when, following the last week of testimony in the Simpson trial, he traveled to Washington and spoke before an adoring crowd at the annual legislative conference of the Congressional Black Caucus. In his speech there, he called the trial in Los Angeles the latest landmark in the long civil rights struggle of African-Americans—a series of events that, as he summarized it, included *Plessy v. Ferguson, Brown v. Board of Education,* the Rodney King trial, and, "yes, even the Simpson case."

It is difficult to determine with precision what impact Cochran's speeches had on the jury. In interviews after the trial, jurors said they had been unaware of Cochran's specific public assertions about the case. Yet Cochran's behavior over the course of the entire case, both in court and especially in public toward the end, attempted to define the case solely in racial terms. By the end of the case, all the jurors did know how contentious a national civil rights issue the trial had become. Thus, Cochran's waving of the bloody shirt of racial resentment must be judged a tactical success. When excused juror Jeanette Harris paraphrased the worries of jurors in the case—"An African-American might say, 'I can't say he's guilty because I want to walk out of here' "—she reflected the heightened political sensitivities about the case, which Cochran helped foment.

Cochran's high public profile had another impact as well: It drove Robert Shapiro crazy. In part, Shapiro's reaction arose from simple jealousy over the attention paid to Cochran, especially in comparison with his own ever more negligible role in the defense. Also, as racial perceptions over the case hardened, Shapiro's position in his own (white) world grew ever more uncomfortable. In this respect, Cochran had nothing but contempt for Shapiro's uneasiness. "I know Shapiro's problem," Cochran said to allies on the defense team, "but I'm a hero in my community."

I had an unusually direct view of Shapiro's dilemma. In May 1995, Mark Fuhrman filed a libel suit against me, The New Yorker, and Shapiro in connection with my original story about Fuhrman the previous year. (Fuhrman would drop his case during the week of the verdict.) Although Shapiro had generally steered clear of me after that issue of The New Yorker ran, the libel case started his competitive juices flowing, and we often talked about it in the courthouse hallway. In short order, however, Shapiro would turn these conversations into diatribes against his colleagues on the defense team, especially Cochran (even more than Bailey). One day during the presentation of the defense case, for example, Shapiro told me that Cochran had interrupted him when he was talking to a lawyer for one of the witnesses. "I'm shaking hands with this lawyer, and you know what he says to me?" Shapiro recounted. "He says, 'We got no time for chitchat. We got to work now.' " Shapiro went on, "I've never been treated this way in my life. It's like they want me to look bad. In front of the jury, they give me questions to ask, and they're bad questions." The heart of Shapiro's complaints always returned, however, to publicity. "Johnnie keeps track of what show everyone is on. He watches everything. He doesn't work. It's unbelievable." Shapiro did have a point about Cochran's obsession with the media (which, of course, was matched by Shapiro's). On September 7, for example, Cochran sent a memo to all the defense attorneys saying, "Effective immediately, per Mr. O. J. Simpson's request, all media appearances must be approved by yours truly. There will be no exceptions to this policy."

Cochran and his allies, for their part, more than returned Shapiro's disdain for them, and with perhaps even greater justification. On another day during the defense case, Shapiro's fellow defense-team members caught him using a miniature Dictaphone in his pocket to record a meeting in the courthouse lockup among Simpson and his lawyers. As Shapiro later admitted, he was surreptitiously documenting these meetings so he could include them in the book he was planning to write about the case. Scheck and Neufeld, who believe strongly in the sanctity of the attorney-client privilege, were beside themselves with outrage at Shapiro over the tape-recording. On the rare occasions that Shapiro deigned to attend defense-team meetings, the atmosphere was poisonous.

To their credit, the prosecutors did not turn on each other in the waning days of the trial, but they didn't entertain any great hopes of victory, either. By and large, they felt doomed by even the small number of excerpts that Ito had allowed from McKinny's tapes. Still, the prosecution put together a smashing start to its brief rebuttal case—one the increasingly stupefied jury seemed barely to notice (and would scarcely comment upon after the trial). The rebuttal case began with the one positive bit of fallout from Darden's glove fiasco. Amateur photographers around the country began searching their files for photographs of Simpson wearing leather gloves at football games. Several found examples, which they sent to the prosecution in Los Angeles. The first, taken on December 29, 1990, at a Chicago Bears game, was the most striking. The glove not only had identical features to the Aris model recovered in 1994, but this glove also looked tight on Simpson's hand, just as the evidence gloves had. Richard Rubin, the glove expert, returned to the stand to say that he was "100 percent certain" that the gloves in the photographs were those rare Aris Lights, style 70263.

Neither side wanted to give the other the last word, so the case wound down, like a dying metronome, with each side calling a final few witnesses. The defense closed on a quasi-comic note, calling a pair of organized-crime informants, the brothers Larry and Tony "The Animal" Fiato. With their earrings and dyed hair, this duo looked like extras from a low-budget crime picture, but they actually served the defense cause very well.

The Fiato brothers had worked as informants in an unrelated criminal case investigated by Detective Tom Lange, Phil Vannatter's partner. In January 1995, just as the Simpson trial was getting under way, the Fiatos were preparing for their testimony in one of these other cases when they started chatting with Vannatter. The topic turned to the Simpson case and the detectives' controversial decision to leave the murder scene and go to O.J.'s home on Rockingham. They claimed that Vannatter said, apparently sarcastically, "We didn't go up there with the intention of saving lives. He was the suspect."

In a final day of testimony, September 19, the defense called four witnesses—Vannatter; Michael Wacks, an FBI agent who was present; and the two Fiato brothers—to testify about this conversation. All essentially agreed about what Vannatter had said, and all pretty much concluded that it seemed the detective had been joking. Yet the whole scene left a seedy impression of Vannatter in particular and the police as a whole. The defense succeeded, at the last moment, in raising a series of embarrassing questions. Was Vannatter's long-questioned justification for going to Rockingham really true? What did he really tell the Fiato brothers? Why was the co–lead detective discussing the Simpson case *at all* with a pair of mafia informants? All these questions hung awkwardly in the air as the jury was about to get the case.

Yet the prosecutors couldn't leave well (or badly) enough alone. Rather than simply ignore the Fiato sideshow, the prosecutors decided to call one final, *final* witness—the last of the trial, and one who served rather well as an emblem for the futility of the government's efforts in this case.

On the morning of September 20, Marcia Clark called Keith D. Bushey, the ramrod-straight police officer who had served as the top LAPD administrator for the western quarter of the city in June 1994. Bushey testified that Detective Ron Phillips had called him at about 2:30 A.M. on June 13 to inform him that Nicole Brown

Simpson's body had been found. Bushey said that on hearing the news, he remembered that several members of John Belushi's family had heard of his death through the news media. Bushey thought that was unfortunate so, he said, he ordered Phillips "to find O. J. Simpson just as soon as humanly possible and notify O. J. Simpson of his ex-wife's death." Clark thus wanted to use Bushey to convince the jury that Vannatter and the other detectives really had been telling the truth all along—that they went over to Rockingham to notify Simpson that his ex-wife had died.

The imperious Bushey never knew what hit him on cross-examination. Johnnie Cochran understood the LAPD better than any of the prosecutors. He knew how the police groveled before celebrities. The sinister brilliance of his examination of Bushey—and, indeed, of his defense in general—was that he made the preferential treatment accorded Simpson look like a different, more nefarious, kind of singling out. Cochran knew that Bushey would have to lie—that he couldn't admit that celebrities won special favors from the LAPD. So Cochran spun those lies to his client's advantage.

"Are you saying that the LAPD department in this case gave preferential treatment by sending four detectives to O. J. Simpson's house in the early morning hours?" Cochran asked.

"No," Bushey replied. "First of all, I don't like the word 'preferential treatment.'"

"Okay," Cochran parried. "That was the word used by the prosecution."

"Well, I don't care . . . ," Bushey answered.

"You don't like the word 'preferential' because on the side of the police car it says 'protect and serve' all the people?"

"That's correct."

"You're supposed to treat all people alike, aren't you?"

"We tried to," Bushey answered glumly.

"And fair? You try?"

"Sure," said Bushey.

Cochran found the heart of the issue a moment later when he asked, "In the course of your responsibilities that morning, were you more concerned about the department's image than you were about investigating these very brutal murders?"

"Certainly not," said Bushey, but the truth was very much the opposite.

The prosecution thus unaccountably completed its presentation in the O. J. Simpson murder case with a pious, double-talking fixture of the LAPD brass. And that might not have been even the worst of it. For in addition to everything else, Keith Bushey was a dead ringer for the most hated man in black Los Angeles—the former chief of the Los Angeles Police Department, Daryl Gates.

|||||

From the day he was hired in the case, Cochran teased the press with the possibility of Simpson testifying in his own defense. The lawyer said repeatedly that he *wanted* O.J. to testify and that O.J. himself *wanted* to testify, but these comments were just public relations. With the exception of Bailey, who actually did want Simpson to take the stand, no one on the defense team ever took the idea very seriously. Bailey thought, with good reason, that Simpson would have no chance of resuming anything like his former life unless he addressed the charges from the witness stand. Cochran and Shapiro were more worried about losing the case, and their view prevailed.

Still, even in jail, Simpson was as obsessed as ever by his image, and Cochran found an opportunity for him to put his point across. As part of the formalities of ending the case, Ito had to ask Simpson on September 22 whether he waived his right to testify. Cochran, in turn, requested that Simpson be allowed to make "a brief statement" as part of his waiver. Even though the jury was not present, Clark objected, saying that "this is a very obvious defense bid to get material admitted through those conjugal visits that is not admitted in court. . . . Please don't do this, Your Honor, I beg you."

Cochran replied with great indignation. "There seems to be this great fear of the truth in this case," he said. "This is still America. And we can talk. We can speak. Nobody can stop us." (A rather odd complaint on behalf of a client who had already written a bestselling book from jail.) Ito caved, and Simpson rose to deliver a sound bite for the evening news.

"Good morning, Your Honor," he said. "As much as I would like to address some of the misrepresentations made about myself and

Nicole concerning our life together, I'm mindful of the mood and the stamina of this jury. I have confidence, a lot more it seems than Ms. Clark has, of their integrity, and that they'll find—as the record stands now—that I did not, would not, and could not have committed this crime. I have four kids—two kids I haven't seen in a year. They asked me every week, 'Dad, how much longer?' "

This was more than even Ito could take, and he cut Simpson off with a curt, "All right."

Simpson said, "I want this trial over."

Even this brief monologue offered a useful insight into Simpson's character. Throughout the trial, his obsession remained the "misrepresentations" about his relationship with Nicole, especially the notion that he was imploring Nicole to come back to him. Typically, too, he attributed his decision not to testify to the "mood and stamina" of the jury, when the real reason had more to do with his lead lawyers' belief in his guilt. The statement was, in short, another snapshot of Simpson's narcissism.

||||||

Tuesday, September 26, 1995, broke chilly and drizzly. During the fall and winter of the previous year, Southern California had been afflicted with some of the coldest and wettest weather in recent history. A normal spring and summer, hot and dry, had followed. Now, on the day that summations were to begin, it appeared that the seasons had changed once more. Jury selection had commenced 365 days earlier. The trial of O. J. Simpson had taken one year.

Even before she uttered her first words to the jury, Marcia Clark was exhausted, with large half moons of purple under each eye. She looked emaciated beneath her simple beige jacket. The chicken salads delivered to her office every lunch hour had often gone untouched. Not so her silver cigarette lighter, the one inscribed with the words TRUTH AND JUSTICE. For all these months, she had fueled herself with an unending relay of Dunhills.

First, Clark thanked the jury, which was customary but not, for her, heartfelt. She and her colleagues had traveled a long way since the optimistic close to jury selection. Over the course of the trial, Clark had felt no warmth from this group, no sympathy for the victims, no core of emotional revulsion at the murders. Clark's instincts about juries had not entirely deserted her, even if enlightenment came far too late. She had come to see that these were fearful jurors, more concerned about the reaction to their verdict than about reaching the right one. They took few notes; they never smiled or frowned; they gave no sense of themselves away—they were too frightened to reveal anything. As the race issue took over the case, the prosecutors knew above all that they needed a courageous jury, and they sensed—correctly, as it turned out—that they didn't have one.

Clark's first words about the facts of the case included a revealing slip of the tongue. "Let me come back to Mark Fuhrman for a minute," she said. Actually, she had not mentioned him before, so she was not really coming "back" to him. It just seemed that way, for the defense had succeeded so completely in making Fuhrman the center of this case. Like it or not, everyone in this trial was always coming back to Mark Fuhrman.

"Did he lie when he testified here in this courtroom saying that he did not use racial epithets in the last ten years?" Clark continued. "Yes. Is he a racist? Yes. Is he the worst LAPD has to offer? Yes. Do we wish that this person was never hired by LAPD? Yes. Should LAPD have ever hired him? No. In fact, do we wish there were no such person on the planet? Yes.

"But the fact that Mark Fuhrman is a racist and lied about it on the witness stand does not mean that we haven't proven the defendant guilty beyond a reasonable doubt, and it would be a tragedy if, with such overwhelming evidence, ladies and gentlemen, as we have presented to you, you found the defendant not guilty in spite of all that, because of the racist attitudes of one police officer."

This immediate and categorical denunciation of Fuhrman was probably the best Clark could have done under the circumstances, but it also underlined how the racial issue paralyzed the prosecution. Yes, Fuhrman was racist, but Simpson was still guilty. The yes/but formulation represented the dominant motif of the summation that followed over the next five hours. Yes, the investigation had been imperfect; yes, the criminalists made mistakes—but the evidence led only to this defendant. Clark was rushed and a little scattered as she attempted to pull all the complex strands of evidence together, but still she delivered an adequate, professional summation—and a persuasive one for a jury willing to listen.

In one passage, Clark drew on the vast changes the trial had wrought in her own life. She thought the jurors might wonder just what Simpson had been doing in the narrow passageway behind Kaelin's room, the place where he knocked into the air conditioner and dropped the glove. "You are thinking, why not drop it in a Dumpster on the way home?" she said. But Clark suggested that this wasn't possible. "He can't. He can't, because he is famous. If someone sees him hanging around near a Dumpster on that night of all nights, they are going to recognize him, and he is going to have a witness." Clark came up with this theory because now she, too, was noticed everywhere she went, and she believed that Simpson, who had far more experience in being famous, had even factored his celebrity into his plans for murder.

||||||

In her fury at Darden after the glove demonstration, Clark had decided for a while that she didn't want him doing any part of the summations. She would do it all herself. But Clark's anger cooled, and she ultimately ceded the domestic-violence portion of the case to him. Ito had decreed that there would be evening sessions during closing statements, so Darden rose to address the jury at shortly after seven in the evening.

Television, of course, was sending the proceedings around the world, but this first nighttime session of the case gave the courtroom a curious intimacy. We were, after all, nearly the only people in that vast and sterile building, and the uniqueness of the experience gave the room a strange glow. Chris Darden captured that mood and that moment. This case—chiefly Cochran's racebaiting—had taken its toll on Darden. The public display of his shortcomings as a lawyer had pained him as well. Darden had a great deal of help with this summation; it was written chiefly by fellow prosecutor Scott Gordon and a private stalking and domestic-violence expert named Gavin de Becker. But just as Darden deserved the blame for his several failures in that courtroom, so too did he earn the credit for this triumph.

Darden used a perfect metaphor for the Simpson marriage: a burning fuse. He noted that the defense had argued that "just because" there was marital discord, "it doesn't mean anything. . . . Well, this isn't a 'just because' issue. This is a 'because' issue. It is because he hit her in the past. And because he slapped her and threw her out of the house and kicked her and punched her and grabbed her around the neck. . . . And it's because he used a base-ball bat to break the windshield of her Mercedes back in 1985. And it's because he kicked her door down in 1993. . . . It's because of a letter he wrote her . . . June the sixth, talking about the IRS. It's be-cause he stalked her." Darden then took each of these domestic-violence incidents in chronological order and punctuated them with the phrase "And the fuse is burning." He played the pair of 911 calls—the wordless slaps from 1989, and the terrified "He's going to kill me!" from four years later.

Darden closed for the night by recalling one of the briefest wit-nesses in the trial—the district attorney's investigator who drilled open Nicole's safe-deposit box after her death. There wasn't much in there: her will; letters of apology from O.J. after his 1989 conviction; and the photographs of Nicole's beaten face from that incident. But Darden asserted that Nicole had a larger purpose for preserving those few items in the way she did. "She put those things there for a reason," Darden said quietly. "She is leaving you a road map to let you know who it is who will even-tually kill her. She knew in 1989. She knew it. And she wants you to know it."

||||||

The defense team held weekly meetings around a big table in Cochran's suite of offices. At these conclaves, Cochran would often take on the persona of a preacher and declaim in mock solemnity about each lawyer's assignment. One day near the end of the case, Cochran was telling Bailey his plans for how they were going to win. "I will bring the brothers and sisters to the table of acquittal," he told Bailey, "but you, sir, are responsible for the Demon."

The Demon was the defense team's nickname for juror number three, Anise Aschenbach, a sixty-year-old woman who was one of only two whites left on the panel. The self-confident and poised Aschenbach had said during jury selection that her advocacy once changed the minds of all eleven of her fellow jurors in another case. Throughout the trial, Aschenbach was the one juror the defense feared might hold out for conviction. Along the way, Cochran and Bailey sensed that she particularly admired Bailey's courtroom style, which led to Cochran's instruction to him. (In fact, the defense missed Aschenbach's signals about Bailey. "I couldn't stand that creep," she told me after the trial.)

Still, the admonition to Bailey illustrated how Johnnie Cochran saw his role in the case. He would take care of the nine black jurors—the brothers and sisters—and one of the white lawyers could handle the rest. In the waning days of the trial, Shapiro lobbied Simpson to be allowed to deliver the second defense summation, but Cochran and the rest of the defense team shot down that idea. Shapiro didn't know the facts well enough; he would only be reading what Barry Scheck had prepared for him. Simpson, too, thought Scheck deserved the white-lawyer slot. (Bailey had played too small a role in the trial even to be considered.)

When Cochran began his address to the jury on Wednesday, September 27, he started in a conventional way. He attacked the prosecutors' time line, principally their theory that Simpson had killed the two victims at 10:15 P.M. He dwelled on the glove demonstration and used a catchy phrase that had been suggested to him by Gerry Uelman: "If it doesn't fit, you must acquit." Cochran continued to ignore or downplay domestic violence. "He is not perfect. He is not proud of some of the things he did," the lawyer said at last. "But they don't add up to murder." Cochran even took a silly turn when he put a black knit cap on his head to suggest the absurdity of someone as famous as O. J. Simpson using a disguise. "If I put this knit cap on, who am I?" Cochran asked. "I'm still Johnnie Cochran with a knit cap." (In fact, wearing a knit cap at night can be an effective disguise—one favored in particular by the navy SEALs, who had been Simpson's tutors on the set of *Frogman* shortly before the murders.)

But Cochran was only warming up to the crux of his argument, about the LAPD. "If you can't trust the messengers, watch out for their messages: Vannatter, the man who carries the blood; Fuhrman, the man who finds the glove." Cochran realized that Fuhrman's role in the case was, in the end, fairly minor, so he threw Vannatter in with the disgraced Fuhrman. Cochran even had a chart for the jury, entitled "Vannatter's Big Lies," and he called the two men the "twins of deception" and then the "twin demons of deception" and finally "the twin *devils* of deception." This was, of course, monstrously unfair to Vannatter, whose errors stemmed more from laziness than malevolence.

This was, in the end, the classic Johnnie Cochran summation— a variant of one he had given many times before. He said the case was really about the police, not his client. The only difference in this case was that the stakes were so much higher. "Your verdict goes far beyond these doors of this courtroom," he advised. "That's not to put any pressure on you, just to tell you what is really happening out there." It was, one supposes, just a sort of courtesy to warn the jurors what their lives might be like if they happened to vote to convict this man.

So what was the jury to do? "Stop this cover-up. Stop this cover-up. If you don't stop it, then who? Do you think the police department is going to stop it? Do you think the D.A.'s office is going to stop it? Do you think we can stop it by ourselves? It has to be stopped by you. . . . Who, then, polices the police? *You* police the police. You police them by your verdict. You are the ones to send the message." Several times he referred to Fuhrman as a "genocidal racist," so that there was only one appropriate point of reference for this man. "There was another man not too long ago in the world who had those same views. . . . This man, this scourge, became one of the worst people in the history of this world, Adolf Hitler, because people didn't care or didn't try to stop him. He had the power over his racism and his antireligion. Nobody wanted to stop him, and it ended up in World War Two." Cochran then exhaled and muttered with disgust, "The conduct of this man"—and it wasn't clear who, Hitler or Fuhrman.

Scheck followed for a brisk tour of the forensic issues in the case. It was, at times, extremely arcane: "The EAP typing system is something that looks at antigens on the outside of that red blood cell." But Scheck did make clear the defense position that the police had cleverly planted the blood on the socks at Rockingham and on the rear gate at Bundy—though at the same time they had incompetently contaminated the blood on the walkway at Bundy. The unifying theme came from Henry Lee. "In the words of Dr. Lee," Scheck said, "something is wrong. Something is terribly wrong with the evidence in this case."

That evening, the last night of the case, the prosecutors gathered on the eighteenth floor to plot strategy for a rebuttal. Bedeviled by dental problems for years, Clark was now finding the pain excruciating. She made an emergency appointment with a dentist at six-thirty that evening, and it turned out she had an abscess. She was knocked out with general anesthesia, operated on, and sent back to the court house at around ten P.M. She stayed until just before four in the morning.

Five hours later, on September 29, the prosecutors spoke for the last time. Frazzled and drained, Clark unwisely tried to respond to each of Scheck's assertions. The defense lawyers interrupted her more than forty times with objections. Ito overruled most of them, but they succeeded in preventing Clark from establishing any kind of rhythm. For once Clark lacked the energy to fight back.

There was one hint of what was to come. Bill Hodgman had spent much of the previous month working on an elaborate chart entitled "Unrefuted Evidence," a summary of all the non-DNA, non-Fuhrman-related evidence in the case. It was arranged in the form of a big pyramid, and Clark saved it for her conclusion. The chart was extremely impressive, and it listed things like Nicole's purchase of the gloves, Park's fruitless buzzing for Simpson, the blood to the left of the shoe prints and the cut on Simpson's left hand. It was a rather complicated graphic, and Clark did not discuss every point on it, so she offered the jurors an option.

"If you would like to take notes on this," Clark said, "I can leave it up for a little while."

Not one juror wrote down a thing.

|||||

When I left Ito's courtroom on September 29 and stood before the steam tables in the cafeteria of the Criminal Courts Building, I had only one thought: Praise be—the last lunch (at least before deliberations). Clark's haggard appearance reflected the feelings of everyone involved with the trial. I ordered my umpteenth chicken burrito and staggered to a table with Sally Ann Stewart, a reporter for *USA Today*. The room was uncharacteristically deserted for that time of day, and we enjoyed the calm as we discussed the end of the trial and the resumption of our normal lives.

A few moments later, though, Johnnie Cochran, Barry Scheck, Carl Douglas, and Larry Schiller arrived. They set their trays down at a centrally located table, and six Fruit of Islam bodyguards, dressed in their trademark bow ties, formed a circle with their backs to Cochran's table and their eyes trained warily outward. The guards had first appeared in the courthouse at the beginning of that final week and had added a new level of uneasiness to an environment that was already extraordinarily charged. In truth, Cochran was probably more miser than provocateur. Cochran had received threats, and what really appealed to him about the Fruit of Islam guards was that they had volunteered their services. Still, after the Fuhrman tapes, and after all of his fiery speeches around the country, Cochran had imported into the courthouse the very symbols of Louis Farrakhan's strident black nationalism. At that Friday lunch, however, the presence of the grim-faced sentries seemed merely ludicrous, for they had only two reporters and Rose, the cashier, to monitor for false moves.

Then, a few minutes later, Robert Shapiro arrived. There had been a time when he was probably the most famous lawyer in America, but by this final Friday, his voluble, visible role had been usurped. Though the other defense lawyers often came and went together, Shapiro arrived and left by himself, and on this day, he paid Rose, took a long look at his colleagues and their sentinels, and sat down by himself at a small table nearby.

Sally and I, feeling a little sorry for him—and always eager to chat with an insider—asked him to sit with us. He picked up his tray, sidled over, and joined in our reveries of life after O.J. His own fantasy, he said, would be to take a month off and join Oscar De La Hoya's training camp at Big Bear Lake. A serious and skilled amateur boxer at the age of fifty-three, he couldn't wait to tear into the heavy bag. As always with Shapiro, though, the topic soon turned to his resentment of his fellow defense lawyers. He said he had been appalled when Cochran brought the Fruit of Islam into his entourage and that he had been disappointed by Cochran's summation the previous day. "It was nothing but race, race, race," he said. "And why am I not reading that in the paper? All I hear is how great his summation was. Why do I keep reading this?" In truth, some reporters had excoriated Cochran's appeal for an acquittal based on racial solidarity, but Shapiro's bitterness was such that he had registered only the favorable words about his colleague.

Meanwhile, Marcia Clark took the Goldman family out for a drink after her rebuttal summation on Friday. She then fled Los Angeles. She took her two boys up the coast to Santa Barbara, to the home of her friend Lynn Reed Baragona. There, Clark slept in peace, played with her kids, and did the crossword puzzle for the first time in more than a year. On Sunday, Clark and Baragona decided to take a trip to the local mall. Amid the upscale stores in that tony Pacific Ocean setting, Clark started to absorb just how famous she had become: As she shopped, she encountered spontaneous outbursts of applause from fellow customers.

Toward the end of the day, Clark and her friend were walking along a long corridor, and a pair of black women started coming toward them from the opposite direction. They were, it seemed, just about the only African-American shoppers in the whole place, and they clearly recognized the Simpson prosecutor. As their paths crossed, one of the black women leaned over and uttered a single word, just loud enough so that Marcia Clark would hear:

"Innocent."

|||||

The jurors selected a foreperson on the afternoon of Friday, September 29, just after Clark completed the last summation. The assignment went to juror number one, Armanda Cooley, a fifty-one-year-old black woman who worked as an administrative assistant for the city of Los Angeles. Cooley was obviously a levelheaded and friendly person, and she had steered clear of most of the jury tempests during the trial. Both sides figured she would be the choice. Judge Ito did not allow the jury to begin considering the evidence on that Friday, however. After they selected the foreperson, Ito sent them back to the hotel; deliberations were set to begin on Monday morning.

Shortly before summations, the sheriff's deputies supervising the jurors at the Inter-Continental Hotel told their charges that they would have to start preparing for the end of their sequestration. Through eight months at the hotel, the jurors had accumulated a great many possessions in their rooms. The deputies told them that by the time of deliberations, all of their belongings would have to fit into one or two suitcases.

Over the last weekend, the deputies made an additional announcement to the jurors. On Monday, and on each day of deliberations to follow, the jurors would be required to pack all of their remaining belongings and take them to the courthouse. This was a major imposition. It also made no sense, because once the jurors reached their verdict, Ito had decided that he was going to delay the announcement overnight. Yet the jurors, beaten down after so many months of confinement, did not protest. They accepted the prospect of rising daily at dawn and packing, then rushing off to court at their usual 7:45 A.M. for as long as it would take to reach a verdict. But this pointlessly strict policy by the sheriff's deputies represented at least a subconscious cue to the jurors to reach a quick decision.

At 9:16 A.M. on Monday, October 2, the twelve members of the jury settled into chairs in the deliberation room just across the back hallway from Ito's courtroom. Twenty-five minutes later, Ito's clerk, Deirdre Robertson, wheeled in a cart piled high with trial exhibits arrayed in black binders. Robertson closed the door and said the jurors could begin discussing the case.

Armanda Cooley, the foreperson, asked her colleagues for advice about how to proceed. She had never before served on a jury. Several of the jurors suggested that they take an immediate straw poll. But Cooley said that a manual she had been given seemed to suggest that the jury should not call for a show of hands. After a little more discussion, it was agreed that Cooley would conduct a vote by secret ballot, just to get a sense of what everyone was thinking.

"Just write 'guilty' or 'not guilty' on a piece of paper and put it in the bowl," Cooley said. After a moment or two, Cooley passed around a glass bowl that Ito's clerks had kept full of candy over the previous months. When the bowl came back to Cooley, her friend Carrie Bess—like Cooley, a single black woman with grown children and a civil-service job—volunteered to tabulate the responses on a blackboard. Cooley called out the votes, and Bess wrote them down:

Ten for acquittal; two for conviction.

Turning for the first time to the facts of the case, Anise Aschenbach (the defense's white "demon") announced she wanted to say something. She had been stewing all weekend. Aschenbach had been so angry during Cochran's summation that she almost got up and told the lawyer to shut up. "I was so outraged at what he said," Aschenbach told her fellow jurors. "He wants us to send the LAPD a message. Does he think we're so stupid that we're going to send a message rather than decide based on what we heard in the case? I hope I was not the only one offended by his remarks."

Her fellow jurors responded to these comments with total silence.

Armanda Cooley decided to distribute the exhibit binders. Jurors began leafing through them and offering comments about the evidence. It wasn't so much a conversation as a series of random observations.

Why wasn't there more blood around the glove Fuhrman said he found at Rockingham?

Goldman had bruises on his knuckles. If they were from fighting back, why didn't O.J. have any bruises on his body? (The prosecution had argued that Goldman had injured his hand flailing against the fence behind him.) The jurors knew that Dave Aldana, the Hispanic man in seat four, was a martial arts expert. He got up and demonstrated how to defend in tae kwon do. He thought Goldman had put up a good fight.

If the glove came off Simpson's hand during the fight, why wasn't it inside out?

Aschenbach volunteered that she was one of the two votes for conviction. (The other never came forward.) Hearing this, Sheila Woods flashed an angry look at her. Woods was the last surviving member of the Jeanette Harris clique. Since Harris had been thrown off the jury, Woods had had little contact with her fellow jurors. "Why did they go after him as a suspect from the beginning?" Woods said to Aschenbach. "They insulted us with their testimony. They went after that man."

Someone mentioned the glove demonstration. Brenda Moran, Gina Rosborough, and Lon Cryer all said they thought it didn't fit on Simpson's hand.

There was only one reference to DNA tests. Both Dave Aldana and Sheila Woods said they didn't think it was reliable when all of the DNA came from the back gate at Bundy. This was important to them. (It was, of course, completely wrong, too. While the molecular weight of the DNA on the back gate was higher than that of the other samples, several other tests of blood at the murder scene tied it to Simpson.)

After about an hour of discussion, the topic turned to the testimony of Allan Park, the limousine driver. Carrie Bess said Park didn't know how many cars had been in Simpson's driveway. A couple of other jurors disagreed about whether Park had seen a black man at the doorway to the house or walking across the driveway. Others were confused by the time that Park said various events occurred. The group decided by consensus that they would like another look at Park's testimony.

Shortly before noon, Cooley sent out a note requesting Park's testimony. She thought the judge would simply send back a transcript the jury could examine, but the judge relayed word that he would have the testimony read in the courtroom starting at 1:00 P.M. The jurors then broke for lunch.

IIIII

As a former prosecutor, I have always hated read-backs. Even when I was trying my own cases, I used to have trouble staying awake when court reporters did their monotone recitals. This day was no different. I took my usual seat and tried to focus on the words as they were spoken. As he had from the beginning, Park struck me as the most powerful government witness in the case. It was absolutely clear that the Bronco was not parked on Rockingham when he arrived to pick up Simpson. Its absence, in my view, doomed O.J. Even worse, from Simpson's perspective, was that Park was fairly certain that the Bronco had returned by the time they left for the airport—an even more incriminating fact.

Still, when Ito called a break after seventy-five minutes of the read-back to give the court reporter's voice a rest, I knew I had to escape. I was sure there were going to be lots of read-backs to come, and I didn't want to embarrass myself by falling asleep in court.

I wandered up to the eighteenth floor and paid a visit to Scott Gordon, the good-natured former Santa Monica cop who was the leading domestic-violence expert in the D.A.'s office. We had been chatting for about ten minutes when his phone rang. I heard only his side of the conversation: "You're shitting me. . . . Don't shit me like this. . . . I know you're shitting me. . . . Really? . . . *Really?*" Finally, he hung up.

"Looks like we have a verdict," he told me.

|||||

Back in the jury room, Cooley had taken advantage of the break to ask if all the questions about Park's testimony had been answered. By consensus, the answer was yes. Suddenly, it seemed, no one had anything more to say. In lieu of returning to the courtroom for the remainder of Park's testimony, Cooley sent a request to Ito for the verdict forms. Before they arrived Cooley conducted another secret ballot, and this time the vote was unanimous. Just to make sure, Cooley asked each juror to repeat their verdict, and they all said, "Not guilty." Cooley filled out the forms and pushed the buzzer to the courtroom three times—the signal for a verdict.

It was shortly before 3:00 P.M. The jurors had discussed the merits of the case against O. J. Simpson for about two hours—less time than most other adults in America.

|||||

Cochran was giving a speech in San Francisco. Bailey was appearing at a snack food distributors' convention in Laguna Beach. Clark was in her office. Though Simpson had eleven lawyers representing him in this case, only Carl Douglas was by his side when Armanda Cooley presented the envelope containing the completed verdict forms to Judge Ito.

"We will accept the verdict from you tomorrow morning at ten," Ito said. "See you tomorrow morning at ten o'clock."

No one—on either side or in the news media—had predicted so swift a verdict. The entire building seemed afflicted with vertigo. After all these months and all the debates over evidence, strategy, rulings, and rumors, only one question remained: What had the jurors done?

I had spent most of the trial believing that it would end in an acquittal or a hung jury. Then the Park testimony threw me. If that's all they needed to hear, I thought, they had voted to convict.

The jurors returned to the Inter-Continental for their 266th, and final, night in residence. The hotel threw the jurors a champagne reception in the presidential suite on the nineteenth floor, then turned their last supper into a steak barbecue. Everyone had a few drinks, which loosened tongues. Reyko Butler, one of the two alternates, couldn't resist asking one of the deliberating jurors how it had all come out. The juror couldn't resist answering: "N," the juror said. Not guilty.

This curiosity extended to the sheriff's deputies as well, who had the same question and received the same answer.

Back at the county jail, Simpson's lawyers gathered in a final vigil with him. Cochran arrived too late to make it to the jail, but Bailey, Kardashian, and Skip Taft sat on the other side of the glass wall for a last chat. As it turned out, Simpson was in good spirits. "All the deputies here are asking for my autograph," Simpson told his lawyers. "They hear from their boys over with the jury that it's going to be the last chance for them to get one."

It was the last leak in the case—from the sheriff's deputies guarding the jury to their colleagues guarding Simpson: O.J. was going to walk.

||||

The scene at the courthouse on the morning of Tuesday, October 3, resembled some sinister carnival. Over the course of the trial, the LAPD had made the Criminal Courts Building ever more isolated. First, they banned all parked cars from the adjacent streets to prevent a car bombing. Then they kept all cars off the main artery of Temple Street, right in front of the building. On this last day, the police shut off all traffic in the immediate vicinity of the courthouse. Crowds of people milled about in the empty streets. Except for the trial, all business in downtown Los Angeles seemed to come to a halt.

In the last half hour before 10:00, more than a hundred people jammed the hallway outside of Ito's courtroom. Bookers for talk shows had taken up more or less permanent residence in that hallway for weeks, and on this day, several stars of the shows joined in the vigil. NBC had forty camera crews ready to roll for reaction to the verdict. ABC had assigned four producers to each juror.

At 9:49 Darden walked into the courtroom alone. Three minutes later, Clark arrived with a retinue of four police bodyguards. At

9:55 Johnnie Cochran, Simpson's sisters, and their Nation of Islam escorts completed the cast in the courtroom.

At one minute before 10:00, the deputies escorted Simpson from his lockup, and he nodded to his family just as he had every day.

For perhaps the first time in the entire trial, Ito appeared and started the proceedings precisely on schedule.

"Counsel," Ito said to the lawyers, "is there anything else we need to take up before we invite the jurors to join us?"

For once, the answer was no.

The jurors filed out in their usual order, expressionless as always. They looked ahead vacantly. None of them met Simpson's eye.

Ito directed Deirdre Robertson to hand the envelope containing the verdict forms to one of the sheriff's deputies, who walked it over to Armanda Cooley. "Madam Foreperson," Ito said, "would you please open the envelope and check the condition of the verdict forms?"

Cooley did so.

"Are they the same forms you signed, and are they in order?"

"Yes, they are."

Ito cautioned the audience that "if there is any disruption during the reading of the verdicts, the bailiffs will have the obligation to remove any persons disrupting these proceedings."

Ito paused. "Mr. Simpson," he instructed, "would you please stand and face the jury." Unbidden, Cochran and the rest of the defense team rose with him. "Mrs. Robertson," Ito cued.

The judge's clerk stumbled as she read the title of the case, then steadied herself as she came to the verdict.

"We the jury in the above-entitled action find the defendant, Orenthal James Simpson, not guilty of the crime of murder in violation of Penal Code Section 187A, a felony, upon Nicole Brown Simpson, a human being, as charged in count one of the information."

At the words "not guilty," Simpson exhaled and gave a sort of half smile. He looked like he was going to cry but didn't. Cochran stood behind him as they faced the jury, and on hearing "not guilty" Cochran pumped his fist quickly, then grabbed Simpson by the shoulder and, in a startlingly intimate gesture, placed his cheek on the back of O.J.'s shoulder. Robert Shapiro looked stricken, crushed. His alienation from his colleagues and client was never more visible than at that moment.

Robertson then proceeded to read the second verdict, that in the murder of Ronald Lyle Goldman. At the second utterance of the words "not guilty," Kim Goldman let out a trembling howl. She grabbed her hair, then buried her head in her father's shoulder.

I was sitting right behind Kim, in the second row. Numb with shock, I stared at Simpson and had a single thought: He's going home. There is no red tape after an acquittal. The handcuffs come off, and you're on your way.

As Robertson finished the formalities and Ito polled the jury, asking them all whether this was their verdict, noise from the audience grew louder. Everyone in all of the families was crying—for joy, for sorrow, at their release from this extraordinary tension.

"The defendant, having been acquitted of both charges," Ito said evenly, "is ordered . . . released forthwith. All right. We'll stand in recess."

The jurors filed out in their usual silence. From his seat, number six, juror Lon Cryer had the longest walk to the door. He kept his head down most of the way, then turned to the defense table and raised his fist in a black power salute. Then he, too, left the courtroom.

|||||

Most of the jurors dissolved into tears when they arrived back in the deliberation room. They hugged and wept and clung to one another for support. After a few minutes, a pair of deputies came to escort them up to the lounge on the eleventh floor, where they had done most of their waiting over the course of the trial. There the tears mostly stopped, and the jurors sat in shell-shocked silence on the couches and easy chairs. Finally, Carrie Bess said something to no one in particular:

"We've got to protect our own."

Larry Schiller, literary entrepreneur, had laid careful plans to cash in quickly on an acquittal. Within an hour of the verdict, Simpson was driven in a white van from downtown to his home in Brentwood. He was accompanied by Robert Kardashian, Schiller, and Schiller's camera.

Schiller and his girlfriend, Kathy Amermann, had both worked as photographers over the years, and Schiller knew that exclusive photographs of the victory party would command a hefty price. In the weeks before the verdict, Schiller arranged to sell first rights to the photos to the supermarket tabloid *Star* for more than $400,000. (Simpson and Schiller split the proceeds, and the photographs bore the copyright marks of both of their companies—Orenthal Productions and Polaris Communications.)

The verdict came on a Tuesday, which was the *Star*'s weekly deadline, but the resourceful Schiller had made contingency plans so the pictures could make it into the next issue. While the jury was deliberating, Schiller had converted the garage at Simpson's home into a photo developing lab and turned the maid's room into a satellite transmission center. All during the evening after the verdict, as friends and family joined Simpson to toast his freedom, Schiller and Amermann snapped dozens of photos, hurriedly developed them in the garage, then transmitted them to the *Star* from Gigi Guarin's old quarters. The following morning, Schiller sent a CD-ROM full of party photographs on a plane to Germany. The Schiller-Simpson joint venture had sold those for an additional fee to the weekly *Stern*.

It was a rather quiet celebration at Rockingham that evening. The small, dedicated group who had stood by Simpson throughout the long trial all paid their respects. There was his family, of course, presided over by his mother and two sisters, as well as his older children, Jason and Arnelle. A. C. Cowlings was there, as was Skip Taft, Simpson's business manager. Most striking were the absences—the golfing buddies, Nicole's friends, the dozens of pals who used to attend Simpson's annual Fourth of July bash at the house. They had all chosen the other side in this case. Those guests who did come gathered around a piano and sang hymns. Simpson mostly stayed in his bedroom, receiving guests in small groups. Only one person stayed by Simpson's side the entire evening. That was Peter Burt, a reporter for the *Star*, whose presence was part of Schiller's deal with the magazine.

After the party, it was Schiller who did not leave Simpson's side. With his camera at the ready, Schiller followed O.J. for the next several days, documenting his life for the resale market. On October 6, three days after the verdict, Schiller's literary agent, Ike Williams, faxed a letter to book publishers offering a sequel to *I Want to Tell You*. Williams said this next book, to be entitled *Now I Can Tell You*, would be "O. J. Simpson's first person account of the trial from his arrest to the not-guilty verdict and his reunion with his family." Like the first book, this one would be "organized and edited by Larry Schiller," but there would be an additional bonus: The Schiller-Simpson joint venture was also offering Schiller's "original and unique" photographs of Simpson's reunion with Sydney and Justin Simpson, which took place on October 4.

However, these literary ventures paled in comparison to the top priority of Simpson's financial team in the wake of the verdict. All through the summer of 1995, Skip Taft and Larry King had engaged in detailed negotiations about a pay-per-view special following the verdict. The two-hour program was to feature King interviewing Simpson live, as well as phone calls from viewers. (It was to take place whether Simpson was acquitted or convicted, but not if the trial ended in a hung jury.) Turner Broadcasting, the parent company of Cable News Network, would buy the rights from Simpson for $25 million. In lieu of a fee for himself, King would arrange for about $1 million of the money to go to his favorite charity, the Cardiac Foundation. Simpson would receive about $4 million personally. According to King and Taft's arrangement, the balance of the money—more than $15 million, after expenses—would go to establish a network of "O. J. Simpson Boys Clubs" in cities across America.

||||||

The photographs of the victory party ran as scheduled in the *Star* and *Stern,* but none of the other schemes came to fruition. There has been no sequel to *I Want to Tell You.* As soon as word leaked out to the public that Larry King was even considering participating in a pay-per-view interview with Simpson, executives at CNN's parent company announced that no such project would take place. Simpson's prospects for any pay-per-view appearance vanished completely when cable-system operators across the country said they would refuse to distribute any broadcast that would enrich the former defendant. The darkly comic notion of "O. J. Simpson Boys Clubs" never materialized.

All of these projects fell victim to the enormous backlash against the verdict in mainstream—that is, white—America. Because of television, the announcement of the verdict became a nationally shared experience—one on par, incredibly, with the assassination of John F. Kennedy. In the days immediately after the end of the case in court, televised images of the verdict itself yielded to images of people watching the verdict. The pictures revealed many scenes of African-Americans cheering the verdict, from college campuses to battered women's shelters. White viewers, by contrast, watched in stunned, generally appalled, silence. Reaction to the verdict was promptly replaced by reaction to the reaction, and then reaction to *that* reaction and so on, which is to say, as Henry Louis Gates, Jr., observed, "black indignation at white anger at black jubilation at Simpson's acquittal." The passing months did not so much heal the wounds in race relations as witness the growth of an ugly scar.

Assessing the "meaning" of the Simpson case became, and remains, a cottage industry. But in evaluating that legacy, it is useful, even necessary, to return to the underlying events—that is, to what happened outside Nicole Brown Simpson's condominium on the night of June 12, 1994. The Simpson case was never some free-floating set of ideas ripe for any number of equally valid interpretations. The case emerged from a set of facts, and those facts matter.

As to the central fact in the case, it is my view that Simpson murdered his ex-wife and her friend on June 12. Any rational analysis of the events and evidence in question leads to that conclusion. This is true whether one considers evidence not presented to the jury—such as the results of Simpson's polygraph examination and his flight with Al Cowlings on June 17—or just the evidence established in court. Notwithstanding the prosecution's many errors, the evidence against Simpson at the trial was overwhelming. Simpson had a violent relationship with his ex-wife, and tensions between them were growing in the weeks leading up to the murders. Simpson had no alibi for the time of the murders, nor was his Bronco parked at his home during that time. Simpson had a cut on his left hand on the day after the murders, and DNA tests showed conclusively that it was Simpson's blood to the left of the shoe prints leaving the scene. Nicole's blood was found on a sock in his bedroom, and Goldman's blood—as well as Simpson's—was found in the Bronco. Hair consistent with Simpson's was found on the killer's cap and on Goldman's shirt. The gloves that Nicole bought for Simpson in 1990 were almost certainly the ones used by her killer.

It is theoretically possible, of course, that Simpson killed the two victims and that the police also planted evidence against him—that he was guilty *and* framed. But I am convinced that did not happen, and that it could not have happened. In their summations, Cochran and Scheck suggested that the police, in their effort to frame Simpson, planted at least the following items: (1) Simpson's blood on the rear gate at Bundy; (2) Goldman's blood in Simpson's Bronco; (3) Nicole's blood on the sock found in his bedroom; (4) Simpson's blood on the same sock; and (5) the infamous glove at Rockingham, which had, as Clark put it in her summation, "all of the evidence on it: Ron Goldman's fibers from his shirt; Ron Goldman's hair; Nicole's hair; the defendant's blood; Ron Goldman's blood; Nicole's blood; and the Bronco fiber." The defense never spelled out how all this nefarious activity took place, but pulling it off would have required more or less the following. The core of the defense case was, of course, that Fuhrman surreptitiously took that glove from the murder scene to the defendant's home. Not only would he have had to transport the glove with its residue of the crime scene, but he would also have had to find some of Simpson's blood (from sources unknown) to deposit upon it and then wipe the glove on the inside of Simpson's locked car (by means unknown)—all the while not knowing whether Simpson had an ironclad alibi for the time of the murders. To me, this possibility is simply not believable, even taking into consideration Fuhrman's repugnant racial views.

The other police conspirators (conspicuously unnamed by the defense) would have had to be equally adept and even more determined. Many of the police officers at the crime scene noticed the blood on the back gate at Bundy; someone would have had to wipe that off and apply Simpson's. The autopsies, where blood samples were taken from the victims, were not performed until June 14, more than a full day after the murders. Someone would have had to take some of Goldman's blood and put it in the Bronco, which was then in police custody. And someone (the same person? another?) would have had to take some of Nicole's blood and dab it on the sock, which was then in a police evidence lab. (When Vannatter took his notorious trip to Brentwood with the blood vial, he only had Simpson's sample, not Nicole's, with him.) All of these illegal actions by the police would have had to take place at a time when everyone involved in the case was under the most relentless media scrutiny in American legal history—and all for the benefit of an unknown killer who, like only 9 percent of the population, happened to share Simpson's shoe size, twelve.

In their comments after the trial, the jurors gamely tried to defend their verdict, insisting that it was based on the evidence, not mere racial solidarity. Brenda Moran and Yolanda Crawford believed that the glove demonstration doomed the government's case. "In plain English, the glove didn't fit," Moran said. Gina Rosborough said, "I believed from the beginning that he was innocent," and the course of the trial confirmed her view. Sheila Woods decried the sloppy lab procedures of the LAPD. Lon Cryer was concerned about evidence contamination and rejected Allan

Park's testimony because he was mistaken about the number of cars in the driveway. As for why he gave Simpson a raised-fist salute at the end of the trial, Cryer said, "It was like a 'Right on to you, Mr. Simpson. Get on with your life. Get your kids. Be happy. Get some closure in your life.'" The three jurors who wrote a joint book about the case—Armanda Cooley, Carrie Bess, and Marsha Rubin-Jackson—attributed the decision to a combination of these factors. Anise Aschenbach, the white juror who initially voted for a conviction, asserted with some sadness that she might have fought on if she had felt any possibility of support from her colleagues. In any event, Aschenbach was deeply troubled by the testimony of Mark Fuhrman and the evidence of his racial views.

All the black jurors denied that race played any role at all in their deliberations or their decision. To me, this is implausible. The perfunctory review of nine months' worth of evidence; the focus on tangential, if not actually irrelevant, parts of that evidence; the simply incorrect view of other evidence; and the constant focus on racial issues both inside and outside the courtroom—all these factors lead me to conclude that race played a far larger role in the verdict than the jurors conceded. As Carrie Bess indicated in her unguarded words after the verdict, they were protecting their own. This is not especially unusual. For better or worse, American jurors have a long and still-flourishing tradition of both taking race into account in making their decisions and denying that they are doing any such thing. The ten whites, one Asian, and one Latino in Simi Valley who in 1992 acquitted the LAPD officers in the Rodney King case denied that race factored into their decisions; so did the ten black and two white jurors who in 1990 acquitted Washington mayor Marion Barry of all but one of the fourteen narcotics charges against him. In 1955, the two white men charged with murdering Emmett Till were acquitted by an all-white Mississippi jury after about an hour of deliberations. A spokesman for the jurors attributed their decision to "the belief that there had been no identification of the dead body as that of Emmett Till." Nor is this phenomenon limited to celebrated cases. In the borough of the Bronx in New York City, where juries are more than 80 percent black and Hispanic, black defendants are acquitted in felony cases 47.6 percent of the time, which is about three times the national acquittal rate of 17 percent for defendants of all races. In these cases, among these jurors, race mattered—and so it was with the Simpson jurors, too.

That race continues to count for so much with African-American jurors should come as no great surprise. Racism in law enforcement has persisted through many decades of American life, and black citizens, and thus black jurors, have stored too many insults for too long. The police in general, and the LAPD in particular, reap what they sow. But the genuine grievances that have led to a tradition of black hostility to officialdom have, in turn, fostered a mode of conspiratorial thinking that outstrips reality. An Emory University study of 1,000 black churchgoers in five major cities in 1990 found that more than a third believed that HIV was a form of genocide propagated by white scientists, a theory shared by 40 percent of African-American college students in Washington, D.C. Understanding the roots of these beliefs should not mean endorsing them. To do so is merely patronizing, a condescending pat on the head to those incapable of recognizing reality. Better, rather, to hold everyone to the same standards, and better, likewise, to speak the truth: Whites didn't concoct HIV—and O. J. Simpson wasn't innocent.

|||||

The backlash against both the jury and Simpson himself was accelerated by Robert Shapiro, who, as was his custom, put his interests ahead of his client's in the immediate aftermath of the verdict. Shapiro left the courthouse on October 3 and traveled to an ABC studio, where he gave a long-promised interview to Barbara Walters. In their conversation, an obviously bitter and angry Shapiro said of the defense effort in the case, "Not only did we play the race card, we dealt it from the bottom of the deck." He remarked further that henceforth, he would neither speak to Bailey nor work with Cochran. Shapiro's remark about the race card was featured prominently in the following day's news stories about the verdict.

Shapiro's conduct was shameful on several levels. His disgust about the "race card" was, first, intellectually dishonest, because it was Shapiro himself who had constructed Simpson's race-based courtroom and media defense in the first place. Second, his statement helped cement the public impression that his client was acquitted because of the jurors' racial sympathies, not because of his innocence, thus virtually guaranteeing that Simpson would have no chance to reestablish anything like his normal life. In my view, Shapiro's analysis of the case was more or less correct, but Simpson had a right to expect that his own lawyer would not portray the case, in substance, as the story of a murderer who got away with it. Finally, Shapiro trivialized the work of his colleagues Barry Scheck and Peter Neufeld, who had constructed a serious forensic and nonracial defense in the case.

None of this mattered more to Shapiro than the opportunity to reingratiate himself with the West Los Angeles world that meant everything to him. After the Walters interview, Shapiro called his old friend Larry Feldman, the lawyer who had defended him in Mark Fuhrman's libel suit. Shapiro boasted that he had just told Walters that the defense team had played the race card from the bottom of the deck. "You're kidding," an appalled Feldman told him. "No, really," said Shapiro, who then broke into self-satisfied laughter.

Notwithstanding the fame and, in some instances, fortune that the case brought them, most of the major participants now regard their experience with considerable bitterness. The most bizarre postscript to the case concerns F. Lee Bailey. In 1994, Shapiro and Bailey shared another client besides O. J. Simpson: Claude Duboc, one of the biggest marijuana dealers in the world. As part of a plea bargain in northern Florida, arranged the month before the murders on Bundy Drive, Duboc agreed to turn over virtually all of his assets to the United States government. Among them were shares in a Canadian company called BioChem Pharma, worth about $6 million at the time of the plea bargain. Also at that time, Duboc believed those shares were likely to appreciate greatly in value, so the prosecutors agreed that Bailey would hold on to the stock for the months until Duboc was formally sentenced.

Two years later, after the verdict in the Simpson case, the value of Duboc's stock had risen by more than $20 million, and Bailey told the prosecutors in Florida that he believed the appreciated portion of the stock assets belonged to him, not the federal government. The deal was never put in writing, so the judge held a hearing in February 1996 to determine the terms of the stock arrangements. The lead witness for the government was Robert Shapiro. He testified that he understood the agreement to hold that the United States, not Bailey, was entitled to the appreciated portion of the stock assets. When Bailey did not produce the stock certificates or the equivalent in cash, the judge threw the sixty-two-year-old lawyer in jail.

Bailey served forty-four days in the federal detention center in Tallahassee. He was released on April 19, only after pledging virtually all of his assets in collateral. However, after a month of living with this nearly impossible financial bind, Bailey gave up his claim to the stock. This financial imbroglio, of course, only intensified the enmity between Shapiro and Bailey. Bailey rages with little prompting at what he regards as Shapiro's betrayal. The cooler Shapiro merely notes that he plans never again to speak with Bailey. He has told friends with a smile, however, that he paid his own way to Florida to testify against Bailey.

Barry Scheck and Peter Neufeld returned to New York after the Simpson trial. They found that their celebrity from the case had not translated into financial support for their Innocence Project, which uses DNA testing to free wrongfully convicted prisoners. When they mentioned to Shapiro the possibility of a Los Angeles fund-raiser for the project, he told them glumly, and probably accurately, "No Jew will give you a dime in this town." The two New Yorkers have also developed the informal specialty of vetting the books on the case written by members of Simpson's defense team. In early 1996, they reacted with shock to a draft of Shapiro's volume, *The Search for Justice,* for it repeatedly violated the attorney-client privilege by quoting conversations with Simpson without his consent. When they passed along their concerns to the author, Shapiro didn't change the substance of the book—but he did add Scheck and Neufeld to the list of former colleagues with whom he no longer speaks.

Alone among the defense lawyers, Johnnie Cochran seemed to survive the trial unscathed. The week after the verdict, he appeared as a national civil rights spokesman on *Meet the Press,* and in subsequent months he traveled the nation and the world giving speeches. However, even Cochran bore a taint from his association with the case—and his client. His book on the case, *Journey to Justice*, was a critical and commercial failure, and his victory at trial did not translate into greater prosperity for his law firm. In early 1997, Cochran virtually abandoned his law practice to become cohost of a nightly program on Court TV. The cable network received considerable criticism for hiring him, and the program—like Cochran's career as a whole—faces an uncertain future.

Lance Ito conducted his next criminal trial the week after the Simpson case ended. He has never commented publicly on the verdict, but friends report that he knows the Simpson trial did not enhance his reputation. His second most noteworthy trial had a sour postscript as well. On April 4, 1996, a federal judge in Los Angeles overturned the state conviction of financier Charles Keating on the ground that Ito had erroneously instructed the jury.

After the verdict, Marcia Clark and Christopher Darden both took leaves of absence from the Los Angeles District Attorney's Office. Both later resigned. Darden wrote a successful book on the trial and will shortly begin a new job as a professor at the Southwestern University School of Law in Los Angeles. He will teach courtroom skills. His brother Michael died of AIDS on November 29, 1995.

Clark's career plans are uncertain. Since the trial, she has given a series of speeches around the United States and Canada and has worked on her own book, for which she received an advance of more than $4 million. It is believed to be the third largest advance in the history of nonfiction publishing, surpassed only by those received by Colin Powell and H. Norman Schwarzkopf. On November 12, 1995, her father left a message on Marcia's answering machine that her ninety-five-year-old grandfather, Pinchas Kleks, had died in Israel. She did not return the call. Her book was long delayed past its original publication date. In early 1997, she announced that she planned to host a television program called *Lady Law*, about women in law enforcement. Few stations expressed an interest in broadcasting the show.

O. J. Simpson still lives at 360 North Rockingham in Brentwood. His children Sydney and Justin reside with him. Simpson's principal commercial venture since the trial, a two-hour video-taped interview with him about the murders, was a commercial failure. At $19.95 each, it sold fewer than 40,000 copies, netting Simpson about $300,000. His contracts with Hertz and NBC were not renewed. He plays golf frequently, but never at his former home course, the Riviera Country Club. (Though he was never formally evicted from the club, members of its governing board informed Skip Taft that Simpson was no longer welcome there.) Simpson sees few of his friends from before the murders, but he does socialize with several of the sheriff's deputies who guarded him in jail. Simpson tells them he remains confident that, in time, he will be able to resume his former career of being O.J.

On the afternoon of October 3, 1995, the day of Simpson's acquittal in the criminal case, the Simpson defense team held a news conference in Judge Ito's courtroom. At the time Simpson was heading home to Brentwood, so Johnnie Cochran presided. Several counsel tables had been placed end to end across the middle of the courtroom, so all thirty or so people on hand could sit in a single row facing the reporters in the spectator benches. The defense team arranged itself as the Soviet Politburo used to for May Day parades in Moscow: the leader—Cochran—in the center with his minions spread out on either side of him in descending order of importance.

Cochran mostly offered banalities in response to questions, but the most startling remarks came from Jason Simpson, O.J.'s son from his first marriage. O.J. had shown little regard for his shy, doughy older son. His athletic career had been almost nonexistent, and he made his living as a chef. In the two years before the murders, Jason had worked at a fashionable Los Angeles restaurant, but O.J. never once came to sample his son's cooking. Still, on the day of the verdict, O.J. allowed Jason to deliver a three-paragraph statement for him.

"I am relieved that this part of the incredible nightmare that occurred on June 12, 1994, is over with," Jason announced on behalf of his father. "My first obligation is to my young children, who will be raised in the way that Nicole and I always planned.

"My second obligation is to my family and to those friends who never wavered in their support. And when things have settled, I will pursue, as my primary goal in life, the killer or killers who slaughtered Nicole and Mr. Goldman. They're out there somewhere. Whatever it takes to identify them and bring them in, I will provide it somehow.

"I only hope someday that—despite every prejudicial thing that has been said about me publicly, both in and out of the courtroom—people will come to understand and believe that I would not, could not and did not kill anyone."

In spirit, this letter of October 3, 1995, reflected the same themes as Simpson's "suicide note," which was read by Robert Kardashian on June 17, 1994. First, of course, it was dishonest, and not merely because in both letters Simpson denied committing the murders. Before Nicole died, Simpson had been a distinctly uninvolved parent to Sydney and Justin. He was not abusive, but he paid the children only sporadic attention. The notion that he had participated in making specific "plans" for their upbringing was simply untrue. Still, the letter anticipated the determined effort he would make to regain custody of the children from Nicole's parents after the criminal trial. It was spite toward the Browns, as much as any desire to be a full-time parent, that motivated Simpson in that quest.

Even more than Simpson's dishonesty, though, the acquittal-day letter to the public revealed his narcissism. It was not enough for Simpson merely to thank the jury and move on to the next chapter in his life. He had to make the preposterous claim that he would not only pursue the real murderer, but make this mission his "primary goal in life." Incredibly, he sought to keep the public spotlight on himself even though he knew he could not possibly deliver on his promise. In the months to come, however, Simpson would finally pay a price for his arrogance.

||||||

Within a few weeks of the murders, in 1994, Sharon Rufo had filed the first wrongful death lawsuit against Simpson. There was some irony in this. Rufo was Goldman's mother, but she had been estranged from her son, Ron, and daughter, Kim, for more than a decade—about half their lives. Sadly, Rufo's was but one of many attempts throughout the Simpson case by peripheral players to cash in on their relationships with the principals. Her haste, though, made her the lead plaintiff when her ex-husband, Fred, and Nicole's parents (as the representatives of her estate) joined her in the suit. *Rufo, et al. v. Simpson* would be a very different case from *California v. Simpson*.

It was virtually unprecedented for a wrongful death civil case to follow so closely after a murder acquittal. Wrongful death lawsuits following criminal *convictions* are extremely rare; I was never able to find a single example of a civil case after a criminal acquittal for murder. In part, this absence stems from the fact that murderers rarely have the money to make it worthwhile for their victims' families to pursue the issue. But it is also true that the families' civil case against Simpson had the feeling of a prosecutorial appeal. True, the double jeopardy clause of the Constitution posed no bar to the second trial, because Simpson faced no threat of official punishment—that is, prison—in the civil case. But public outrage about the verdict in the criminal case was the fuel that powered the civil case to trial.

The most important moment in the civil case may have come long before this second trial began. In October of 1995, one of the Marciano brothers, who own the Guess clothing company, called his lawyer Daniel Petrocelli and asked for permission to recommend him to Fred Goldman. Petrocelli and Goldman hit it off, and the lawyer obtained permission from his firm to invest a great deal of time and money in a case that might never pay off. Petrocelli had been primarily a civil litigator, and he was largely unknown to much of the Los Angeles legal community, much less the public at large. But his skill and passion dominated the civil case.

He also had important advantages. Most significantly, the burden of proof in a civil case is a preponderance of the evidence— that is, it must be more likely than not that the plaintiff's assertions are true—while criminal cases must be proved beyond a reasonable doubt. Also, because Simpson had been acquitted of the murders, he no longer had a Fifth Amendment privilege to refuse to testify about them. Petrocelli thus could take Simpson's deposition before the trial and call him to testify in front of the civil jury. Still, despite these inherent advantages, the civil trial also made it clear that Petrocelli's team was simply a more skilled collection of attorneys than the one assembled by Gil Garcetti. Petrocelli's exhaustive preparation, combined with his crisp competence in the courtroom, made Darden and Clark look much diminished by comparison.

Petrocelli also had one thing going for him that the prosecutors certainly did not: good luck. The most important example of fortune's favor toward the civil plaintiffs went back to a little-remembered incident from the criminal trial. Late in the criminal case, William Bodziak, the FBI's expert on foot and shoe impressions, had testified powerfully before the jury. Bodziak had studied the bloody shoe prints that the killer had left behind at the murder scene. He concluded that they had been made by a size-twelve Bruno Magli shoe known both as the Lyon and the Lorenzo. Simpson, of course, wore size-twelve shoes, but the prosecution could never prove that he had actually purchased or worn this model. In an excruciating moment for the prosecutors, Samuel Poser, a shoe salesman at Bloomingdale's in New York, had testified that he sold the relevant Bruno Magli model, that Simpson had been a frequent customer of his, and that Simpson usually paid cash for shoes (meaning that no credit card receipt would survive). So did Simpson ever buy a pair of these rare Bruno Maglis? Poser couldn't remember—so his testimony ended with an unsatisfying thud. The inability of the prosecutors to tie Simpson to a specific pair of the Bruno Maglis remained a great source of frustration to them.

Several months after the trial, however, fate smiled on the plaintiffs. The *National Enquirer* published a photograph of Simpson at a Buffalo Bills game on September 26, 1993, about nine months before the murders. On his feet—unmistakably—were the Bruno Maglis. A freelance photographer, Harry Scull, had stumbled upon the old photographs after the criminal trial and then sold them to the highest bidder. Here, finally, Simpson was tied to the murderer's shoes.

The photograph presented Simpson with a dilemma, which he resolved in a characteristic way. At his pretrial deposition for the Simpson case, Petrocelli logically asked Simpson if he had ever owned a pair of the Bruno Maglis. What should Simpson have said? Simpson was and is a great clotheshorse. His vast walk-in closet at Rockingham held more than forty pairs of shoes at the time of the murders. A logical answer for Simpson—indeed, for many people—would have been that he couldn't remember every pair of shoes he had owned in the past several years. But Simpson was too arrogant for that approach. Confronted during his deposition, Simpson said with certainty that he had never owned that model of Bruno Maglis. What's more, he said, he would never have worn a pair of those "ugly ass" shoes.

|||||

Shortly after eight-thirty every morning in the civil trial, a bailiff with a microphone tartly announced that the jurors were taking their seats. Judge Hiroshi Fujisaki then ordered the proceedings to begin; sometimes he didn't even pause to say "Good morning." There were two breaks in the morning, a break for lunch, and two more breaks in the afternoon. Court adjourned promptly at four-thirty, day after productive day.

Fujisaki was the anti-Ito—disciplined, laconic, unwilling to listen to argument (even when he probably should have done so). The original judge in the civil case had been Alan B. Haber, an expansive and intellectual jurist, but Simpson's lawyers had exercised their prerogative to reject him and asked the chief judge to assign a new judge. The L.A. legal folklore about the consequences of "papering" a judge has it that you wind up with an even more unsympathetic judge than the one you decided to eliminate. So it was for the defense with Fujisaki. The Simpson civil trial turned out to be his last case before retirement. He was not worried about preserving (or making) a reputation. All he seemed to want in that courtroom was rough justice—and given the ever more overwhelming evidence against Simpson, rough justice did not favor the defense.

Early in the trial, the figure who stood out most clearly was Robert Baker, Simpson's lead lawyer. With his perfectly sculpted swirl of gray hair and his impeccable suits, Baker looked like the kind of actor who always plays a senator in the movies. By his side was his son, Phillip, who is a junior lawyer in Baker's firm and a young duplicate of his father. Together, they whispered and snickered, father tutoring son in the art of contempt for the adversary. As often as not in the civil case, one of Baker's real adversaries was

Judge Fujisaki. Trim and fatigued, sixty but looking older, Fujisaki had none of the nervous hunger for public affection displayed by Ito in the criminal case, and even less of Ito's deference to the lawyers hired to defend Simpson. Fujisaki would barely turn his head when he said "Overruled" to one of the Simpson team's many objections. The senior Baker, for his part, lacked Johnnie Cochran's silken adaptability to such momentary setbacks. Indeed, Baker soon abandoned even the pretense of deference to the man who made his life so difficult. Confronted with one quickly overruled objection after another, Baker would respond, sneeringly, "Thanks for your consideration, Your Honor."

For the criminal trial, of course, Baker's predecessors had devised a famously daring defense strategy, claiming that O. J. Simpson was framed for murder by a conspiracy of racist police officers. From the beginning of the second trial, though, it was clear that Baker would have to take another tack. In part, this was because of pretrial rulings by Judge Fujisaki, who found the racism of Detective Mark Fuhrman to be irrelevant to the trial unless the defense could show that Fuhrman's views had a discernible impact on the investigation—something Simpson's lawyers failed to do. There was also the racial makeup of the people in Fujisaki's courtroom in Santa Monica. Through most of the trial, there were just three black faces present: the defendant, one juror, and one alternate. (In the atmosphere of obsessive census-taking that came to envelop the Simpson legal saga, it was usually also noted that one juror was Hispanic and another a "half-black, half-Asian Jamaican immigrant.") The "race card" was absent also because of the man who would have been called upon to deal it. As a member of the virtually whites-only Los Angeles Country Club, Robert Baker would have had a certain credibility problem if he were to pose, like Cochran, as the deliverer of black Los Angeles from the depredations of the city's police.

But Baker fashioned a defense that was, in its way, no less audacious than that offered by Cochran and Robert Shapiro. Simpson as black martyr was gone, replaced by Simpson as star. Baker's (and Simpson's) theory was that the defendant was too grand a celebrity—too irresistible to women—to have suffered over the departure of his ex-wife. The attempt was to turn the domestic violence theme on its head. O.J. wasn't pursuing Nicole, the theory went; she was after him.

|||||

Baker specializes in defending insurance companies in medical malpractice cases, so he was accustomed to making uncomfortable arguments before juries. Lawyers like Baker have to say things like "The baby wasn't *so* brain-damaged by the hospital's error," and in this case he appeared to have few qualms about disparaging the deceased. In his opening statement to the jury, on October 24, 1996, Baker told the story of a marriage that was basically one of predator and prey, of Nicole pursuing O.J. According to Baker's highly selective account of their relationship, Nicole and O.J. separated for the first time in 1992, after seven years of marriage, and afterward O.J. became "Nicole's confidant." Baker said that Simpson steered his ex-wife through a variety of troubles—chiefly "boyfriend problems," including an unwanted pregnancy, which she terminated after seeking her ex-husband's counsel. By 1993, Baker said, Nicole had begun pursuing Simpson, attempting to revive their marriage. Baker read the jury a letter Nicole had written to O.J.: "I love you, I cherish you, and I want to make you smile." Simpson agreed to attempt a reconciliation, but Nicole made it difficult. "Nicole was having parties, visiting people . . . who were prostitutes, inviting drug dealers into her house with his children there," Baker said. Baker even made the jury a promise: "You'll hear the name Heidi Fleiss, you'll hear 'prostitute,' you'll hear 'drugs.' It's all in there."

The implication of Baker's opening statement was that the killer came out of Nicole's sordid world (even if no evidence of any such connection had emerged in the nearly three years since the murders). But Baker's subtext was even uglier—a twist on the once common defense of consent in rape cases. O.J. was a concerned dad, Nicole was a tramp. He was a star, she was a groupie. He played it safe, she took chances. In short, the bitch asked for it.

The sine qua non of Baker's strategy was Simpson's own testimony—just as his silence had been critical to the success of the race-card strategy in the criminal case. Head bowed at the defense table, Simpson could be transformed by Johnnie Cochran into the symbol of all black victimhood. If O.J. had taken the stand, Cochran could not have hidden his client's life of privilege and ease. But Simpson's life in Brentwood was indispensable to Baker's tack. Simpson would have to be as much exhibit as witness—so charming and desirable that the jury would have to dismiss the notion of him as a scorned and vengeful lover.

Baker's strategy (unlike Cochran's) had the advantage of requiring Simpson to do no more than show himself as he really is. Baker was right about one thing: Simpson was a star, even after the criminal trial. Around the Santa Monica courthouse, the regulars—local lawyers, off-duty cops, surly clerks—hung around the metal detectors hoping for a glimpse of Simpson as he walked by. Simpson has been so famous for so long that he excels at the quick wink of acknowledgment, the feigned intimacy with strangers, the scribbled autograph. He charmed everyone, even the stone-faced bailiffs who guarded the courtroom. Roger Cossack, the cohost of CNN's *Burden of Proof,* had dealt with Simpson only in passing before O.J. sidled up to him during a break early in the trial. "The first thing he said to me was 'So when are we playing golf?' " Cossack recalled. "And—you can't help it—you do think for a second, 'Hey, golf with O. J. Simpson!' " Still, Cossack never took him up on the offer.

||||||

For the few days of Simpson's testimony, the case provoked a media frenzy reminiscent of the first trial. From the quiet streets of Santa Monica, the satellite trucks beamed predawn reports to local television stations, and the technicians once more piled up O.J.-driven overtime. In the crush outside the courthouse after Simpson left the stand on his first day of testimony, Kim Goldman, Ron's sister, was hit on the head and bruised by an overaggressive cameraman. Inside the courtroom, the atmosphere was tense.

Simpson's adversaries tried hard to unnerve him on the witness stand. Fred Goldman, Ron's outspoken father, sat with his lawyers right behind the podium, so Simpson had to look at Goldman during much of his three days of testimony. Petrocelli, who was the plaintiffs' main inquisitor, was immune to Simpson's charm. Petrocelli was fiercely bland—neither young nor old, neither handsome nor plain, neither tall nor short. He handled the grisly, familiar details of the Simpson case—the photographs of Nicole sprawled in a pool of blood, her trembling cries to a 911 operator—with the dispassion of a lawyer in a contracts case. In the weeks leading up to Simpson's testimony, Petrocelli's doggedness was obviously paying off. The plaintiffs' presentation of evidence rarely faced even mildly effective cross-examination, and witnesses who had taken days, or even weeks, on the stand before Judge Ito completed their testimony in a small fraction of that time in Santa Monica. Of course, the stakes in this case for Simpson were lower than those in the criminal trial: money damages, not jail. But still, by raising only a perfunctory defense to the DNA and other physical evidence the plaintiffs introduced, Baker was betting almost everything on the testimony of his client.

Petrocelli delivered his questions to Simpson with aggressive but businesslike precision. His task was to get the jury to see the other side of stardom—the narcissism, the malignant self-obsession that, according to the plaintiffs' theory, drove Simpson to kill what he could not have. Petrocelli made a strong case that Simpson's account of the night of the murders—and of his life with Nicole—bore little relation to reality. The defendant's "story," as Petrocelli repeatedly referred to it, conflicted with telephone records, the recollections of other witnesses, and Simpson's own prior statements. The examination also illuminated the surreal nature of Simpson's celebrity existence. When Simpson returned to Los Angeles from New York two days before the murders, he said breezily, he had been carrying "at least seven thousand dollars in cash," and when he traveled to Chicago on the night of the murders he had left four or five thousand dollars in cash "underneath my sweater" in a walk-in closet. Petrocelli confronted Simpson with a passage from a quickie autobiography published in 1970, *OJ: The Education of a Rich Rookie*. First, though, he asked whether Simpson had been aware of his "image" in the public eye.

"Yeah," Simpson replied. "I always know people like me, yes."

"You wrote when you first began your football career, back in the first book that you authored, 'I have been praised, kidded, and criticized about being image-conscious. And I plead guilty to the charge.' True?"

"At that time, yes," Simpson replied.

"And you wrote that, quote, 'I tried all the images.' End of quote. True?"

"I don't recall that, no."

"It's in your book," Petrocelli pursued.

"I didn't write the book," Simpson said, with some impatience.

Petrocelli tried to clarify. The book had O. J. Simpson's name on it. Was Simpson saying that he didn't believe what the book said he believed? How much did he have to do with the book?

"In general, I okayed the book," Simpson explained finally. "I think I read the galley of the book before it went to press."

Petrocelli confronted Simpson with an interview he gave ESPN about the 1989 incident after which he pleaded no contest to beating Nicole. "We were both guilty," Simpson said in the 1989 broadcast. "No one was hurt, it was no big deal, and we both got on with our lives."

Petrocelli charged that Simpson's account of the beating was "absolutely false."

"I disagree with you on that," the witness replied.

"Did Nicole get hurt?"

"She had some bruises," Simpson conceded.

Eventually, Petrocelli got Simpson to admit that he had minimized his behavior in the ESPN interview. Why did he not tell the truth?

"It was a sports show," Simpson explained.

||||||

Simpson may have followed Baker's strategy too well in his testimony. He longed to show off. During a break early in his testimony, he told Erik Menendez's defense lawyer, Leslie Abramson, who was seated in the media section, "I wish I could talk more." Unsurprisingly, Simpson forcefully denied committing the murders. But he also wound up denying that he had engaged in *any* conduct that would diminish his stature before the jury. He presented himself as virtually flawless—as the celebrity of his own imagination. "I like to think I was a guy . . . people could come to," Simpson testified at one point. "I liked to treat everybody the way I wanted to be treated. My basic philosophy was 'Do unto others.' " When he was asked initially about violence in his marriage, the first thing he mentioned was that Nicole had hit him. He went on to deny that Nicole had been afraid of him on the night in 1993 when she called 911. "I will debate forever that she was not frightened of me that night," he said. Simpson even denied having ever hit Nicole. All Simpson would concede was that he had "rassled" with her— or, as he put it another time, had been "wrongly physical with her."

Petrocelli's phlegmatic style served him well here. Simpson raised his voice on just one occasion during his testimony. O.J. and Nicole divorced in mid-1992, and attempted a reconciliation about a year later. Petrocelli asked Simpson who had initiated the reconciliation. "She was incessably [sic] pursuing me," Simpson said.

He returned to this theme several times, prompting Petrocelli to ask:

"Are you sure you were not pursuing this time?"

"No. I think everyone, including our family, knows it was her pursuing me."

"You sure about that?"

"I think everybody knows that."

"I'm just asking if you're sure."

"I'm a thousand percent sure," Simpson insisted.

"How many percent?" Petrocelli asked, recognizing that the ferocity of Simpson's denials might convey the opposite of what he intended.

"A thousand percent sure," Simpson repeated.

Moments later, Petrocelli mentioned a *National Enquirer* story from the fall of 1993 which stated that O.J. had begged Nicole to resume their relationship. "That really upset you?"

"Yes," Simpson said, at top volume. "It certainly did."

"And it upset you because it was false, right?"

"Exactly. That's why it upset me."

Petrocelli knew where Simpson was going, and he didn't want to stand in the way. He asked, "She begged—you did not beg her?"

"Exactly right," came Simpson's chilling reply.

The contrast was striking. Simpson's demeanor was casual when he was accused of beating Nicole, but furious when he was asked if he had begged her. He had been famous for thirty years; he became the author (at least nominally) of an autobiography when he was just twenty-two. He could not abide the picture of himself as a vulnerable supplicant. He did not—would not—beg.

Baker did not question Simpson at all after Petrocelli first called him to the stand in November. Baker decided instead to present his client's full life story when the defense made its case in January, after the Christmas break. By the end of Simpson's first round of testimony, though, it appeared that he was offering little more than his idealized public image to refute the evidence against him. The defense came down to "Trust me." How did Simpson cut his hand on the night of the murders? He couldn't really say—except that he was sure that it wasn't in attacking Ron and Nicole. Wasn't he photographed, several months before the crime, wearing the murderer's model of Bruno Magli shoes? Simpson said that that was what the picture showed—but it was a doctored image. Wasn't that Simpson's blood at the murder scene, in his Bronco, and on his driveway? Simpson conceded that it was—and offered no explanation for how it got there. At one point, Petrocelli accused Simpson of acting in response to his questions. Hadn't he acted in television shows and movies? "I don't think I've ever called myself an actor in my life," Simpson replied. "I always said I was a personality."

|||||

The case changed dramatically over the course of the two-week Christmas break. First, Orange County Superior Court Judge Nancy Wieben Stock ruled that Simpson, as the biological father of Sydney and Justin, had the immediate right to resume primary custody of them. This decision was more or less preordained by the state of the law. The Browns had to show "clear and convincing" evidence that Simpson was an unfit parent—that he was abusive, neglectful, or unable to care for the children. In the custody trial, the Browns attempted to make the case that Simpson's history of abuse of Nicole made him unsuited to resume custody. But the judge had no basis to find that Simpson posed a danger to the children. Moreover, the Browns themselves had hardly behaved flawlessly in the months since the murders. Louis Brown, Nicole's father, accepted $162,500 from A Current Affair to narrate O.J. and Nicole's wedding video for broadcast. He also sold Nicole's diaries to the *National Enquirer* for $100,000. Nicole's sister Dominique, who also still lived with her parents, sold topless photographs of Nicole to the *Enquirer* for $32,500 and tipped off a photographer when the children were placing flowers at their mother's grave. The custody decision transformed the financial calculus of the case. Now, instead of merely taking money from a single, high-living defendant, the jury would be asked, in effect, to take money out of Sydney and Justin's pocket as well.

But the plaintiffs received some good news over the holidays as well. Early in the defense case, Baker had called a so-called photographic expert named Robert Groden to testify about the single photograph of Simpson in the Bruno Magli shoes, the one taken by Harry Scull. Groden's conclusion was that the photograph had been doctored to place the shoes on Simpson's feet. Groden was an inept and unreliable witness. A JFK assassination buff without any formal training in photography, he was mauled by the plaintiffs in cross-examination. But the plaintiff had to deal with the fact that the defense had at least put forth an expert (of sorts) to question the authenticity of this crucial piece of evidence.

Over the holidays, though, the plaintiffs received word that there were more photographs of Simpson wearing the shoes—a lot more. Another freelance photographer in Buffalo, E. J. Flammer, had searched his files and found thirty different photographs of Simpson wearing the shoes on September 26, 1993. What was more, he had published one of the photos in a Buffalo Bills newsletter in November 1993, months before the murders. This was extraordinary evidence for the plaintiffs on several levels. First, it established beyond doubt that Simpson had worn the same extremely rare shoes as the murderer. (Only 299 pairs of the size-twelve model had been sold in the United States between 1991 and 1993.) Second, the new evidence proved that Simpson had lied—both in his deposition and in front of the jury—about not owning the shoes. Finally, the evidence damaged Baker's credibility before the jury—as well as that of the other defense lawyers—because they had used Groden's testimony, which the new photographs completely discredited. (For this, one can only feel sorry for Baker, though he can be faulted for being gullible enough to believe his client's protestations.)

The discovery of the E. J. Flammer pictures transformed the case. The plaintiffs could have imagined no more compelling way to prove that Simpson had lied—nor any more important subject. (And after the Flammer photographs came to light, other free-lancers came forward with even more photographs of Simpson wearing the Bruno Maglis on September 26, 1993. Not wanting to waste time, the plaintiffs never even introduced these other photographs.) When Simpson returned to the witness stand, he compounded his troubles by continuing to deny—even in the face of the Flammer photographs—that he had ever owned the shoes. In summation, Petrocelli shed his lawyerly reserve and mocked Simpson's lies and evasions on the witness stand. Most important, Petrocelli showed how Simpson's version of events conflicted completely with the other evidence in the case. He showed the jury a chart itemizing sixty points on which the jury had to believe either Simpson—or other, more credible witnesses.

The issue of race, which had mostly disappeared from the civil case, returned to it in its final days. The single black juror on the case was removed at the request of the defense when the Los Angeles District Attorney's office reported to Judge Fujisaki that the juror's daughter was employed as a legal secretary for the prosecutors. Then two of the black women jurors in the criminal case, Brenda Moran and Gina Rosborough, wrote to at least two of the civil jurors advising them to make a deal with the same agent who represented them. The civil jurors reported this wildly inappropriate approach to the judge, and he in turn set in motion a criminal investigation of the ex-jurors, which included a search of Brenda Moran's home. The upshot of this frenzied activity on the eve of the jury's decision was that the civil jury wound up including not a single black juror, and that two black jurors from the first case were facing possible criminal charges. These events served as a reminder of the still-poisoned racial atmosphere surrounding the case.

|||||

The jury deliberated for nearly a week. As if consciously rebuking the criminal jurors for their brief consideration of the case, the civil jurors asked to review a great deal of the evidence in the case, especially about the DNA tests. On the afternoon of Tuesday, February 4, 1997, the foreman pressed the buzzer indicating to the judge that the jury had reached a verdict.

Judge Fujisaki gave the families time to assemble; it was not until shortly after seven in the evening that the judge summoned the jurors back into the courtroom. In a final, surreal coda to the strange Simpson story, the jury returned at precisely the moment when President Clinton was concluding his State of the Union address. The President was shaking hands in the House chamber at 7:12 P.M. Pacific time, when the verdict was read in court.

I was sitting in the outdoor ABC broadcast position, across the street from the courthouse, when the verdict against Simpson was announced. I was facing the camera, so I could not see what was going on behind me, and I did not really know what was occurring there until news of the verdict was broadcast. At that moment, I heard a huge, angry shout of vindication. It turned out that a crowd of several hundred had gathered, and the nearly all-white group took it upon itself to issue a raucous rejoinder to the African-Americans who had cheered Simpson's acquittal. It was payback time—and a moment of surpassing ugliness. In truth, though, it was a fitting culmination to this divisive national experience.

The jury awarded $8.5 million in compensatory damages to the Goldman family for the wrongful death of their son. (The Browns had sought no compensatory damages because doing so would have required Sydney and Justin to testify against their father.) The trial ended on a tragicomic note. Fujisaki held a two-day hearing on Simpson's financial condition so that the jury could decide whether to assess punitive damages for the murders, and if so in what amount. Ironically, here at the end of the case, Simpson's lawyers finally seemed to have the better of the argument. The core of the disagreement between the parties involved Simpson's potential for earning money in the future. The plaintiffs called an expert who said that Simpson could expect to make about two and a half million dollars a year on autograph sales and endorsement fees for the next twenty years—an amount with a net present value of about $25 million.

To me, this testimony was entertainingly absurd. The expert pointed out that Simpson had certainly tried to cash in on his notoriety, even going so far as to trademark his name and a few catch-phrases like, "Team O.J.: Justice for All." And it was true that Simpson and Larry Schiller had cashed in as much as they could in the immediate aftermath of the case. But the civil verdict only confirmed Simpson's status as a pariah in mainstream American society. Skip Taft, Simpson's business manager, testified that Simpson had no offers of any significance on the horizon. That was undoubtedly true. It was a measure of the jury's revulsion toward Simpson that they accepted the plaintiff's estimate of Simpson's earning power without apparent question. Likewise, the jury seems to have given little thought to the question of how Simpson will support Sydney and Justin. The jury awarded $12.5 million to each plaintiff, dividing in half the windfall the plaintiffs asserted that Simpson could expect over the next twenty years. Simpson owes a total of $33.5 million, an amount he cannot possibly afford.

In comments after the case, the jury gave cogent reasons for their decision: Simpson had not been a credible witness; he had denied facts that other evidence in the case established beyond doubt; the DNA evidence was compelling. It was a familiar and persuasive litany. Almost lost in the cacophony of the day's events were the statements of the only other African-American in the well of the courtroom on the final day of the trial. It turned out that the black alternate, a middle-aged woman, had a different view of the case from her colleagues who had deliberated. She would have ruled for the defendant.

ACKNOWLEDGMENTS

My debts begin with my colleagues at *The New Yorker*. I owe my entire career in journalism to Tina Brown, who took a chance on me four years ago and never stopped encouraging me. I thank Pat Crow for editing my Simpson stories for the magazine, and Elizabeth Dobell for providing skillful and diligent editorial research. I benefited throughout the case from the wise counsel of Maurie Perl, Jill Bernstein, and Melissa Pranger. My thanks also to Pam McCarthy and Dorothy Wickenden. I am grateful to David Remnick for his friendship, for his sensitive reading of the manuscript, and most of all for the example of his own work as a writer. My Los Angeles colleagues, Caroline Graham and Charlotte Reynolds, made me feel like family. Over the long life of the case, it seemed that everyone involved had a lawyer. I, however, had the best: Devereux Chatillon at *The New Yorker*, and Bradley Phillips, Michael Doyen, and Steven Weisburd of Munger, Tolles and Olson.

This book was written during a fellowship at the Freedom Forum Media Studies Center at Columbia University. I am grateful to all my colleagues there, especially its leaders during my tenure, Everette Dennis, Nancy Hicks Maynard, and Nancy Woodhull. Matt Dallek provided terrific research assistance and welcome companionship. My gratitude also to Nancy Grimes for her help at an earlier stage. I thank the West Publishing Company for providing me with on-line access to the trial transcript.

I could not have had a more supportive publisher. At Random House, Ann Godoff steered this project (and me) with confidence, savvy, and good cheer. The copy-editing team of Beth Pearson and Veronica Windholz greatly improved the manuscript. To Elsa Burt, Enrica Gadler, Ivan Held, Carol Schneider, and the boss, Harry Evans, my thanks for their enthusiasm. My agent, Esther Newberg, was (and is) always three steps ahead of everybody.

I must have done something right in my life to deserve friends like Michael Lynton, Jamie Alter, and Eloise Lynton, who allowed me to become the second-most-notorious houseguest in Los Angeles.

Thank you, also, to Wendy Gray and the Pirate.

I have been covering the Simpson case for almost half of my daughter's life and about two-thirds of my son's. Ellen brought great sophistication to her analysis of the case ("I think O. J. Simpson should be in time-out for a long time!") and Adam a healthy skepticism for the whole endeavor ("No O.J., Daddy!"). They have flourished so much despite their father's frequent absences because of their mother, Amy McIntosh. In addition to her duties at home, my beloved McIntosh has also scaled her own professional heights during this period and still found time to edit this manuscript with care. I treasure the adventure of our life together.

New York City
July 1996

SOURCES AND BIBLIOGRAPHY

This book is based principally on my observations and interviews during the two years I covered the Simpson case. During this time, I interviewed more than two hundred people for this book. Many of them spoke to me on the condition that I not report what they said until Simpson's criminal trial had ended. All quotations from private conversations come either from the person who made the comment or a person who heard it. All quotations from court proceedings come from the official court transcript. In Chapter 2, all of the statements by the police officers come from their grand jury, preliminary hearing, or trial testimony, but my account is also based on my interviews with the participants and the internal police reports of the investigation.

In addition to my own efforts, I have steeped myself in the voluminous media coverage of the case. I wish to acknowledge my great debt to my colleagues in the Simpson press corps. In addition to the works cited by name below, I also studied the continuing coverage of the case by a number of journalists. The *Los Angeles Times* served as the newspaper of record on the case, and I learned a great deal from the work of Jim Newton, Andrea Ford, Henry Weinstein, Tim Rutten, Stephanie Simon, Ralph Frammolino, and especially Bill Boyarsky in his invaluable column, "The Spin." Also in the *Times*, I profited from the conscientious and thoughtful analysis of the case by (and my own conversations with) Professors Peter Arenella and Laurie Levenson. My work as a magazine writer was made more difficult by David Margolick's brilliant and witty daily coverage of the trial in *The New York Times*; my thanks to him nonetheless. I also express my appreciation to Linda Deutsch and Michael Fleeman of the Associated Press; Mark Miller and Donna Foote of *Newsweek*; Elaine Lafferty and Jim Willwerth of *Time*; Michelle Caruso of the New York *Daily News*; Ann Bollinger of the *New York Post*; Sally Ann Stewart of *USA Today*; Shirley Perlman and Joe Demma of *Newsday*; Lorraine Adams of *The Washington Post*; and the inimitable Dominick Dunne of *Vanity Fair*.

I watched a lot of television, too. I always learned a great deal from my friends Dan Abrams and Kristin Jeannette-Meyers and all of their colleagues at Court TV, as well as from Jack Ford at NBC, Cynthia McFadden at ABC, and Bill Whitaker at CBS. Thanks, too, to Jim Moret and the Simpson coverage team at CNN. For assisting me in tracking down videotapes and transcripts of television coverage of the case, I thank Tracy Day of ABC, Stacie Griffith of NBC, Tom Mazzarelli of CNN, and Sybil Mac-Donald of KCBS in Los Angeles.

I drew on the following books and articles in my analysis of the case and its context.

BOOKS

Abramson, Jeffrey, ed. *Postmortem*. New York: Basic Books, 1996.

Bailey, F. Lee. *To Be a Trial Lawyer*. New York: John Wiley and Sons, 1994.

———, with Harvey Aronson. *The Defense Never Rests*. New York: Signet, 1972.

———, with John Greenya. *For the Defense*. New York: Atheneum, 1975.

Barich, Bill. *Big Dreams: Into the Heart of California*. New York: Vintage Books, 1994.

Berry, Barbara Cochran, with Joanne Parrent. *Life After Johnnie Cochran*. New York: Basic Books, 1995.

Bugliosi, Vincent, with Curt Gentry. *Helter Skelter*. New York: Pocket Books, 1975.

———. *Outrage*. New York: W. W. Norton & Co., 1996.

Cooley, Armanda, Carrie Bess, and Marsha Rubin-Jackson. *Madam Foreman*. Beverly Hills: Dove Books, 1995.

Darden, Christopher, with Jess Walter. *In Contempt*. New York: Regan Books, 1996.

Davis, Mike. *City of Quartz: Excavating the Future in Los Angeles*. New York: Vintage Books, 1992.

Dershowitz, Alan M. *The Abuse Excuse*. Boston: Little, Brown & Co., 1994.

———. *The Best Defense*. New York: Random House, 1982.

———. *Reasonable Doubts*. New York: Simon & Schuster, 1996.

Deutsch, Linda, and Michael Fleeman. *Verdict*. Kansas City: Andrews and McMeel, 1995.

Didion, Joan. *After Henry*. New York: Vintage International, 1992.

———. *Slouching Towards Bethlehem*. New York: Farrar, Straus and Giroux, 1968.

———. *The White Album*. New York: Farrar, Straus and Giroux, 1979.

Domanick, Joe. *To Protect and to Serve: The LAPD at War in the City of Dreams*. New York: Pocket Books, 1994.

Dutton, Donald G., with Susan K. Golant. *The Batterer: A Psychological Profile*. New York: Basic Books, 1995.

Elias, Tom, and Dennis Schatzman. *The Simpson Trial in Black and White*. Los Angeles: General Publishing Group, 1996.

Eliot, Marc. *Kato Kaelin: The Whole Truth*. New York: Harper Paperbacks, 1995.

Fox, Larry. *The O. J. Simpson Story: Born to Run*. New York: Dodd, Mead & Co., 1974.

Gebhard, David, and Robert Winter. *Los Angeles: An Architectural Guide*. Salt Lake City: Gibbs-Smith Publisher, 1994.

George, Lynell. *No Crystal Stair: African-Americans in the City of Angels*. New York: Anchor Books, 1994.

Horne, Gerald. *Fire This Time: The Watts Uprising and the 1960s*. Charlottesville: University Press of Virginia, 1995.

Kennedy, Tracy, Judith Kennedy, and Alan Abrahamson. *Mistrial of the Century*. Beverly Hills: Dove Books, 1995.

Knox, Michael, with Mike Walker. *The Private Diary of an OJ Juror*. Beverly Hills: Dove Books, 1995.

Lardner, George, Jr. *The Stalking of Kristin*. New York: Atlantic Monthly Press, 1995.

Los Angeles Times staff. *In Pursuit of Justice*. Los Angeles: Los Angeles Times, 1995.

McWilliams, Carey. *Southern California Country: An Island on the Land*. Freeport, New York: Books for Libraries Press, 1970.

Ovnick, Merry. *Los Angeles: The End of the Rainbow*. Los Angeles: Balcony Press, 1994.

Reid, David, ed. *Sex, Death and God in L.A.* Berkeley: University of California Press, 1994.

Resnick, Faye, with Mike Walker. *Nicole Brown Simpson: The Private Diary of a Life Interrupted*. Beverly Hills: Dove Books, 1994.

Shapiro, Robert L., with Larkin Warren. *The Search for Justice*. New York: Warner Books, 1996.

Simpson, O. J. *I Want to Tell You*. Boston: Little, Brown & Co., 1995.

———, with Pete Axthelm. *OJ: The Education of a Rich Rookie*. New York: Macmillan, 1970.

Sonenshein, Raphael J. *Politics in Black and White: Race and Power in Los Angeles*. Princeton, New Jersey: Princeton University Press, 1993.

Starr, Kevin. *Endangered Dreams: The Great Depression in California*. New York: Oxford University Press, 1996.

———. *Material Dreams: Southern California Through the 1920s*. New York: Oxford University Press, 1990.

Turner, Patricia A. *I Heard It Through the Grapevine: Rumor in African-American Culture*. Berkeley: University of California Press, 1993.

Uelman, Gerald F. *Lessons from the Trial: The People v. O. J. Simpson.* Kansas City: Andrews and McMeel, 1996.

Vernon, Robert. *L.A. Justice: Lessons from the Firestorm.* Colorado Springs: Focus on the Family Publishing, 1993.

Weller, Sheila. *Raging Heart.* New York: Pocket Books, 1995.

ARTICLES

Colvin, Richard Lee, and Tina Daunt. "Shapiro Now Faces His Defining Moment," *Los Angeles Times,* June 26, 1994, p. A1.

Dunne, John Gregory. "The Simpsons," *The New York Review of Books,* September 22, 1994, p. 34.

Gates, Henry Louis, Jr. "Thirteen Ways of Looking at a Black Man," *The New Yorker,* October 23, 1995, p. 56.

Goodman, Michael J. "For the Defense, Johnnie Cochran," *Los Angeles Times Magazine,* January 29, 1995, p. 10.

Hancock, LynNell, et al. "Putting Working Moms in Custody," *Newsweek,* March 13, 1995, p. 54.

Holden, Benjamin A., et al. "Race Seems to Play an Increasing Role in Many Jury Verdicts," *The Wall Street Journal,* October 4, 1995, p. A1.

Jervey, Gay. "Michael and Reggie's Magician," *The American Lawyer,* May 1994, p. 56.

Jones, Tamara. "The Silent Persuader: Johnnie Cochran," *The Washington Post,* October 3, 1995, p. B1.

Katz, Jon. "Guilty," *Wired,* September 1995, p. 130.

Krikorian, Greg. "Co-Workers Paint Different Portrait of Mark Fuhrman," *Los Angeles Times,* November 8, 1995, p. A1.

Lafferty, Elaine, et al. "The Simpson Verdict," *Time,* October 16, 1995, p. 48.

Lopez, Robert J. and Jesse Katz. "Nicole Brown Anti-Abuse Charity Beset by Problems," *Los Angeles Times,* July 10, 1995, p. A1.

Margolick, David. "Trial Lawyer Now Forced to Fight His Fame While Battling for His Client," *The New York Times,* January 20, 1995, p. A12.

———. "Prosecutor of Distinction," *The New York Times,* January 22, 1995, p. A17.

Newton, Jim. "Jackson Being Persecuted, Ministers Say," *Los Angeles Times,* February 19, 1994, p. A5.

Noble, Kenneth B. "A Showman in the Courtroom, for Whom Race Is a Defining Issue," *The New York Times,* January 20, 1995, p. A13.

Parloff, Roger. "How Barry Scheck and Peter Neufeld Tripped Up the DNA Experts," *The American Lawyer*, December 1989, p. 50.

Perlman, Shirley. "Judge Ito Steals the Show," *Newsday*, November 13, 1994, p. A7.

Reibstein, Larry, et al. "Disorder in the Court," *Newsweek*, April 17, 1995, p. 26.

Schaeffer, Danna Wilner. "How to Be Marcia Clark," *Mirabella*, January/February 1996, p. 30.

Shapiro, Robert L. "Using the Media to Your Advantage," *The Champion*, January/February 1993, p. 7.

Silverman, Ira, and Fredric Dannen. "A Complicated Life," *The New Yorker*, March 11, 1996, p. 44.

Sipchen, Bob. "Schiller's Twist," *Los Angeles Times*, February 3, 1995, p. E1.

Simpson, O. J. "The Playboy Interview," *Playboy*, December 1976, p. 77.

Turow, Scott. "Simpson Prosecutors Pay for Their Blunders," *The New York Times*, October 4, 1995, p. A 31.

Weathers, Diane. "The Other Side of Johnnie Cochran," *Essence*, November 1995, p. 87.

INDEX

About the Author

JEFFREY TOOBIN is the bestselling author of *The Oath, The Nine, Too Close to Call, A Vast Conspiracy,* and *The Run of His Life*. He is a staff writer at *The New Yorker* and the senior legal analyst at CNN. He lives with his family in New York.

3-25